GUIDE

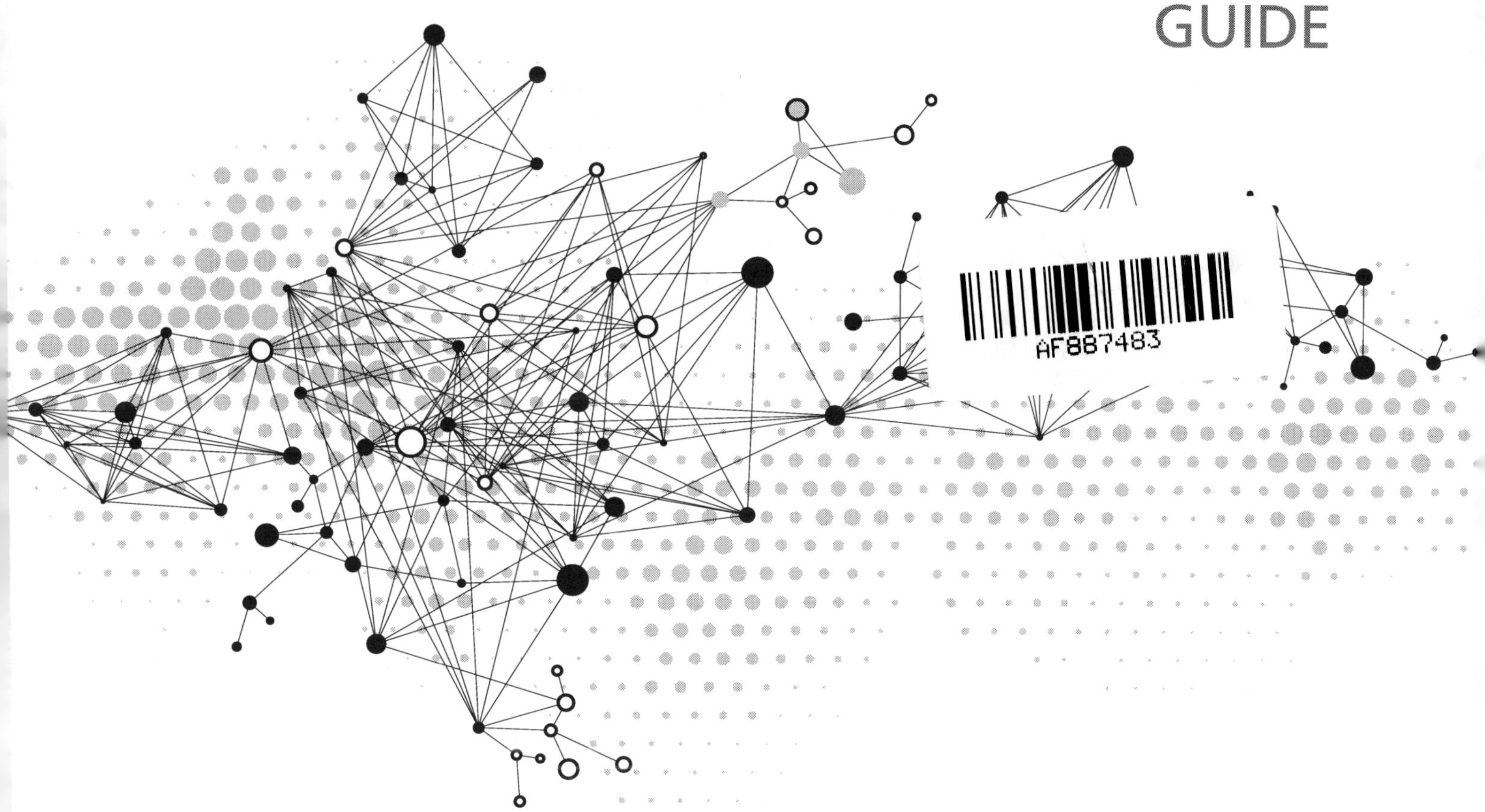

FINANCIAL SOUNDNESS INDICATORS COMPILATION GUIDE

2019

INTERNATIONAL MONETARY FUND

Cataloging-in-Publication Data
IMF Library

Names: International Monetary Fund, publisher.
Title: Financial soundness indicators compilation guide.
Description: [Washington, DC] : International Monetary Fund, 2019. | Revision of the 2006 FSI Guide. | Includes bibliographical references.
Identifiers: ISBN 9781484436209 (paper)
Subjects: LCSH: Financial institutions—Auditing. | Economic indicators.
Classification: LCC HF5686.F46 F352 2019

ISBN: 978-1-48439-620-9 (paper)
ISBN: 978-1-51351-095-8 (PDF)
ISBN: 978-1-51351-094-1 (ePub)

Please send orders to:
International Monetary Fund, Publication Services
P.O. Box 92780, Washington, D.C. 20090, U.S.A.
Tel.: (202) 623-7430 Fax: (202) 623-7201
E-mail: publications@imf.org
Internet: www.elibrary.imf.org
www.bookstore.imf.org

Contents

Annexes

Annex Tables

Figures

Preface

In the late 1990s, the International Monetary Fund (IMF) launched an ambitious data collection effort—the Financial Soundness Indicators (FSIs)—to monitor the soundness of the system-wide financial sector, from a macroprudential vantage point. The FSIs included indicators of capital adequacy, asset quality, profitability, liquidity, and market risk sensitivity. The *2006 Financial Soundness Indicators Compilation Guide* (*2006 Guide*) provided guidance about the source supervisory statistics, consolidation options, and compilation and dissemination advice, while simultaneously aiming at cross-country comparability. The initiative succeeded in persuading policymakers about the value of FSIs for tracking financial soundness trends that could inform financial stability analysis and policies—with a corresponding growth in the number of economies compiling and reporting these indicators.

However, the global financial crisis that started in 2007–2008 revealed to the international community the need to enhance this and other financial sector data collections and bridge necessary data gaps, including supplementing them with tail and macroeconomic measures, to strengthen macrofinancial surveillance. The response included IMF revisions to the original list of FSIs and the IMF/Financial Stability Board G-20 Data Gaps Initiative (DGI)—endorsed by the G-20 finance ministers and Central Bank governors and the IMF's International Monetary and Financial Committee. Inter alia, these initiatives have yielded a revised list of FSIs including new international standards, operationalizing the measurement of concentration and tail risk in the financial system, and enhancing the coverage of FSIs. These efforts have been carried out in consultation and close collaboration with a broad-based group of national and international experts, international standard setting bodies, IMF's relevant departments and all FSI-reporting countries, and concerned international organizations.

This *2019 Financial Soundness Indicators Compilation Guide* (*Guide*) includes new indicators to expand the coverage of the financial sector, including other financial intermediaries, money market funds, insurance corporations, pension funds, nonfinancial corporations, and households. In all, the *Guide* recommends the compilation of 50 FSIs—13 of them new. Additions such as new capital, liquidity and asset quality metrics, and concentration and distribution measures will serve to enhance the forward-looking aspect of FSIs and contribute to increase policy focus on stability of the financial system.

Acknowledgments

This *Guide* was prepared by staff of the Financial Institutions Division of the Statistics Department (STA) under the general direction of Gabriel Quirós Romero (STA Deputy Director) and Marco A. Espinosa-Vega (Division Chief). René Piché (Deputy Division Chief) and José Cartas (Senior Economist) managed the project.

The primary contributors to this *Guide* include Evrim Bese Goksu, José Cartas, Thomas Elkjaer, Artak Harutyunyan, Phousnith Khay, André Mialou, José Carlos Moreno-Ramírez, Naoto Osawa, Renato Pérez, René Piché, Josep Puigvert, Samah Torchani, and Giovanni Ugazio.

The *Guide* has benefited from the review and comments of STA staff—including Francien Berry, Brian Kwok Chung Yee, Bidisha Das, Agus Firmansyah, Antonio Galicia-Escotto, Elizabeth Holmquist, Laurent Kemoe, Diane Kostroch, Mahmut Kutlukaya, Justin Matz, and Clement Ncuti—and the following Monetary and Capital Markets Department staff: Sergei Antoshin, Rachid Awad, Liliana Beatriz Schumacher, Luis Brandao-Marques, John Charles Caparusso, Fabio Cortes, Salim Darbar, Jennifer Elliott, Ellen Gaston, Javier Hamman, Abdullah Haron, David Hofman, Tumer Kapan, Dimitrios Laliotis, Mindaugas Leika, Hiroko Oura, Antonio Pancorbo, Irman Pardede, Maral Shamloo, Galen Sher, Laura Valderrama, Felix Vardy, Peter Windsor, and TengTeng Xu.

Comments by members of the FSI Reference Group, Michael Andrews and Russell Krueger, are gratefully acknowledged.

Finally, this manual benefited from the comments from numerous officials in member countries and international organizations, which are gratefully acknowledged. Also, we wish to thank participants at the April 2017 Users' Workshop on Financial Soundness Indicators and Meeting of the FSI Reference Group in Washington, D.C., convened to assist in the revision of the *2006 Guide*.

The revision also benefited from the outstanding administrative assistance by Brian Bowling and Tonia Takyi.

Louis Marc Ducharme
Chief Statistician and Data Officer, and Director
Statistics Department
International Monetary Fund

Acronyms

2006 Guide	*2006 Financial Soundness Indicators Compilation Guide*
AMC	Asset Management Company
ASF	Available Stable Funding
AT1	Additional Tier 1 Capital
BCBS	Basel Committee on Banking Supervision
BIS	Bank for International Settlements
BPM6	*Balance of Payments and International Investment Position Manual,* sixth edition
CAMELS	Capital Adequacy, Asset Quality, Management Soundness, Earnings and Profitability, Liquidity, and Sensitivity to Market Risk
CAR	Capital Adequacy Ratio
CBCSDC	Cross-Border, Cross-Sector, Domestically Controlled Consolidation Basis
CBCSDI	Cross-Border, Cross-Sector, Domestically Incorporated Consolidation Basis
CBDC	Cross-Border, Domestically Controlled Consolidation Basis
CBDI	Cross-Border, Domestically Incorporated Consolidation Basis
CCP	Central Clearing Counterparties
CDM	Concentration and Distribution Measures
CET1	Common Equity Tier 1
CPPI	Commercial Property Price Index
DCR	Displaced Commercial Risk
DGI	Data Gaps Initiative
DL	Domestic Location Consolidation Basis
DM	Distribution Measure
DQAF	Data Quality Assessment Framework
DT	Deposit Taker
EBIT	Earnings Before Interest and Tax
ECL	Expected Credit Loss
ED	Exposure at Default
ES	Expected Shortfall
FBB	Foreign Bank Branches
FC	Financial Corporation
FISIM	Financial Intermediation Services Indirectly Measured
FSAP	Financial Sector Assessment Program
FSI	Financial Soundness Indicator
FVOCI	Fair Value Through Other Comprehensive Income
FVTPL	Fair Value Through Profit or Loss
GDP	Gross Domestic Product
GFC	Global Financial Crisis
GFSM 2014	*Government Finance Statistics Manual 2014*

GNF	Global Note Facility
G-SIFI	Global Systemically Important Financial Institutions
Guide	*2019 Financial Soundness Indicators Compilation Guide*
HH	Household
HQLA	High Quality Liquid Assets
IAG	Inter-Agency Group on Economic and Financial Statistics
IAH	Investment Account Holders
IAS	International Accounting Standards
IASB	International Accounting Standards Board
IBS	International Banking Statistics
IC	Insurance Corporation
ICAAP	Internal Capital Adequacy Assessment Process
IDT	Islamic Deposit Takers
IFRS	International Financial Reporting Standards
IFSB	Islamic Financial Services Board
IIP	International Investment Position
IMF	International Monetary Fund
IRB	Internal Ratings-Based Approach
IRR	Investment Equalization Reserves
ISIC	International Standard Industrial Classification of All Economic Activities
LCR	Liquidity Coverage Ratio
LGD	Loss Given Default
LOC	Letter of Credit
MFSMCG	*Monetary and Financial Statistics Manual and Compilation Guide 2016*
MMF	Money Market Fund
NAV	Net Asset Value
NFC	Nonfinancial Corporation
NIF	Note Issuance Facilities
NPI	Nonprofit Institution
NPISH	Nonprofit Institutions Serving Households
NPLs	Nonperforming Loans
NSFR	Net Stable Funding Ratio
NSO	National Statistics Office
OCI	Other Comprehensive Income
OFC	Other Financial Corporation
OTC	Over-the-Counter
PD	Probability of Default
PER	Profit Equalization Reserves
PF	Pension Fund
PLS	Profit and Loss Sharing
PSIA	Profit Sharing Investment Accounts
PSIFI	Prudential and Structural Islamic Financial Indicators
Repo	Repurchase Agreement
ROA	Return on Assets
ROE	Return on Equity
RPPI	Residential Property Price Index
RSF	Required Stable Funding
RUF	Revolving Underwriting Facility
RWA	Risk-Weighted Assets

SCR	Solvency Capital Requirement
SLDR	Spread Between Reference Lending and Deposit Rates
SNA	System of National Accounts
SRF	Standardized Report Form
VaR	Value-at-Risk

1 Introduction

I. Overview

1.1 This *2019 Financial Soundness Indicators Compilation Guide* (*Guide*) provides guidance on the concepts and definitions, data sources and methods for the compilation and dissemination of financial soundness indicators (FSIs). (Table 1.1 contains the set of core and additional FSIs.)

1.2 FSIs are indicators of the current financial health and soundness of the financial institutions in a country, and of their corporate and household counterparts. They include both aggregated individual institution data and indicators that are representative of the markets in which the financial institutions operate. Supervisory data are important sources for calculation of FSIs. FSIs are calculated and disseminated to support macroprudential analysis. They focus on indicators of financial soundness directly relevant for the financial sector. The reason is twofold: FSIs have traditionally been associated to financial institutions and the necessary data sources are sufficiently available. For the same reasons, this *Guide* gives less emphasis to non-financial corporations or other areas of the financial sector, like shadow banking.

1.3 The *Guide* has benefited from extensive consultations with FSI compilers and users, including (i) presentation to the IMF Board of the 2013 Board paper on the outcomes of STA consultations on revising the current list of FSIs in response to the global financial crisis, adoption of the Basel III Accord and the G-20 Data Gaps Initiative; (ii) the April 2017 Statistics Department Workshop on Financial Soundness Indicators—A Users' Perspective; and (iii) consultations with the FSI Reference Group of experts, G-20 representatives, and Inter-Agency Group on Economic and Financial Statistics (IAG). The new *Guide* incorporates changes in international regulatory standards, including new capital and liquidity requirements, and provides more practical advice on compilation issues.

1.4 The *Guide* is more prescriptive—to facilitate the compilation and cross-country comparability of these data— and more forward looking than *2006 Financial Soundness Indicators Compilation Guide* (*2006 Guide*) to assist users in their macrofinancial surveillance efforts for financial stability purposes.

1.5 The *Guide* reflects advances in the regulatory framework, most prominently embodied in the Basel III reform—including new definitions and measures of capital and new global liquidity standards. Recommendations on accounting practices have been updated to reflect new and revised International Financial Reporting Standards (IFRS). The *Guide*, consistent with current Basel Committee guidance, recommends that the distinction between general and specific provisions, which is a concept not included in the IFRS 9 expected loss model, should be determined in line with national supervisory standards.

II. Background

1.6 A well-functioning financial system can act as an engine of growth through the provision of efficient maturity and liquidity transformation, credit origination, and other services. However, financial intermediation is also vulnerable to liquidity risks arising from the use of short term liabilities to fund longer-term assets, and potentially inadequate capital buffers to absorb unexpected losses. If unchecked, these vulnerabilities can result in full-fledged economic crisis.

1.7 Vulnerabilities at the institution level have long been recognized, resulting in prudential standards and supervisory oversight. The IMF introduced FSIs in the late 1990s to identify emerging risks in the financial sector, at the aggregate level. The core FSIs for deposit takers were inspired by a common supervisory rating system known as CAMELS.[1] As noted in the *2006 Guide*, "The long-established surveillance of individual institutions is being supplemented by the monitoring of risks to the stability of national financial systems arising from the collective behavior of individual institutions."[2]

[1] The acronym CAMELS stands for Capital adequacy, Asset quality, Management capability, Earnings, Liquidity, and Sensitivity to market risk.

[2] *2006 Guide*, paragraph 1.6.

1.8 FSIs steadily became a staple of macrofinancial analysis, featuring in a number of countries' Financial Stability Reports, and IMF surveillance work, including Article IV Consultation Reports, Global Financial Stability Reports, and Financial Sector Assessment Programs (FSAPs).

1.9 The global financial crisis exposed a number of weaknesses in the approach to identification and mitigation of financial sector risks. Insufficient attention had been devoted to aggregate risks in the financial system, and to the linkages between the real and financial sectors. In addition, large international banks were found to hold insufficient capital against their risk exposures, particularly through special purpose vehicles, securitized assets, and derivatives. Some instruments included in regulatory capital proved not to be truly loss-absorbing in the crisis, and it became clear that in some jurisdictions banks and their supervisors had paid insufficient attention to liquidity risk in the long period of benign market conditions preceding the crisis.

1.10 In sum, the crisis brought to the fore the need to strengthen financial regulation, which in turn triggered revision of the FSIs to reflect the new international standards on capital and liquidity that were more risk-based and forward looking, and to supplement the new FSIs with tail risk measures. The new FSIs are well aligned with enhanced regulatory practices that are more risk sensitive and forward looking and are supplemented with concentration and distribution measures. New FSIs expand coverage of money market funds, insurance corporations, pensions as well as the nonfinancial corporate and household sectors, potentially providing greater insights into the linkages between the financial and real sectors.

1.11 Because risks evolve, there is little doubt that future editions of FSIs will need to cover new topics such as digital financial intermediation and other emerging risks. As international consensus emerges around prudential standards and supervisory approaches to new risks, new or revised FSIs will be developed to provide relevant statistics for financial stability analysis.

Table 1.1 Financial Soundness Indicators: The Core and Additional

	Core Set
	Deposit Takers
Capital Adequacy	Regulatory capital to risk-weighted assets Tier 1 capital to risk-weighted assets Nonperforming loans net of provisions to capital Common Equity Tier 1 capital to risk-weighted assets Tier 1 capital to assets
Asset Quality	Nonperforming loans to total gross loans Loan concentration by economic activity Provisions to nonperforming loans
Earnings and Profitability	Return on assets Return on equity Interest margin to gross income Noninterest expenses to gross income
Liquidity	Liquid assets to total assets (liquid asset ratio) for all DTs Liquid assets to short term liabilities for all DTs Liquidity Coverage Ratio for the DTs that have implemented Basel III liquidity standards Net Stable Funding Ratio for the DTs that have implemented Basel III liquidity standards
Sensitivity to Market Risk	Net open position in foreign exchange to capital
	Real Estate Markets
	Residential real estate prices
	Additional Set
Deposit Takers	Large exposures to capital Geographical distribution of loans to total loans Gross asset position in financial derivatives to capital Gross liability position in financial derivatives to capital Trading income to total income Personnel expenses to noninterest expenses Spread between reference lending and deposit rates

Table 1.1 Financial Soundness Indicators: The Core and Additional *(concluded)*

	Spread between highest and lowest interbank rate Customer deposits to total (noninterbank) loans Foreign-currency-denominated loans to total loans Foreign-currency-denominated liabilities to total liabilities Credit growth to private sector
Other Financial Corporations	Assets to total financial system assets (for total of OFCs and by subsectors) Assets to gross domestic product (GDP) (for total of OFCs and by subsectors)
Other Financial Corporations Money Market Funds	Sectoral distribution of investments Maturity distribution of investments
Other Financial Corporations Insurance Corporations	Shareholder equity to total invested assets (life and non-life insurance) Combined ratio (non-life insurance only) Return on assets (life insurance only) Return on equity (life and non-life insurance)
Other Financial Corporations Pension Funds	Liquid assets to estimated pension payments in the next year Return on assets
Nonfinancial Corporations	Total debt to equity External debt to equity Foreign currency debt to equity Total debt to GDP Return on equity Earnings to interest and principal expenses Earnings to interest expenses
Households (HH)	Household debt to GDP Household debt service and principal payments to income Household debt to household disposable income
Real Estate Markets	Commercial real estate prices Residential real estate loans to total loans Commercial real estate loans to total loans

Source: IMF staff.
Note: DT = deposit taker; OFC = other financial corporation.

III. The Structure of the *Guide*

1.12 The *Guide* is presented in four parts: the foundational blocks, including accounting principles underlying data compilation and consolidation bases—Chapters 2–6; specific guidance on how to calculate the individual FSIs and metadata reporting—Chapters 7–10; compilation and dissemination issues likely to be faced by compilers—Chapter 11; and the intersection of FSIs and macroprudential analysis—Chapter 12–13.

1.13 The *Guide* is provided to facilitate the compilation and dissemination of the FSIs agreed by the IMF Executive Board, the IMF/FSB G-20 Data Gaps Initiative (DGI) and the FSI Reference Group. Specifically, the content of each chapter is as follows:

IV. Foundational Blocks

1.14 Chapter 2 of the *Guide* describes in more detail key aspects of the *System of National Accounts 2008* essential for sectoral analysis, including institutional units, residency, institutional sectors, and the financial corporation subsectors. The financial corporations subsector, together with financial instruments and markets and government regulation, comprises the financial sector. The Core FSIs focus on the deposit- taking component of the financial corporations subsector, with additional FSIs providing insights into non-DT financial corporations. The section on the payment system, which appeared in the original *2006 Guide*, has been removed from the *Guide* due to its lesser relevance to the compilers.

1.15 Chapter 3 updates and consolidates the coverage of Basel prudential standards relevant for the compilation of FSIs. Previously, the focus was on the original Basel Capital Accord and Basel II, and the information was spread over several chapters. Now, Chapter 3 includes some of the most recent Basel Committee on Banking Supervision enhancements to the Basel II and Basel III frameworks, with a special focus on capital and liquidity standards.

1.16 Three main contributions stand out in this chapter: an overview of the evolution of the Basel

Accords from Basel I to Basel III tailored to FSI compilers; a detailed description of capital and liquidity standards relevant for the compilation of FSIs and a careful description of the aggregation of capital components under different Basel Accords.

1.17 Chapter 4 incorporates advances on accounting practices and defers for the most part to IFRS standards. The major exception is the treatment of general and specific provisions, concepts that are not found in the expected loss model of IFRS 9. Continuing the practice from the previous *Guide*, and in line with current Basel Committee Guidance, the *Guide* recommends following national supervisory practices with respect to loan classification and provisioning. The chapter defines short-term maturity as up to three months (e.g., short-term liabilities should include liabilities with remaining maturity of three months or less) addressing a confusion in the *2006 Guide* which in some places defined short term maturity as one year or less.

1.18 Chapter 5 aligns the description of financial assets and liabilities with the *System of National Accounts 2008*. The chapter includes sectoral financial statements and memorandum series for money market funds, insurance corporations, and pension funds to guide the source data collection for the compilation of FSIs in each of these subsectors. The chapter provides guidance on a number of technical issues, generally following IFRS and Basel Committee guidance, but in some cases deferring to national supervisory standards.

1.19 The chapter on Aggregation and Consolidation of Data (Chapter 6) is more explicit about the fact that the most relevant type of consolidation for DTs will generally be the cross-border, cross-sector, domestically incorporated consolidation basis (CBCSDI). While the *2006 Guide* deferred to countries on the choice of whether to include insurance subsidiaries in their consolidation exercise, this *Guide* recommends exclusion of insurance companies from the deposit takers for consolidation purposes, to promote cross-country comparability of data. This exclusion is in line with supervisory practices whereby banks' insurance subsidiaries are generally not consolidated for supervisory reporting.

V. Description of Financial Soundness Indicators

1.20 Chapter 7 focuses on the core FSI for DTs and features the definition, analytical interpretation, data sources, and compilation issues for each of the core FSIs for DTs.

1.21 Chapter 8 presents the recommended "additional set" of FSIs for DTs. Many of these indicators were part of the indicators known as "encouraged indicators" of the *2006 Guide* with two exceptions: the indicator Tier 1 capital to assets (leverage ratio) is now part of the core FSI for DT (Chapter 7); net open position in equity to capital has been discontinued. In addition, credit growth of private sector is now part of the "additional set" of FSIs, recognizing its role as a leading indicator in financial stability analysis.

1.22 Chapter 9, Specification of Financial Soundness Indicators for Other Financial Corporations, features FSIs for non-DT financial corporations. Many of these indicators were part of the FSIs for other sectors in the *2006 Guide*. One of the main innovations in this *Guide* is the development of a comprehensive set of reporting requirements and FSIs for OFCs—in contrast with the focus on the reporting of total OFC assets in the *2006 Guide*. OFC FSIs now include FSIs for Money Market Funds (MMFs), Insurance Corporations (ICs—separately for life and nonlife), and Pension Funds (PFs). Chapter 9 recommends that OFCs balance sheets be compiled on a residency-based basis for all OFC subsectors, except for countries with OFCs that have significant cross-border activities, for which cross-border consolidation is relevant.

1.23 Chapter 10 focuses on selected soundness indicators of non-financial corporations, households, and real estate markets. This chapter provides a compilation methodology for a revised set of indicators for NFCs to provide more information to data users on developments in debt positions and debt servicing capacity of NFCs. Changes to the FSIs for NFCs include (i) external debt to equity and foreign currency debt to equity ratios are introduced supplementing the existing total debt to equity ratio, (ii) two new indicators: total debt to GDP and earnings to interest expenses are introduced, and (iii) two indicators (net foreign exchange exposure to equity and number of applications for protection from creditors) were dropped due to limited reporting and comparability.

1.24 Chapter 10 provides a compilation methodology for a revised set of indicators for the households sector to better capture the financial health of the HH sector for macroprudential analysis and systemic risk monitoring. In addition to two existing FSIs for the HH sector (HH debt to GDP and HH debt-service and principal payments to income), the revised set of FSIs for the HH sector includes an additional indicator on the HH debt to income.

1.25 The *2006 Guide* did not recommend a single approach for the real estate price indices but described a range of techniques that could be implemented based on national circumstances. The *Guide* explicitly recommends the compilation of FSIs for (i) residential real estate price index (residential property price index, RPPI) and (ii) commercial real estate price index (commercial property price index, CPPI). Given the increasing policy focus on monitoring residential real estate prices that has been reflected in the inclusion of RPPI in the FSI category for SDDS Plus, RPPI is now included among the core FSIs.

VI. Compilation and Dissemination Issues

1.26 Chapter 11 merges Chapters 10–12 in the *2006 Guide*. The chapter shortens the discussion on strategic and managerial issues related to the data collection and compilation and provides more specific recommendations regarding the data frequency and timeliness.

VII. The Intersection of FSIs and Macroprudential Analysis

1.27 Chapter 12, "Concentration and Distribution Measures," (CDMs) is prescriptive and provides concrete guidance for the computation of the selected FSIs for which to apply specific CDMs. The chapter also discusses ways to overcome confidentiality concerns about CDM reporting.

1.28 Chapter 13 provides a comparison between macro-prudential and micro-prudential policies. The chapter discusses the potential and existing uses of FSIs in the context of calibration of macroprudential tools as well as financial stability analysis with references to the recent macroprudential literature.

1.29 The chapter also discusses the uses of FSIs as inputs and outputs to analytical approaches (e.g., stress testing, and network analysis), their relevance to macroprudential indicators and macroprudential toolkits, and provides examples of uses of FSIs at the national macroprudential policy and financial stability analysis. Finally, Chapter 13 outlines challenges hampering an enhanced use of FSIs.

1.30 Finally, Table 1.2 presents a mapping of the 2006 to the 2019 FSIs.

Table 1.2 Financial Soundness Indicators: Mapping from the 2006 Guide

Core Set		
	Deposit Takers	Mapping from the 2006 Guide[1]
Capital Adequacy	Regulatory capital to risk-weighted assets	Basel III capital definitions introduced
	Tier 1 capital to risk-weighted assets	Basel III capital definitions introduced
	Nonperforming loans net of provisions to capital	Follow supervisory guidance to allocate IFRS allowance for expected credit loss to specific and general provisions Clarification that the denominator is total regulatory capital (previously capital and reserves)
	Common Equity Tier 1 capital to risk-weighted assets	New FSI
	Tier 1 capital to assets	New FSI, replaces the encouraged FSI capital to assets. Jurisdictions implementing the Basel III leverage ratio to use the Basel definition of "exposure" as the denominator
Asset Quality	Nonperforming loans to total gross loans	Unchanged
	Loan concentration by economic activity	Revised specification, ratio of lending to three largest economic sectors to total loans
	Provisions to nonperforming loans	New FSI. Follow supervisory guidance to allocate IFRS allowance for expected credit loss to specific and general provisions
Earnings and Profitability	Return on assets	Unchanged
	Return on equity	Based on net income after tax figures
	Interest margin to gross income	Unchanged
	Noninterest expenses to gross income	Unchanged

Table 1.2 Financial Soundness Indicators: Mapping from the 2006 Guide *(continued)*

Core Set		
	Deposit Takers	**Mapping from the 2006 Guide[1]**
Liquidity	Liquid assets to total assets (liquid asset ratio)	Unchanged
	Liquid assets to short term liabilities	Unchanged
	Liquidity Coverage Ratio	New FSI, introduces Basel III liquidity definitions
	Net Stable Funding Ratio	New FSI, introduces Basel III liquidity definitions
Sensitivity to Market Risk	Net open position in foreign exchange to capital	Unchanged
Real Estate Markets	Residential real estate prices	Now a core FSI specific to residential real estate prices Previously an encouraged FSI
Additional Set		
Deposit Takers	Large exposures to capital	Now only one recommended approach to compiling the numerator, summing all exposures exceeding 10 percent of Tier 1 capital. Denominator is now Tier 1 capital rather than total capital, aligning with more recent Basel Committee guidance
	Geographical distribution of loans to total loans	Unchanged
	Gross asset position in financial derivatives to capital	Clarification that the denominator is total regulatory capital (previously capital and reserves)
	Gross liability position in financial derivatives to capital	Clarification that the denominator is total regulatory capital (previously capital and reserves)
	Trading income to total income	Unchanged
	Personnel expenses to noninterest expenses	Unchanged
	Spread between reference lending and deposit rates	Unchanged
	Spread between highest and lowest interbank rate	Unchanged
	Customer deposits to total (noninterbank) loans	Unchanged
	Foreign-currency-denominated loans to total loans	Unchanged
	Foreign-currency-denominated liabilities to total liabilities	Unchanged
	Credit growth to private sector	New FSI
Other Financial Corporations	Assets to total financial system assets (for total of OFCs and by subsectors)	New FSIs provide additional detail relative to the previous encouraged FSI for the other financial corporations, reported for total OFCs and subsectors.
	Assets to gross domestic product (GDP) (for total of OFCs and by subsectors)	New FSIs provides additional detail relative to the previous encouraged FSI for the other financial corporations, reported for total OFCs and subsectors.
Money Market Funds	Sectoral distribution of investments	New FSI
	Maturity distribution of investments	New FSI
Insurance Corporations	Shareholder equity to total invested assets (life and non-life insurance)	New FSI
	Combined ratio (non-life insurance only)	New FSI
	Return on assets (life insurance only)	New FSI
	Return on equity (life and non-life insurance)	New FSI

Table 1.2 Financial Soundness Indicators: Mapping from the 2006 Guide *(concluded)*

Additional Set		
		Mapping from the 2006 Guide[1]
Pension Funds	Liquid assets to estimated pension payments in the next year	New FSI
	Return on assets	New FSI
Nonfinancial Corporations Sector	Total debt to equity	Unchanged
	External debt to equity	New FSI
	Foreign currency debt to equity	New FSI
	Total debt to GDP	New FSI
	Return on equity	Unchanged
	Earnings to interest and principal expenses	Unchanged
	Earnings to interest expenses	New FSI
Households	Household debt to GDP	Unchanged
	Household debt service and principal payments to income	Unchanged
	Household debt to household disposable income	New FSI
Real Estate Markets	Commercial real estate prices	Unchanged
	Residential real estate loans to total loans	Unchanged
	Commercial real estate loans to total loans	Unchanged

Source: IMF staff.

Note: IFRS = international financial reporting standards.

[1] The FSIs from the *2006 Guide* not in this table have been dropped.

2 Institutional Sectors and the Financial System

I. Introduction

2.1 This chapter starts by defining institutional units (as holders and issuers of financial assets) and classifying them into sectors following the overarching macroeconomic statistics principles in the *2008 System of National Accounts (2008 SNA)*. Subsequently, the concept of residence is used to establish the economic boundary for compiling FSIs. It determines the foreign/domestic breakdown of assets and liabilities of financial corporations (FCs). Next, resident institutional units are classified into institutional sectors and subsectors. This allows the presentation of FCs' claims on and liabilities to the different sectors of the domestic economy. Finally, the chapter identifies and defines the main types of players and markets that typically constitute a financial system.

II. Institutional Units

2.2 An institutional unit is an economic entity capable, in its own right, of decision-making autonomy in owning assets, incurring liabilities and engaging in economic activities and in transactions with other entities.

2.3 Institutional units, as owners of financial assets and issuers of liabilities, constitute the structural building blocks for macroeconomic statistical frameworks. Two main types of units may qualify as institutional units: persons or groups of persons in the form of households, and legal or social entities.

Households

2.4 A household is a group of persons who share the same living accommodation, pool some, or all, of their income and wealth and consume certain types of goods and services collectively, mainly housing and food. A household may consist of an individual or more than one person.

Legal or Social Entities

2.5 The second type of institutional unit is a legal or social entity that engages in economic activities and transactions in its own right. A legal or social entity is one whose existence is recognized by law or society independently of the persons, or other entities, that may own or control it. Such units are responsible and accountable for the economic decisions or actions they take, although their autonomy may be constrained to some extent by other institutional units.

2.6 Three categories of legal or social entities constituting institutional units can be identified: (1) corporations; (2) nonprofit institutions (NPIs); and (3) government units. The status of an institutional unit cannot always be inferred from its name. It is necessary to examine its economic objectives, functions, and behavior. (For detail see *Monetary and Financial Statistics Manual and Compilation Guide [MFSMCG]* paragraphs 3.3-3.50).

III. Residence

2.7 The delineation between resident and nonresident units determines which units are part of the reporting population and facilitates the estimation of the external position of the FCs sector. The key concepts for defining the residence of an institutional unit are *economic territory* and *center of predominant economic interest*.[1] Residence is not based on nationality of the account holder, nor on the currency of denomination of accounts.

Economic Territory

2.8 An economic territory can be any geographic area or jurisdiction for which statistics are required. The most commonly used concept of economic territory is the area under the effective economic control of a single government. It includes special zones (e.g., free trade zones and offshore financial centers).[2] The connection of entities to an economic territory

---

[1] The concept and coverage of residence in the *Guide* are identical to those in the *2008 SNA*, the *MFSMCG*, and the *BPM6*.

[2] For the government's own statistical needs, data on activities in these zones may be excluded or shown separately.

is determined from aspects such as physical presence and being subject to the jurisdiction of the government of the territory. Economic territory may be larger or smaller than the physical or political borders of a country, for example, a currency or economic union, or part of a country.[3]

2.9 Economic territory has the dimensions of physical location, as well as legal jurisdiction, so that corporations created under the law are part of that economy. The concepts of economic territory and residence are designed to ensure that each institutional unit is a resident in one economic territory, determined by its center of predominant economic interest.

Residence of Institutional Units

2.10 The residence of each institutional unit is the economic territory with which it has the strongest connection, expressed as its center of predominant economic interest.

2.11 An institutional unit has a center of predominant economic interest in an economic territory when there exists, within the economic territory, some location, dwelling, place of production, or other premises on which or from which the unit engages and intends to continue engaging, either indefinitely or over a finite, but long, period of time, in economic activities and transactions on a significant scale. Actual or intended location for one year or more is used as an operational definition. Although the choice of a specific time period is somewhat arbitrary, it is adopted in *BPM6* (see paragraph 4.114) to avoid uncertainty and facilitate international consistency.

Resident units

2.12 An institutional unit is considered a resident if it has already engaged in economic activities and transactions on a significant scale in the territory for one year or more, or if it intends to do so.

2.13 A household is a resident in the economic territory in which the household members maintain or intend to maintain a dwelling or succession of dwellings treated and used by members of the household as their principal dwelling. The residence of individual persons is determined by that of the household of which they form part and not by their place of work. All members of the same household have the same residence as the household itself, even though they may cross borders to work or otherwise spend periods of time abroad.

2.14 Corporations and NPIs normally may be expected to have a center of predominant economic interest in the economy in which they are legally constituted and registered. Corporations may be resident in economies different from their shareholders. Subsidiaries may be resident in different economies from their parent corporations. As a general principle, an enterprise is resident in an economic territory when it is engaged in a significant amount of production of goods or services from a location in the territory. They must maintain at least one production establishment in the territory and plan to operate it indefinitely or over a long period of time (usually one year or more). Additional factors to consider are the maintenance of a set of accounts covering local productive activities and being subject to the income tax system in the economy in which it is located. Unincorporated enterprises that are not quasi-corporations[4] are not separate institutional units from their owners and, therefore, have the same residence as their owners. When a nonresident unit has substantial operations over a significant period in an economic territory, but no separate legal entity for those operations, a branch may be identified as an institutional unit.

2.15 Apart from these general definitions, there are special cases where individuals or institutional units should be considered residents of the territory, and their accounts incorporated in the domestic assets and liabilities of the FCs.[5]

Nonresident units

2.16 Institutional units that have their center of predominant economic interest outside the economic

[3] The economic territory includes: (1) the land area; (2) airspace; (3) territorial waters, including areas over which jurisdiction is exercised over fishing rights and rights to fuel or minerals; (4) in maritime territory, islands that belong to the territory; and (5) territorial enclaves in the rest of the world, such as embassies, consulates, military bases, scientific stations, information and immigration offices, aid agencies, and central bank representative offices with diplomatic status (*MFSMCG* paragraph 3.53).

[4] Quasi-corporations are unincorporated enterprises that function in all (or almost all) respects as if they were incorporated. For a quasi-corporation to exist, it must be possible to develop a full set of accounts, including balance sheets, to distinguish it from its owners. (For details, see *MFSMCG* paragraphs 3.18–3.20.)

[5] For those special cases, see *MFSMCG* paragraphs 3.62–3.86.

territory are nonresidents. Their accounts are recorded as part of foreign assets or foreign liabilities of the resident FCs, irrespective of the nationality of the account holder and of the currency of denomination of the accounts.[6]

IV. Institutional Sectors

Definition

2.17 Classifying institutional units into institutional sectors is key in all macroeconomic statistical frameworks. Sectoring of institutional units involves grouping together institutional units with similar economic objectives, functions, and behavior into institutional sectors. In the FSIs, it is necessary to delineate the FCs sector and its subsectors, to identify their financial health and soundness.

2.18 Resident institutional units are grouped into mutually exclusive sectors. For FSI compilation purposes, the key sectors comprise: (1) financial corporations (FCs); (2) nonfinancial corporations (NFCs); (3) general government; (4) households; and (5) nonprofit institutions serving households (NPISHs).[7] All resident institutional units are allocated to only one institutional sector. A unit engaged in activities belonging to more than one sector and not having a separate set of accounts for each activity must be classified entirely in a single sector, based on the most prominent economic activity in which it engages.

2.19 Financial corporations include deposit takers (DTs), and other financial corporations (OFCs);[8] and OFCs are split into additional subsectors as discussed in the next section.

[6]In addition to cases in which it is straightforward to identify the accounts of nonresidents, there are several cases in which it is not clear-cut that the account holder is a nonresident of the economy. (For those cases, see *MFSMCG* paragraphs 3.89–3.99.)

[7]The households sector in the *Guide* includes NPISH.

[8]As well as accurately portraying the type of institutions covered, the *Guide* uses the term "deposit takers" rather than "other depository corporations" (ODC) as used in the *MFSMCG* because of the possible difference in coverage of institutions. In reflecting analytical interest in broad money, ODCs are defined as including all those entities that issue liabilities included in the national definition of money. This may exclude (include) institutional units that are otherwise included (excluded) within the *Guide*'s definition (e.g., certain offshore banks). Notably, money market funds are explicitly excluded from the *Guide*'s coverage of deposit takers (see paragraph 2.47) but can be included in the *MFSMCG*'s coverage of ODCs. Any institutional unit classified as an ODC that does not meet the *Guide*'s definition of a deposit taker should be classified as OFCs.

Financial Corporations

2.20 The FCs sector consists of all resident corporations, including quasi-corporations, that are principally engaged in providing financial services to other institutional units. Units providing financial services do not usually produce other goods and services and financial services are not provided as secondary production.

2.21 FCs are distinguished from nonfinancial corporations at the first level of sectoring, because FCs are engaged principally in providing financial services, including financial intermediation, which are inherently different from other types of productive activity.

Nonfinancial Corporations

2.22 The nonfinancial corporations (NFCs) sector encompasses corporations and quasi-corporations whose principal activity is the production of market goods or nonfinancial services.

2.23 The NFCs sector is composed of the following resident institutional units: (1) all resident nonfinancial corporations, regardless of the residence of their shareholders; (2) the branches of nonresident enterprises that are engaged in nonfinancial production in the economic territory on a long-term basis; and (3) all resident NPIs that are market producers of goods or nonfinancial services.

General Government

2.24 Government units are unique kinds of legal entities established by political process that have legislative, judicial, or executive authority over other institutional units within a given area. The principal functions of government units are to assume responsibility for the provision of goods and services to the community or individual households primarily on a nonmarket basis, redistribute income and wealth by means of transfers, engage in nonmarket production, and finance their activities out of taxation or other compulsory transfers.

2.25 The general government sector consists of resident institutional units that fulfill the functions of government as their primary activity. The general government sector comprises all government units of central, state, provincial, regional and local government, and social security funds, as well as all resident nonmarket NPIs controlled by government units.[9]

2.26 Resident public corporations include entities in the deposit-taking and other sectors that are subject to control by government units, defined as the ability to determine general corporate policy by choosing directors, if necessary.[10]

V. Financial Sector

Definition

2.27 The financial sector consists of institutional units, financial instruments and markets, and government regulation, interacting to facilitate intermediation between providers and users of funds.

2.28 Financial markets facilitate the transfer of productive resource between entities or sectors with surplus resources to those in need of resource, and in doing so support the productive potential and development of the economy. Markets provide a setting within which financial claims can be traded under established rules of conduct, and can facilitate the management of credit, market and, other risks. They also play an important role in identifying market prices ("price discovery").

2.29 Although many definitions in the *Guide* draw from the *MFSMCG*, the definition of the financial sector is not equivalent across the two frameworks. Also the definition of DTs in the *Guide* could deviate from their regulatory definitions in some countries.

Central Bank

2.30 The central bank is the national financial institution exercising control over key aspects of the financial sector. Its functions generally include (1) issuing currency, (2) conducting monetary policy, including by regulating money supply and credit, (3) managing international reserves, (4) providing credit to deposit-taking corporations, and (5) acting as banker to government, by holding central government deposits and providing credit in the form of overdrafts, advances, and purchases of securities. FSIs are not computed for the central bank.

Deposit Takers

2.31 Deposit takers have financial intermediation as their principal activity. To this end, they obtain funds through the acceptance of deposits or other financial instruments such as short-term certificates of deposits,[11] bills, bonds, other debt securities, or other financial instruments. DTs may also be subject to license and regulatory requirements.

2.32 Within a financial system, the role of deposit takers (DTs) is central. They often provide a location for the placement and borrowing of funds and, as such, are a source of liquid assets and funds to the rest of the economy. They are important for the transmission of monetary policy. They also provide payments services that are relied upon by all other entities for the conduct of their business. Thus, failures of deposit takers can have a significant impact on the activities of all other financial and nonfinancial entities and on the confidence in, and the functioning of, the financial system. This makes the analysis of the health and soundness of deposit takers central to any assessment of financial system stability.

2.33 In the *Guide*, DTs comprise all deposit-taking institutions, regardless of whether liabilities issued are included in the national definition of broad money. On the other hand, in the *MFSMCG*, other depository corporations (ODCs) are defined as financial corporations that issue liabilities in the form of deposits included in broad money. For deposits that are not included in broad money, FCs are defined as OFCs. One notable exception is of MMF shares and units which are highly liquid and close substitutes for transferable and other deposits. In the *MFSMCG*, MMF shares and units are thus included in broad money and all MMFs as defined in paragraph 2.51 are classified as ODCs. By contrast, MMFs are defined as OFCs in the *Guide* because the nature of their business might differ from that of DTs, and because legal and regulatory systems and prudential requirements can differ.

[9] For detailed classification of the general government sector and its subsectors see the *Government Finance Statistics Manual 2014 (GFSM 2014)* paragraphs 2.76–2.78.

[10] For indicators of control and how to apply them to establish control of government over corporations, see *GFSM 2014* Box 2.2.

[11] The *Guide* definition for DTs follows closely the *SNA 2008* definition of *depository corporations, with the exception of the central bank.*

2.34 DTs, as defined in the *Guide*, in some jurisdictions may cover institutions outside of the banking system, defined de facto or de jure. For instance, in certain countries, the definition of DTs may cover institutions that do not have a "banking license" but that can still accept deposits. These DTs often fall outside the scope of banking supervision and may be subject to a prudential regime that varies from that applied to banks.

2.35 For compiling FSIs, dealing with data for DTs not regulated as banks (non-bank DTs) adds complexity, and may prove costly if regulatory-based information is not available. The *Guide* recommends two options for dealing with non-bank DTs: (i) report annually information on their number, asset size, and control in the IMF report form on the institutional coverage of FSIs; or (ii) compile a subset of FSIs for these institutions and disseminate this information separately. The latter option is recommended when non-bank DTs comprise a significant part of the financial sector in terms of size or number of customers served.

Commercial banks

2.36 A commercial bank is the most common designation of a deposit-taking corporation but use of the term "bank" in the name of an entity does not imply it is actually a commercial bank—it should be classified as a bank based on the types of activities undertaken and not based on the name alone. The range of activities in which a commercial bank can participate varies widely among countries, depending on national banking regulations and practices, and the sophistication of a country's financial system. The most common services provided by commercial banks are accepting deposits and granting loans or other forms of finance to corporations and households. In many countries, they are required to hold reserves at the central bank, often determined as a certain proportion of their deposit liabilities.

Other deposit-taking corporations

2.37 Corporations and quasi-corporations that may be classified as other deposit-taking corporations include (1) merchant banks; (2) savings and loan associations, building societies, and mortgage banks; (3) credit unions, and credit cooperatives; (4) municipal credit institutions; (5) rural banks and agricultural banks; and (6) electronic money institutions, among others.[12]

Special cases

Offshore banks

2.38 "Offshore banks" is a term for deposit-taking corporations established in jurisdictions that provide legal and fiscal advantages, such as low or no taxation and less stringent regulations in terms of reserve requirements or foreign exchange restrictions. They engage in various types of financial transactions, including deposit taking and the extension of loans typically denominated in currencies other than the currency of the economy in which they are located. They may be restricted from accepting deposits from residents of the economy in which they are located.

2.39 Offshore banks engaged in trade and finance are residents of the economies in which they are located. The *Guide* recommends that offshore banks are included in the DTs if they take deposits. If they do not take deposits, they should be classified as OFCs.

Banks in distress

2.40 Under financial difficulties, some deposit-taking corporations may operate under the control of receivers or regulators and others may have been closed. The deposit-taking corporations are deemed to continue to exist until a formal bankruptcy or reorganization has taken place. Until such corporations are liquidated or reorganized, their deposits may be frozen.

2.41 The deposit-taking corporations in liquidation or reorganization may retain claims on various sectors of the economy, which may be transferred to a restructuring agency or may be acquired by other depository corporations. Reorganization, sale, or merger of such depository corporations may result in all or part of the funds eventually becoming available to depositors and possibly other creditors.

2.42 The *Guide* recommends that banks whose deposits liabilities are frozen during liquidation or reorganization continue to be included in the DTs subsector as long as they own financial assets and liabilities. It is recognized that in practice, it is usually

[12] For detailed descriptions of those entities, see *MFSMCG* paragraphs 3.129–3.137.

difficult to get data on the accounts of banks in liquidation reported on a regular basis. Moreover, reported values of assets and liabilities of banks in liquidation may not reflect true market value of those instruments.

2.43 If DTs in distress constitute a significant share of the domestic financial system, the authorities may consider compiling data both including and excluding these institutions, particularly if the liquidation process is very lengthy.[13]

Other Financial Corporations

2.44 In recent years, the OFCs sector has increased its importance within the financial system, engaging in a wide range of financial intermediary, or auxiliary, activities outside the banking system. These activities include so-called "shadow banking," which can be broadly defined as credit intermediation involving entities and activities outside the regulated banking system. Total assets of all OFCs, plus selected financial statement and memorandum series for money market funds, insurance corporations and pension funds, are used in the compilation of FSIs.

Money Market Funds

2.45 Money market funds (MMFs) are collective investment schemes that raise funds by issuing shares or units to the public. The proceeds are invested primarily in money market instruments, MMF shares or units, bank deposits, tradable debt instruments with a residual maturity of not more than one year, and instruments that pursue a rate of return that approaches the interest rates of money market instruments. For an investment fund to be recognized as an MMF, there needs to be (1) a certain degree of capital certainty (reliable store of value); and (2) the possibility to withdraw funds immediately or on short notice. If the conditions above are not met, the institution is not classified as an MMF but as a non-MMF investment fund.

Non-MMF Investment Funds

2.46 Non-MMF investment funds are collective investment schemes that raise funds by issuing shares or units to the public excluding MMFs. The proceeds are invested predominantly in long-term financial assets, such as equity shares, bonds, and mortgage loans, and nonfinancial assets, such as real estate. Non-MMF investment funds may also invest a small percentage of their total assets in highly liquid short-term financial instruments to ensure that requests to redeem shares or units are met without delay. They can be run under several denominations, such as mutual funds, investment pools, investment trusts, unit trusts, and institutions, for collective investment.

Insurance Corporations

2.47 Insurance corporations provide financial benefits to policyholders through risk-sharing and risk-transfer contracts. Main types of insurance include *life or long-term insurance; non-life or property and casualty, or general insurance; and reinsurance.* Also included in this subsector are captive insurance companies, which serve only their owners; deposit insurers; issuers of deposit guarantees; and other issuers of standardized guarantees that are separate institutional units and function like insurers by constituting reserves and charging premiums proportional to the cost of the service provided. Insurance corporations may also operate pension plans, as indicated in the next subsection.

2.48 Life insurance corporations invest premiums to build up portfolios of financial assets to be used to meet future claims of policy holders, spreading risks of the policy holders over time. Life insurance corporations offer products that are purely insurance as well as products with a savings component. "Term insurance" provides a guaranteed death benefit for a specified time period. Non-unit linked insurance (or traditional insurance) is a contract that provides life insurance with a fixed payment in case of death or at maturity. Unit-linked insurance is an insurance contract, which provides a combination of (traditional) life insurance and an investment component with the investment risk being entirely borne by the policyholder. Returns on the investment component depend on market performance.

2.49 Non-life insurance corporations provide financial benefits to policy holders in the event of accidents, fire, property loss, health-related expenses, and so on, spreading current risk or expenses among clients. Some individual insurance corporations sell both life and non-life insurance, in which case they are called *composite insurance companies.*

[13] For example, this could be considered if DTs, which are in distress over a long period of time, have large foreign exchange exposures (but "active" DTs do not).

2.50 Reinsurance corporations insure the insurance policies written by other insurance corporations in exchange for insurance premiums. Insurance corporations purchase reinsurance to offset policy risk, thereby capping the net loss incurred if the insured event occurs.

Pension Funds

2.51 The pension funds subsector consists of autonomous pension funds that are separate funds (i.e., separate institutional units) established for purposes of providing incomes on retirement for specific groups of employees which are organized, and directed, by private or public employers or jointly by the employers and their employees.[14] Pension schemes may be administered by a separately constituted pension fund, or a fund that is operated by the employer. Governments also sometimes organize pension schemes for their employees, which are independent of the social security system.

2.52 Pension schemes may be funded or unfunded. Funded pension schemes have separate pools of financial assets, or reserves, assigned for the payment of benefits. Unfunded pension schemes have no separated pool of assets and are not a separate institutional unit from the administrator of the scheme. They are administered by employers or the government, who do not create specific pension-fund reserves for the payment of benefits.

2.53 There are three types of funded pension schemes: (1) those operated by FCs, typically insurance or asset-management corporations; (2) those operated as autonomous pension funds; and (3) those operated as non-autonomous pension funds. If funded, all three types of pension funds will hold reserves dedicated to the payment of pensions and other retirement benefits to the beneficiaries.

2.54 Depending on how the benefits are determined, pension plans may operate as defined benefit plans or defined contribution plans. Under a *defined benefit plan*, the future retirement benefits are determined by specific factors such as the participants' length of service and salaries and age at retirement. Under *a defined contribution plan*, the benefits to be received by a participant are based on contributions to the pension fund and the investment performance of the fund. *Hybrid schemes* are a combination of a defined benefit plan and a defined contribution plan, where the risk of the scheme to provide an adequate income in retirement is shared by the employer and the employee.

Other Financial Intermediaries

2.55 Other financial intermediaries, except insurance corporations and pension funds, consist of FCs that are engaged in providing financial services by incurring liabilities, in forms other than currency and deposits, for the purpose of acquiring on their own account financial assets, by engaging in financial transactions on the market. It is a feature of a financial intermediary that transactions on both sides of the balance sheet are carried out in open markets.

2.56 FCs in the other financial intermediaries subsector generally raise funds on wholesale financial markets or through the sale of securities, and usually not in the form of deposits, and use the funds to extend loans and acquire other financial assets. The intermediaries often specialize in lending to borrowers in particular sectors of the economy and for specialized financial arrangements. Units classified as other financial intermediaries include finance companies, financial leasing companies, investment banks, venture capital and private equity firms, underwriters and dealers, central clearing counterparties (CCPs), financial derivative intermediaries, securitization vehicles, specialized financial intermediaries, asset management companies (AMCs), and bank restructuring agencies.[15]

Financial Auxiliaries

2.57 Financial auxiliaries are principally engaged in facilitating transactions in financial assets and

[14]In contrast, nonautonomous pension funds are not separate institutional units and are therefore not separated from the entity which has organized them, and so their assets and liabilities are reflected in the accounts of that entity. Excluded from the pension fund subsector are nonautonomous pension funds managed by the employer, government sponsored pension schemes funded through social security schemes (pay-as-you-go schemes), and arrangements organized by nongovernment employers for which the reserves of the fund are simply included among the employer's own resources or are invested in securities issued by that employer.

[15]For detailed descriptions of those entities, see *MFSMCG* paragraphs 3.155–3.163.

liabilities by providing the regulatory context for these transactions but in circumstances that do not involve the auxiliary taking ownership of the financial assets and liabilities being transacted. Financial auxiliaries do not act as intermediaries.

2.58 Some of the most common types of financial auxiliaries include public exchanges, securities markets, clearing houses, brokers, agents, foreign exchange companies (or bureau de change), insurance and pension funds auxiliaries (e.g., agents, adjusters, and actuarial services), financial derivative corporations, representative offices of foreign banks, corporations primarily involved in the operation of electronic payment mechanisms, third-party payment processors (e.g., online payment corporations, and financial payment corporations including money-transfer or remittance services), supervisory agencies, regulatory bodies, managers of pension funds and of mutual funds, head offices of FCs, solicitor nominee companies, and peer-to-peer lending companies.[16]

Captive Financial Institutions and Money Lenders

2.59 Captive financial institutions and money lenders consist of institutional units providing financial services other than insurance where most of either their assets or liabilities are not transacted on open financial markets but arise from transactions with related parties. This category includes entities transacting within only a limited group of units or subsidiaries of the same holding corporation, or entities that extend loans from own funds provided by only one sponsor.[17]

2.60 Captive financial institutions are corporate subsidiaries that act as financial agents for their parent corporations, raising funds to lend to their parent corporations or for purchase of parent corporations' accounts receivables. Captive insurance companies and pension funds that serve their owners are not included in this subsector but classified as insurance corporations and pension funds. Captive financial institutions are sometimes operated by deposit-taking corporations for engaging in specialized activities or for regulatory reasons. If they do not qualify to be treated as units separate from their parent corporations they are included within the balance sheets of the parent corporations unless they are resident in an economy different from that where the parent is resident. They are classified in the OFC subsector if they qualify to be treated as separate institutional units.

2.61 Holding companies are units that hold the assets of a group of subsidiary corporations as their principal activity, and do not provide any other service to the enterprises in which the equity is held (i.e., they do not administer or manage other units). Holding companies are always allocated to the FCs sector and treated as captive financial institutions, even if all the subsidiary corporations are nonfinancial corporations.

VI. Financial Markets

2.62 A financial market can be defined as a market in which entities can trade financial claims under some established rules of conduct. There are various types of financial markets depending on the nature of the claims being traded. The two main categories include the money and capital markets (primary and secondary). Other financial markets include derivatives, commodities and the foreign exchange market.

2.63 The money market involves short-term lending and borrowing of funds. It provides short-term liquidity to governments and financial and nonfinancial corporations. Instruments traded in a money market have a short maturity and include treasury bills, central bank bills, certificates of deposit, bankers' acceptances, and commercial paper. They also include borrowing through repurchase agreements. An active money market allows entities to manage their liquidity in an efficient manner, by facilitating investment of excess holdings of cash in interest-bearing assets, which can be drawn upon when needed, and by providing a source of funds for those short of liquidity, or who wish to finance short-term positions in other markets.

2.64 One specific money market is the interbank market, where banks lend to each other their excess liquidity, often overnight and usually on an unsecured basis. An efficient interbank market facilitates banks' liquidity management and contributes to monetary policy design.

[16] For detailed descriptions of those entities, see *MFSMCG* paragraphs 3.167–3.179.

[17] Trusts, corporations engaged in lending, pawnshops or pawnbrokers, Special Purpose Entities, and Sovereign wealth funds (SWFs) are also included in this sector.

2.65 Capital markets are the markets where financial instruments such as bonds and shares are issued to secure long term financing, and where they are traded. Capital markets include bond markets and equity markets. The bond market is the market in longer-term debt instruments issued by governments, and financial and nonfinancial corporations. The bond market allows a borrower to obtain long-term funds through the issuance of debt securities, while providing investors with an opportunity to purchase and sell these securities. For borrowers, such a market provides an alternative to bank lending as a form of long-term finance. An active bond market also allows credit risks to be spread over a wide range of investors, reducing the potential for credit risk concentration and providing borrowers with up-to-date information on the market views of their credit-worthiness. Bonds also provide an investment opportunity for those investors that have a long-term investment horizon, such as pension funds with long-term liabilities.

2.66 The equity market is where equity securities are traded. An active equity market is an important source of capital to the issuer and allows the investor to benefit from the future growth of the business through dividend payments and/or an increase in the value of the equity. Turnover serves as an indicator of liquidity in equity markets.

2.67 Financial derivatives markets are used to trade financial risks such as those arising from foreign exchange and interest rates, to entities more able or willing to bear them. Credit risk can also be traded, through credit derivatives. Derivatives comprise forwards, options, swaps, and sometimes combinations of these three elements, with the value of the derivative instrument depending mainly on the price of the underlying item—the reference price. These markets can broaden financial market activity by providing a way to transfer financial risk that otherwise would have deterred an investor from purchasing the security. Since financial derivatives transfer risk, financial stability can be threatened by an accumulation of risk exposures by derivatives counterparties, particular if the risks have not been fully understood or properly priced.

2.68 In financial markets, liquidity is important, because it allows investors to manage their portfolios and risks more efficiently, which tends to reduce the borrowing cost. There are several dimensions to market liquidity, including tightness, depth, immediacy, and resilience. Tightness is a market's ability to match supply and demand efficiently and can be measured by the bid-ask spread. Market depth relates to the ability of a market to absorb large trade volumes without a significant impact on prices and can be approximated by the amounts traded over a period of time (turnover) and quote sizes. Immediacy is the speed with which orders can be executed and settled, and resilience is the speed with which price fluctuations arising from imbalances in trades are dissipated.

3 Basel Capital and Liquidity Standards for Deposit Takers

I. Introduction

3.1 This chapter discusses prudential standards relating to capital and liquidity developed by the Basel Committee on Banking Supervision (BCBS)—the international standard setter for banks—which are relevant to compiling FSIs.[1] An overview of the concepts and key terminology is provided, but much of the technical detail, which will not in the normal course be required by compilers, has been omitted. Compilers requiring additional detail are referred to the publications of the BCBS.[2]

3.2 International standards are not themselves binding or enforceable, but rather are implemented, on a voluntary basis, by national authorities. Compilers will rely on national definitions and standards for capital, liquidity, leverage and large exposures related series, drawing on supervisory data rather than themselves calculating the various elements of Basel Committee-prescribed methodology.

3.3 Despite the expected reliance on supervisory data, it is important for compilers to have a broad understanding of the Basel concepts and principles related to capital and liquidity. Compilers need to be able to document in the metadata which version of the Basel Capital Accord provides the foundation for the national capital adequacy regime. They also need to identify whether their jurisdiction has exercised any of the many elements of national discretion, and if there are any national variations from the relevant Basel regime (other than the elements of express national discretion).

II. Evolution of the Basel Capital Accord

3.4 There were three novel elements to the original Basel Capital Accord. Prior to 1988, there were no agreed international standards with respect to deposit takers, and national approaches to capital adequacy were not linked to the riskiness of individual institutions. The Accord (i) introduced commonly accepted definitions of the elements of regulatory capital; (ii) linked capital requirements to risk through the introduction of risk weights—factors approximating risk applied to the assets of the bank to determine required capital; and (iii) established a minimum capital requirement of 8 percent of risk weighted assets for internationally active banks, which soon became a de facto standard for almost all banks through its widespread adoption by national authorities.

3.5 The Basel I capital requirement was to be met by Tier 1 capital—the most permanent and loss absorbing instruments; and Tier 2 capital—instruments with some shortcomings with respect to the key features of capital—to a limit of 50 percent of total capital.

3.6 The 1996 Amendment to Incorporate Market Risks partially addressed one of the early criticisms of the original Accord—banks are exposed to many risks, but Basel I originally considered only credit risk. To maintain consistency with the original approach, the calculation of market risk exposure was expressed in the form of a risk-weighted asset equivalent. A new element of capital, Tier 3, was introduced at national

[1] The Islamic Financial Services Board (IFSB) is the international standard setter for institutions offering Islamic financial services. ISFB 15, *Revised Capital Adequacy for Institutions Offering Islamic Financial Services,* establishes capital adequacy standards, which, with differences required for Islamic finance, parallel the standards of the Basel Committee. IFSB *Guidance Note 6* addresses the application of the Basel III liquidity ratios, LCR and NSFR, to institutions offering Islamic financial services.

[2] Key publications include (i) *International Convergence of Capital Measurement and Capital Standards* (1988), and *Amendment to the Capital Accord to Incorporate Market Risks* (1996), collectively referred to as Basel I; (ii) *International Convergence of Capital Measurement and Capital Standards: A Revised Framework* (2004), commonly referred to as Basel II; (iii) *Basel III: A Global Regulatory Framework for More Resilient Banks and Banking Systems* (2010); and (iv) *Basel III: Finalising Post-Crisis Reforms* (2017).

discretion, with use limited solely to supporting market risks.[3]

3.7 Basel II, while retaining the original definitions of capital and 8 percent minimum, more thoroughly addressed the criticism that Basel I focused on only one (two after 1996) of the many risks faced by banks. It also responded to criticisms that the risk weightings were insufficiently granular, not distinguishing, for example, between the risk of an AAA-rated corporate exposure and a CCC-rated (one notch above default) exposure—each was weighted at 100 percent.

3.8 Basel II also reflected feedback from large and complex banks, which indicated that the risk weights and capital required by Basel I bore little resemblance to how risks were internally assessed, and capital allocated in managing risk in the bank. In response, Basel II introduced the advanced measurement approaches, permitting the use of banks' internal models, subject to supervisory approval, in the determination of capital requirements for credit and operational risks.[4] Allowing the use of models aligned capital more closely with complex banks' actual risk management practices, while the Basel II Standardized Approach introduced additional granularity for smaller or less complex banks by using external credit ratings to further differentiate the risk of credit exposures.

3.9 Basel II required banks to hold capital against three "Pillar 1" risks—credit, market and operational risks, and introduced requirements for banks to identify other risk exposures and capital requirements in "Pillar 2." The Pillar 2 concept requires banks, whether using the standardized or advanced approaches, to undertake an internal capital adequacy assessment process (ICAAP). This requires the identification of all material risks faced by the bank, and the allocation of capital against those risks.

3.10 In the immediate aftermath of the global financial crisis, *Enhancements to the Basel II Framework* (2009), often called Basel II.5, addressed some issues that had proven particularly problematic. Requirements for retention of a portion of the credit risk for securitized assets or application of penal risk weights ensured that banks originating asset-backed securities retained an interest in the credit risk of the underlying assets. More stringent requirements were introduced to ensure that assets securitized or sold truly had a "clean break" from the bank before the assets were removed from the bank's risk-weighted assets for regulatory purposes. Additional capital charges were introduced for some elements of market risk, and the advanced method of calculation of market risk capital charges was revised to require consideration of stress scenarios.

3.11 Basel III (2010) was a more far-reaching response to the lessons of the crisis, requiring banks to hold more, higher quality capital (Figure 3.1), introducing a leverage ratio and two new liquidity ratios. While the original 8 percent capital adequacy limit from Basel I and II was retained, effectively the minimum capital requirement became 10.5 percent of risk-weighted assets through the introduction of the capital conservation buffer (Table 3.1). In addition, other capital buffers can result in higher minimum requirements for the system overall, and for individual banks. The countercyclical capital buffer is a Basel III macroprudential tool, which can be used by authorities to require banks to hold additional capital in a period of increasing risks. Higher minimum capital requirements for

Figure 3.1 Basel Capital Requirements

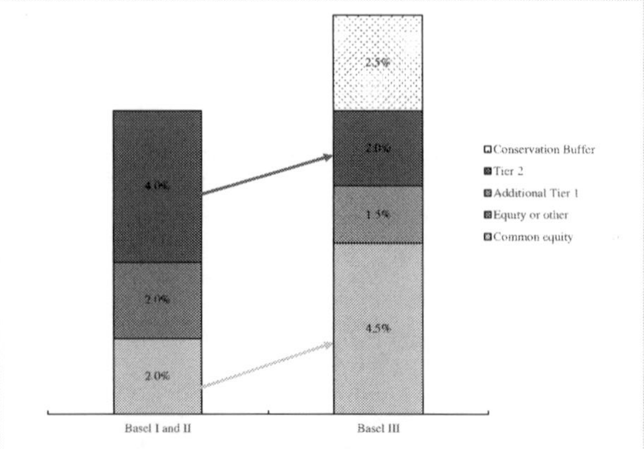

Source: IMF and BCBS.

[3] Tier 3 capital was eliminated in Basel III. Few countries adopted Tier 3 capital as part of their national frameworks, and the national discretion to allow Tier 3 capital no longer exists. Compilers generally should not require details of Tier 3 capital, so it is excluded from this discussion. Compilers requiring more information on Tier 3 capital should consult their national supervisory standards and BCBS *Amendment to the Capital Accord to Incorporate Market Risks* (1996).

[4] Use of internal models for market risk had been introduced in *Amendment to the Capital Accord to Incorporate Market Risks* (1996).

Table 3.1 Basel III Capital Ratios (percent of risk-weighted assets)

	CET1	Tier 1 Capital	Total Capital
Minimum	4.5	6	8
Capital conservation buffer	2.5	2.5	2.5
Minimum plus capital conservation buffer	7	8.5	10.5

Source: BCBS (2011).
Note: CET1 = Common Equity Tier 1.

large and complex banks result from the application of buffers for globally and domestically systemically important banks.

3.12 Basel III introduced a Common Equity Tier 1 (CET1) capital requirement of 4.5 percent of risk-weighted assets, which is effectively 7 percent since the 2.5 percent capital conservation buffer must be met with CET1. This, plus the requirement for Tier 1 capital of at least 6 percent of risk-weighted assets, increased the minimum capital available to absorb losses on a going-concern basis. To ensure going concern loss absorption, instruments qualifying as Additional Tier 1 (AT1) capital must be subject to write-down or conversion to common equity. This meant that some hybrid instruments previously qualifying at Tier 1 capital were no longer eligible, requiring banks to raise more high-quality capital.

3.13 Basel III introduced for the first time agreed international standards for liquidity. Reflecting that banks and their supervisors had paid insufficient attention to liquidity risk during the long period of benign market conditions preceding the crisis, the stress-scenario- based liquidity coverage ratio (LCR) and net stable funding ratio (NSFR) require banks not only to hold higher levels of high quality liquid assets (HQLA), but also require increased focus on liquidity risk management. At minimum, calculation of the LCR and NSFR requires banks to apply liquidity stress scenarios to their balances sheets and requires supervisory review of banks' application of these stress-tests. These liquidity ratios are discussed in more detail in paragraphs 3.49–3.55.

3.14 *Basel III: Finalisation of Post Crisis Reforms* (2017) is in some ways even more far-reaching than the original 2010 Basel III reforms. Key elements are (i) a far more granular approach to credit risk weights in the standardized approach; (ii) a new Standardized Credit Risk Assessment providing an alternative to the use of external credit ratings in risk weightings; (iii) constraints on the use of internal models intended to reduce variability in risk-weighted asset calculations across banks; (iv) an output floor for internal model calculation of capital for credit risk of 72.5 percent of the requirement determined using the standardized approach; and (v) a single new method for calculating operational risk capital charges that replaces all previous options.

3.15 Annex 3.1 summarizes key aspects of Basel I, II, and III.

III. Concepts and Terminology

Regulatory Capital

3.16 Capital is similar to, but not the same as, the accounting concept of equity. Capital represents a buffer between the value of banks' liabilities and assets, similar to the accounting definition of equity as the difference between the value of assets and liabilities. From a supervisory perspective, the purpose of capital is to absorb unexpected losses so that the providers of banks' liabilities—commonly depositors—will be repaid in full even if the providers of capital—owners and subordinated debt holders—incur losses.

3.17 Regulatory capital differs from accounting equity because of the supervisory focus on absorbing losses. Certain accounting liabilities may be loss absorbing, for example, debt which is subordinated to the claims of other creditors (including depositors), so liabilities meeting specific criteria are included in regulatory capital.

3.18 The distinguishing elements of regulatory capital are its permanence, its freedom from fixed charges against income, and its ability to absorb losses. The highest quality capital, common equity, exists for the life of the bank unless repurchased at the discretion of the bank, receives dividends only on a discretionary basis, and ranks last in the priority of claims and thus has the highest loss absorption capacity.

3.19 Other capital instruments generally are deficient with respect to one or more of these key qualities. For example, subordinated debt must have a minimum term to maturity of five years to qualify as capital. It is not permanent, and as a debt instrument has a contractually agreed interest rate and thus has a fixed charge against income. It ranks behind other creditors, and, while not subject to loss while the bank continues in normal operation, will absorb losses on a gone concern basis.

3.20 The value of some assets is deducted from regulatory capital. This is because intangible assets such as goodwill, and deferred tax assets, which only have value to a profit-making bank, are normally written-off—they are completely worthless—when a bank is liquidated. The value of these assets is deducted from capital so that the amount of capital recognized for regulatory purposes has already been reduced by the losses expected in liquidation from the write-off of intangible and other specified types of asset.

3.21 While there are many specific and technical requirements, in general, regulatory capital (i) includes all elements of accounting equity; (ii) includes liability instruments meeting prescribed criteria to ensure their ability to absorb losses either on a going concern basis or in liquidation (gone concern basis); and (iii) is reduced by the value of assets likely to be worthless in liquidation.

3.22 To prevent the double counting of capital, capital requirements should be applied on a consolidated basis. Intra-group positions are eliminated in an accounting consolidation, so capital in subsidiaries created through the parent bank's ownership of its equity (and possibly qualifying debt instruments) is eliminated. The amount of any investment in a subsidiary which is not consolidated with the accounts of the parent should be deducted from the parent bank's capital.[5]

3.23 The original Basel Accord defined two tiers of capital; Tier 1, comprising the highest quality capital; and Tier 2, comprising instruments with some, but not all, of the characteristics of capital discussed earlier. The elements of Tier 1 and Tier 2 capital remained unchanged in Basel II. Despite modifications in Basel III, the two tier approach remains central to the Basel standard.

3.24 Under Basel I and II, total regulatory capital can be expressed as:

(Tier 1 capital – goodwill) + Tier 2 capital – adjustments.

Regulatory adjustments are deductions from capital, which except for goodwill, are deducted from total capital in Basel I, and 50 percent from Tier 1 and 50 percent from Tier 2 capital in Basel II.

3.25 Under Basel III, total regulatory capital is still the sum of Tier 1 plus Tier 2 capital, less adjustments; however, all regulatory adjustments are deducted from their respective components. Basel III regulatory capital can be expressed as:

(CET 1 capital – adjustments) + (AT 1 – adjustments) + (Tier 2 capital – adjustments)

3.26 Tier 1 capital (Basel I definition continued in Basel II) consists of equity capital and disclosed reserves that are considered freely available to meet claims against the bank. It comprises paid-up shares and common stock-issued and fully paid ordinary shares/common stock and perpetual noncumulative preference shares—and disclosed reserves created or increased by appropriations of retained earnings or other surplus. The latter include, among others, share premiums, retained profit, general reserves, and legal reserves, and are considered to be freely and immediately available to meet claims against the bank.[6] Tier 1 capital excludes revaluation reserves and cumulative preference shares.

[5] While consolidation of the accounts of the parent and its subsidiaries is the usual accounting treatment, supervisors generally require that the accounts of banking and insurance entities not be consolidated. This is because the banking and insurance businesses are so different that neither banking nor insurance prudential standards and supervisory analysis can be meaningfully applied to accounts consolidating material amounts of the two types of business.

[6] Tier 1 capital may also include general funds, such as funds for general banking risk, subject to four criteria: (1) allocations to the funds must be made out of post-tax retained earnings or out of pre-tax earnings adjusted for all potential tax liabilities; (2) the funds and movements into or out of them must be disclosed separately in the bank's published accounts; (3) the funds must be available to a bank to meet losses for unrestricted and immediate use as soon as they occur; and (4) losses cannot be charged directly to the funds but must be taken through the profit and loss account.

3.27 CET1 capital (Basel III definition) consists of the sum of common shares, retained earnings, accumulated other comprehensive income and other disclosed reserves, and common shares issued by subsidiaries of the bank that are consolidated with the bank and held by third parties that meet the criteria for inclusion in CET1, less regulatory adjustments.

3.28 AT1 capital (Basel III definition) consists of subordinated instruments with no maturity and neither secured nor covered by a guarantee of the issuer. To be eligible for inclusion in additional Tier 1, financial instruments must, among other criteria, be: (1) issued and paid in; (2) subordinated to depositors and general creditors of the bank; (3) neither secured nor covered by a guarantee of the issuer or other arrangement that legally or economically enhances the seniority of the claim vis-à-vis bank creditors; and (4) perpetual, that is, there is no maturity and there are no incentives to redeem.

3.29 Tier 2 capital (Basel I definition continued in Basel II) consists of financial instruments and reserves that are available to absorb losses, but which might not be permanent, have uncertain values, might entail costs if sold, or which otherwise lack the full loss-absorption capacity of Tier 1 capital items. These include (1) undisclosed reserves, that is, that part of accumulated retained earnings that banks in some countries may be permitted to maintain as an undisclosed reserve; (2) asset revaluation reserves with regard to fixed assets, and with regard to long-term holdings of equities valued in the balance sheet at historic cost but for which there are "latent" revaluation gains; (3) general provisions/general loan loss reserves (up to 1.25 percent of risk-weighted assets);[7] (4) hybrid instruments that combine the characteristics of debt and equity and are available to meet losses;[8] and (5) unsecured subordinated debt with a minimum original fixed term of maturity of more than five years and limited-life redeemable preference shares. Tier 2 capital and subordinated debt cannot exceed 100 percent and 50 percent, respectively, of Tier 1 capital.

3.30 Tier 2 capital (Basel III definition) consists of the sum of: (1) unsecured subordinated debt with a minimum original maturity of at least five years and limited-life redeemable preference shares; (2) stock surplus resulting from the issuance of instruments included in Tier 2 capital; (3) instruments issued by subsidiaries that are consolidated with the bank and held by third parties that meet the criteria for inclusion in Tier 2 capital; (4) general provisions or loan-loss reserves held against future unidentified losses, not ascribed to particular assets or known liabilities;[9] and (5) regulatory adjustments applied in the calculation of Tier 2 capital.

3.31 The adjustments to regulatory capital in Basel I and II include deducting the value of goodwill from Tier 1 capital, and deduction from total capital (50 percent from Tier 1 and 50 percent from Tier 2 in Basel II) of the value of investments in unconsolidated banking and financial subsidiaries to prevent the multiple use of the same capital resources within the same banking group.[10] National authorities have the discretion to add to these supervisory deductions investment in the capital of other banks and financial institutions, and other intangible assets. Basel III introduced a wider set of deductions to buttress the quality of the capital in times of stress. These deductions include: (1) goodwill; (2) deferred tax assets; (3) defined benefit pension plan deficits; (4) excess minority interest in subsidiaries; (5) profit revaluation of own debt; and (6) threshold deductions (other deferred taxes arising from timing differences, mortgage servicing rights, and investments in unconsolidated subsidiaries) taken as the excess over 10 percent of CET1 individually and the excess of 15 percent of CET1 when considered in aggregate.

[7] Provisions held against specific assets are excluded from this definition of capital.

[8] Eligible capital instruments should meet the following requirements: (1) they are unsecured, subordinated, and fully paid-up; (2) they are not redeemable at the initiative of the holder or without the prior consent of the supervisory authority; (3) they are available to participate in losses without the bank being obliged to cease trading (unlike conventional subordinated debt); (4) although the capital instrument may carry an obligation to pay interest that cannot permanently be reduced or waived (unlike dividends on ordinary shareholders' equity), it should allow service obligations to be deferred (as with cumulative preference shares) where the profitability of the bank would not support payment.

[9] Up to 1.25 percent of risk-weighted assets calculated under the standardized approach, and up to 0.6 percent of risk-weighted assets calculated under the IRB approach. At national discretion, lower limits may apply.

[10] The assets representing the investment in subsidiary companies whose capital had been deducted from that of the parent would not be included in risk-weighted assets for the calculation of capital adequacy, or total assets when calculating the leverage ratio.

Risk-Weighted Assets

Credit Risk

3.32 Basel I introduced the concept of adjusting assets through the application of a weighting factor to approximate risk. Banks are required to hold the specified minimum capital relative to their risk-weighted (or risk-adjusted) assets, rather than their total assets. Basel I initially considered only credit risk, with the 1996 Amendment incorporating market risk by expressing the measure of market risk as a risk-weighted asset equivalent. Basel II introduced an expression of the measure of operational risk as a risk-weighted asset equivalent. Applying the Basel minimum 8 percent capital adequacy standard, a bank would require $8 in capital for each $100 in 100 percent risk-weighted commercial loans ($100 * 1.00 * 0.08), $2 in capital for each $100 in 20 percent risk-weighted debt of another bank ($100 * 0.20 * 0.08), and no capital for $100 in 0 risk-weighted government bonds ($100*0.0*0.08). Total capital requirements can be calculated as follows:

*Total Risk-Weighted Assets * 0.08 = Minimum Capital Requirement*

3.33 There are four Basel I groupings of assets with corresponding credit-risk weights (Table 3.2). Basel II and Basel III have introduced more granular versions of the original Basel I approach to credit-risk

Table 3.2 Basel I Risk Weights for On-balance-Sheet Assets

Risk Weight (Percent)	Asset Category
0	Cash, including, at national discretion, gold bullion held in own vaults or on an allocated basis to the extent backed by bullion liabilities Claims on central governments and central banks denominated in national currency and funded in that currency Other claims on OECD central governments and central banks Claims collateralized by cash of OECD central-government securities or guaranteed by OECD central governments
0, 10, 20, or 50 (At National Discretion)	Claims on domestic public sector entities, excluding central governments, and loans guaranteed by such entities
20	Claims on multilateral development banks and claims guaranteed by or collateralized by securities issued by such banks Claims on banks incorporated in the OECD and loans guaranteed by OECD-incorporated banks Claims on banks incorporated in countries outside the OECD with a residual maturity of up to one year and loans with a residual maturity of up to one year, guaranteed by banks incorporated in countries outside the OECD; claims on non domestic OECD public sector entities, excluding central governments, and loans guaranteed by such entities Cash items in process of collection
50	Loans fully secured by mortgage on residential property that is or will be occupied by the borrower or that is rented
100	Claims on the private sector Claims on banks incorporated outside the OECD with a residual maturity of over one year Claims on central governments outside the OECD (unless denominated in national currency—and funded in that currency—see above) Claims on commercial companies owned by the public sector Premises, plant and equipment, and other fixed assets Real estate and other investments (including nonconsolidated investment participations in other companies) Capital instruments issued by other banks (unless deducted from capital) All other assets

Source: BCBS (1988).

Note: OECD = Organisation for Economic Co-operation and Development.

weighting, breaking the original four groupings of assets into an increasing number of categories in efforts to make the standardized approaches more nuanced. An illustration of the increasing granularity is provided in Annex 3.2. Basel II also introduced a treatment of risk-mitigants, whereby risk weights can be adjusted to reflect the value of collateral and guarantees. Compilers requiring additional detail on the standardized approaches to risk weights and the treatment of risk-mitigants should refer to national supervisory standards and the relevant version of the Capital Accord.

3.34 All versions of Basel employ conversion factors to determine a credit equivalent amount for off-balance-sheet items (Table 3.3). This credit equivalent amount is then subject to risk weighting in accordance with the factor applicable to the counterparty.

3.35 In addition to a more granular standardized approach, Basel II introduced internal ratings–based approaches (IRB) for credit risk, which use models to determine risk weightings. Subject to supervisory approval, banks may use data from their own internal ratings–based models as inputs into the function determining the capital requirement for credit risk exposures. In the advanced IRB approach, the bank provides the key risk inputs of probability of default (PD), loss given default (LGD), exposure at default (ED), and effective maturity (M). In the foundation IRB approach, the bank provides only the estimates of PD, with the supervisory authority prescribing the other risk inputs.

3.36 Compilers should ensure that the metadata indicates whether the national supervisory standards make the advanced approaches are available to banks. Compilers should not normally require details of the internal ratings–based approach to credit risk, but if required, should refer to national supervisory standards and the BCBS publications *International Convergence of Capital Measurement and Capital Standards: A Revised Framework* (Basel II, 2004), and *Basel III: Finalizing Post-Crisis Reforms* (2017).

Market Risk

3.37 Market risk is the risk of losses in on- and off-balance-sheet positions arising from movements in market prices. The 1996 *Amendment to the Capital Accord to Incorporate Market Risks* introduced capital charges for interest rate–related instruments and equities in the trading book (instruments not held primarily for the collection of cash flows), and to total

Table 3.3 Credit Conversion Factors for Off-Balance-Sheet Items

Instruments	Credit conversion factors (in percent)
Direct credit substitutes, eg general guarantees of indebtedness (including standby letters of credit serving as financial guarantees for loans and securities) and acceptances (including endorsements with the character of acceptances).	100
Sale and repurchase agreements and asset sales with recourse where the credit risk remains with the bank.	100
The lending of banks' securities or the posting of securities as collateral by banks, including instances where these arise out of repo-style transactions.	100
Forward asset purchases, forward deposits and partly paid shares and securities, which represent commitments with certain drawdown.	100
Off-balance sheet items that are credit substitutes not explicitly included in any other category.	100
Note issuance facilities and revolving underwriting facilities regardless of the maturity of the underlying facility.	50
Transaction-related contingent items such as performance bonds, bid bonds, warranties and standby letters of credit related to particular transactions.	50
Commitments, regardless of the maturity of the underlying facility, unless they qualify for a lower CCF.	40
The issuing and confirming banks of short-term self-liquidating trade letters of credit arising from the movement of goods (e.g. documentary credits collateralized by the underlying shipment).	20
Commitments that are unconditionally cancellable at any time by the bank without prior notice, or that effectively provide for automatic cancellation due to deterioration in a borrower's creditworthiness.	10

Source: Basel III

(trading book plus banking book) currency and commodities positions. Banks can measure their market risk exposure and calculate the required capital using the standardized approach or, subject to supervisory approval, internal models. The market risk requirements remained unchanged in Basel II. A revised approach to market risk, including a new standardized approach and revisions to the requirements for internal models was introduced in 2016.[11]

3.38 Under Basel I and II, in the standardized framework, the capital charge is calculated using fixed risk factors. The capital charge for foreign currency exposure, for example, is calculated as 8 percent of the overall net currency positions.[12] For interest rate and equity risk (including derivatives), a specific risk (issuer risk) charge is added to the general market risk charge.

3.39 Under Basel I and II, banks with well-established risk management practices are allowed, subject to supervisory approvals, to calculate market risk regulatory capital requirement using their own value at risk (VaR) estimates.[13] Supervisory approval is subject to certain conditions, including daily VaR back-tests, that is, to test the validity of the VaR measure by comparing VaR figures to actual or hypothetical outcomes.

3.40 Reflecting experience in the global financial crisis with models significantly underestimating actual volatility and the probabilities of extreme tail events, the 2009 revisions to Basel II, often called Basel II.5, introduced a number of changes to the calculation of capital requirements for market risk. These included (1) the calculation of VaR under stressed market conditions; (2) a new incremental risk charge to capture default and credit mitigation risk; (3) for securitized products, the application of the same capital charge applied for exposures in the banking book; and (4) an incremental charge for credit risk in the trading book to minimize capital arbitrage by eliminating the difference in capital requirements for identical instruments held in the trading book and banking book.

3.41 The new capital standards for market risk introduced in 2016 revised the required methodology for internal models, and also introduced a much more detailed standardized approach. Reflecting experience in the global financial crisis, the approach shifted from VaR to expected shortfall (ES) to better capture tail risk. In addition, both the internal model and standardized approach introduced varying liquidity horizons to incorporate the risk of market illiquidity, and, following on from Basel II.5, made technical revisions to more clearly identify the boundary between the trading book and banking book.

3.42 In January 2019, the BCBS published a revised standard for minimum capital requirements for market risk. The main changes were the introduction of a new standardized approach and simplified standardized approach to enhance market risk sensitivity, clearer delineation of the boundary between the trading book and the banking book, and more detailed and stringent requirements for banks' internal market risk models and the processes for supervisory review.

3.43 Compilers should be aware of whether capital charges for market risk have been incorporated into national supervisory standards and should disclose in the metadata whether the approach is based on the Basel I and II approach, the Basel II.5 revisions, or Basel III. Any national variations from the Basel regime should be noted. Compilers will generally not need the details of the standardized or internal model calculations of market risk capital requirements but if required should refer to the relevant Basel publications.

Operational Risk

3.44 Operational risk is defined as the risk of loss resulting from inadequate internal procedures or from external events. This definition includes legal risk but excludes strategic and reputational risks. Capital charges for operational risk were introduced in Basel II. Initially banks were to choose from three methods to calculate the capital required for operational risk: (1) the basic indicator approach; (2) the standardized approach, and (3) the advanced measurement approaches. The advanced measurement approaches were later withdrawn, reflecting that the state of the art of operational risk management was not as advanced as credit and market risk management. Basel III introduced in 2017 a new standardized approach, using business line revenues and assumed or observed

[11] BCBS, *Minimum Capital Requirements for Market Risk* (2016).

[12] The overall net open position is measured by aggregating (1) the sum of the net short positions or the sum of the net long positions, whichever is the greater; plus (2) the net position (short or long) in gold, regardless of sign.

[13] VaR measures the maximum likely loss in a given period of time in the event of extreme market moves. It is calculated at a confidence level of 99 percent over a 10-day holding period, using at least 250 days of data.

operational loss experience as inputs, replacing the two other options for calculating operational risk.

3.45 Compliers should disclose in the metadata whether capital charges for operational risk have been adopted in national supervisory frameworks, and, if so, which calculation methods are available to banks. Further detail on operational risk capital charges should not normally be needed by compilers but, if required, can be obtained from national supervisory standards and BCBS *Basel III: Finalising Post-Crisis Reforms* (2017).

Leverage Ratio

3.46 Basel III introduced a non-risk-based leverage ratio to serve as a supplementary measure to the risk-based capital requirements. Banks were initially required only to disclose their leverage ratio as defined in the original 2010 Basel III text. The capital measure (numerator) is Tier 1 capital (Basel III definition), and the exposure measure (denominator) comprises all balance sheet assets, derivatives exposures, securities financing transaction exposures, and off-balance-sheet items. Exposure as defined in Basel III provides a more comprehensive measure of risk than on- and off-balance-sheet items by requiring the use of the accounting measure of exposure plus regulatory requirements with respect to derivatives, repurchase agreements and securities finance, committed credit facilities, direct credit substitutes, and other specified items. The exposure measure was revised in December 2017.

3.47 By 2018, banks were required to hold Tier 1 capital equal to at least 3 percent of the exposure measure as originally defined and have until 2022 to meet the 3 percent requirement using the revised exposure definition. In addition, the December 2017 revisions introduced a requirement for a leverage buffer for global systemically important banks (G-SIB). The leverage buffer add-on is equal to half of the G-SIB buffer the bank is required to hold. For example, a G-SIB with a capital buffer of 1 percent would be required to meet a leverage limit of 3.5 percent—the broadly applicable 3 percent leverage limit, plus a leverage buffer equivalent to half of the applicable G-SIB buffer. Implementation will be phased in through 2022. There is the option, at national discretion, of early adoption of the revised exposure measure.

3.48 Compilers will rely on supervisory sources for leverage data but should note in the metadata whether the national definition is aligned with either the original or revised Basel definition.

Liquidity Standards

3.49 Basel III introduced two internationally harmonized global liquidity standards: the LCR and NSFR. These two ratios are calculated using prescribed stress-scenarios and agreed international definitions of HQLA. National implementation may vary, and compilers should rely on national supervisory standards. Some jurisdictions may apply the LCR and NSFR requirements only to a sub-set of banks, for example, only large internationally active banks. As described in Chapter 7, the LCR and NSFR FSIs should be compiled based on aggregation of those banks to which the standards apply.

Liquidity coverage ratio

3.50 The LCR is intended to promote resilience to potential liquidity disruptions over a 30 day horizon. The LCR standard is defined by dividing the stock of HQLA by net cash outflows over a 30-day time period under stressed conditions. Unlike other liquidity FSIs (except the net stable funding ratio discussed further), the LCR is not a ratio of balance sheet items, but rather the result of a supervisor-prescribed stress scenario. Compilers will rely on supervisory data sources.

3.51 Phased implementation ends in 2019, meaning that HQLA must equal or exceed a stressed one-month cash outflow using run-off rates prescribed by the supervisory authority.

3.52 HQLA are those assets that can be easily and immediately converted into cash at little or no loss of value. Basel III sets out fundamental and market-related characteristics and operational requirements that HQLA should possess or satisfy. These assets should be unencumbered, liquid in markets during a time of stress and, ideally, eligible as collateral for the central bank standing liquidity facilities.

3.53 Implementing the LCR will be challenging in many countries because of a lack of assets that would meet the Basel definition of HQLA.[14] Compilers should provide in the metadata definitions of HQLA if these differ from the Basel standard. Full details of the Basel definition are available in the 2010 Basel III text.

Net stable funding ratio

3.54 The NSFR is defined as the ratio of the available amount of stable funding relative to the amount of required stable funding over a one-year time horizon. Like the LCR, but in contrast to other liquidity FSIs, the NSFR is not a ratio of balance sheet items, but the outcome of a supervisor-prescribed stress scenario applied to individual banks. It is intended to limit overreliance on short-term wholesale funding, encourage assessment of funding risks across all on- and off- balance sheet items, and promote funding stability. The NSFR should be greater than 100 percent and complements the short-term horizon of the LCR.

3.55 Available stable funding (ASF) is defined as the portion of a banks' capital and liabilities that are expected to remain with the bank in a stress scenario over a one-year horizon. Calibration of the presumed degree of stability considers the funding tenor, the funding type, and counterparty. Required stable funding is institution-specific, reflecting the liquidity characteristics and residual maturities of its assets and its off-balance-sheet exposures. Compilers will rely on supervisory data and will not generally need to be familiar with the highly detailed specification of available stable funding and required stable funding (RSF). Additional detail, if required, can be obtained from national supervisory standards and BCBS *Basel III: The Net Stable Funding Ratio* (2014).

[14]This will be a significant problem in countries that do not have liquid domestic securities markets. Also, it is a problem for Islamic financial institutions that are constrained from holding interest-bearing instruments.

IV. Aggregation of Capital Components under Different Basel Accords

3.56 In some countries, there may be different prudential standards for different types or classes of bank. If differing capital definitions are in force, for example, Basel III for larger banks and an earlier definition for savings or mutual banks, this will create a problem for aggregating internal data based on different regulatory frameworks. Table 3.4 summarizes the recommended approach for aggregating on different regulatory frameworks.

Table 3.4 Recommended Aggregation of Capital Components under Basel III and Basel II (or Basel I) for Deriving Sectoral Data

Basel I	Basel II	Basel III	Sectoral data calculated by aggregation of capital data under different Basel standards
Tier I	Tier I	CET1*	Sectoral CET1 = Common Equity Under Basel I and II + Basel III CET1*
		Tier 1 (CET1*+ AT1*)	Sectoral Tier 1 = Basel I Tier 1 + Basel II Tier 1 + Basel III Tier 1
Tier 2	Tier 2	Tier 2*	Sectoral Tier 2 = Basel I Tier 2 + Basel II Tier 2 + Basel III Tier 2*
Tier 3	Tier 3	Tier 3 is eliminated	Sectoral Tier 3 (if applicable) = Basel I Tier 3 + Basel II Tier 3
Supervisory adjustments (except for goodwill) are deducted from total regulatory capital	Supervisory adjustments (except for goodwill) are deducted 50 percent Tier 1 and 50 percent Tier 2	Supervisory adjustments are deducted from each component of regulatory capital	Sectoral supervisory adjustments = Basel I supervisory adjustments + Basel II supervisory adjustments (as applicable)
Basel I total regulatory capital = Tier 1 + Tier 2 + Tier 3 (if applicable) – supervisory adjustments	Basel II total regulatory capital=Tier 1 + Tier 2 + Tier 3 (if applicable) – supervisory adjustments	Basel III total regulatory capital = Tier 1 (CET1* + AT1*) + Tier 2*	Sectoral Total Regulatory Capital = Sectoral Tier 1 + Sectoral Tier 2 + Sectoral Tier 3 (if applicable) – Sectoral supervisory adjustments (as applicable)

Source: IMF staff.

Note: AT1 = Additional Tier 1; CET1 = Common Equity Tier 1.

*Net of supervisory adjustments.

ANNEX

3.1 The Basel Regulatory Frameworks

Basel I	Basel II	Basel III
Capital adequacy framework *Definition of capital* • Tier 1 capital (equity and disclosed reserves) • Tier 2 capital (undisclosed and revaluation reserves, general provisions up to 1.25 percent of risk-weighted assets, subordinated debt) • Tier 3 capital (medium-term debt with lock-in provisions) • Supervisory deductions (goodwill and other intangibles) applied to Tier 1 capital • Investment in unconsolidated subsidiaries deducted from total capital	**Capital adequacy framework** *Definition of capital* • No changes from Basel I except (i) significant investments in capital instruments of insurance companies and minority investments in the capital instruments of banking, securities and other financial entities are to be deducted 50 percent from Tier 1 and 50 percent from Tier 2 capital; and (ii) banks using the advanced approaches must deduct any shortfall in provisions relative to expected loss from capital (50 percent Tier 1, 50 percent Tier 2), and may include any surplus in Tier 2, to a maximum of 0.6 percent of RWA.	**Capital adequacy framework** *Definition of capital* • Common Equity Tier 1 (equity and disclosed reserves) • Additional Tier 1 (subordinated instruments with no maturity) • Tier 2 (long-term subordinated debt) • Wider set of supervisory deductions that apply to CET1 and AT1 • Capital conservation buffer • Countercyclical capital buffer • Systemic risk charge for G-SIFIs • Tier 3 capital is eliminated
Credit risk • Simple fixed risk-weights • Four risk categories • From 0 to 100 percent	*Credit risk* • More sensitive measures of risk • Standardized approach • Internal ratings-based approach • Foundation IRB approach • Advanced IRB approach	*Credit risk* • More granular Standardized Approach, and introduction of an alternative to external ratings. • Restrict the use of Advanced IRB approach for exposures to banks, financial institutions and certain large corporates. • Equity exposures are subject to the standardized approach only.
Market risk • Explicit cushion for price risks, in particular from trading activities	*Market risk* • No changes from Basel I	*Market risk* • More integrated management of market risk • New standardized and simplified standardized approaches • Clearer delineation of the boundary between the trading book and banking book.
	Operational risk • Basic indicator approach • Standardized approach • Advanced measurement approach	*Operational risk* • New Standardized approach replaces all other options
		Leverage ratio • Simple, transparent, and non-risk-based leverage ratio
		New liquidity framework • Short-term ratio (LCR) • Longer-term ratio (NSFR)
	Supervisory review process • Cover other risks (concentration, reputational, etc.) • Supervision should go beyond capital requirements compliance	**Supervisory review process** • Enhanced oversight of credit and market risks
	Disclosure requirements • To encourage market discipline	**Disclosure requirements** • Additional disclosures for credit, market, and liquidity risk supplement Basel II disclosures

Source: IMF staff.

Note: AT1 = Additional Tier 1; CET1 = Common Equity Tier 1; G-SIFI = global systemically important financial institution; IRB = internal rating based.

ANNEX

3.2 Illustration of Increasing Granularity in Standardized Approaches to Credit Risk

	Basel I		Basel II Standardized		Basel III Standardized	
	Category	**Risk weight**	**Category**	**Risk weight**	**Category**	**Risk weight**
Residential mortgages	Loans fully secured by mortgage on residential property	50 percent	Loans fully secured by mortgages on residential property	35 percent	LTV ≤ 50	20 percent*
						30 percent#
					50 < LTV ≤ 60	25 percent*
						35 percent#
					60 < LTV ≤ 80	30 percent*
						45 percent#
					80 < LTV ≤ 90	40 percent*
						60 percent#
					90 < LTV ≤ 100	50 percent*
						75 percent#
					LTV >100	70 percent*
						105 percent#
Commercial loans	All loans	100 percent	AAA to AA–	20 percent	AAA to AA–	20 percent
			A+ to A–	50 percent	A+ to A–	50 percent
			BBB+ to BB–	100 percent	BBB+ to BBB–	75 percent
					BB+ to BB–	100 percent
			Below BB–	150 percent	Below BB–	150 percent
			Unrated	100 percent	Unrated	100 percent
					SME	85 percent
					Project finance	80 – 130 percent
					Object finance	100 percent
					Commodities finance	100 percent

Sources: Basel I, Basel II, *Basel III: Finalizing Post Crisis Reforms.*

* Risk weights for mortgages where repayment is not dependent on cash flow from renting the property.

\# Risk weights for mortgages where repayment is dependent on cash flow from renting the property.

4 Accounting Principles for Financial Soundness Indicators

I. Introduction

4.1 A consistent set of accounting principles is required for compiling position and flow data for calculating financial soundness indicators (FSIs) and is a precondition for aggregating data from different institutional units within a sector of an economy. Consistent accounting principles ensure the methodological soundness of the calculated indicators and facilitate cross-country comparability, even when different accounting standards are applied in different economies. This chapter provides guidance on accounting principles to be followed when compiling FSIs for deposit takers (DTs) and OFCs drawing on the existing International Financial Reporting Standards (IFRS) issued by the International Accounting Standard Board (IASB). The accounting principles underlying the FSI compilation for nonfinancial corporations (NFCs) and households are typically sourced from national accounts statistics, discussed in Chapter 10.[1]

4.2 Although there is still no full-fledged adherence to internationally agreed financial reporting standards, countries are converging toward IFRS as the accounting principles to be used for preparing financial statements. The *Guide* defers to IFRS as the overarching framework for compiling FSIs for DTs and OFCs but recognizes that not all countries adhere to them, and some follow generally accepted national accounting practices instead. The *Guide* further defers to supervisory standards, particularly with respect to allowance for losses. Reporters are encouraged to provide metadata indicating the statistical and financial reporting standards used, including any critical assumptions and significant differences from IFRS.

[1] The accounting rules applied in national accounts are presented in the *2008 System of National Accounts* (*2008 SNA*), paragraphs 2.43–2.72.

II. Flows and Positions

4.3 Flow data refer to economic actions and effects of events within a period of time. Flows include transactions in goods, services, income, transfers, and nonfinancial and financial assets; holding gains and losses arising from price or exchange rate movements; and other changes in the volume of assets and liabilities, such as losses from extraordinary events. Under certain circumstances, potential costs can also be included.[2]

4.4 Position data are the value of outstanding stocks, which refers to holdings of nonfinancial and financial assets, and liabilities at a specific point in time.

III. Time of Recognition of Flows and Positions

Recognition and Derecognition of Financial Assets and Liabilities

4.5 Assets are resources controlled by an entity as a result of past events, and from which future economic benefits are expected to flow to the entity or institutional unit. Financial assets are a subset of economic assets that consist of financial claims. Most financial assets are financial claims arising from contractual relationships entered into when one institutional unit provides funds or other resources to another. These contracts are the basis of creditor/debtor relationships through which asset owners acquire unconditional claims on economic resources of other institutional units.

4.6 Each claim represented by a financial asset has a corresponding liability. A liability is a present

[2] The *2008 SNA* (paragraphs 2.21–2.35) provides a more complete definition of transactions and other flows.

obligation of an entity arising from past events, the settlement of which is expected to result in an outflow of resources from the entity. A liability is established when one unit (the debtor) is obliged, under specific circumstances, to provide funds or other resources to another unit (the creditor). Usually, a liability is established through a legally binding contract that specifies the terms and conditions of the payment(s) to be made, and the payment is unconditional.

4.7 Whether assets and liabilities exist and are outstanding is determined at any moment in time by the concept of ownership. Two types of ownership can be distinguished: legal and economic ownership.[3] The legal owner of nonfinancial and financial assets and liabilities is the institutional unit entitled by law and sustainable under the law to claim title to the instrument. The economic owner of nonfinancial and financial assets and liabilities is the institutional unit entitled to claim the benefits associated with their use by virtue of accepting the associated risks. Every nonfinancial and financial asset and liability has both a legal and an economic owner. In most cases, the economic owner and the legal owner are the same. Where they are not, the legal owner has passed to the economic owner the risk involved in using the resource in an economic activity, as well as the associated benefits.[4]

4.8 An entity shall recognize financial assets or liabilities in its financial statements when the entity becomes party to the contractual provisions of the instruments. IFRS 10 requires an entity to consolidate entities, which it controls.[5] Thus, the consolidated financial statements of the parent entity would recognize financial assets and liabilities when entities it controls become party to the contractual provisions of the instruments. While the *Guide* generally defers to IFRS on consolidation, in the case of the DT sector, it recommends supervisory consolidation (Chapter 6). Purchase or sale of financial assets shall be recognized and derecognized using the trade date (i.e., the date of the transaction) or, if not feasible, the settlement date (i.e., the time of delivery of the financial assets and payment of consideration).[6] Trade date accounting presupposes that the purchaser of the instrument assumes the risks and rewards to the instrument on the day of the transaction, not the day of delivery of the instrument.

4.9 Financial liabilities are removed (derecognized) from the financial statement of an institutional unit when such liabilities are extinguished. In other words, financial liabilities are removed when the obligations specified in the contracts are discharged, cancelled, or expired.

Accrual Accounting

4.10 Accrual accounting is the main method used in the *Guide*, in IFRS and for the compilation of other macroeconomic statistics. Accrual accounting records flows and changes in the corresponding stocks at the time economic value is created, transformed, exchanged, transferred, or extinguished. Under accrual accounting, flows and positions are recorded when a change in economic ownership takes place. The effects of economic events are thus recorded in the period in which they occur, irrespective of whether payment was made. Existing assets and liabilities are recognized, but contingent positions are not.[7]

4.11 The change of economic ownership is central to determine the time of recording of transactions in financial assets on an accrual basis. Economic ownership takes account of the risks and rewards of ownership. As already stated, a change in economic ownership means that, in practice, an entity has transferred substantially all the risks and rewards of ownership to another entity. Accrual accounting is adopted because by matching the time of recognition with the

[3] Economic ownership is also referred to as beneficial ownership, as the holder retains claims to the risks and rewards of ownership. See *Monetary and Financial Statistics Manual and Compilation Guide*, paragraph 4.9.

[4] In general, a change in legal ownership also involves a change in economic ownership. In some cases, however, a change of economic ownership takes place even though the legal ownership remains unchanged (e.g., financial leases). In other cases, there is no change in economic ownership, even though there is a change in legal ownership (e.g., repurchase agreements).

[5] Control exists when an entity is exposed, or has rights, to variable returns from its involvement with the investee and has the ability to affect those returns through its power over the investee. See IFRS 10, paragraph 6.

[6] IFRS allow the use of trade or settlement date for recognition of regular way sales and purchases (IFRS 9, paragraphs 3.1.1 and 3.1.2). If both parties use the same basis, then recognition and derecognition will occur simultaneously. However, if one party records on a trade date basis while the other party records on a settlement day basis, there will be a mismatch in their respective recognition and derecognition of the instrument.

[7] See IAS 37 *Provisions, Contingent Liabilities and Contingent Assets*, paragraphs 27–35.

time of resource flows and the time of gains and losses in value, the economic consequences of transactions and events on the current condition of the reporting entities is best observed. The simultaneous recognition of the transfer of rights and values between the buyer and seller also results in symmetrical reporting of value, which reduces the possibility of discrepancies in the accounts.

4.12 When a transaction occurs in assets, the entities should record the change in position on the date of the transaction (the trade date). If an existing asset is sold by one entity to another, the first entity derecognizes, and the second entity recognizes the asset on the date of the transaction, which is when the economic risks and rewards associated with the instrument are transferred. The date of recording may actually be specified to ensure matching entries in the books of both parties. If no precise date can be fixed on which the change in ownership occurs, the date on which the creditor receives payment in cash or in some other asset (settlement date) is decisive.

4.13 A financial claim is created and exists until payment is made or forgiven. An asset transaction is recorded when a service is rendered, interest accrues, or an event occurs that creates a transfer claim (i.e., taxation). Similar to interest, service charges can accrue continuously. After dividends are declared payable, they are recorded as liabilities/assets until paid.

Accrual of Interest

4.14 The *Guide* recommends that interest costs accrue continuously on debt instruments, matching the cost of funds with the provision of funds and increasing the principal amount outstanding until the interest is paid.[8] As set forth in IFRS 9, an entity should recognize interest income by applying the effective interest method. For fixed-rate instruments, the effective interest rate is the rate of interest that exactly discounts estimated future cash payments or receipts through the expected life of the financial asset or financial liabilities to the gross carrying amount of a financial asset or to the amortized cost of a financial liability.[9] For variable-rate instruments, the yield will vary over time in line with the terms of the contract. With the exception of instruments meeting the IFRS 9 criteria for hedge accounting, no adjustment should be made to interest income for any gains or losses arising from financial derivatives contracts, as these are recognized as gains and losses on financial instruments (see paragraph 5.19).

4.15 These recommendations for the accrual of interest are based on IFRS 9.[10] However, it is recognized that for data compiled under IFRS when an instrument is traded, interest accrues to the new creditor at the effective yield at the time of acquisition of the instrument and not at the effective yield at the time of issuance. This would open up the possibility that there could be asymmetric reporting of interest income for traded financial instruments by debtor and creditor deposit takers.[11]

4.16 Interest costs that accrue in a recording period should be recorded as an expense (income) in that period. For position data, there are three possibilities for measuring accrued interest costs:

a. Interest earned is paid within the reporting period, with no impact on end-period positions
b. Interest earned is not paid because it is not yet due, with the consequence that the positions increase by the amount of interest that has accrued during the reporting period
c. Interest earned is not paid when due, with the consequence that the positions increase by the amount of interest costs that has accrued during

[8] Interest accrual on nonperforming assets is discussed in paragraph 5.15. In many countries supervisory standards prohibit recognition of accrued interest income on non-performing assets. Reflecting this, the *Guide* recommends that interest accrued on non-performing assets be credited to the provisions for accrual of interest on non-performing assets account rather than income. Only when interest is actually paid is the provision account reduced and the amount taken into income.

[9] See IFRS 9, Appendix A.

[10] Under IFRS, certain fees are treated as an integral part of the effective yield of a financial instrument, and hence affect the rate at which interest accrues.

[11] One possibility is to calculate interest income as the amount the debtors will have to pay to their creditors over and above the repayment of the amounts advanced by the creditors. A second possibility is to define interest as the income that follows from applying, at any point in time, the discount rate of future receivables implicit in the instrument's market value. Finally, a third alternative is to calculate interest as the income that follows from applying the discount rate implicit in the cost at which the instrument was acquired (see *BPM6*, paragraph 11.52).

the period (excluding any specific provisions against such interest, see paragraph 5.15).

The *Guide* recommends including interest costs that have accrued and are not yet payable as part of the value of the underlying instruments (aforementioned second bullet point).

Arrears

4.17 When principal or interest payments are not made when due (e.g., on a loan) arrears are created. Arrears should continue to be recorded from their creation date,[12] until they are extinguished, such as when they are repaid, rescheduled, or forgiven by the creditor. Arrears should continue to be recorded in the underlying instrument, with the exception of interest on nonperforming assets (see paragraph 5.14).[13]

4.18 If debt payments are guaranteed by a third party (guarantor) and the debtor defaults, the debtor records an arrear until the creditor invokes the guarantee, at which time the debt is attributed to the guarantor. In other words, the arrear of the original debtor is extinguished as though repaid. Depending on the contractual arrangements, in the event of a guarantee being exercised, the debt is not classified as arrears of the guarantor but instead as a short-term debt liability until any grace period for payment ends.

Contingencies

4.19 Many types of contractual financial arrangements between institutional units do not give rise to unconditional requirements, either to make payments or to provide other economic assets.[14] In this context, "conditional" means that the claim becomes effective only if a stipulated condition (or conditions) arise. These arrangements, which are often referred to as *contingent items* (or *off-balance-sheet exposures*), are not recognized as financial assets or liabilities in the *Guide*, because they are not actual claims and there are no certain future economic benefits that can be measured reliably.

4.20 Off-balance-sheet exposures represent potential exposures to risks. The types of contingent arrangements for which data should be collected on the basis of the maximum potential exposure are described below.

4.21 *Loan and other payment guarantees* are commitments to make payments to third parties when another party, such as a client of the guarantor, fails to perform some contractual obligations. These are contingent liabilities because payment is required only if the client fails to perform, and until such time no liability is recorded on the balance sheet of the guarantor. A common type of risk assumed by a deposit-taking guarantor is commercial risk or financial performance risk of the borrower.

4.22 Included under payment guarantees are *letters of credit* (LoCs). Stand-by LoCs are guarantees to make payment upon nonperformance by the client, provided all the conditions in the letter have been met. LoCs are an important mechanism for international trade whereby a bank makes payment to a supplier on behalf of the bank's customer upon documentary proof of delivery of the specified items in accordance with the terms of the LoC. Irrevocable LoCs provide certainty of payment if the original terms are met, while revocable LoCs, which are seldom used as they do not provide certainty of payment, allow the terms of the letter to be changed without prior approval of the beneficiary. Also included are performance bonds that normally cover only part of the contract value but in effect guarantee a buyer of goods, such as an importer, that the seller, such as an exporter, will meet the terms of the contract. Performance bonds are also used in construction to protect the owner by providing a bank guarantee of payment for remedial work, to the limit of bond, that may be required if the contractor does not complete a project or completes it with material deficiencies.

4.23 *Lines of credit* and *credit commitments,* including undisbursed loan commitments, are contingencies that provide a guarantee that undrawn funds will

[12] It is recognized that, in some instances, arrears arise for operational reasons rather than due to a reluctance or inability to pay. Nonetheless, in principle, when outstanding at the reference date, they should be recorded as arrears.

[13] There are often supervisory rules that restrict the ability to recognize arrears as income when a loan has been rescheduled, for example, requiring that a specified number of payments be made before the arrears can be extinguished. The *Guide* defers to supervisory requirements for the reporting of non-performing loans and the recognition of income on non-performing and rescheduled loans.

[14] In the *Guide*, financial derivatives instruments, including credit derivatives, are actual—not contingent—positions. For a definition of financial derivatives, see Chapter 5, paragraphs 5.55–5.65.

be available in the future, but no financial liability/asset exists until such funds are actually advanced.

4.24 Included under credit commitments are unutilized back-up facilities such as *note issuance facilities* (NIFs) that provide guarantees that parties will be able to sell short-term debt securities (notes) that they issue and that the financial corporations providing the facility will purchase any notes not sold in the market. Other non-guarantee facilities providing contingent credit or back-up purchase facilities are revolving underwriting facilities (RUFs), multiple options facilities, and global note facilities (GNFs). Both banks and nonbank financial institutions provide such back-up purchase facilities.

Provisions for Loan Losses and Other Impaired Assets

4.25 IFRS 9, which came into effect from January 2018, prescribes an expected credit loss (ECL) treatment for establishing a loss allowance for financial assets.[15] Previously, accounting standards (i.e. IAS 39) had used an incurred credit loss approach, whereby loss allowances were established only when there was objective evidence of impairment. This evidence would typically be payments in arrears but could also comprise qualitative information such as the bankruptcy of the debtor even if payments were not yet in arrears.

4.26 Supervisory treatment of provisions for loan losses has long taken an expected loss approach. This reflects the certain knowledge from experience in banking that losses will be incurred on some assets even if there is currently no evidence of impairment of those assets. The divergence between the expected loss approach favored by supervisors, and the incurred loss approach mandated by IAS 39, resulted in differences in the provision amounts determined in accordance with supervisory standards, and allowance for loss amounts determined in accordance with accounting standards.

4.27 Supervisory requirements, which often include minimum provisioning amounts for loans over a specified number of days in arrears, may result in higher specific provisions than the allowance for loss determined in accordance with the accounting requirements. This may occur, for example, because a bank might expect to recover through the sale of collateral an amount sufficient to repay the entire loan, thus requiring no allowance for loss under accounting standards, yet under supervisory requirements, minimum provisions may be required in accordance with the number of days payment is in arrears.

4.28 Supervisory requirements also frequently require a general provision amount, for example, 1 percent of the total portfolio. This recognizes that there will be losses in a portfolio even if individually impaired loans have not yet been identified, which is conceptually similar to, but differing in practice from, the expected loss approach of IFRS 9.

4.29 The combination of prescribed minimum provisions and requirement for general provisions may result in higher levels of provisions determined in accordance with supervisory requirements than the allowance for loss amounts determined in accordance with IAS 39 and IFRS 9 accounting principles. Under Basel I, any excess of provisions above the allowance for loss calculated in accordance with accounting principles was treated as a general provision. This amount, to a maximum of 1.25 percent of risk-weighted assets, was included as an element of Tier 2 capital for regulatory purposes.

4.30 Basel II introduced a divergent treatment between the Standardized Approach and the Internal Ratings-Based Approach with respect to specific and general provisions. Basel I treatment was retained for institutions using the Standardized Approach. For institutions on the advanced approaches, the difference between provisions (e.g., specific provisions, portfolio-specific general provisions such as country risk provisions or general provisions) and expected losses may be included in or must be deducted from regulatory capital. The excess, to a maximum of 0.6 percent of risk-weighted assets, is included in Tier 2 capital. Any shortfall in provisions relative to expected loss would be deducted from capital, 50 percent from Tier 1, and 50 percent from Tier 2. Banks using the advanced approaches for a portion of their portfolio and the standardized approach for the balance should attribute total general provisions on a pro rata basis

[15] The Financial Accounting Standards Board, which governs United States Generally Accepted Accounting Principles, has adopted a similar, but not identical approach, Current Expected Credit Losses, to become effective in 2020 for some banks, and more broadly in 2021. Early adoption is permitted from 2019.

to the advanced and standardized portfolios. There are options and elements of national discretion, and the *Guide* defers to supervisory requirements for the treatment of provisions and expected loss.[16] Basel III retained the Basel II approach, with the difference that any shortfall in provisions is to be deducted from CET1.

4.31 Under IFRS 9, the loss allowance is a cumulative account, with increases or decreases in loss allowance recognized in profit and loss. There are differing accounting treatments depending on the type of financial instrument.

4.32 For financial assets measured at amortized cost—typically loans and leases as well as securities held for the intention of collecting the cash flows—the loss allowance is netted against the carrying amount of the assets. Thus, under IFRS 9, the net amount is reported on the statement of financial position (balance sheet). However, for compiling FSIs, the *Guide* recommends that loans be reported without any deduction for loss allowance—that is, they should be reported at a gross value. The loss allowance for off-balance-sheet items such as loan commitments or guarantees is recognized as a provision (liability). For securities measured at fair value through other comprehensive income (FVOCI)—typically debt instruments—provision expense is recognized in profit or loss using the same credit impairment methodology as for financial assets measured at amortized cost. Other changes in the carrying amount due to fair value measurement are recognized in OCI; the cumulative fair value gain or loss recognized in OCI is recycled from OCI to profit or loss when the related financial asset is derecognized.

4.33 Adoption of the ECL approach in IFRS bridges some of the conceptual differences between the accounting and supervisory approaches to loss allowance (provisioning), but there continues to be a wide gulf in specific application. This is compounded by the diversity across jurisdictions in the application of accounting and supervisory standards.[17]

4.34 At the time of writing, the BCBS has prescribed an interim approach continuing the existing Basel I, II, and III determinations described earlier, recommending that national authorities issue guidance on the allocation of IFRS 9 ECL to general and specific provisions.[18] Thus, the concepts of general and specific provisions continue to be relevant to the FSIs, which include provisions (non-performing loans net of provisions to regulatory capital, paragraph 7.27, and provisions to non-performing loans, paragraph 7.39), and compilers should follow the supervisory practices prescribed in their jurisdiction for the determination of specific provision amounts. Data should be obtained from supervisory sources, and details of the national treatment of specific and general provisions should be provided in the metadata.

IV. Valuation

4.35 The accounting principles for the recognition and measurement of financial assets and liabilities discussed in the *Guide* follow IFRS 9. In the *Guide*, *valuation* corresponds to the IFRS concept of *measurement*. Measurement involves assigning monetary amounts at which the elements of the financial statements are to be recognized and carried on the balance sheet.[19]

Amortized Cost and Fair Value

4.36 IFRS 9 requires measurement (valuation in the terms of the *Guide*) using amortized cost, fair value through other comprehensive income, or fair value through profit and loss. Determination of the appropriate approach is based on the entity's business model for managing the financial assets, and the contractual cash flow characteristics of the financial asset.

4.37 Financial assets are valued (measured) at amortized cost if the asset is held to collect contractual cash flows and the contractual terms give rise, on specified dates to cash flows that are solely payments of principal and interest. Fair value through other comprehensive income is to be used if the business model includes both collecting contractual cash flows and selling financial assets, and the contractual terms give rise, on specified dates to cash flows that are solely payments of principal and interest. Financial assets not meeting the criteria for valuation (measurement) at amortized cost or fair value through

[16] For further details, see Basel II paragraphs 381–383.

[17] See BCBC *Regulatory treatment of accounting provisions—interim approach and transitional arrangements* (March 2017).

[18] See footnote 18.

[19] See IFRS *Conceptual Framework for Financial Reporting*, paragraph 4.54.

other comprehensive income are to be measured at fair value through profit and loss.[20]

4.38 Amortized cost is the amount at which the financial asset or financial liability is measured at initial recognition minus the principal repayments, plus or minus the cumulative amortization using the effective interest method of any difference between that initial amount and the maturity amount and, for financial assets, adjusted for any loss allowance.[21] Interest income (or accrued interest) is calculated using the effective interest method and is recognized in profit and loss. Changes in fair value of assets valued at amortized cost are recognized in profit and loss only when the asset is derecognized or reclassified. The *Guide* recommends that financial assets other than loans (lines 19–22 in Table 5.1) that are valued at amortized cost be presented net of allowance for loss, which is consistent with IFRS 9. As noted earlier, however, the *Guide* recommends that loans (line 18 in Table 5.1) be presented net of specific provisions, with subtotals provided on gross loans by category and the amount of specific provisions. As discussed earlier in this chapter, this treatment varies from IFRS 9 as the allowance for loss calculated using the IFRS 9 ECL model does not include the supervisory concepts of specific and general provisions. The allocation of IFRS 9 loan loss allowance between specific and general provisions should follow national supervisory guidance. Specific provisions are netted against gross loans (line 18.i in Table 5.1), and general provisions are recorded as a liability item in line 30.

4.39 Fair value is a market-equivalent value. It is "the price that would be received to sell an asset or paid to transfer a liability in an orderly transaction between market participants at the measurement date."[22] Under IFRS 9, assets and liabilities that are not valued at amortized cost are to be measured at fair value. For measuring fair value, an entity assumes that market participants would use it when pricing the asset or liability under current market conditions, including assumptions about risk. Fair value measurement of a nonfinancial asset takes into account its highest and best use from the markets participant's perspective.

4.40 Fair value measurement assumes an orderly and hypothetical transaction between market participants at the measurement date under current market conditions, and that the transaction takes place in the principal market for the asset or liability, or in the absence of a principal market, the most advantageous market for the asset or liability.

4.41 The fair value of a financial liability, or an entity's own equity instruments, assumes it is transferred to another market participant without settlement, extinguishment, or cancellation of the liability when transferred. Fair value of a liability reflects non-performance risk, including an entity's own credit risk and assuming the same non-performance risk before and after the transfer of the liability.

4.42 Three valuation techniques are widely used for calculating fair value: (1) the *market approach*, which uses the prices and other relevant information generated by market transactions involving identical or comparable assets, liabilities, or a group of assets and liabilities; (2) the *cost approach*, which reflects the amount that would be required to replace the service capacity of an asset (current replacement cost); and (3) the *income approach*, which converts future cash flows of income and expenses into a single current (discounted) amount, reflecting current market conditions and expectations about those future amounts.[23]

4.43 To increase consistency and comparability in fair value measurements, IFRS establish a fair value hierarchy. Entities are required to use Level 1 if possible and may only use Level 3 if the required inputs are not available to enable use of Level 1 or 2. *Level 1 inputs*, the highest priority, are (unadjusted) quoted prices in active markets for identical assets or liabilities that the entity can access at the measurement date. *Level 2 inputs*, medium priority, are inputs other than quoted prices included within Level 1 that are directly or indirectly observable for the asset or liability, such as similar instruments or identical instruments in markets that are not active. *Level 3 inputs*, the lowest priority, are unobservable inputs for the asset or

[20] There are options for adoption of an alternative method at time of recognition for some specific types of asset. See IFRS 9, paragraphs 4.1.4 and 5.7.5–5.7.6.

[21] IFRS 9, Appendix A.

[22] IFRS 13 *Fair Value Measurement*, paragraph 9.

[23] See IFRS 13, paragraphs B5–B11.

liability, which should be developed using the best information available to the entity.[24]

Transactions

4.44 Transactions are generally valued (measured) at the fair value of the consideration given or received.[25] Consistent with IFRS 9, the *Guide* recommends that, for initial recognition, an entity should measure financial assets or financial liabilities at fair value plus or minus, in the case of a financial asset or financial liability not at fair value through profit or loss, *transaction costs* that are directly attributable to the acquisition or issue of the financial asset or financial liability.[26] If part of the consideration given or received is for something other than the financial instrument, an entity shall measure the fair value of the financial instrument.[27] Under IFRS 9, at initial recognition, entities must classify financial assets into: amortized cost; fair value through other comprehensive income (FVOCI); or fair value through profit or loss (FVTPL).

4.45 As noted earlier, the basis for the classification is twofold: (1) the business model for managing the financial asset, and (2) the contractual cash flow characteristics of the financial asset.[28] Some financial instruments, such as loans and deposits, are measured at amortized cost because they are held to collect cash flows and have contractual terms giving rise to payments of principal and interest. These instruments are measured using Level 3 inputs, specifically discounted cash flow using market rates of interest, as there are generally no observable market prices.

4.46 Positions of all financial assets that are not measured at amortized cost must be recorded at fair value, either as FVTPL or as FVOCI. FVTPL applies to all financial assets that: (1) the entity holds to sell, or (2) the entity has elected to value at fair value at initial recognition to address an accounting mismatch. FVOCI includes financial assets (debt instruments and equity) held with the purpose to collect contractual cash flows and to sell the financial asset.

[24]See IFRS 13, paragraphs 72–90.
[25]See IFRS 9, Initial Measurement Section 5.1.
[26]IFRS 9, paragraph 5.1.1.
[27]IFRS 9, paragraph B51.1.
[28]See IFRS 9, paragraph 4.1.1.

Derivatives and Hedge Accounting

4.47 Under IFRS 9, all derivatives, including those linked to unquoted equity investments, are measured at fair value. Changes in the value of derivatives must be recognized in profit or loss, unless the entity has selected to apply hedge accounting designating a derivative as a hedging instrument.

4.48 Hedge accounting recognizes the offsetting effects on profit or loss of changes in the fair values of the hedging instrument and the hedged items. Through hedge accounting, an entity can match the risk exposure in some instruments (the hedged instruments) due to changes in its fair value or future cash flows, with an opposite gain or loss on the hedging instruments. Implementation of hedge accounting rules results in netting or reclassification of hedged items and hedging instruments in the balance sheet presentation. There are three types of hedging relationships recognized in IFRS 9: (1) fair value hedge, (2) cash flow hedge, and (3) hedge of a net investment in a foreign operation.

V. Recording of Gains and Losses

4.49 Financial assets are classified into assets measured at amortized cost and assets measured at fair value. Where assets are measured at fair value, gains and losses are either recognized in profit or loss (FVTPL) or other comprehensive income (FVOCI).

4.50 The requirements for reporting gains or losses recognized at FVOCI are different for debt instruments and equity investment. For debt instruments at FVOCI, unrealized gains and losses are recognized in other comprehensive income. For equity investments at FVOCI, realized gains and losses are allocated directly to retained earnings.

4.51 Gain and losses on financial liabilities designated at FVTPL must be split into the amount of change in fair value attributable to changes in credit risk of the liability presented in other comprehensive income, and the remaining amount presented in profit or loss.

VI. Domestic and Foreign Currencies, Unit of Account, and Exchange Rate Conversion

4.52 Domestic currency is the one that is legal tender in the economy and issued by the monetary authority for that economy or for the common currency area to which the economy belongs.[29] Any currencies that do not meet this definition are foreign currencies to that economy. Under this definition, an economy that uses as its legal tender a currency issued by a monetary authority of another economy—such as U.S. dollars—or of a currency area to which it does not belong should classify the currency as a foreign one, even though domestic transactions are settled in it.

4.53 In the *Guide*, the currency composition of assets and liabilities is determined primarily by characteristics of their currency of denomination. Foreign currency instruments are those denominated in a currency other than the domestic currency. Foreign-currency-linked instruments are those payable in domestic currency but with the amounts payable linked to a foreign currency and, therefore, are considered to be denominated in foreign currency. Domestic currency instruments are those denominated in the domestic currency and not linked to a foreign currency. In the instance of debt instruments with interest payable in a foreign currency, but principal payable in a domestic currency, or vice versa, only the present value of the amounts payable in a foreign currency should be classified as a foreign currency instrument.

4.54 From the perspective of the national compiler, the domestic currency unit is the obvious choice in which to calculate FSIs. Such data are compatible with the national accounts and most of the economy's other economic and monetary statistics, which are expressed in that unit.

4.55 The calculation of FSIs can be complicated by the fact that transactions, other flows, and positions may be expressed initially in a variety of currencies or in other standards of value. Their conversion into a reference unit of account is a requisite for the construction of a consistent and analytically meaningful set of FSI statistics. Assets and liabilities shall be translated at the closing rate at the date of the financial statement position. Income and expenses presented in the income statement and other comprehensive income shall be translated at the exchange rate at the dates of the transactions. The most appropriate exchange rate to be used for conversion of position data denominated in foreign currency into the unit of account is the market (spot) exchange rate prevailing on the reference date to which the position relates. The midpoint between buying and selling rates is preferred to ensure consistency of approach among the reporting population.

4.56 For conversion of an instrument in a multiple rate system,[30] the rate on the closing date of the actual exchange rate applicable to the specific liabilities or assets should be used. If this information is not available, the average rates for the shortest period applicable should be used. If only information on aggregated transactions over a period is available, then the average exchange rate over this period is a suitable proxy.

VII. Maturity

4.57 Maturity is relevant for financial stability analysis, both from a liquidity viewpoint (e.g., in calculating the value of liabilities falling due in the short term) and from an asset/liability mismatch perspective (e.g., in estimating the effect of changes in interest rates on profitability).[31] In the *Guide*, short-term is defined as a maturity of three months or less.[32]

[29] A common currency area, or currency union, consists of more than one economy and has a regional central decision making body, usually a currency union central bank, with the authority to conduct a single monetary policy and to issue the legal tender of the area. To belong to this area, an economy must be a member of the decision making body (see *BPM6*, paragraph A3.9).

[30] A multiple exchange rate system is one in which there are schedules of exchange rates, set by the authorities, and where different exchange rates are applied to various categories of transactions/transactors.

[31] In the latter case, maturity may not capture the interest rate mismatch of some instruments if they have a repricing period that is shorter than the term to maturity. For example, a five-year bond with interest adjusted quarterly in relation to a reference rate would have a short-term maturity for interest rate risk analysis, but long-term maturity from the perspective of the timing of liabilities falling due.

[32] For financial instruments, inter alia, this category includes amounts payable on demand and those debt instruments redeemable at short notice. There is no universal definition of short-term liabilities, with one year being another common definition. In line with the focus on financial stability, the *Guide* recommends three months or less as a maturity better suited to capturing in the FSIs liquid assets to total assets, and liquid assets to short term liabilities, the ability to deal with a short-term market disruption.

4.58 One approach is to determine the maturity classification of financial instruments on the basis of the time until repayments of principal (and interest) are due—known as remaining maturity (and sometimes referred to as residual maturity).[33] Another approach uses the maturity at issuance—known as original maturity—thus indicating whether the funds were raised in the short-term or long-term markets. The *Guide* recommends calculating short-term liabilities based on residual maturity; if this information is unavailable, original maturity can be used as an alternative and should be noted in the metadata.

[33] Strictly defined, the outstanding amount of short-term assets or liabilities on a remaining maturity basis is the present value of payments due in one year or less. In practice, the outstanding amount of short-term assets or liabilities on a remaining maturity basis can be measured by adding the present value of short-term debt (original maturity) to the present value of long-term debt (original maturity) to be paid in one year or less.

5 Sectoral Financial Statements for Financial Soundness Indicators

I. Introduction

5.1 The balance sheet, or the stock of assets and liabilities, and income and expense statements of deposit takers (DTs) and other financial corporations (OFCs) are fundamental to understanding their financial condition.[1] Data series obtained from such statements can be used to calculate most of the FSI ratios for financial corporations, although additional series are needed to complete the full set. In addition to data reported by individual institutions, other data are required to make adjustments at the group level, primarily to eliminate transactions and positions among institutions within the same group.[2] Data for constructing the financial statements for nonfinancial corporations (NFCs) and households (HHs) are mainly obtained from the system of national accounts (SNA), in particular the financial accounts.

5.2 This chapter first outlines a common accounting framework for financial reporting. It then presents detailed sectoral financial statements and defines the line-item series required to calculate the FSI ratios. Where necessary, the chapter also draws on other macroeconomic statistical methodologies, supervisory and macroprudential requirements.

5.3 As highlighted in Chapter 4, countries are converging toward International Financial Reporting Standards (IFRS), but they still have different accounting systems and rely on a wide variety of data sources when compiling FSIs. Indeed, some data series may not even be collected, and others may not meet the definitions suggested in the *Guide*. In such circumstances, the data that most closely approximate the principles in the *Guide* should be used. It should be noted that such differences in accounting frameworks may hamper cross-country comparability and reinforce the relevance of disseminating metadata to improve transparency and help users interpret the FSIs.

5.4 The sectoral financial statements and detailed definitions provided in the *Guide* fulfill several aims. First, they support compilation efforts at the national level as they specify the definitions of data series required for calculating FSIs. Second, this guidance sets out a consistent framework that draws on relevant international standards and takes account of analytical needs, providing a benchmark to national compilers, even if their own national standards differ; such a benchmark can be used as a reference when disseminating metadata. Third, this approach helps foster comparability of data across countries.

II. Financial Statements

Income and Expense Statement

5.5 This statement includes income and expenses related to the operations of the entity. After expenses have been deducted along with any dividends paid or payable to shareholders, any remaining income is transferred to the capital and reserves as retained earnings. As noted in Chapter 4, for FSI compilation, income and expenses are recorded on an accrual basis. As defined in the *Guide*, net income before dividends measures the increase or decrease in net assets of the sector during the period.

5.6 What the *Guide* defines as *income and expense statement* corresponds to the IAS 1 concept of *statement of comprehensive income*, presented as a single statement or as two statements: *statement of profit or loss* and a *statement of other comprehensive income*.[3]

[1] The terms "balance sheet" and "income and expense statement" in the *Guide* broadly correspond to statement of financial position and statement of comprehensive income as defined in International Accounting Standard (IAS) 1.

[2] Group-level data are discussed in more detail in Chapter 6.

[3] See IAS 1, paragraph 81. The profit or loss section represents the traditional profit and loss concepts, while the other comprehensive income section presents items of income and expense that are not recognized in profit or loss, such as foreign currency translation gains or losses, as required or permitted by other IFRS.

Balance Sheet

5.7 The balance sheet (known in IAS 1 as *statement of financial position)* is the statement of assets, liabilities, and capital at the end of each accounting period:

a. Assets comprise both nonfinancial and financial assets (including financial derivatives).

b. Liabilities include debt liabilities, financial derivatives, and general provisions.

c. The difference between the book value of assets and liabilities is known in the *Guide* as capital and reserves and coincides with the IFRS term "equity."[4] This represents the "cushion" to absorb any losses arising from the income and expense statement, or for other reasons. If liabilities exceed assets, then the entity is balance-sheet insolvent.

5.8 Some liabilities and assets of corporations are contingent on a certain event(s) occurring and are therefore recorded off-balance sheet (see paragraphs 4.19–4.24). As noted in Chapter 4, such items require monitoring to assess the full financial risk exposure of the corporation.

5.9 Measures of profitability and capital depend on the accounting definitions and recognition rules adopted. In developing the guidance on definitions set out further, the *Guide* defers to IFRS and to the banking supervision standards set by the Basel Committee on Banking Supervision (BCBS). Box 5.1 summarizes these sources and complements them with a

[4] In the *2008 SNA*, the equivalent term is "equity and investment fund shares" together with "net worth." In the *Guide*, the term "equity and investment fund shares" is used only to denote equity assets.

Box 5.1 Measurement Frameworks

In determining the most relevant measurement framework for the compilation of FSIs, three basic standards can be drawn upon—national accounting, commercial accounting, and banking supervision.

National accounts data

The system of national accounts (SNA) consists of a coherent, consistent, and integrated set of macroeconomic accounts based on internationally agreed concepts, definitions, classifications, and accounting rules. The SNA provides a comprehensive accounting framework of aggregated macroeconomic data. Central to the development of national accounts and the related methodologies is the concept of residency; there are five resident institutional sectors and the rest of the world.

The main source of information on national accounting is the System of National Accounts 2008 (2008 SNA) (United Nations and others, 2008). Other related methodologies include The Monetary and Financial Statistics Manual and Compilation Guide 2016 (MFSMCG) (IMF, 2016); Balance of Payments and International Investment Manual, sixth edition (BPM6) (IMF, 2009); Government Finance Statistics Manual 2014 (GFSM) (IMF, 20014); and External Debt Statistics: Guide for Compilers and Users (Bank for International Settlements and others, 2013).

International accounting standards

International Financial Reporting Standards (IFRS), formerly international accounting standards (IAS), are a series of standards for commercial accounting that provide concepts that underlie the preparation and presentation of financial statements of commercial, industrial, and business reporting enterprises, whether in the public or the private sector.[1] Over time, IFRS are replacing or supplementing IAS, with 17 IFRS and 25 IAS in force at end-July 2018. There may also be specific national accounting standards in jurisdictions that have not adopted IFRS, or that have included some national variations from IFRS.

The IFRS, including earlier IAS, are available from the International Accounting Standards Board (IASB), www.iasb.org.

Banking supervision

In 1988, the Basel Committee on Banking Supervision (BCBS) agreed on standards governing the capital adequacy of internationally active banks. This original capital accord, which was amended in 1996 to incorporate market risk, provides a framework for the measurement of capital in relation to the perceived credit and market risk of the assets owned by the bank. Two fundamental objectives lie at the heart of the BCBS's work. First, the framework is intended to strengthen the soundness and stability of the international banking system. Second, the framework is intended to be fair and, through a high degree of consistency in its application to banks in different countries, to diminish sources of competitive inequality among international banks.

Box 5.1 Measurement Frameworks *(concluded)*

While banking supervisors rely on commercial accounting standards for financial statements from banks, they commonly prescribe specific treatments which may vary from IFRS with respect to the classification and provisioning of loans and other assets and require detailed reporting on various asset and liability items, including deposits and liquid assets. Supervisory reporting provides the source data for many of the memoranda series required to compile the FSIs.

The main sources of information on the BCBS's capital adequacy requirements are the "International Convergence of Capital Measurement and Capital Standards" (BCBS, 1988), "Amendment to the Capital Accord to Incorporate Market Risks" (BCBS, 1996), "International Convergence of Capital Measurement and Capital Standards: A Revised Framework" (often known as Basel II, BCBS 2004), "Basel III: A Global Regulatory Framework for More Resilient Banks and Banking Systems" (BCBS 2010), and "Basel III: Finalizing Post-Crisis Reforms" (BCBS 2017).[2]

Financial soundness indicators

Unlike commercial accounting and supervisory approaches which concern individual entities, the FSI framework, like the national accounts, focuses on aggregated sector information.

However, whereas the national accounts embrace symmetric recording of flows and positions within and across sectors, commercial accounting and supervisory approaches—the basis for compiling FSIs for DTs and OFCs—do not.

While the national accounts aim at recording all economic activity, the FSI framework, like commercial and supervisory standards, favors a consolidated approach for financial corporations to avoid the double counting of capital and activity.

[1] The effective date of IFRS was January 1, 2001, which may have resulted in breaks in series. The IASs and IFRS are voluntary standards that are implemented by national authorities. The European Union and some other countries adopted IFRS in 2005, while other countries have adopted IFRS at later dates. In some cases, elements of IFRS have been adapted to local conditions, or not fully implemented, or may not be applicable to all entities even when IFRS has been adopted, for example, publicly traded companies. Thus, national commercial accounting standards may differ from IFRS in important respects.
[2] All are available on the BIS website (https://www.bis.org/bcbs/index.htm?m=3%7C14).

brief description of the national accounts framework and their relevance to the compilation of FSIs.

III. Sectoral Financial Statements

5.10 Sectoral financial statements are shown on an institutional sector basis. While the income and expense statements and the balance sheets for financial corporations have a considerable degree of overlap in terms of line-item series identified, there are significant differences in presentation and composition between DTs and subsectors of OFCs, which have implications for the calculation of FSIs.[5] Furthermore, it is not possible to aggregate separate information from individual institutional units to construct sectoral financial statements for NFCs and HHs; their data are sourced from SNA estimates. The DT sector is presented first because of its central role in the financial system and the wider range of series from the sectoral financial statements required to calculate FSIs for DTs.

5.11 The line-item series in the financial statements for which definitions are provided are those required to calculate the FSIs set out in Chapters 7 to 10, either directly or as important building blocks in calculating the required aggregates. The advantage of defining these series within the framework of a financial statement is the accounting rigor that is imposed—the series are defined to ensure that the integrity of a double-entry recording system is maintained—while promoting a consistency of approach in the classification and coverage of transactions and positions.

5.12 To avoid duplication, each series is defined only once, even if it appears in multiple sectoral financial statements. Most of the definitions are provided in the section covering the DTs' financial statement, set out in Table 5.1. They are also applicable to the sectoral financial statement of OFCs, such as

[5] For instance, interest margin is an important FSI series for DTs, but not for insurance corporations, whose main source of revenue is premium income.

money market funds (Table 5.2), insurance corporations (Table 5.3), and pension funds (Table 5.4). Data for NFCs aggregate (Table 5.5) and HHs (Table 5.6) are largely sourced from SNA estimates. When disseminating data, compilers are encouraged to document any material differences between national practice and the guidance provided.

Deposit Takers

Income and expense statement

5.13 For DTs, the main source of revenue and expense is interest. *Interest income/expense* is a form of income that accrues on debt instruments such as deposits, loans, debt securities, and other accounts receivable/payable. It includes fees and commissions that are an integral part of the effective yield of a financial instrument, as discussed in paragraph 5.18. For the borrower, it is the cost (known as an interest cost) of the use of another entity's funds. Interest income and expense may also include gains (and losses) on instruments meeting the criteria for hedge accounting pursuant to IFRS 9. As explained in Chapter 4 (paragraph 4.14), interest is recorded as accruing continuously. As shown in Table 5.1, the difference between

Table 5.1 Deposit Takers

Income and Expense Statement	Balance Sheet
1. Interest income[1]	14. **Total assets** (= 15 + 16 = 23 + 31)
i. Gross interest income	15. *Nonfinancial assets*
ii. *less* Provisions for accrued interest on nonperforming assets	16. *Financial assets* (= 17 through 22)
2. Interest expense[1]	17. Currency and deposits[1]
3. *Net interest income* (= 1 – 2)	18. Loans (after specific provisions) (= 18.i – 18.ii)
4. Noninterest income	i. Gross loans[1]
i. Fees and commissions receivable[1]	i.i. Interbank loans[2]
ii. Gains or losses on financial instruments	i.i.i. Resident
iii. Prorated earnings	i.i.ii. Nonresident
iv. Other income[1]	i.ii. Noninterbank loans
5. *Gross income* (= 3 + 4)	i.ii.i. Central bank
6. Noninterest expenses	i.ii.ii. General government
i. Personnel costs	i.ii.iii. Other financial corporations
ii. Other expenses	i.ii.iv. Nonfinancial corporations
7. Provisions (net)	i.ii.v. Other domestic sectors
i. Loan loss provisions	i.ii.vi. Nonresidents
ii. Other financial asset provisions	ii. Specific provisions[3]
8. *Net income (before taxes)* (= 5 – (6 + 7))	19. Debt securities[1]
9. Income tax	20. Equity and investment fund shares
10. *Net income after tax* (= 8 – 9)	21. Financial derivatives[1]
11. Other comprehensive income (loss) net of tax	22. Other financial assets[1]
12. Dividends payable	23. *Liabilities* (= 28 + 29 + 30)
13. *Retained earnings* (= 10 – 12)	24. Currency and deposits
	i. Customer deposits
	ii. Interbank deposits[2]
	ii.i. Resident
	ii.ii. Nonresident
	iii. Other currency and deposits
	25. Loans
	26. Debt securities
	27. Other liabilities
	28. *Debt* (= 24 through 27)
	29. Financial derivatives and employee stock options
	30. General and other provisions
	31. *Capital and reserves*
	32. **Balance sheet total (= 23 + 31 = 14)**

Table 5.1 Deposit Takers (*concluded*)

Memorandum Series
Other series required to calculate FSIs
Supervisory-based series
33. Tier 1 capital *less* corresponding supervisory deductions[4]
34. Common Equity Tier 1 capital *less* corresponding supervisory deductions[4]
35. Additional Tier 1 capital *less* corresponding supervisory deductions[4]
36. Tier 2 capital *less* corresponding supervisory deductions[4]
37. Tier 3 capital
38. Other supervisory deductions[5]
39. Total regulatory capital (= 33 + 36 + 37 – 38)
40. Risk-weighted assets
41. Basel III total exposure measure
42. High-quality liquid assets
43. Total net cash outflows over the next 30 calendar days
44. Available amount of stable funding
45. Required amount of stable funding
46. Large exposures
Series that provide a further analysis of the balance sheet
47. Liquid assets
48. Short-term liabilities
49. Nonperforming loans
50. Residential real estate loans
51. Commercial real estate loans
52. Geographic distribution of loans[6]
53. Foreign currency loans
54. Foreign currency liabilities
55. Net open position in foreign currency for on-balance-sheet items
56. Total net open position in foreign currency
57. Credit to the private sector
58. Loan concentration by economic activity
59. Reference lending rates
60. Reference deposit rates
61. Highest interbank rate
62. Lowest interbank rate

Source: IMF staff.

Note: DT = deposit taker; NPLs = nonperforming loans.

[1] To understand the interconnections among DTs, separate identification of income and claims on other DTs in the reporting population is encouraged.

[2] Interbank loans and deposits comprise those loans to or deposits from any other DT. Nonperforming interbank loans should be included in line 49.

[3] If only gross loans data are available, including the accrual of interest on NPLs, any provisions for accrued interest on NPLs should be included in this line item and, if significant, separately identified.

[4] Depending on the regulatory framework.

[5] Sum of supervisory deductions not already deducted from the corresponding regulatory capital component.

[6] While individual country circumstances will vary, data on the distribution of lending by regional groupings of countries are encouraged, with additional country information where relevant (see paragraph 8.9).

Table 5.2 Other Financial Corporations: Money Market Funds

Income and Expense Statement	Balance Sheet
1. Interest income 2. Interest expenses 3. Noninterest income 4. *Gross income* (= 1 – 2 + 3) 5. Noninterest expenses and provisions 6. *Net income (before taxes) (= 4 – 5)* 7. Income tax 8. *Net income after tax* (= 6 – 7) 9. Other comprehensive income (loss) net of tax	10. **Total assets** (= 11 + 12 = 23) 11. *Nonfinancial assets* 12. *Financial assets (= 13 through 18)* 13. Currency and deposits 14. Loans 15. Debt securities 16. Equity and investment fund shares 17. Financial derivatives 18. Other financial assets 19. *Liabilities* (= 20 + 21 + 22) 20. Loans 21. Financial derivatives and employee stock options 22. Investment fund shares issued 23. **Balance sheet total (= 19 = 10)**
Memorandum Series ***Other series required to calculate additional FSIs*** Sectoral distribution of investments (percentage) i. Central bank ii. Deposit takers iii. Other financial corporations iv. Central government v. Other general government vi. Nonfinancial corporations vii. Nonresidents Maturity distribution of investments (percentage) i. 1–30 days ii. 31–90 days iii. >90 days GDP	

Source: IMF staff.

Table 5.3 Other Financial Corporations: Insurance Corporations

Income and Expense Statement	Balance Sheet
1. Premiums earned, net of reinsurance (= 1.i – 1.ii + 1.iii) i. Gross premium earned ii. Reinsurers' share of gross premiums earned iii. Transfer of premium reserves from other companies 2. Claims incurred, net of reinsurance (= 2.i – 2.ii + 2.iii + 2.iv) i. Gross claim payments ii. Reinsurers' share of gross claim payments iii. Changes in reserves for claims outstanding iv. Transfer of premium reserves to other companies 3. Net change in technical reserves for future claims 4. *Net income from insurance activity* (= 1 – 2 + 3) 5. Other operating income (= 5.i + 5.ii + 5.iii) i. Commissions received ii. Real estate income iii. Gains and losses from the sales of fixed assets iv. Other income 6. *Gross income* (= 4 + 5) 7. Other operating expenses (= 7.i + 7.ii + 7.iii + 7.iv) i. Personnel costs ii. Underwriting expenses iii. Real estate expenses or nonfinancial asset depreciation iv. Other expenses 8. Investment income (net) (= 8.i + 8.ii – 8.iii) i. From financial investments ii. From other investments iii. Interest cost 9. Gain/losses due to revaluations of financial assets/liabilities 10. *Net income (before taxes)* (= 6 – 7 + 8 + 9) 11. Income tax 12. *Net income after tax* (= 10 – 11) 13. Other comprehensive income (loss) net of tax	14. **Total assets** (= 15 + 16 = 31) 15. *Nonfinancial Assets* *of which* i. Property, own use ii. Property for investment 16. *Financial assets* (= 17 through 23) 17. Currency and deposits 18. Loans 19. Debt securities 20. Equity and investment fund shares 21. Reinsurance claims (= 21.i + 21.ii) i. Reinsurance recoverable ii. Reinsurance receivable 22. Financial derivatives 23. Other financial assets 24. *Liabilities* (= 25 through 29) 25. Loans 26. Debt securities 27. Financial derivatives and employee stock options 28. Other liabilities 29. Insurance, pensions, and standardized guarantee schemes (= 29.i + 29.ii + 29.iii + 29.iv) i. Net equity of households in life insurance reserves ii. Prepayment of insurance premiums and insurance payable iii. Pension fund reserves iv. Other technical provisions 30. Capital and reserves 31. **Balance sheet total** (= 24 + 30 = 14) **Memorandum Series** Other series required to calculate additional FSIs 32. GDP

Source: IMF staff.

Table 5.4 Other Financial Corporations: Pension Funds

Income and Expense Statement	Balance Sheet
1. Investment income (= 1.i + 1.ii + 1.iii) i. Interest income ii. Other income from investments iii. Net change in fair value of investments 2. Investment expense (= 2.i + 2.ii) i. Investment management expenses ii. Taxation on investments 3. *Net investment income* (= 1 – 2) 4. Other income 5. Total administrative expenses 6. Net actuarial gains/losses 7. *Net income (before taxes)* (= 3 + 4 – 5 + 6) 8. Income tax 9. *Net income after tax* (= 7 – 8) 10. Other comprehensive income (loss) net of tax	11. **Total assets** (= 12 + 13 = 30) 12. *Nonfinancial assets* (= 12.i + 12.ii) i. Property, own use ii. Property for investment 13. *Financial assets* (= 14 through 22) 14. Currency and deposits 15. Loans 16. Debt securities 17. Equity and investment fund shares 18. Contributions receivable 19. Insurance, pensions, and standardized guarantee schemes 20. Financial derivatives 21. Pension benefit surplus 22. Other financial assets 23. *Liabilities* (= 24 through 27) 24. Loans 25. Debt securities 26. Financial derivatives and employee stock options 27. Other liabilities 28. Net equity of households in pension fund reserves (= 28.i + 28.ii + 28.iii) i. Defined contribution ii. Defined benefit iii. Hybrid schemes 29. *Net worth* (= 11 – 23 – 28) 30. **Balance sheet total** (= 23 + 28 + 29 = 11)
Memorandum Series *Other series required to calculate additional FSIs:* 31. Liquid assets 32. Estimated pension payments in the next 12 months. 33. GDP	

Source: IMF staff.

Table 5.5 Nonfinancial Corporations

Income and Expense Statement	Balance Sheet
1. Revenue from sales of goods and services (excluding indirect sales taxes) 2. Cost of sales 3. *Net operating income* (= 1 – 2) 4. Interest income 5. Interest expenses 6. Other income (net) 7. *Net income (before taxes)* (= 3 + 4 – 5 + 6) 8. Corporate income taxes 9. *Net income after taxes* (= 7 – 8) 10. Dividends payable 11. *Retained earnings* (= 9 – 10)	12. **Total assets** (= 13 + 14) 13. *Nonfinancial assets* (13.i through 13.v) i. Real estate property ii. Equipment iii. Intellectual property products iv. Inventories v. Other 14. *Financial assets* (= 15 through 20) 15. Currency and deposits 16. Debt securities 17. Equity and investment fund shares 18. Trade credit 19. Financial derivatives 20. Other financial assets 21. *Liabilities* (= 26 + 27 + 28) 22. Loans 23. Debt securities 24. Trade credit 25. Other liabilities 26. *Debt* (= 22 through 25) 27. Financial derivatives and employee stock options 28. General and specific provisions 29. *Capital and reserves* 30. **Balance sheet total** (= 21 + 29 = 12)
Memorandum series *Other series required to calculate additional FSIs:* 31. Earnings before interest and taxes 32. Total debt to nonresidents 33. Total debt in foreign currency 34. Debt-service payments (principal and interest) 35. Interest income receivable from other nonfinancial corporations 36. GDP	

Source: IMF staff.

Table 5.6 Households

Income and Expenses	Balance Sheet
Sources of income 1. Wages and salaries 2. Property income receivable 3. Current transfers (e.g., from government) 4. Other 5. *Less* taxes, including social security contributions, and other current transfers 6. *Gross disposable income* (= 1 + 2 + 3 + 4 – 5)	7. **Total assets** (= 8 + 9) 8. *Nonfinancial assets* (= 8.i + 8.ii + 8.iii) i. Real estate ii. Consumer durable goods iii. Other 9. *Financial assets* (= 10 through 15) 10. Currency and deposits 11. Debt securities 12. Loans 13. Equity and investment fund shares 14. Insurance, pensions, and standardized guarantee schemes 15. Other financial assets 16. *Liabilities* (= 19 + 20) 17. Loans 18. Other debt instruments 19. *Debt* (= 17 + 18) 20. Other liabilities 21. *Net worth* (= 7 – 16)
Memorandum Series ***Other series required to calculate additional FSIs:*** 22. Debt-service payments (interest and principal) 23. Debt collateralized by real estate 24. GDP	

Source: IMF staff.

interest income and interest expense is known as *net interest income.*

5.14 A specific issue arises as to whether interest should accrue on nonperforming assets, and if so, whether this should affect net interest income. The *Guide* recommends that interest on a nonperforming asset should be recorded on a cash payment, not accrual, basis. Interest income should not include accrued interest on nonperforming assets because doing so would overstate net interest income relative to the actual interest-earning capacity of the DT.[6]

5.15 Table 5.1 includes the line items for *gross interest income* (line 1.i), including accrued interest on nonperforming assets, and *provisions for interest accrual on nonperforming assets*, (line 1.ii). The latter should be deducted from the former to eliminate the interest accruing on nonperforming assets in the interest income line. If the debtor subsequently pays interest on nonperforming assets to the DT, interest income should be recognized in the period when payments are received and, if significant, should be referred to in any accompanying explanatory documentation.[7] If any interest is accrued before an asset was classified as nonperforming, this accrual should be reversed. If data are available only on interest income, excluding interest accrual on nonperforming assets, then only the interest income (line 1 in Table 5.1) should be reported.

5.16 *Noninterest income* is all other income received by the DT. Included are *fees and commissions* from the provision of services, *gains and losses on financial*

[6] The *Guide* recognizes that while in many countries classification of an asset as nonperforming is strong evidence for it to be placed on a nonaccrual basis, the provision of collateral or other guarantees might lead the DT to consider that debtors will continue to meet their obligations. While accepting that national practices do vary on this matter, for compiling FSIs, the *Guide* recommends that an asset cease accruing interest upon its classification as nonperforming, and to subsequently record interest income only if the debtor makes an interest payment.

[7] Where interest ceases to accrue on claims on other DTs in the reporting population, to avoid asymmetric reporting of net income at the sector level, additional information on the amounts involved should be reported—both the provisions and any amounts subsequently paid.

instruments, *prorated earnings*, and *other income*.[8] Net interest income together with noninterest income is equal to *gross income*.

5.17 *Fees and commissions* are for services such as payment services; intermediary services (e.g., those associated with lines of credit and letters of credit); services related to transactions in securities (e.g., brokerage, placements and underwriting of new issues, arrangement of swaps and other financial derivatives, and security lending); and services related to asset management (e.g., portfolio management and safe custody).[9]

5.18 Accounting rules for the recognition of revenues from financial service fees are set out in the IFRS framework, distinguishing between: (1) *fees that are an integral part of the effective interest rate of a financial instrument*, generally treated as an adjustment to the effective interest rate; (2) *fees earned as services are provided*, such as those charged for servicing a loan; and (3) *fees that are earned on the execution of a significant act*, such as commissions on the sale of securities to a client, or placement fees for arranging a loan between a borrower and an investor. While fees in (1) are treated as interest income through an adjustment to the effective interest rate, fees in (2) and (3) are included in fees and commissions receivable.

5.19 *Gains and losses on financial instruments* are those arising during the period under review. The *Guide* recommends recording in this item any realized and unrealized gains and losses arising during each period on all financial instruments (financial assets and liabilities, in domestic and foreign currencies) held at fair value through profit and loss on the balance sheet.[10] Gains and losses on equity in associates, unconsolidated subsidiaries, and any reverse equity investments that are designated at FVOCI are excluded.[11] Gains and losses on foreign exchange instruments and on financial derivatives, such as interest rate swaps, with the exception of instruments meeting the qualifying criteria for hedge accounting under IFRS 9, are also included. Gains and losses on financial instruments exclude any interest included in the net interest income account as accrued for that instrument in the reporting period, as such amounts have already been accounted for as interest income. Gains and losses on financial assets held at fair value through other comprehensive income are excluded, and recorded instead in line 11, other comprehensive income.

5.20 Volatility in other comprehensive income can be indicative of a buildup of unrealized gains and losses.

5.21 For those financial instruments for which gains and losses can be recorded only when realized, the gain or loss should be measured as the difference between the transaction value and the market value recorded on the balance sheet at the end of the previous period. Any realized valuation gains or losses on disposal/derecognition are reported through the profit or loss section of the income and expense statement. Any unrealized gains or losses that developed over previous periods are included in other comprehensive income in accordance with IFRS 9. In addition, all gains or losses in the reporting period—that is, since the previous end-period—that are realized on any other financial assets (except for those related to associates, unconsolidated subsidiaries, and reverse equity investments, which are all recorded directly in capital and reserves) should also be included within the gains and losses on the financial instruments line. This includes gains and losses on loan sales.

5.22 *Prorated earnings* cover the proportion of net income after tax from associates, unconsolidated subsidiaries, and reverse equity investments, and— for domestic-based data—foreign branches.[12, 13] Prorated

[8] Such gains and losses are not classified as income in the *2008 SNA*.

[9] Implicit fees and commissions, such as those corresponding to the *2008 SNA* concept of "financial intermediation services indirectly measured" (FISIM), are not included in this item. In other words, interest income is not adjusted for any FISIM estimates.

[10] IFRS 9, paragraphs 5.7.1–5.7.4, indicates that financial assets or liabilities measured at fair value through profit and loss are to be recognized in profit and loss (except if they are part of a hedging relationship, or special cases of equity investment); while gain or losses on financial assets measured at amortized cost are to be recognized in profit or loss only when the financial asset is derecognized.

[11] Associates and subsidiaries are defined in Chapter 6.

[12] Unless the taxes on net income are payable by the investor, in which instance this item covers net income before tax.

[13] This item also covers income reflecting the withdrawal of income by the owner from a quasi-corporation. Only withdrawal of income from the net income earned by the quasi corporation should be included.

earnings are calculated on the basis of the share of equity owned.[14]

5.23 *Other income* covers (1) dividends declared payable by other corporations or cooperatives in which DTs have an equity stake,[15] (2) gains or losses on sales of fixed assets in the current period (measured as the difference between the sale value and the balance sheet value at the previous end-period), (3) rental and royalty income receivable (including income from buildings, other structures, and equipment; from land and subsoil assets; and from other produced and non-produced assets); and (4) any amounts receivable by DTs arising from compensation for damage or injury.

5.24 In addition, total other comprehensive income (or loss) that would be reported in an IFRS Statement of Comprehensive Income should be reported on line 11. This will include items to be subsequently reclassified to net income such as the net change in unrealized gains (losses) on financial assets at fair value through other comprehensive income (available-for-sale securities under IAS 39); the net change in unrealized foreign currency translation gains (losses) on investments in foreign operations, net of hedging activities; and the net change in gains (losses) on derivatives designated as cash flow hedges; as well as items specified in IFRS that will not subsequently be reclassified to net income such as actuarial gains (losses) on employee benefits plans; and the change in net unrealized gains (losses) on equity securities designated at fair value through other comprehensive income.

5.25 *Noninterest expenses* cover all expenses other than interest expenses, including *fees and commissions*. They include operating expenses relating to the ordinary banking business (other than interest expenses and fees and commissions that are an integral part of the effective yield of a financial instrument) such as (1) personnel (or staff) costs; (2) expenses for property and equipment (ordinary and regular maintenance and repair);[16] rentals paid on building, other structures, and equipment (and related depreciation);[17] and rents paid on land; (3) other expenditures related to the operations, including purchases of goods and services (e.g., advertising costs, staff training, service expenses, and fees for other services provided), and royalties paid for the use of other produced or non-produced assets (excluding those expenses classified as personnel costs); and (4) taxes other than income taxes—such as taxes on the ownership or use of land and buildings or on labor employed (including payroll and other employee-related taxes payable by the employer)—less any subsidies related to operating activity, such as subsidies received from general government. Also included are any fines and penalties imposed on DTs, by courts of law or otherwise, and any amounts payable by DTs as compensation to other institutional units for injury and damage. For DTs, operating expenses also include any premiums paid to a deposit insurance fund.

5.26 *Personnel costs* include the total remuneration, in cash or in kind, payable by the enterprise in return for work done by employees during the accounting period. Included are wages and salaries, including paid annual leave and paid sick leave; profit sharing and bonuses; allowances for housing and cars; as well as free or subsidized goods and services (except those required for employees to carry out their work); and social security contributions for such items as medical care and pensions. Also included are unfunded employee social insurance benefits, such as the continued payment of normal or reduced wages during periods of absence from work as a result of illness or accidents, redundancy payments, accruals for holidays, long service leave, and so on. Employee stock options (see paragraph 5.63) are a way of paying wages and salaries in kind and should be considered as personnel expenses when granted.

[14] Any earnings from deposit-taking associates that are covered in the reporting population should be excluded from this line at the sector level.

[15] To avoid double counting of income before taxes, in the sector-level data, dividends receivable from other DTs in the reporting population should be excluded from this item and instead included (with a negative sign) in the dividends payable line—so, the data for dividends payable by, and receivable from, other DTs in the reporting population will net to zero in this line.

[16] Such expenses are different in nature, and so recorded differently, from expenditures on gross fixed capital formation, which add to nonfinancial assets in the balance sheet.

[17] There are differences between the national accounts and commercial accounts measurements of depreciation. The *Guide* does not make a judgment as to the preferred method. The national accounts approach is based on current market prices, whereas the commercial accounts approach is based on historic prices but allows for periodic reviews with adjustments to the schedule of depreciation as necessary.

5.27 *Loan loss provisions* are net new allowances for losses that DTs make in the reporting period to reflect increases in expected credit loss (ECL, an expense) or decreases in ECL (income). As discussed in Chapter 4, the concept of ECL does not include a distinction between general and specific allowance for loan loss. Consistent with IFRS 9, DTs should recognize ECL using a forward-looking approach. ECL is the sum of (1) the 12-month expected credit losses for financial instruments whose credit loss has not increased significantly since initial recognition and (2) full-lifetime expected credit losses if the credit risk on a financial instrument has increased significantly since initial recognition.[18]

5.28 The *Guide* relies on national practices in identifying loan loss provisions and distinguishing between specific and general provisions and recommends that such practices be clearly documented (paragraph 4.38). Provisions for the accrual of interest on nonperforming assets should not be included under loan loss provisions, as they are identified within (and excluded from) net interest income.[19] While provisions for losses or future expenses reduce net income, overshooting of expected losses or expenses in any one period could be reversed in subsequent periods subject to national practice, increasing income in those periods.

5.29 *Other financial asset provisions* include the expense incurred to establish an expected credit loss allowance against any other financial assets that are within the scope of IFRS 9. This includes financial assets valued at amortized cost such as securities held for the purpose of collecting the cash flows. Consistent with IFRS 9, allowance for loss on these assets is recognized in the profit and loss and netted against the assets.[20] This category also includes any net new provisions made for supervisory purposes to take account of changes in the volatility of bid-ask spreads or other factors relating to closing out a position in less-liquid tradable instruments. Gross income *less* noninterest expenses and provisions for expected credit losses on loans and other financial assets[21] equates to *net income before taxes*.

5.30 Some events are extraordinary in relation to the business ordinarily carried out by the enterprise. These may include the recovery of written-off loans and (although rare) catastrophic losses arising from a natural or other disaster. Extraordinary items can include income but will usually be an expense item. However, IAS 1 prevents the reporting of extraordinary items in the statements presenting profit or loss and other comprehensive income, or in the notes.[22] Therefore, those *extraordinary items* are to be presented in Table 5.1 as part of other income in (line 4.iv), or as part of other expenses in (line 6.ii). If the volume of those extraordinary events is significant, metadata explaining them should accompany the dissemination of the FSIs.

5.31 *Income taxes* are those taxes that accrue in the period under review and are related to the income, profits, and capital gains of DTs. Once taxes are deducted from net income, the total is equal to *net income after taxes*.

5.32 *Dividends* are amounts payable for the period under review to the owners of DTs after all other expenses have been met, leaving *retained earnings* (net income after taxes less dividends payable) to be posted to the retained earnings account of capital and reserves.

Balance sheet

Nonfinancial assets

5.33 *Nonfinancial assets* are all economic assets other than financial assets. Nonfinancial assets provide benefits to their owners but do not represent claims on other institutional units. It is expected that balance sheets of DTs and OFCs show a small proportion of nonfinancial assets within the total.[23]

[18] See IFRS 9, paragraphs 5.5.3 and 5.5.5.

[19] As noted in paragraph 5.15, for any interest that has accrued in earlier periods but is subsequently considered to be an expected identifiable loss, the provision for the loss should be included in line 7 of Table 5.1, and not as a provision for accrued interest on nonperforming assets.

[20] This reduces the carrying value of the security in the balance sheet.

[21] Provisions should usually represent as an expense. However, in any one period, they might add to income if there is a reduction in expected loss or recovery exceeding the net value of an asset for which an allowance for loss had previously been established.

[22] See IAS 1, paragraph 87.

[23] For some financial instruments used by Islamic banks, Islamic banks may record nonfinancial assets used for leasing or installment sales agreements in relation to financial instruments. This can result in larger proportions of nonfinancial assets as a component of the balance sheet compared to data from countries without Islamic banks. See IFSB *PSIFI Compilation Guide*.

Nonfinancial assets are further discussed when presenting the sectoral balance sheet for NFCs (paragraph 5.141).

5.34 Some nonfinancial assets of DTs might be goods and real estate property acquired in the process of collecting impaired loans. These are not part of the fixed and other nonfinancial assets used in the normal conduct of their business, but assets that will be sold to (totally or partially) recover the outstanding loans.

Financial assets and liabilities

5.35 *Financial assets* are a subset of economic assets that are financial instruments. Most financial assets are financial claims arising from contractual relationships created when one institutional unit provides funds or other resources to another.[24] These contracts are the basis of creditor/debtor relationships through which asset owners acquire unconditional claims on economic resources of other institutional units. When a financial claim is created, a liability of equal value is simultaneously incurred by the debtor as the counterpart to the financial asset.

5.36 The identification and presentation of the different types of financial assets and liabilities can vary depending on analytical needs and national accounting practices. In the list of FSI ratios, the primary focus is on instruments by functional type, such as loans, debt securities, or derivatives. Thus, in the *Guide*, the primary classifications of financial assets and liabilities are *currency and deposits, loans, debt securities, equity and investment fund shares (assets), financial derivatives,* and *other assets/liabilities.*

5.37 *Currency* consists of notes and coins that are of fixed nominal values and are issued or authorized by central banks or governments. Currency is divided into domestic currency and foreign currency. Domestic currency is the legal tender in the economy and is issued by the central bank (or government) of that economy or of the common currency area to which the economy belongs. Foreign currency represents claims on nonresident central banks or governments. Gold and commemorative coins that are not in circulation as legal tender are classified as nonfinancial assets rather than as currency.

[24] In the SNA, by convention, financial assets also include monetary gold, which is gold bullion held by monetary authorities as a reserve asset and for which there is no counterpart liability.

5.38 *Deposits* are standard, non-negotiable contracts open to the public at large that represent the placements of funds available for later withdrawal. They include all claims on the central bank, government units, and some OFCs, that are represented by evidence of deposit. Claims of one DT on another are excluded from deposits and are instead recorded as interbank loans (paragraph 5.47). Deposits comprise *transferable* and *nontransferable* deposits. *Transferable deposits* comprise all deposits that are (1) exchangeable for banknotes and coins on demand at par and without penalty or restriction; and (2) directly usable for making third-party payments by check, draft, giro order, direct debit/credit, or other direct payment facility.[25] *Nontransferable deposits* comprise deposits that cannot be used for third-party payments or have restrictions on the number or size of such third-party payment. Most common nontransferable deposits include, among others: (1) sight deposits that permit immediate cash withdrawals but are not useable for direct third-party payments; (2) savings deposits, which pay interest but cannot be used for direct payments to third-parties;[26] (3) fixed-term deposits, which can have maturities ranging from a month to a few years; (4) non-negotiable certificates of deposits; (5) repayable margin payments in cash related to different financial contracts, such as financial derivatives; and (6) repurchase agreements that resemble a deposit where the DT is the cash-taker.[27]

5.39 Volatility of deposits refers to the likelihood that depositors will, at short notice, withdraw funds in response to a perceived weakness in an individual DT or in the banking system. Determining such

[25] Money market funds shares can be regarded as functionally equivalent to deposits. However, in the *Guide*, they are classified as equity and investment fund shares because their characteristics, and hence regulation, are different from that of DTs.

[26] Deposits that are called "savings deposits" but are equipped with automatic transfer service features are considered transferable deposits.

[27] In Islamic finance, much of the deposit-like funding provided by the public to banks is not in the form of interest-bearing deposit accounts but rather as "profit-sharing investment accounts" in which the bank shares with the funders the earnings generated by the deposited funds. Although such accounts are commonly used like deposit accounts, they differ because they have quasi-investment characteristics and do not guarantee specific interest-like payments. This means that funders share in the risks in the bank's investments, which changes the financial soundness profile of the bank.

likelihood in advance is difficult, but typically the key factors taken into account are the type of depositor, the existence of insurance coverage, and the maturity of the deposits (remaining maturity). Experience suggests that some types of depositors are less likely to move their funds than others.[28] Additionally, deposits covered by credible insurance schemes are more likely to be a stable form of funding for DTs than those not covered. Also, deposits with a long-remaining maturity are likely to be more stable, although the lower the penalties for withdrawal, the less relevant this factor is in determining the likelihood of withdrawal.

5.40 *Customer deposits* are usually considered to be a more stable type of deposit and can be employed to fund long-term lending. This series is required to calculate the ratio of customer deposits to loans, an additional FSI. The *Guide* recommends that the type of depositor be the primary factor in defining customer deposits, because of both its relevance and its general applicability. Thus, customer deposits include all deposits placed by residents or nonresidents, except those placed by (resident and nonresident) financial corporations, central governments, and central banks. The depositors in the excluded sectors are more likely to monitor DTs' financial information, are less likely to be covered by deposit insurance, and perhaps have a fiduciary responsibility to safeguard their assets. They are, therefore, more prone than other depositors to shifting deposits as risks increase. Perhaps because of deposit insurance, household depositors tend to be less aware of the risks, while commercial depositors may have other relationships with banks that make them more reluctant than institutional investors to move funds. Provided it can be determined that the penalties for withdrawal are high, customer deposits could also include those from the excluded sectors that have a remaining maturity of more than one year.[29,30]

[28] This is reflected is the Basel III liquidity standards, with different run-off rates prescribed when calculating the Liquidity Coverage Ratio to approximate the relative "stickiness" of different types of deposit.

[29] Another approach that could yield a similar outcome would be to determine customer deposits by type of deposit, that is: (1) deposits known for their stability such as demand deposits, small-scale savings, and time deposits; and (2) deposits covered by a (credible) deposit insurance scheme.

[30] For Islamic banks, the characteristics of customer deposits noted in this paragraph also exist, but customer behavior will also be affected to some extent by the risk-bearing nature of some of funding provided by customers, as noted in footnote 25.

5.41 *Loans* are financial assets that are (1) created when a creditor lends funds directly to a debtor, and (2) evidenced by documents that are not negotiable.[31] Collateral, in the form of either a financial asset (e.g., security) or nonfinancial asset (e.g., land and building), may be provided under a loan transaction, though it is not an essential feature. Loans collateralized by real estate should be separately identified to assist in financial stability analysis. The loan category includes commercial loans, overdrafts, installment loans, hire-purchase credit, loans to finance trade credit, financial leases, and repurchase agreements.[32] Undrawn lines of credit are not recognized as an asset, and therefore not as loans, because they are only potential claims. Accounts receivable/payable, which are treated as a separate category of financial assets, are excluded from loans. To meet the requirements of the FSI list, loans to other DTs (resident and nonresident) are distinguished in Table 5.1 from other loans as interbank loans (line 18.i.i), which are attributed by sector on a residency basis, as defined in Chapter 2.

5.42 Loans that have become negotiable are to be reclassified from loans to debt securities. For such reclassification, there needs to be firm evidence of secondary market trading, including the existence of market makers, and frequent quotations of the instruments, such as provided by bid-offer spreads. A transfer or one-time sale of a loan, for example, to a special purpose vehicle for securitization, would not normally constitute a basis for reclassifying the loan as a security.

5.43 Two forms of loans require further discussion. A *finance lease* is a contract under which the lessor—the financial corporation providing the financing—as the legal owner of an asset, conveys substantially all the risks and rewards of ownership of the asset to the lessee, who becomes the economic owner of the asset. Under a finance lease, the lessor recognizes assets held under a finance lease as a receivable at an amount

[31] A financial asset is negotiable if its legal ownership is readily capable of being transferred from one unit to another unit by delivery or endorsement. Loans may be traded or securitized, but their legal form is not designed for negotiability in the same way as debt securities.

[32] Except those repurchase agreements that resemble a standard deposit, where the DT receives cash from a client and provides a security as collateral.

equal to the net investment in the lease. Payments under a finance lease are treated not as rentals on the asset but as finance income over the lease term of a finance lease, based on a pattern reflecting a constant periodic rate of return on the net investment.[33]

5.44 A *securities repurchase agreement* (repo) is an arrangement involving the provision of securities in exchange for cash with a commitment to repurchase the same or similar securities at a fixed price either on a specified future date or with an "open" maturity.[34] Repos convey the legal ownership of the securities to the cash provider, which entitles the cash provider to sell the securities to a third party (on-selling). Despite conveyance of the legal ownership to the cash provider, the economic ownership is retained by the cash taker (i.e., the securities provider), as the cash taker retains the market risk and ownership benefits, other than the right of sale, including holding gains or losses and interest income on the securities. Because of these features, repurchase agreements should be recorded as loans collateralized by the securities underlying the agreement.[35] The securities should remain on the balance sheet of the cash taker and a new financial asset (i.e., a loan) should be recorded as an asset of the cash provider offsetting the reduction in cash and a liability, offsetting the cash received, of the cash taker. Although repurchase agreements are usually classified as loans, those resembling a standard deposit, where the client of the DTs is the cash-provider, should be classified as deposits. If securities acquired under a repo or securities-lending arrangement are sold to third parties, the security taker should record on the balance sheet a liability equal to the current market value of the security that was sold (short position).[36]

5.45 A *gold swap*, under which gold is exchanged for other assets (usually foreign exchange), is similar in nature to a repo and is to be recorded as a collateralized loan.

5.46 *Securities lending* is similar to a repo. Ownership of the security is transferred to the borrower with the execution of an agreement to return it. The lender earns a fee for the transaction and typically takes collateral in the form of other securities, or less commonly, cash or other instruments. If the security-taker provides cash as collateral, then the arrangement is treated in the same way as a repo, with the securities involved remaining on the balance sheet of the security provider. In the more typical case of non-cash collateral being provided, the ownership of both the securities lent and collateral provided changes hands; the borrowed securities are recorded on the balance sheet of the borrower, and the securities provided as collateral are recorded on the balance sheet of the lender.

5.47 *Interbank loans* are loans granted to other DTs, usually with a short-term maturity. For the compilation of the FSI Customers Deposits to Total Loans, and to monitor interbank exposures, interbank loans should be identified separately from other loans because their behavior often differs from that of loans with non-DT entities, and because they can be a channel for transmission of stress between banks.

5.48 *Specific loan loss provisions* are the outstanding amount of provisions made against the value of individual non-performing loans, collectively assessed groups of loans, and non-performing loans to other DTs (see also paragraph 5.27) in accordance with requirements specified by the DT supervisory authority.[37, 38, 39] In some economies, provisions are constituted

---

[33] See IFRS 9, paragraph 3.2.7.

[34] "Open" maturity is when both parties agree daily to renew or terminate the agreement. Such an arrangement avoids settlement costs if both parties wish to rollover the repo on a continuing basis.

[35] Repos may be used for a variety of purposes. An extended discussion of repos and securities lending can be found in Chapter 4 of the *Monetary and Financial Statistics Manual and Compilation Guide* (*MFSMCG*), paragraphs 4.71–4.84.

[36] IFRS 9, paragraph BA.7.

[37] As discussed in Chapter 4, IFRS 9 focuses on the concept of ECL. In line with BCBS guidance, compilers should follow national supervisory standards in identifying specific and general provisions. The *Guide* recommends that interest on NPLs should not accrue, so specific loan provisions should not in principle include specific provisions for interest accrual on NPLs.

[38] If the accounting practice is not to accrue interest on NPLs, but to include the interest in the value of the loan on the balance sheet offset by an item such as interest in suspense, it is suggested that the interest in suspense be included together with the data for specific loan provisions on the balance sheet. If this approach is adopted, it should be explained in the metadata.

[39] In jurisdictions such as the EU that have elected to treat all ECL as specific provisions, it will be necessary to report a subset of provisions which are only those held against non-performing loans. In jurisdictions that prescribe an allocation of ECL to general and specific provisions, for example considering as specific provisions that portion of ECL attributable to loans having a significant increase in credit risk since initial recognition, the supervisory prescription of specific provisions should be used.

against nonperforming and performing loans, without the possibility of separately identifying them. For such cases, the *Guide* defers to the national legal framework for provisioning, which should be documented in the metadata. The *Guide* recommends reporting specific loan loss provisions as a negative asset item, netting from total gross loans (line 18.ii in Table 5.1).

5.49 *Debt securities* are negotiable financial instruments serving as evidence that units have obligations to settle by means of providing cash, a financial instrument, or some other item of economic value, and give the holder an unconditional right to receive interest and/or principal payments. They include bills, bonds and debentures, commercial paper, negotiable certificates of deposit, asset-backed securities, loans that have become de facto negotiable, preferred stocks or shares that pay a fixed income but do not provide for participation in the residual value of the corporation, bankers' acceptances, and similar instruments normally traded in the financial markets.[40] Some corporate bonds are convertible into shares of the same corporation at the option of the bondholder; if the conversion option is traded separately, then it is recorded as a separate asset and classified as a financial derivative.

5.50 Common types of debt securities are those sold on: (1) a *coupon basis*, stipulating that periodic interest, or coupon, payments will be made during the life of the instrument and that the principal will be repaid at maturity; (2) an *amortized basis*, stipulating that interest and principal payments will be made in installments during the life of the instrument; (3) a *discount*, or *zero coupon, basis*, whereby a security is issued at a price that is less than the face (or par) value of the security, and all interest and principal are paid at maturity; or (4) an *indexed basis*, which ties the amount of interest or principal payment to a reference index, such as a price index or an exchange rate index, or to the price of a commodity (e.g., gold). The *Guide* defers to IFRS regarding the accrual of interest and the related asset classification and measurement of all types of debt securities.

[40]The *Handbook on Securities Statistics* (jointly published by the BIS, ECB, and IMF) deals with the conceptual framework for the compilation and presentation of securities statistics, elaborating on issues such as issuers, holders, currency, maturity, and type of interest rate.

5.51 Table 5.1, line 19, includes all the above instruments under the heading of debt securities. However, it is recognized that national practices might separately identify certain types of instruments, such as mortgage-backed securities, government securities, and securities considered to be of a liquid nature.

5.52 *Equity* comprises all instruments and records acknowledging claims on the residual value of a corporation after the claims of all creditors have been met. Ownership of equity in legal entities is usually evidenced by shares, stocks, participations, depository receipts, or similar documents.[41] Shares and stocks have the same meaning. Participating preferred shares are those that provide for participation in the residual value on the dissolution of an incorporated enterprise; such shares are also equity securities, whether or not the income is fixed or determined according to a formula.[42] Buybacks by a DT of its own equity securities reduce the number of equity securities outstanding.

5.53 Equity assets include equity investments in associates, unconsolidated subsidiaries, and reverse equity investments, as well as other equity investments in DTs. In the context of domestic data, equity assets include any share capital provided to foreign branches.

5.54 *Investment fund shares* comprise shares or units of all kinds issued by money market funds (MMFs) and non-MMF investment funds, which are collective investment schemes that raise funds from the public. The fundamental difference between them is that MMFs typically invest in low-risk liquid money market instruments with a residual maturity of less than one year, are often transferable, and are often regarded as close substitutes for deposits. Non-MMFs investment funds typically invest in longer-term financial assets and possibly real estate. MMF and

[41]Depository receipts allow a nonresident institutional unit to introduce its equity (or debt) into another market in a form more readily acceptable to the investors in that market, often including translating the price of securities into the currency of the receiving economy, and adjusting issues to national legal and reporting standards. Depository receipts are classified according to the underlying financial instrument backing them (i.e., debt and equity).

[42]Accounting standard setters agree that not everything commonly called equity qualifies as such. For instance, mandatorily redeemable preferred stocks are liabilities, and so are various kinds of puttable stock, where the stocks are being essentially used as currency.

non-MMF investment fund shares or units represent a claim on a proportion of the value of an established investment fund.

5.55 *Financial derivatives* are financial instruments that are linked to another specific financial instrument, indicator, or commodity, and through which specific financial risks (e.g., interest rate risk, foreign exchange risk, equity and commodity price risk, and credit risk) can be traded in their own right in financial markets. The value of a financial derivative depends on the price of the underlying item: the reference price. The reference price may relate to a commodity, a financial asset, an interest rate, an exchange rate, another derivative, or a spread between two prices. The derivative contract may also refer to an index or a basket of prices. Unlike debt instruments, no principal amount is advanced that has to be repaid, and no investment income accrues. Financial derivatives are used for several purposes, including risk management, hedging, arbitrage between markets, and speculation.

5.56 There are two broad types of financial derivatives: *forward-type contracts* and *options*. A major difference between a forward contract and an option is that, whereas either party to a forward is a potential debtor, the buyer of an option acquires an asset and the option's writer incurs a liability. Option contracts can expire without worth; options are exercised only if settling a contract is advantageous for the option's holder.

5.57 A *forward-type contract* (forward) is an unconditional contract by which two parties agree to exchange a specific quantity of an underlying item (financial or real) at an agreed-upon contract price (the strike price) on a specified date. Forward-type contracts include forwards, futures, and swaps. *Forward rate agreements* and *forward foreign exchange contracts* are common types of forward-type contracts. A *swap contract* involves the counterparties exchanging, in accordance with prearranged terms, cash flows based on the reference prices of the underlying items.[43] Swap contracts classified as forward-type contracts include currency swaps, interest rate swaps, cross-currency interest rate swaps, and equity swaps.

5.58 *Futures* are forward-type contracts traded on organized exchanges, while forward contracts are bought and sold in over-the-counter (OTC) trading conducted directly between the parties, although clearing may occur through a central counterparty. For futures, the exchanges facilitate trading by determining the standardized terms and conditions of the contract, acting as the counterparty to all trades, and requiring margins to be deposited and paid to mitigate against risk.

5.59 At the inception of a forward-type contract, risk exposures of equal market value are exchanged, so a contract typically has zero value at inception. As time passes, market rates change, and the price of the underlying item changes and the market value of the forward contract will change (although it may be restored to zero by periodic settlements during its life). The classification of a forward-type contract may change between asset and liability positions.

5.60 An *off-market swap* has a nonzero value at inception as a result of having reference rates priced differently from current market values (i.e., "off-the-market"). The economic nature of an off-market swap is equivalent to a combination of a loan and an on-market financial derivative. Therefore, off-market swaps should be recorded as two stock positions in the sectoral balance sheets—a loan and an on-market financial derivative.

5.61 In an *option contract* (option), the purchaser acquires from the seller a right to buy or sell, depending on whether the option is a call (a contract to buy) or a put (a contract to sell) a specified underlying item at a strike price on or before a specified date. The purchaser of an option pays a premium to the writer of the option. Throughout the life of the contract, the writer of the option has a liability and the buyer an asset, although the option can expire worthless; the option will be exercised only if settling the contract is advantageous for the purchaser.

5.62 Options can be contrasted with forward-type contracts in that: (1) at inception, a premium is paid for an option representing a non-zero value for the contract, unlike a forward-type contract where there is usually no up-front payment and the derivative contract begins with a zero value reflecting the mutual net exchange of

[43] Other types of arrangements also called swaps, but not meeting the definition given earlier, include gold swaps, central bank swap arrangements and other similar arrangements, and credit default swaps, a type of option contract.

claims and obligations between the parties to the forward contract; (2) during the life of an option contract, the buyer is always the creditor and the writer is always the debtor; whereas for a forward-type contract, either party can be creditor or debtor, and it may change during the life of the contract; and (3) at maturity, redemption is determined by the buyer of the option, whereas it is unconditional for a forward-type contract.

5.63 *Employee stock options* are options to buy the equity of a company, offered to employees of the company as a form of remuneration and as an incentive to perform their duties in the best interests of the corporation's shareholders. This *Guide* recommends treatment of employee stock options as an increase in equity with an offsetting debit comprising the fair value of the stock option at the date the options are exercised.[44]

5.64 If an instrument such as a security or a loan contains an embedded derivative that is inseparable from the underlying instrument, valuation and classification varies for assets and liabilities.[45] For financial liabilities, an embedded derivative is accounted for separately from the host contract as a derivative (FVTPL) if it is not closely related to the host contract in terms of economic risk and characteristics. Examples are bonds that are convertible into shares and securities with options for repayment of principal in currencies that differ from those in which the securities were issued. For financial assets, if the host is an asset that falls within the scope of IFRS 9, there is no bifurcation and the embedded instrument is measured in its entirety in accordance with IFRS 9. If the host does not fall within the scope of IFRS 9, the derivative is accounted for separately from the host (FVTPL).

5.65 Financial derivative contracts are usually settled by net payments of cash rather than by the delivery of the underlying items. Exchange-traded contracts, such as commodity futures, are often settled before maturity. Cash settlement is a logical consequence of the use of financial derivatives to trade risks independently of the ownership of underlying items. Some financial derivative contracts—particularly those involving foreign currency—are, however, settled by delivery of the underlying items. Once a financial derivative reaches its settlement date, any unpaid overdue amount is reclassified as accounts receivable/payable, as its value is fixed, and thus the nature of the claim becomes debt. Gross market values for financial derivative assets and liabilities should be recorded on the balance sheet, and any valuation gains and losses should be recorded in the income and expense statement.

5.66 *Other financial assets* (or *other liabilities* from the debtor perspective) cover prepayments of insurance premiums and miscellaneous other items due to be received or paid. Miscellaneous other items receivable or payable include accrued but unpaid taxes, dividends (including dividends declared but not yet payable), purchases and sales of securities, rent, wages and salaries, social contributions, social benefits, and similar payments.

5.67 *Trade credit and advances* are mostly relevant to NFCs and separately identified as asset and liability items in their balance sheets. For other sectors, it is included in other financial assets and liabilities, but will generally not be relevant to the DT sector. Trade credit and advances are claims (or obligations) that arise from the sale (or purchase) of goods and services for which payment is not yet due. They consist of (1) trade credit extended directly by the suppliers of goods and services to their customers, and (2) advances for work that is in progress (or is yet to be undertaken) and prepayment by customers for goods and services not yet provided. Trade credit does not include loans, debt securities, or other liabilities that are issued to finance trade credit. So, trade-related loans provided by a third party, such as a DT, to an exporter or importer are not included in this category but are included under loans. If significant allowances are made against these assets, particularly trade credit, compilers are encouraged to separately identify these allowances.[46]

5.68 *General provisions for losses on financial assets* and *other provisions* are presented in the *Guide* as liability items and classified as a separate component (line 30 in Table 5.1), although they are "internal

[44] See IFRS 2 *Share-based Payment*.

[45] Refer to IFRS 9, Section 4.3, Embedded Derivatives.

[46] The ECL approach applies to trade receivables. Refer to IFRS 9, paragraph 5.5.15.

accounts" to reflect losses on certain assets rather than liabilities to creditors. The *Guide* defers to national supervisory standards for the allocation of allowances for ECL to general and specific provisions. When specific and general provisions are created, they are included in the income and expense statement as an expense (see paragraph 5.27). The counterpart for the created specific provisions reduces the net value of the relevant asset on the balance sheet, while the counterpart for the created general provisions shows as a liability item in the balance sheet.

5.69 *Debt* is defined as the outstanding amount of those actual current and non-contingent liabilities that require payment of principal or interest by the debtor at some point(s) in the future. Thus, for DTs, debt comprises those financial liabilities that are deposits, loans, debt securities, and other liabilities.

5.70 *Capital and reserves* is defined as the equity interest of the owners in an enterprise and is the difference between total assets and liabilities. It represents the amount available to absorb unidentified losses.

5.71 In the *Guide*, total capital and reserves include the following:

a. *Funds contributed by owners* comprise the total amount from the initial and any subsequent issuance of shares, stocks, or other forms of ownership. This item is valued as the nominal amount of proceeds from the initial and subsequent issuances. It is not revalued.
b. *Retained earnings* reflect all previous years' after-tax profits that have not been distributed to shareholders or appropriated as general or special reserves. This item is also valued at the nominal amount of earnings that have been retained and is not revalued.
c. *Current year result* represents the accumulation of profit or loss since the beginning of the business year.
d. *General and special reserves* are reserves that reflect appropriations from retained earnings.[47]

5.72 Under consolidated reporting at group level, when the parent has less than full ownership of a subsidiary, the capital and reserves attributable to minority shareholders in the subsidiary are included in capital and reserves, because the focus of FSIs is on the total capital and reserves of the DTs in the reporting population.

Memorandum series

5.73 Some of the series required to calculate the FSIs are not directly available from the financial statements described earlier. They are included as memorandum items to the financial statements. These series fall into two categories: (1) supervisory-based series, and (2) series that provide for further analysis of the balance sheet.

Supervisory-based series

5.74 These are series to be directly sourced from supervisory information because the definitions conform to supervisory guidance. For supervisory-based series, the *Guide* relies on the definitions and concepts of the BCBS as implemented by national authorities. Due to the many elements of national discretion in the various Basel standards and many jurisdictions' adoption of definitions and requirements that vary in areas aside from national discretion in the relevant Basel standard, compilers will rely on national supervisory standards for these series, and should therefore document in the metadata the exercise of national discretion as well as any elements that vary from the relevant Basel standard.

5.75 Chapter 3, which describes the regulatory framework for DTs, provides detail with respect to the elements of regulatory capital, the calculation of risk-weighted assets, and liquidity ratios. This section focuses on their most relevant features. The BCBS has developed specific definitions of *regulatory capital* to be used as numerators in regulatory capital adequacy ratios (see paragraph 3.24 and 3.25). The definitions extend beyond purely capital and reserve account items identified on the balance sheet, to include several specified types of subordinated debt instruments and reserves. Banks are expected to have total regulatory capital of at least 8 percent of risk-weighted assets, with specific minimums for its components. Based on the Basel regulatory framework, regulatory capital consists of three components.

[47] In many cases, general reserves are required by law to provide the entity and its creditors with an added measure of protection from the effects of losses. Special reserves also provide added protection, but from the effects of losses that may arise from specific activities of the corporation.

5.76 *Tier 1 capital* under Basel I and Basel II comprises equity capital and freely available disclosed reserves (see paragraph 3.26). Tier 1 capital should already reflect the corresponding *supervisory deductions*, such as goodwill (see paragraph 5.80). Regarding total capital, supervisory deductions cover investments in unconsolidated banking and financial subsidiaries and, at the discretion of national authorities, investment in capital of other banks and financial institutions.[48]

5.77 Under Basel III, Tier 1 capital is split into two components: (1) *Common equity tier 1* (CET1) capital, and (2) *Additional tier 1* (AT1) capital (see paragraphs 3.27 and 3.28). Both components of Tier 1 are measured net of supervisory deductions. *CET1* capital consists predominantly of common shares, retained earnings, and accumulated other comprehensive income and other disclosed reserves. *AT1* capital consists of instruments that are subordinated, have fully discretionary non-cumulative dividends or coupons, and have neither a maturity date nor an incentive to redeem.

5.78 *Tier 2 capital* under Basel I and II consists of financial instruments and reserves that are available to absorb losses, but might not be permanent and have uncertain values, might entail costs if sold, or which otherwise lack the full loss-absorption capacity of Tier 1 capital items (see paragraphs 3.29 and 3.30). The balance of Tier 2 capital should reflect the corresponding supervisory deductions. Tier 2 capital and subordinated debt cannot exceed 100 percent and 50 percent, respectively, of Tier 1 capital. The composition of Tier 2 capital was modified under Basel III, in order to strengthen the loss absorption capacity of banks (see paragraph 3.30).

5.79 *Tier 3 capital* was introduced in the 1996 amendment to Basel I (see paragraph 3.6). At the discretion of national authorities, it can be used solely to support market risk. It consists of medium-term subordinated debt and is limited to 250 percent of the bank's Tier 1 capital. Tier 3 capital is eliminated under Basel III.

[48] In the absence of data on Tier 1 capital (as in the case of units not subject to Basel capital adequacy guidelines), the data for funds contributed by owners together with retained earnings (including those earnings appropriated to reserves) could be used.

5.80 *Supervisory deductions* cover goodwill (see next paragraph) and all other intangibles, as a deduction from Tier 1 capital (CET1 in Basel III). With regard to total regulatory capital, supervisory deductions cover investments in unconsolidated banking and financial subsidiaries and, at the discretion of national authorities, investment in capital of other banks and financial institutions, and other specified types of asset. The data reported in *Supervisory deductions* (line 38 of Table 5.1) is the amount, if any, not already deducted from the components of regulatory capital Tier 1 (CET1 and AT1) and Tier 2, in accordance with paragraphs 5.76 to 5.78.

5.81 *Goodwill* is defined as the excess of the fair (paid) value for a business entity over the book value of the acquired net assets. Accounting standard setters consider goodwill to be an asset. However, goodwill is an intangible asset, and as such not available to absorb losses.[49]

5.82 *Risk-weighted assets* arise from the application to all on- and off-balance- sheet assets of specified risk weights in Basel I and the Standardized approaches in Basel II and III, and an approved methodology for risk modeling of specified assets in the internal-ratings-based approaches of Basel II (see paragraphs 3.32–3.36). Assets are weighted by factors representing their credit riskiness and potential for default. Through the use of credit conversion factors, the credit risk of off-balance-sheet exposures, such as credit line commitments and letters of credit that serve as financial guarantees, is also taken into account in determining regulatory capital requirements. The calculation of risk-weighted assets evolved from fixed coefficients for credit risk in Basel I to basic and more sophisticated methods of measuring credit, market, and operational risks in Basel II and III.

5.83 The measure of total regulatory capital will differ from the measure of capital and reserves in the sectoral balance sheet of Table 5.1. In this context, some general statements can be made:

a. Both regulatory capital and the sectoral balance sheet measure of capital cover paid-in capital,

[49] Consistent with IFRS, if the cost of the acquired entity is lower than the market or fair value of its net assets (negative goodwill), any excess that remains after a rigorous valuation of the net assets acquired is a gain in profit or loss.

reserves (both disclosed and undisclosed), valuation adjustments, retained earnings, and current year result. However, the amounts posted to reserves can differ due to different accounting approaches and regulatory frameworks, such as the treatment of gains or losses on financial instruments.

b. The regulatory measure of capital can include general provisions (up to 1.25 or 0.6 percent of risk-weighted assets, in the standardized or advanced approaches, respectively). As discussed in Chapter 4, the concept of general provisions is not included in the IFRS 9 ECL model. In line with the BCBS transitional guidance on IFRS 9, compilers should rely on national supervisory standards for the identification of specific and general provisions. Specific provisions should be obtained from supervisory data as a memorandum item.

c. Goodwill is deducted from the regulatory measure of capital, while in the sectoral balance sheet, it is recorded as intangible assets and, therefore, implicitly included in the total measure of capital and reserves.

d. The regulatory measure covers certain debt instruments, such as subordinated debt, which are classified as liabilities in the sectoral balance sheet measure.

e. At the sector level, only intragroup equity investments (between units within the same group) are excluded from the sectoral balance sheet measure. That means equity investments in DTs that are not within the same group are included in balance sheet capital. As noted earlier, at national discretion, investments in unrelated DTs may or may not be deducted from regulatory capital calculations.

f. Non-DTs may be consolidated for the calculation of regulatory capital (or investments in such entities deducted from regulatory capital), but this is not preferred for the calculation of the sectoral balance sheet measure.

5.84 *Off-balance-sheet exposures* include contractual financial arrangements that are often referred to as contingencies and are not defined as financial assets or liabilities. These arrangements comprise commitments (including liquidity facilities), unconditionally cancellable commitments, direct credit substitutes, acceptances, stand-by letters of credit, trade letters of credit, failed transactions, and unsettled securities. Off-balance-sheet items are a source of potentially significant leverage.

5.85 *High-quality liquid assets* is a supervisory concept defined in Basel III as those unencumbered assets that can be converted easily and immediately into cash at little or no loss of value. The Basel III text sets out specific market-related characteristics and operational requirements that high-quality liquid assets should possess or satisfy.

5.86 *Total net cash outflows* is a supervisory concept defined in Basel III as the total expected cash outflows minus total expected cash inflows in the specified stress scenario for the subsequent 30 calendar days.[50]

5.87 *Stable funding* is a supervisory concept defined in Basel III as the portion of those types and amounts of equity and liability financing expected to be reliable sources of funds over a one-year time horizon under conditions of extended stress.

5.88 *Large exposures* are defined as the sum of all exposure values of a DT to a counterparty or to a group of connected counterparties, if it is equal to or above 10 percent of the DT's eligible capital base.[51] Specific principles are outlined for the measurement of exposure values. Off-balance-sheet exposures should be converted into credit exposure equivalents through the use of credit conversion factors.

Series that provide a further analysis of the balance sheet

5.89 In order to calculate some core and additional FSIs, there is a need for a number of series that are subtotals of the balance sheet line items and that provide for further analysis of the balance sheet.

5.90 *Liquid assets* are those assets that are readily available to an entity to meet a demand for cash. While it may be possible to raise funds through borrowing, conditions in the market may not always be favorable,

[50] For the calculation of total expected cash outflows and inflows, see BCBS *Basel III: The Liquidity Coverage Ratio and Liquidity Monitoring Tools* (2013).

[51] BCBS, *Standards—Supervisory Framework for Measuring and Controlling Large Exposures*, April 2014, page 4.

and experience has shown the necessity for DTs to maintain a prudent level of liquid assets. For a financial asset to be classified as a liquid asset, the holder must have the reasonable certainty that it can be converted into cash with speed and without significant loss under normal business conditions. The financial assets included in this item go beyond the supervisory definition of high-quality liquid assets.

5.91 Whether an instrument is considered liquid or not depends on judgment and is influenced by market conditions. For example, cash, transferable deposits, and deposits that permit immediate cash withdrawals are typically liquid and are included in liquid assets, while non-traded instruments with a long time until maturity are not. Other deposits provide certainty of value but may not be readily convertible into cash because of restrictions on withdrawals prior to maturity. Conversely, tradable securities, particularly those issued by the government or the central bank, might be readily converted into cash through sale on the secondary market, but their realizable value depends on the market price at the time of sale.

5.92 In the *Guide*, *liquid assets* comprise (1) currency; (2) deposits and other financial assets that are available either on demand or within three months or less; and (3) securities that are traded in liquid markets (including repo markets) that can be readily converted into cash, with insignificant risk of change in value under normal business conditions. Typically, securities issued by the government or the central bank in their own currency meet the criteria to be classified as liquid assets, and in a number of markets high credit-quality private securities, including those issued by financial institutions, may also meet the criteria.

5.93 *Short-term liabilities* are the short-term element of DTs' debt liabilities (line 28 in Table 5.1) and the net (short-term, if possible) market value of financial derivatives positions (liabilities (line 29) *less* assets (line 21) in Table 5.1). The definition includes short-term liabilities to other DTs in the reporting population. Consistent with the definition of liquid assets, *short-term liabilities* could be withdrawn either on demand or within three months or less. Preferably, "short term" should be defined on a remaining maturity basis, although original maturity can be used as a (more limited) alternative.

5.94 *Nonperforming loans* (NPLs) are defined as those loans for which (1) payments of interest or principal are past due by 90 days or more; or (2) interest payments equal to 90 days or more have been capitalized (reinvested into the principal amount), refinanced, or rolled over (payment delayed by agreement); or (3) evidence exists to reclassify them as nonperforming even in the absence of a 90-day past due payment, such as when the debtor files for bankruptcy. The amount of loans recorded as nonperforming should be the gross value of the loan as recorded on the balance sheet, not just the overdue amount.

5.95 Once a loan is classified as nonperforming, it (and/or any replacement loans) should remain classified as such until payments are received, or the principal is written-off on this or subsequent loans that replace the original. It is recognized that some national supervisory practices might be stricter in that loans are classified as nonperforming until payments are received for specified periods of time, for example, until three consecutive payments have been made.

5.96 Replacement loans include loans arising from rescheduling or refinancing the original loan(s) (restructured loans) and loans provided to make payments on the original loan. While these loans may be granted on easier than normal commercial terms, provided the terms and conditions of the replacement loan are complied with by the debtor, and subject to national supervisory guidance, the loan is no longer classified as an NPL.

5.97 *Residential real estate loans* are those loans that are collateralized by residential real estate. Residential real estate includes houses, apartments and other dwellings (e.g., houseboats and mobile homes), and any associated land intended for occupancy by individual HHs.

5.98 *Commercial real estate loans* are those loans that are collateralized by commercial real estate, as well as loans to construction companies and loans to companies active in the development of real estate (including those companies involved in the development of multi-household dwellings). Commercial real estate includes buildings, structures, and associated land used by enterprises for retail, wholesale, manufacturing, or other such purposes.

5.99 The counter parties to Total gross loans can be broken down into the different institutional *sectors of the economy*, and nonresidents, as defined in Chapter 2. This classification follows primarily the sectoral classification of the SNA: (1) deposit-taking corporations except the central bank (DTs in the *Guide*); central bank; the seven subsectors of the financial corporations sector that are not DTs (subsumed in the *Guide* as OFCs), general government, NFCs, and other domestic sectors (HHs and NPISHs), plus nonresidents.[52, 53]

5.100 The *geographic distribution of loans* refers to an attribution of loans on the basis of the residence of the immediate counterpart—that is, the country of residence of the debtor. While country circumstances will differ, a regional classification of lending is encouraged, with perhaps additional detail on lending to residents of other countries that may be of particular relevance, such as neighboring countries. The regional grouping is based on the IMF's *World Economic Outlook* classification.

5.101 For DTs, *foreign currency loans* and *foreign currency liabilities* are those assets and liabilities that are denominated in a currency other than the domestic currency, and those that are denominated in domestic currency but with the amounts to be paid linked to a foreign currency (foreign currency linked). By convention, those loans, and liabilities that are denominated in a foreign currency but with the amounts to be paid linked to a domestic currency (domestic currency linked) are also included in foreign currency loans and liabilities. For related financial derivative liabilities, it is recommended that the net fair value position (liabilities *less* assets) be included in the foreign currency liability measure rather than the gross liability position, because of the market practice of creating offsetting contracts, and the possibility of a forward-type instrument switching from an asset to a liability position and vice versa from one period to the next.

[52]These are money market funds, non-MMF investment funds, other financial intermediaries except insurance corporations and pension funds, financial auxiliaries, captive financial institutions and money lenders, insurance corporations, and pension funds.
[53]The NFC sector could be disaggregated by type of industry.

5.102 The *net open position in foreign currency* for on-balance-sheet items and the *total net open position in foreign currency* are calculated by summing the net position for each foreign currency into a single unit of account (the reporting currency). The calculation is described in more detail in Chapter 7 (paragraphs 7.77–7.83).

5.103 *Credit to the private sector* includes gross loans extended by DTs to the private nonfinancial sector, plus debt securities issued by private NFCs and held by DTs. The data should be compiled on a domestic consolidated basis. The private sector comprises private NFCs, HHs, and NPISHs. An alternative source for compiling this underlying series is the standardized report form (for other depository corporations) used for transmitting monetary data to the IMF for publication in *International Financial Statistics*, which many economies report to the IMF Statistics Department on a monthly basis.

Other Financial Corporations

5.104 As described in Chapter 2, the OFC sector comprises a wide and diverse range of institutions performing financial intermediary, or auxiliary, activities outside the deposit-taking system. Two FSIs for OFCs show the relative importance of the OFC sector (and its subsectors) within the domestic financial sector and within the total economy; no sectoral financial statements are needed to calculate these two FSIs. Additionally, specific FSIs should be compiled for three subsectors of the OFC sector, for which separate financial statements are required, namely: (1) MMFs, (2) insurance corporations (ICs), and (3) pension funds (PFs). They are set out in Tables 5.2 to 5.4.

5.105 The definition of the series presented in these sectoral balance sheets and income and expenses statements are the same as for the corresponding series in Table 5.1, albeit somewhat simplified and adapted to the specific requirements for each subsector. The given discussion touches only on those items previously not presented when describing the financial statements of DTs.

Money market funds

5.106 Table 5.2 presents a summarized sectoral financial statement for MMFs. The typical sectoral balance sheet of MMFs is dominated by financial assets largely comprising holdings of high-quality, short-term maturity, debt securities. The main liability of MMFs is the amount due to investors, who are entitled to receive the value of each share with its accumulated income (or loss) or net asset value (NAV). Total other comprehensive income (or loss) that would be reported in an IFRS Statement of Comprehensive Income should be included in line 9.

5.107 The *sectoral distribution of investments* as a percent of their total investments provides an indication of the concentration of MMFs investments. Potentially, this can provide a very rough approximation of asset quality—a higher proportion of government and central bank exposures suggests less risk and possibly greater liquidity relative to a higher proportion of exposure to nonfinancial corporations. The distribution of the financial investments held by MMFs is based on the economic sectors of the *2008 SNA*, and is the same (except for the non-inclusion of other domestic sectors) as the one used for the sectoral distribution of loans by DTs: central bank, DTs, OFCs, general government, NFCs, and non-residents.

5.108 The liquidity profile of MMFs' investments (beyond the "less than one year" investment rule) can be monitored through the *maturity distribution of investments*, as a percentage of total investments. MMFs' investments are split into three groups: (1) from 1 to 30 days; (2) from 31 to 90 days; and (3) more than 90 days. The *Guide* recommends compiling these data on a remaining maturity basis, although using original maturity can also be an alternative.

Insurance corporations

5.109 Summarized sectoral financial statements for ICs are presented in Table 5.3, including memorandum items needed for calculating some additional FSIs. The financial statement presented in Table 5.3 should be *separately* compiled for life insurance and non-life insurance (including reinsurance).

Income and expense

5.110 *Premiums earned* constitute, together with investment income, the main source of revenue for ICs. It constitutes all premiums received and receivable (after the deduction of any taxes or other duties levied on direct insurance premiums) to cover all types of insurance services, which are recognized as income during the reporting period. Premiums earned (line 1 in Table 5.3) should be reported net of reinsurance ceded (line 1.ii in Table 5.3) and including transfer of premium reserves from other insurers (line 1.iii in Table 5.3).

5.111 *Claims incurred* are financial obligations of the insurers with respect to the beneficiary, concerning the risks realized by events during the period, as defined by the policy. They include both gross claims paid during the period plus changes in reserves for claims outstanding and the transfer of premium reserves to other companies, typically reinsurers. They are presented on a net basis, subtracting the reinsurers' share of gross claims.

5.112 Another expense item for ICs is the *net change in technical reserves* needed to provide for future claims for unearned premiums, life insurance, outstanding claims, and other types of technical reserves.

5.113 *Other operating income* includes all income not due to premiums or investments, such as income from commissions or rents received on real estate holdings.

5.114 *Other operating expenses* include personnel costs, underwriting expenses, depreciation of nonfinancial assets, and any other operating costs not related to claims or investments.

5.115 *Investment income* corresponds to the income earned from holdings of financial (debt securities, equity, investment fund shares, etc.) and nonfinancial (property) assets, associated with both unit-linked and non-unit-linked products. It is presented on a net basis, subtracting the interest cost on liabilities, such as loans received, the costs of managing own property, and the income on unit-linked products that is passed on to policyholders. For non-unit-linked (non-participating) insurance, all risk and income of the investments are borne by the ICs; while the investment income of unit-linked (participating) insurance is passed-through to policy holders, who bear risk and income of the investments.

5.116 *Gains and losses on revaluation of financial assets* are those arising during the period under review. Similar to the investment income, it is necessary to distinguish gains and losses on revaluations of those financial assets allocated to non-unit-linked (non-participating) insurance (appropriated by the ICs) from those allocated to unit-linked insurance (participating—appropriated by policy holders).

5.117 The calculation of net income before and after taxes is similar to the one performed for DTs, although with a presentation adapted to the need of ICs. Relevant items here are the net income from insurance activity (premiums *less* claims *less* net change in technical reserves), net operating income, and the net income on own investments.

5.118 Total other comprehensive income (or loss) that would be reported in an IFRS Statement of Comprehensive Income should be included in line 13.

Balance sheet

5.119 Beyond the different categories of the sectoral balance sheet already described for DTs, some items need to be highlighted for the case of ICs.

5.120 *Nonfinancial assets* include both property for own use and also property held for investment purposes, generally real estate. Investments in real estate may be channeled through real estate investment funds, and not only through direct investment. In such cases, the claims on real estate investment funds are classified as equity and investment fund shares.

5.121 *Reinsurance claims* on the asset side record the reinsurance claims recoverable from reinsurers, and the claims on other insurers for reinsurance sold for which premiums have not yet been paid. On the liability side, *insurance, pensions, and standardized guarantee schemes* comprise reserves created to cover: (1) life insurance and annuities entitlements, which are assets of HHs; (2) non-life insurance payable for claims not yet settled, or not yet presented; (3) prepayment of non-life insurance premiums not yet used; (4) pension fund reserves, in cases where ICs offer pension schemes; and (5) any other technical reserve.

5.122 As in the case of DTs, *capital and reserves* represents the equity interest of ICs' owners and is calculated as the difference between total assets and total liabilities.

Pension funds

5.123 Summarized sectoral financial statements for PFs are presented in Table 5.4, including memorandum items needed for calculating some additional FSIs.

Income and expense

5.124 *Investment income* represents the main source of income for PFs. It is composed of interest income on financial instruments, other types of income on financial instruments (e.g., capital gains on equity), and income from investments in property (real estate). It also includes the net change in the fair value of investments of PFs. In the case of defined benefit schemes, PFs bear all gains and losses of their investments, since their liabilities to beneficiaries are determined by the defined benefit. In the case of defined contribution schemes, PFs pass through the gains and losses of the investment to the pension beneficiaries, who are entitled to future payments based on the return of their contributions.

5.125 *Investment expenses* are mainly constituted by expenses for managing investments and taxation of the return on investments.

5.126 *Net actuarial gains/losses* are part of the PFs' net income. They measure gains or losses arising from differences between the long-term estimates and the actual events, or changes in actuarial assumptions, during the reporting period. Gains or losses on actuarial liabilities can occur because long-term assumptions (e.g., mortality, salary increases, and retirement rates) were not met. Usually, actuarial assumptions are subject to legal constraints and regulatory/supervisory approval.

5.127 Total other comprehensive income (or loss) that would be reported in an IFRS Statement of Comprehensive Income should be included in line 10.

Balance sheet

5.128 As for the case of ICs, PFs hold *nonfinancial assets* for own use, but also for investment purposes, mainly real estate.

5.129 The main liability of PFs are financial claims that both existing and future pensioners hold against PFs to pay pensions. These are the *net equity of households in pension funds reserves.* These reserves show the extent of financial claims both existing and future pensioners hold against the PF to pay pensions. Beyond pensions, some schemes may have other related liabilities, such as for health benefits, which are included under entitlements to non-pension benefits. For pragmatic reasons, liabilities for non-pension entitlements may be included with those for pension entitlements. PF entitlements are measured as the present value of the amounts expected to be paid out based on actuarial assumptions. The reserves created for pension benefits can be distinguished between reserves for: (1) defined contribution plans, (2) defined benefit plans, and (3) hybrid schemes.[54]

5.130 The difference between total assets and total non-pension-related liabilities constitute the *net total assets* of a PF.

5.131 The difference between the net total assets of a PF and its pension fund reserves is recorded as the *net worth* of the PF, which can be positive (net assets larger than pension reserves) or negative (net assets below pension reserves).

Memorandum series

5.132 *Liquid assets* of PFs comprise: (1) currency; (2) deposits and other financial assets that are available either on demand or within one year or less; and (3) securities that are traded in liquid markets. The *Guide* recommends the compilation of liquid assets on a remaining maturity basis, although original maturity may be an alternative.

5.133 *Estimated pension payments in the next 12 months* are the sum of the actuarially expected payments to beneficiaries by PFs during the next year.

Nonfinancial Corporations

5.134 The data for constructing income statements and a sectoral balance sheet for NFCs are sourced from the SNA, more specifically from financial accounts. Efficiency and methodological problems will arise when trying to aggregate individual NFCs financial statements. As mentioned in the *2008 SNA*, "It may be difficult, if not impossible, to achieve micro databases and macroeconomic accounts that are fully compatible with each other in practice. Nevertheless, as a general objective, the concepts, definitions and classifications used in economic accounting should, so far as possible, be the same at both a micro and macro level to facilitate the interface between the two kinds of data."[55]

5.135 Therefore, sectoral income statements and balance sheets for NFCs are estimates obtained from national account data, rather than the result of the sum of individual financial statements, as is the case for DTs or for some subsectors of OFCs. Table 5.5 sets out a simplified income and expense statement and a sectoral balance sheet for NFCs, which is needed for the calculation of the additional FSIs for NFCs. The balance sheet is presented with assets, liabilities, and capital and reserves (which includes the SNA concept of net worth), as the difference between assets and liabilities.

Income and expense

5.136 *Operating income* of an NFC is the revenue from the *sales of goods and services* (excluding taxes on goods and services) less the *cost of those sales.* The cost of sales include: (1) personnel (staff) costs; (2) costs of materials purchased for the production process; (3) depreciation of installations and equipment; (4) fixed and variable production overheads; (5) rentals paid on land, buildings, and equipment; (6) royalties paid; (7) distribution costs, including transportation and advertising expenses; and (8) any other costs associated with production and sales, including professional fees, insurance, research and development costs, taxes other than income taxes, and so on.

5.137 In addition to operating income, other sources of income include *net interest income* (interest income *less* interest expense) and *other income (net). Net interest income* is the difference between interest income and interest expenses. *Interest*

[54] PFs may reinsure part of their PF reserve liabilities with ICs, in which case they would show a claim on ICs on the asset side of their balance sheet.

[55] 2008 *SNA*, paragraph 1.62.

income is the income received by NFCs as remuneration on their holdings of deposits and debt securities, and on loans made by NFCs to their customers or other institutional units. *Interest expenses* comprise the cost incurred by an entity for borrowed funds and represents interest accrued and payable on any type of borrowings during the period under consideration.

5.138 *Other income* (net) encompasses rents, rentals, and royalties receivable (payable); income from holdings of shares and other equity; gains or losses arising during the period on financial instruments and on the sales of fixed assets; and any amounts receivable (payable) by nonfinancial corporations arising from compensation for damage or injury.

Balance sheet

5.139 The definitions of balance sheet series presented in Table 5.5 are the same as for the corresponding series in Table 5.1.

5.140 *Total assets* comprise financial and nonfinancial assets (paragraphs 5.33 and 5.35).

5.141 *Nonfinancial assets* for NFCs distinguish between (1) real estate property, (2) equipment, (3) intellectual property products, (4) inventories, (5) valuables, and (6) other nonfinancial assets.

5.142 The sectoral balance sheet for NFCs separately identifies *trade credit*. Trade credit and advances include: (1) trade credit extended directly to purchasers of goods and services; and (2) advances for work that is in progress or is to be undertaken, such as progress payments made during construction or for prepayments of goods and services. Trade credit does not include loans, debt securities, or other liabilities that are issued to finance trade credit.

5.143 Regarding coverage, *equity and investment fund shares* include such claims on associates, unconsolidated subsidiaries, any reverse equity investments, and, for data compiled on a domestic basis, any share capital provided to foreign branches.

5.144 For non-financial corporations, *capital and reserves* are otherwise known as equity. They represent the claims of the shareholders on the residual value of a corporation after the claims of all creditors have been met. In the sectoral balance sheet, capital and reserves are presented at book value (i.e., as the difference between total assets and liabilities). In the SNA, equity is treated as a liability of the issuing institutional unit, with the difference between the corporation's book value (capital and reserves) and its market value recorded as the corporation's *net worth*.

Memorandum series

5.145 *Interest income receivable from other nonfinancial corporations* is that amount of interest income (item 35 in Table 5.5) that is receivable from other nonfinancial corporations that are also in the reporting population.

5.146 *Earnings before interest and tax* (EBIT) is defined as net operating income (item 3 in Table 5.5) plus interest income (item 4 in Table 5.5) plus other income (net) (item 6 in Table 5.5) *less* interest income receivable from other NFCs (item 35 in Table 5.5). Interest expenses are excluded by definition. Interest receivable from other NFCs is deducted from EBIT data to ensure that sector earnings are not inflated by such intrasector income.

5.147 *Total debt to nonresidents* is the outstanding amount of those actual current, and not contingent, liabilities that require payment(s) of principal or interest by the debtor at some point(s) in the future and that are owed to nonresidents by resident NFCs. The data for compiling the external debt for NFCs are sourced from data compiled to be consistent with the *External Debt Statistics Guide*.[56]

5.148 *Total debt in foreign currency* is the part of NFCs' total debt with principal and interest payments denominated in a currency other than the domestic

[56]The *External Debt Statistics: Guide for Compilers and Users* provides guidance on the concepts, definitions, and classification of external debt data, as well as the source and techniques for compiling these data and the analytical uses.

currency, regardless as to whether the creditor is resident or a nonresident.

5.149 *Debt-service payments* are interest and principal payments made on outstanding debt liabilities within the specified period of the statement. Principal payments always reduce the amount of debt outstanding. Interest payments are those periodic payments that meet interest costs arising from the use of another entity's funds.[57]

Households

5.150 Households (HH)s' micro data are typically derived from sample surveys that may be subject to significant response and reporting errors. It may be particularly difficult to obtain reliable and meaningful data about the activities of small unincorporated enterprises owned by HHs. Aggregates based on HH surveys have to be adjusted for certain typical biases, such as the underreporting of certain types of expenditure and also to make them consistent with macro data. Therefore, the data to derive a simple sectoral financial statement for HHs are sourced from the SNA's financial accounts.

5.151 Table 5.6 sets out a simplified sectoral financial statement for HHs, needed for the calculation of the additional FSIs for HHs.

Income and expense

5.152 The main source of *income* for HHs is *wages and salaries* (gross of any income tax) from employment. These are payable in cash or kind and are a component of compensation for employment. Other major sources of income include *property income receivable* (interest, dividends, and rent) and *current transfers,* including those from general government. *Other* income sources include operating income from production activity (gross of consumption of fixed capital).[58]

5.153 *Gross disposable income* includes these sources of income *less* current taxes on income and wealth, contributions for social insurance (e.g., for old-age insurance paid by HHs to general government), and other current transfers (e.g., payments of fines, penalties, and subscriptions to NPISHs).

Balance sheet

5.154 HHs' *nonfinancial assets* are mainly composed by their ownership of real estate, consumer durable goods, and other nonfinancial assets. HHs' *financial assets* and *liabilities* correspond broadly to the series defined in Table 5.1. Within HHs, unincorporated enterprises may own other (non-real estate) fixed assets, but these tend to be small relative to housing.

5.155 *Insurance, pensions, and standardized guarantee schemes* represent a special case of financial assets held by HHs. They mostly correspond to the contributions from HHs to life insurance, annuity, and pension entitlements, and are claims of HHs on ICs and PFs.

5.156 *Total household debt* comprises all the loans granted to the HH sector; including mortgages loans, consumer loans, credit cards debts, and other debts. Countries that do not have HHs debt data sourced from SNA may consider using mirror data from the financial corporations sector and indicate so in the metadata.

5.157 *Net worth* is defined as the value of the assets owned by HHs *less* their liabilities.

Memorandum series

5.158 *Household debt-service and principal payments* are the debt service payments made by HHs

[57] For long-term debt instruments, interest costs paid periodically are defined as those to be paid by the debtor to the creditor annually or more frequently; for short-term instruments, that is, with an original maturity of one year or less, interest costs paid periodically are defined as those to be paid by the debtor to the creditor before the redemption date of the instrument.

[58] Production within the HH sector takes place within enterprises that are directly owned and controlled by members of HHs, either individually or in partnership with others. When members of HHs work as employees for corporations, quasi corporations, or the government, the production to which they contribute takes place outside the HH sector.

on outstanding debt liabilities within a specified period of time. Such payments always reduce the amount of debt outstanding. Interest payments are those periodic payments that meet interest costs arising from the use of another entity's funds, and principal payments are all other payments that reduce the amount of principal outstanding. Countries that do not have data on debt-service and principal payments from national accounts sources, may use data sourced from financial corporations and indicate so in the metadata. *Debt collateralized by real estate* covers all debt for which real estate is used as a form of collateral. This includes borrowing for the purchase, refinancing, or construction of buildings and structures (including alterations and additions to such), and for land.

6 Aggregation and Consolidation of Data

I. Introduction

6.1 The analytical interpretation of financial soundness indicators (FSIs) is affected by (1) the consolidation basis used for their compilation; and (2) the group-consolidation adjustments in the source data. The first aspect determines the reporting population[1] for FSIs compilation, whereas the second affects the calculation of the FSI underlying series. The two aspects are interrelated: the consolidation basis defines the perimeter of institutions for which the group-consolidation adjustments are required.

6.2 This chapter presents definitions of corporation ownership and control, approaches for compiling FSIs, as well as recommended consolidation basis for: (1) deposit takers (DTs); (2) OFCs; (3) nonfinancial corporations (NFCs); and (4) households.

II. Aggregation and Consolidation

6.3 *Aggregation* refers to the summations of position or flow data. For sector-level data, aggregation is the sum of the positions and flows of all individual reporting groups/entities within the sector.[2] Thus, the sector and subsector totals equal the sum of their component elements and the data on claims and liabilities among the groups/entities of the sector are preserved; as well as total flows (e.g., all interest payments) between them. The sectoral financial statements described in Chapter 5 are aggregates, where positions and flows are the sums of flows and positions of all the reporting units in the sector.

[1] The term "reporting population" refers to all entities included in the sector information. The reporting population can vary depending on the institutional coverage of the sector.

[2] In some instances, data on an economic sector can be compiled using information reported by a sample of reporters, together with estimates for those units in the sector that do not report. Statistically, the more representative the sample is of the total population, the greater the likelihood of estimating reliable information for the nonreporters.

6.4 *Group-consolidation*, in contrast, refers to the elimination of positions and flows between units that are part of the same reporting group. If related institutional units are grouped together to form one individual reporting group (e.g., foreign branches of domestic banks are grouped with their parent bank), then all positions and flows within that reporting group are eliminated from the reported information. For FSIs, data are consolidated by reporting group at various levels. For instance, the reporting group for DTs includes their branches, but some levels may include or exclude domestic and foreign controlled banks, DT and non-DT affiliates, or non-resident branches and affiliates. Inclusion or exclusion of these entities define the consolidation basis explained in Section IV.

6.5 The concepts of aggregation and consolidation should be distinguished from the concepts of gross and net recording. *Gross recording* refers to the presentation of assets and liabilities at their full value, that is, where claims on a particular institutional unit or group of units are not netted against the liabilities to that unit or group.[3] *Net recording* refers to the offsetting of these assets and liabilities, and is not recommended by the *Guide*; however, compilation on a net basis may be unavoidable due to lack of source data.

6.6 FSI compilation involves aggregation of group-consolidated data. Reporting entities provide group-consolidated data to the compiling agency, which then aggregates these data to produce sector totals for the financial statements (income and expense statement and balance sheet) and the memorandum series, as described in Chapter 5.

[3] This is the approach followed by the *2008 System of National Accounts* (*2008 SNA*) and other statistical manuals, such as the *Monetary and Financial Statistics Manual and Compilation Guide* (*MFSMCG*).

6.7 Before discussing consolidation of data in more detail, some definitions associated with reporting groups are required, as these terms are used throughout the rest of this chapter.

III. Ownership and Control of Corporations

6.8 It is common for corporations to own shares in other corporations, establishing ownership relationships among them. The ownership of a corporation is distributed among the institutional units that own its shares in proportion to the shareholdings.

6.9 *Control* of a corporation exists when an entity is exposed, or has rights, to variable returns from its involvement with the corporation and has the ability to affect those returns through its power over the corporation.[4] This IFRS definition encompasses but is somewhat broader than existing monetary and national statistics definitions of control: the ability to determine its general corporate policy and operations by choosing (or removing) appropriate directors.[5] The *Guide* defers to IFRS[6] as in practice compilers will not determine control, but will rely on consolidated financial reporting by parent corporations prepared in accordance with IFRS.[7] Control is unambiguously established through ownership of more than half of the voting shares; or otherwise controlling more than half of the shareholders voting power (including indirect ownership, that is, through ownership of a second corporation that in turn has a majority of the voting shares). Exceptionally, control could also be established with ownership of less than half the voting shares, such as through special legislation, decree, regulation, privileged voting rights ("golden share"), or loan arrangements that effectively establish control.[8] However, it is not possible to stipulate a minimum shareholding below 50 percent that will guarantee control in all cases. Some of the common forms of relationships between entities are listed further.

6.10 *Branches* are operating entities that do not have a separate legal status from their parent corporations and are thus integral part of them. They are set up in a location where there is a legal representative of the parent and must meet certain requirements before they can operate. A branch of a nonresident DT is identified for statistical purposes as a separate institutional unit in the economy where it operates. Branches of nonresident DTs are always under foreign control.

6.11 *Subsidiaries* are entities controlled by another entity.[9] A corporation is said to be a subsidiary of its parent when the parent is exposed, or has rights, to variable returns from its involvement with the corporation and has the ability to affect those returns through its power over the corporation. As the relationship of a parent corporation to a subsidiary is defined in terms of control rather than ownership, the relationship must be transitive; in other words, if a corporation has a majority shareholding in a subsidiary, and this subsidiary has itself a majority shareholding in a third corporation, the former corporation must be able to control the latter through its subsidiary, even if it does not have a majority shareholding.[10]

6.12 *Associates* are corporations over which the investor has a significant degree of influence, being the power to participate in the financial and operating policy decision of the investee; but not control or joint control as is the case of subsidiaries. Significant influence is usually assumed to arise when the investor controls between 10 and 50 percent of the shareholders' voting power. In this way, the investor has some influence over the corporate policy and management of the associate. By definition, a corporation is able to exert less influence over an associate than over a subsidiary.

6.13 *Equity investment* or minority interest refers to the holding of shares in a corporation with the purpose of gains from dividends or stock appreciation, with the threshold being established at less than 10 percent. Equity holders receive voting rights, but not enough to influence the operations of the company where they have invested. Therefore, equity investment is considered solely as a financial investment. If

[4] IFRS 10, paragraph 6.
[5] See *MFSMCG*, paragraph 3.21.
[6] Or national standards if these have different definitions of control.
[7] Similarly, when supervisory requirements exclude some entities such as insurance companies from the consolidated reporting of deposit-takers, compilers will rely on the supervisory series for the DT sector, thus ensuring consistent compilation of FSIs for the jurisdictions' DT sector.
[8] For exceptional cases where control of a corporation can be achieved with less than half of the voting power, see *2008 SNA*, paragraphs 4.69–4.71.
[9] IFRS 10, Appendix A.
[10] See *2008 SNA*, paragraph 4.74.

the ownership stake reaches the threshold for classification as an associate (10 percent of voting power) but is expected to be of a temporary nature, the investment continues to be classified as non-associate equity investment. However, for FSI compilation purposes, if the equity investment has reached the level to be classified as an associate for two successive periods, the implication is that the investment is not temporary.

6.14 *Joint arrangements* are entities where two or more parties have joint control. Joint arrangements are classified either as joint operations or joint ventures. In a joint operation, the parties, called joint operators, have joint control and have rights to the assets, and obligations for the liabilities, relating to the arrangement. Joint operators recognize in their financial statements their share of the assets, liabilities, revenues, and expenses attributable to the joint operation. In a joint venture, the parties, called joint venturers, have joint control and have rights to the net assets of the arrangement. Joint venturers recognize their interest in the joint venture as an investment, and account for it using the equity method.[11]

6.15 *Holding companies* are units that hold the assets of subsidiary corporations but do not undertake any management activities. Their principal activity is to own and direct the group and they are not directly engaged in deposit taking. The *Guide* distinguishes between unregulated holding companies, and holding companies subject to prudential regulation, for example the EU Capital Requirement Regulation. In the former case, in line with the *Guide*'s focus on the health and soundness of DTs as a sector, unregulated holding companies should in principle be excluded from the DT sector, even if the business of the subsidiaries they own is primarily deposit taking. Such holding corporations should be part of the OFC's sector. In the latter case, such holding companies are the regulated parents and provide the consolidated supervisory data that is the foundation for the FSIs.

Domestic and Foreign Control

6.16 When discussing reporting populations in more detail, definitions of domestic and foreign control are required.

6.17 Units can be controlled by domestic or foreign parent corporations, which may be financial institutions, or regulated or unregulated holding companies. The *Guide* uses the term "domestically incorporated" to refer to both domestic and foreign controlled entities, reflecting the emphasis on the jurisdiction of incorporation rather than the residency of shareholders.

6.18 Deposit-taking entities are defined in the *Guide* as *foreign controlled* if they are subsidiaries or branches of a foreign parent DT, that is, a DT controlled by nonresident institutional units, either directly or indirectly as described in paragraph 6.11. Deposit-taking entities and their subsidiaries and branches are defined as *domestically controlled* if they are directly or indirectly controlled by resident shareholders.

6.19 In the rare instances that the parent is located in both the domestic and foreign economies, such subsidiaries are classified as domestically controlled. A conceptual difficulty related to branches is that they are not actually "controlled" by a parent company, since they are an organizational part of the parent company and not an independent legal unit. For the sake of simplification, the *Guide* assumes that a branch is "owned" or "controlled" by its "parent company," although they both may belong to the same legal unit. When the branch is located and operating in a different economy than its parent, it is a foreign controlled branch.

6.20 Foreign controlled DTs, in addition to supervision by the host supervisory authority, are typically subject to supervision by their parent supervisory authority, as recommended in the BCBS minimum standards for the supervision of international banking groups and their cross-border establishments.[12] This criterion should be taken into account if there is uncertainty as to whether a DT is domestically or foreign controlled. If a resident DT is controlled by a non-resident bank holding company that is subject to banking supervision in that foreign economy, then it should be classified as foreign controlled.

IV. Consolidation Basis

6.21 Depending on different analytical needs and source data availability, various consolidation basis

[11] For additional detail, refer to IFRS 11.

[12] See BCBS, *Minimum standards for the supervision of international banking groups and their cross-border establishments*, Basel, 1992.

may be used for compiling FSIs. The consolidation basis determines the reporting population for FSI compilation. Which units are included under a specific consolidation basis depends, among other factors, on ownership and control, including whether a unit is a branch, subsidiary or associate, and whether it is domestic or foreign controlled.

6.22 Accounting, financial supervisory standards, and macroeconomic statistical frameworks operate with related, but different, understandings of consolidation and consolidation basis.

6.23 Accounting standards take a conglomerate view of a group and require that a group encompasses a parent company and all its subsidiaries, regardless of whether these entities belong to the financial sector or the nonfinancial sectors.

6.24 Financial supervisory standards take a prudential view of a group financial position, which is often narrower than the accounting approach. In banking regulation, for instance, the supervisory scope prescribed by the BCBS[13] for internationally active banks includes "*on a fully consolidated basis, any holding company that is the parent entity within a banking group to ensure that it captures the risk of the whole banking group.*" Under this functional approach, an individual reporting bank of a given nationality must consolidate all its positions independently of the residency of the institutional units that are part of the banking group.

6.25 The macroeconomic statistical frameworks take an economic activity view at the level of the institutional unit and not at the corporate group level, and generally do not consolidate beyond the institutional unit level.

6.26 This *Guide* uses different consolidation standards depending on the institutional sector to which the particular FSI refers to. Broadly speaking, for DTs and OFCs FSIs, the standard is closer to the financial supervisory approach. For nonfinancial corporations and households, the standard follows the macroeconomic statistics approach. The following sections provide detailed explanations on the recommended consolidation basis by institutional sector, starting with DTs.

[13]See BCBS, *International convergence of capital measurement and capital standards*, June 2006, paragraph 21.

Consolidation Basis for Deposit Takers

6.27 This *Guide* recommends that DT's data be compiled on a consolidated group basis. *Consolidated group reporting* by a resident DT includes coverage of its own activities and those of its branches and financial subsidiaries (except insurance corporations),[14] with any transactions and positions among these entities eliminated on consolidation. Consolidation is based on the concept of control by a parent of other operating units. Such an approach is an essential element of banking supervision[15] and is adopted to preserve the integrity of capital in DTs by eliminating double counting of capital (double gearing), and to avoid the double counting of income and assets arising from the intra-group activity of DTs. It is for this reason that the *Guide* recommends that DTs' data be compiled on a consolidated group basis. For FSIs, a consolidation basis for DTs has two fundamental dimensions: cross-sector and cross-border consolidation.

6.28 *Cross-sector consolidation* involves a parent DT and its financial subsidiaries (DT and non-DT). If such non-DT subsidiaries (e.g., a leasing company or a money market fund) are included in the group data of its parent DT, the data are referred to as *cross-sector data*. The cross-sector dimension highlights financial strengths and weaknesses of groups considering their full range of financial activities: weak non-DTs financial subsidiaries might generate stress for the DT parents.

6.29 *Cross-border consolidation* involves a parent DT and its nonresident financial subsidiaries and branches, in addition to the resident ones. A branch or subsidiary may be resident in another economy than its parent. When such units are included in the group reporting, the data are referred to as *cross-border data*.

[14]The exclusion of insurance companies follows supervisory practices whereby banks' insurance subsidiaries are not consolidated for supervisory reporting. The reason is that banking and insurance are two very different activities with different prudential standards. This means that key FSIs such as those based on regulatory standards calculated using data consolidating banking and insurance would be meaningless from the supervisory and macroprudential perspective because of the very different capital and liquidity requirements for the two types of business. For this reason, the *Guide* follows supervisory practice in recommending that the banking and insurance elements of a group be reported as separate units.

[15]See BCBS, *Core Principles for Effective Banking Supervision*, Principle 12, (2012).

6.30 When compiling FSIs for DTs the *Guide* recommends cross-border, cross-sector, domestically incorporated consolidation (CBCSDI). This is consistent with BCBS guidance requiring application of the same supervisory standards to domestic and foreign-owned banks, and for effective consolidated supervision of all domestic and foreign operations of a banking group. In addition, the *Guide* recognizes a second option, domestic location (DL),[16] for countries with DTs that have (i) very few or no foreign branches or subsidiaries, and (ii) very few or no cross-sector subsidiaries. Compiling on both a CBCSDI and DL basis would be consistent with BCBS guidance and the common supervisory practice of requiring reporting on both a consolidated basis (CBCSDI) and bank solo basis (DL). Comparison of the FSIs from these two consolidations can help to identify the potential resilience of the parent banks (DL) and potential vulnerabilities arising in activities outside of the parent banks (CBCSDI). However, for IMF reporting purposes, all relevant FSIs should be compiled using the recommended CBCSDI consolidation basis. Reporting different FSIs using different consolidation basis may impact the analysis of the DT sector's soundness and should be avoided. In the instances when a different consolidation basis must be used, this should be clearly indicated in the metadata.

6.31 A third alternative is cross-border, cross-sector, domestically controlled (CBCSDC). This approach is **only appropriate for financial sectors with no material foreign-controlled DTs.** The exclusion of foreign controlled domestically incorporated DTs means that potentially significant risks are not captured in the FSIs if these are a material part of the financial system.

6.32 CBCSDI and DL are the focus of the *Guide*, but the option of other consolidation basis remains available for compilers, not least because due to legal constraints some countries have no alternative but to report on an "other" consolidation basis. Nevertheless, the *Guide* strongly emphasizes the need to promote cross-country convergence, and any deviation from the recommended CBCSDI consolidation basis should be in exceptional cases only.

[16]This approach was called "domestically consolidated data" in the *2006 Guide*.

Cross-border, Cross-sector, domestically incorporated consolidation basis (CBCSDI)

6.33 For financial stability analysis, it is often relevant to look at domestically incorporated DTs and their resident and non-resident branches and subsidiaries in the financial sector as one economic group that reports consolidated data. This approach focuses on domestically incorporated entities and provides an indication of their financial soundness regardless of where their business is undertaken and the kind of financial activities of the subsidiaries. Banking supervisory data frequently rely on this form of consolidation, as it is consistent with BCBS requirements for effective consolidated supervision.[17]

CBCSDI comprises:

- Domestically incorporated, domestically controlled DTs, including domestic branches and DT subsidiaries (D1), domestic financial non-DTs subsidiaries, excluding insurance companies (D2); and their foreign branches (F1), foreign DT subsidiaries (F2), and foreign financial non-DT subsidiaries, excluding insurance companies (F3).
- Domestically incorporated foreign controlled DTs, including domestic branches and DT subsidiaries (D3), domestic financial non-DTs subsidiaries, excluding insurance companies (D4); and their foreign branches (F4), foreign DT subsidiaries (F5), and foreign financial non-DT subsidiaries, excluding insurance companies (F6).

Figure 6.1 presents a schematic presentation of the CBCSDI consolidation basis.

Cross-border, cross-sector, domestically controlled consolidation basis (CBCSDC)

6.34 A relevant alternative consolidation basis for DTs, the *CBCSDC*, is more narrowly focused on the financial soundness of domestically controlled DTs and their ownership related entities, whether domestic or abroad. For financial stability analysis, CBCSDC may be particularly relevant

[17]Under the BCBS framework, insurance activities are not included within "financial activities," and "financial entities" do not include insurance entities; as a result, insurance corporations are treated separately from deposit takers, sometimes even if they are subsidiaries of a deposit taker. See BCBS, *International Convergence of Capital Measurement and Capital Standards—A Revised Framework*, Basel, 2004, footnote 5, paragraph 24.

Figure 6.1 Cross-Border, Cross-Sector, Domestically Incorporated Consolidation Basis (CBCSDI)[1]

	Domestic Economy		Foreign Economies		
Domestically controlled	DTs + branches + DT subsidiaries D1	Non-DTs Subsidiaries D2	Branches F1	DT subsidiaries F2	Non-DT subsidiaries F3
Foreign controlled	DTs + branches + DT subsidiaries D3	Non-DTs Subsidiaries D4	Branches F4	DT subsidiaries F5	Non-DT subsidiaries F6

Source: IMF staff.

Note: DT = deposit taker.

[1] Domestically incorporated = domestically controlled + foreign controlled.

Figure 6.2 Cross-Border, Cross-Sector, Domestically Controlled Consolidation Basis (CBCSDC)

	Domestic Economy		Foreign Economies		
Domestically controlled	DTs + branches + DT subsidiaries D1	Non-DTs Subsidiaries D2	Branches F1	DT subsidiaries F2	Non-DT subsidiaries F3
Foreign controlled	*DTs* *+ branches* *+ DT* *subsidiaries* *Branches of* *foreign DTs* *D3*	*Non-DTs* *Subsidiaries* *D4*	*Branches* *F4*	*DT subsidiaries* *F5*	*Non-DT* *subsidiaries* *F6*

Source: IMF staff.

Note: DT = deposit taker.

Note: Entities in italics are excluded from this consolidation basis.

when domestic controlled DTs have large branches and subsidiaries abroad, while there are few and irrelevant foreign controlled DTs in the domestic economy. In these cases, the risks associated with failure of foreign entities of the domestically controlled DTs could pose a systemic risk to the domestic financial sector, where the domestic authorities ultimately might need to provide financial support to the group. If foreign controlled DTs are few and small, their potential impact on financial stability would be minimal.

CBCSDC comprises:

- Domestically controlled DTs, including domestic branches and DT subsidiaries (D1), domestic financial Non-DTs subsidiaries, excluding insurance companies (D2); and their foreign branches (F1), foreign DT subsidiaries, (F2), and foreign financial Non-DT subsidiaries, excluding insurance companies (F3).

Figure 6.2 shows a schematic presentation of the CBCSDC consolidation basis.

Domestic location consolidation basis (DL)

6.35 Another relevant consolidation basis for DTs, *DL* consolidation basis, has no cross-sector or no cross-border dimensions. DL includes both domestically incorporated DTs and branches of foreign banks.[18] Specially, it includes both domestic- and foreign-controlled, domestically incorporated DTs and domestic foreign bank branches.

DL comprises:

- Domestically controlled DTs, including domestic branches and DT subsidiaries (D1).
- Foreign controlled DTs, including domestic branches, DT subsidiaries, and branches of foreign DTs (D3).

Figure 6.3 shows a schematic presentation of the DL.

6.36 DL data generally aligns with the supervisory reporting framework in jurisdictions that have not introduced consolidated reporting. It excludes cross-border and cross-sector entities and is relevant for financial stability analysis when the non-DT domestic subsidiaries and foreign operations of domestic DTs are few and small. DL data only covers cross-border and cross-sectoral risks in an indirect and limited way: through the net profit/loss from the unconsolidated operations, while the direct risks and benefits to DTs are not identified. If DL data involves intra-group consolidation adjustments between parent DTs and their domestic DT subsidiaries, these should be noted in the metadata.

Other consolidation basis

6.37 Sometimes, countries may choose a consolidation basis that is not recommended in the *Guide*. For instance, a country may choose a cross-border, domestically incorporated (CBDI) consolidation basis for compiling FSIs for its DT sector. CBDI covers domestically incorporated DTs (both domestic and foreign controlled), and their branches and deposit- taking subsidiaries (both residents and non-residents). In such cases, the *Guide* recommends that for cross-country comparability purposes, an explanation on the differences from the recommended consolidation basis be included in the associated metadata.

6.38 Adopting different consolidation basis has important implications as they would lead to different reporting populations (institutional coverage), and thus to different sectoral data for calculating FSIs. Therefore, FSIs compiled on different consolidation basis may complicate cross-country comparisons of data. In countries where the applied consolidation basis differs substantially from the recommended basis, the difference should be clearly explained in the metadata and the data should be characterized as using other consolidation basis.

[18] The data source will be supervisory series, as supervisory authorities generally require branches of foreign banks to submit regular prudential returns.

Figure 6.3 Domestic Location Consolidation Basis (DL)

	Domestic Economy		Foreign Economies		
Domestically controlled	DTs + branches + DT subsidiaries D1	*Non-DTs Subsidiaries D2*	*Branches F1*	*DT subsidiaries F2*	*Non-DT subsidiaries F3*
Foreign controlled	DTs + branches + DT subsidiaries Branches of foreign DTs D3	*Non-DTs Subsidiaries D4*	*Branches F4*	*DT subsidiaries F5*	*Non-DT subsidiaries F6*

Source: IMF staff.

Note: DT = deposit taker.

Note: Entities in italics are excluded from this consolidation basis.

Other Financial Corporations

6.39 The FSIs that measure the relative importance of the OFC sector and some of its subsectors (money market funds [MMFs], insurance corporations, pension funds) are calculated on a residency and institutional basis. Therefore, flows and positions within a group are not consolidated, and data can be presented on an *aggregated resident-based approach.* However, for countries with OFC with significant cross-border activities, cross-border consolidation may be relevant. In this case, it is recommended to use CBDI or, in jurisdictions where foreign-owned corporations are few and small, cross-border, domestically controlled consolidation basis (CBDC).[19]

6.40 Under an *aggregated resident-based approach,* the headquarters office consolidates its transactions and positions only with resident branch offices (i.e., without subsidiaries, associates, and nonresident branches). Under this approach, data are reported at the level of institutional-unit resident in the economy and aggregated by the compiling agency to provide totals of the sectors. This is the approach adopted in the *2008 SNA,* the sectoral balance sheets in monetary statistics, and related national accounts methodologies.

6.41 MMFs generally do not have controlling interests in other MMFs; therefore, the *Guide* recommends compiling FSIs for MMFs on an aggregated resident-based approach. Similarly, it is not expected that pension funds have other pension funds as subsidiaries, so FSIs for them should also be compiled on an aggregated resident-based approach.

6.42 For the insurance company's subsector, the *Guide* recommends using a CBDI consolidation basis. Data under a CBDI consolidation basis for the insurance companies consist of the consolidated data for the following units: domestically incorporated, domestic and foreign controlled insurance companies, and their resident and nonresident subsidiaries in the insurance sector.

Nonfinancial Corporations and Households

6.43 Both for the NFC and the household sectors the FSIs are compiled using the *aggregated resident-based approach.* The activities and positions of these resident entities in the domestic economy are captured by macroeconomic statistics, which are residency based, and data for these sectors are typically readily available from national accounts statistics.

6.44 The residency-based approach differs from DL consolidation. For instance, under the residency-based approach, all transactions and positions between headquarters and resident subsidiaries are not consolidated because these are separate institutional units, while under DL these subsidiaries are part of the reporting group of the parent deposit taker.

[19] No cross-sector consolidation is recommended in this case.

ANNEX

6.1 Intra-Group Consolidation

6.45 CBCSDI, CBCSDC, DL, and CBDI involve intra group consolidation, which allows for presenting statistics for a set of units as if they formed a single encompassing unit. Intra group consolidation needs to be done at a very detailed level to ensure consistency between the consolidated items and units. FSI compilers would usually not conduct the intra group consolidation, but rather rely on the consolidation being carried out by the reporting group. Nevertheless, it is useful for compilers to understand how consolidation adjustments are carried out in broad terms, in particular for the DT sector.

A. Consolidation of the Income Statement

6.46 When producing group consolidated income statements for use in calculating FSIs, the following items are offset between units in the reporting group in order to eliminate intra group transactions and gains and losses from intra group data:

- Provisions for accrued interest on nonperforming loans and loan (and other claims) loss provisions.
- Fees and commissions receivable and payable.
- Gains and losses on financial instruments issued by other entities of the group, including ownership of equity.
- The investing DT's prorated share of the earnings of its subsidiaries in the reporting group.
- Any other intra group income receivable and expense payable.
- Gross interest income and expense should, in principle, be consolidated. However, because net interest income (i.e., gross interest income less interest expense) is used for calculating the corresponding FSIs, there should be in principle no need for consolidation since the net calculation should produce a zero result, assuming that all units within the group consistently record interest income and expense.

B. Consolidation of the Balance Sheet

6.47 For the purpose of producing a group consolidated balance sheet, the following adjustments are required to eliminate intra group positions, as listed below:

- Claims on and liabilities to units of the deposit-taking group:
- Currency and deposits
- Loans
- Debt securities
- Financial derivatives
- Other claims and liabilities
- Specific provisions on loans to other units of the deposit-taking group.
- Equity investment in other units of the deposit taking group.

C. Consolidation of Memorandum Series

6.48 Regarding the memorandum series required for deposit takers, the following adjustments are required for intra group consolidation, offsetting claims on and liabilities to entities of the same group:

- Regulatory capital, comprising Common Equity Tier 1 (CET1), Additional Tier 1 (AT1), and Tier 2 capital; should be adjusted for the participation of the parent DT in the different tiers of the regulatory capital of its subsidiaries. Although financial non-deposit-taking subsidiaries do not compute regulatory capital, for consolidation purposes their capital should be harmonized to the banking supervisory concepts, and equivalents to CET1, AT1, and Tier 2 should be used to present regulatory capital of the group on a net basis.

- Financial instrument positions between units of the same group should be risk weighted and deducted from total risk-weighted assets of the group.
- Nonperforming loans.
- Foreign currency denominated loans and liabilities.
- Other memo items, except liquid assets and short-term liabilities, because these represent the potential for liquidity drain in the short term, even if it is between entities in the same reporting group.

D. Specific Issues Arising from Group Consolidation

6.49 While aggregation of data is a simple concept, consolidation is more complex, particularly when the parent owns less than 100 percent of its subsidiary; or when consolidating the activities of the parent with an associate; or in the special case of a deposit-taking parent with insurance subsidiaries.

6.50 Accounting and bank supervisory guidelines generally follow the full consolidation approach for subsidiaries, and a prorated approach for the profit and capital of associates. There is, however, generally a divergence between accounting and supervisory approaches to consolidation of financial conglomerates including both bank and insurance entities. Full consolidation is required by IFRS 10, which exempts only investment entities, commonly called non-operating holdings companies, from preparing consolidated financial statements. Supervisory authorities, however, often require financial reporting that does not consolidate banking and insurance units. As noted earlier, this is because the business are so different that prudential requirements cannot meaningfully be applied to an entity consolidating both insurance and banking. Compilers will rely on supervisory data series, and thus will follow national supervisory guidance which generally will not consolidate the insurance subsidiaries of bank parents.

6.51 When consolidating the activities of less than 100 percent owned subsidiaries, the *Guide* defers to IFRS 10 Consolidated Financial Statements, except when supervisory treatment differs. In accordance with IFRS 10, full consolidation should be undertaken of any entities controlled by the parent. Non-controlling interests should not be separately identified in earnings or in the balance sheet as a liability item, but rather reported in the consolidated statement of financial position (balance sheet) within equity, separately from the equity of the owners of the parent. For DTs, such full consolidation is consistent with the Basel Capital Accord for the measurement of capital and reflects the focus on the total capital and reserves of the DT as a consolidated group.

6.52 IFRS require use of the equity method to account for associates. Under the equity method, the investment in an associate is initially recognized at cost and adjusted thereafter for the post-acquisition change in the investor's share of the investee's net assets. The investor's profit or loss includes its share of the investee's profit or loss and the investor's other comprehensive income includes its share of the investee's other comprehensive income. Thus, if the owner of the investment has a 50 percent stake in a unit, half of the profit should appear as income from the equity investment. There should be similar treatment for any equity investment by an associate in a parent (reverse equity investment).

ANNEX

6.2 Numerical Example on Intra-Group Consolidation

6.53 This annex provides a numerical example to illustrate the guidance given in Annex 6.1 on intra-group consolidation. The example is based on the CBCSDI consolidation basis. The tables in the example present *two steps*: (1) compilation of the group consolidated data and (2) calculation of *sectoral* data by aggregation. (The *sectoral* data are the source to compile FSIs.)

6.54 For this example, we assume that the population for which FSIs are compiled consists of:

- Deposit taker 1 (DT1): foreign controlled (having no subsidiaries)
- Deposit taker 2 (DT2): domestically controlled
- Deposit taker 3 (DT3): a domestic subsidiary of DT2
- Deposit taker 4 (DT4): a foreign subsidiary of DT2
- Non-deposit taker 1 (NonDT1): a domestic subsidiary of DT2
- Non-deposit taker 2 (NonDT2): a foreign subsidiary of DT2

6.55 CBCSDI includes all these institutions. In contrast, other consolidation basis would exclude some of them. For example, on a CBCSDC basis DT1 would be excluded because it is a foreign controlled entity; also, on a CBDI basis, non-deposit takers will be excluded, that is, Non-DT1 and Non-DT2.

6.56 The example uses three tables for consolidating the following data:

- Table 6.1: Consolidation of Income and Expense Statements
- Table 6.2: Consolidation of Balance Sheets
- Table 6.3: Consolidation of Memorandum Series

6.57 The income and expense, balance sheet and memorandum series data of each financial institution are presented in the columns of Tables 6.1–6.3 as follows:

- The first five columns are the institutions belonging to the group controlled by DT2, that is DT2 (as parent), DT3, DT4, NonDT1, and NonDT2
- The sixth column is the DT2 group consolidated data (Step 1). It contains the aggregated data of the group minus the adjustments needed in the consolidation process.[20]
- The seventh column contains the data for DT1, a deposit taker with no subsidiaries and, therefore, with no need for consolidation.
- The last column aggregates columns 6 and 7, resulting in the sectoral data used to compile FSIs

6.58 Adjustments in the income and expense statements (Table 6.1)

6.59 For the purposes of compiling data for use in calculating FSIs, a number of adjustments are required to the income statement to eliminate intragroup transactions and related gains and losses. These adjustments are described below:

- Provisions for accrued interest on nonperforming assets (among entities in DT2 group);
- Fees and commissions receivable/payable (among entities in DT2 group);
- Gains and losses on financial instruments (among entities in DT2 group);
- Prorated earnings (among entities in DT2 group);
- Other income (among entities in DT2 group);
- Noninterest expenses (among entities in DT2 group);
- Provisions (among entities in DT2 group);

[20] In reality, this step will be repeated for every deposit-taking group resident in the economy for which FSIs are compiled.

Table 6A.1 Consolidation of Income and Expense Statements

(Millions of US dollars, unless otherwise stated)	DT2	DT3	DT4	Non-DT1	Non-DT2	Step 1: DT2 Group Consolidated Data	DT1	Step 2: Sectoral Data
	A	B	C	D	E	F (= A + B + C + D + E ± Group Consolidated Adjustment)	G	H (= F + G)
1. Interest income	810	481	210	171	242	1,919	859	2,778
i. Gross interest income[1]	825	495	220	180	255	1,975	880	2,855
ii. Less provisions for accrued interest on nonperforming assets	15	14	10	9	13	56	21	77
Of which: among entities in DT2 group	***3***	***2***	***0***	***0***	***0***	***Eliminated***	–	–
2. Interest expense	540	258	116	107	130	1,151	490	1,641
3. Net interest income (= 1 – 2)	*270*	*223*	*94*	*64*	*112*	*768*	*369*	*1,137*
4. Noninterest income	1,023	695	186	191	340	2,227	533	2,760
i. Fees and commissions receivable	300	225	78	80	170	839	154	993
Of which: among entities in DT2 group	***7***	***3***	***2***	***0***	***2***	***Eliminated***	–	–
ii. Gains or losses on financial instruments	100	290	60	50	85	566	110	676
Of which: among entities in DT2 group	***6***	***5***	***3***	***3***	***2***	***Eliminated***	–	–
iii. Prorated earnings	463	72	0	0	17	404	70	474
Of which: among entities in DT2 group	***148***	–	–	–	–	***Eliminated***	–	–
iv. Other income	160	108	48	61	68	418	199	617
Of which: among entities in DT2 group	***8***	***4***	***6***	***4***	***5***	***Eliminated***	–	–
5. Gross income (= 3 + 4)	*1,293*	*918*	*280*	*255*	*452*	*2,995*	*902*	*3,897*
6. Noninterest expenses	1,080	730	235	195	328	2,527	840	3,367
i. Personnel costs	300	380	185	150	85	1,100	420	1,520
ii. Other expenses[2]	780	350	50	45	243	1,427	420	1,847
Of which: among entities in DT2 group	***4***	***9***	***12***	***10***	***6***	***Eliminated***	–	–
7. Provisions (net)	80	65	45	23	35	242	84	326
i. Loan loss provisions	80	65	45	23	35	242	84	326
Of which: among entities in DT2 group	***4***	***2***	***0***	***0***	***0***	***Eliminated***	–	–
ii. Other financial asset provisions	0	0	0	0	0	0	0	0
8. Net income (before taxes) (= 5 – (6 + 7))	*133*	*123*	*0*	*37*	*89*	*226*	*–22*	*204*
9. Income tax	13	12	0	4	9	38	0	38
10. Net income after tax (= 8 – 9)	*120*	*111*	*0*	*33*	*80*	*188*	*–22*	*166*
11. Other comprehensive income (loss) net of tax								
12. Dividends payable	0	0	0	0	0	0	0	0
13. Retained earnings (= 10 – 12)	*120*	*111*	*0*	*33*	*80*	*188*	*–22*	*166*

Source: IMF staff estimates.

Note: DT = deposit taker.

[1] Neither gross interest income nor interest expense among group members adjusted for consolidation, and thus interest payments by one group member to another is netted out in the calculation of net interest income.

[2] Other expenses also include fees and commissions payable.

Table 6A.2 Consolidation of Balance Sheets

	DT2	DT3	DT4	Non-DT1	Non-DT2	Step 1: DT2 Group Consolidated Data	DT1	Step 2: Sectoral Data
						F		H
(Millions of US dollars, unless otherwise stated)	A	B	C	D	E	(= A + B + C + D + E ± Group Consolidated Adjustment)	G	(= F + G)
14. **Total assets** (= 15 + 16 = 23 + 31)	25,025	9,817	6,738	4,180	5,497	48,023	19,357	67,380
15. Nonfinancial assets	*1,475*	*772*	*300*	*785*	*1,304*	*4,636*	*1,125*	*5,761*
16. Financial assets (=17 to 22)	*23,550*	*9,045*	*6,438*	*3,395*	*4,193*	*43,387*	*18,232*	*61,619*
17. Currency and deposits	4,350	1,050	580	498	798	6,741	3,270	10,011
Of which: among entities in DT2 group	***250***	***70***	***30***	***75***	***110***	***Eliminated***	–	–
18. Loans (after specific provisions)	13,183	6,621	4,660	1,763	2,495	28,407	11,799	40,206
i. Gross loans	13,400	6,744	4,710	1,838	2,585	28,942	12,029	40,971
i.i. Interbank loans	900	620	50	0	25	1,260	1,350	2,610
i.i.i. Resident	250	110	50	0	25	100	270	370
Of which: among entities in DT2 group	***150***	***110***	***50***	***0***	***25***	***Eliminated***	–	–
i.i.ii. Nonresident	650	510	0	0	0	*1,160*	1,080	2,240
i.ii. Noninterbank loans	12,500	6,124	4,660	1,838	2,560	27,682	10,679	38,361
i.ii.i. Central bank	0	0	0	0	0	*0*	0	0
i.ii.ii. General government	4,000	1,380	500	78	0	*5,958*	878	6,836
i.ii.iii. Other financial corporations	2,000	500	280	420	500	*3,700*	675	4,375
i.ii.iv. Nonfinancial corporations	2,000	1,808	1,500	620	150	*6,078*	8,653	14,731
i.ii.v. Other domestic sectors	2,500	1,700	1,400	720	610	*6,930*	473	7,403
i.ii.vi. Nonresidents	2,000	736	980	0	1,300	*5,016*	0	5,016
Of which: among entities in DT2 group	0	0	0	0	0	***Eliminated***	–	–
ii. Specific provisions	217	123	50	75	90	535	230	765
Of which: among entities in DT2 group	***12***	***8***	***0***	***0***	***0***	***Eliminated***	–	–
19. Debt securities	2,717	1,000	870	990	820	6,192	2,660	8,852
Of which: among entities in DT2 group	***70***	***0***	***60***	***0***	***75***	***Eliminated***	–	–
20. Equity and investment fund shares	3,000	170	150	87	0	1,263	135	*1,398*
Of which: among entities in DT2 group	***2,144***	***0***	***0***	***0***	***0***	***Eliminated***	–	–
21. Financial derivatives	200	136	120	0	0	421	270	691
Of which: among entities in DT2 group	***0***	***0***	***35***	***0***	***0***	***Eliminated***	–	–
22. Other financial assets	100	68	58	57	80	363	98	461
Of which: among entities in DT2 group	0	0	0	0	0	***Eliminated***	–	–
23. Liabilities (= 28 + 29 + 30)	*21,175*	*8,297*	*6,228*	*3,260*	*4,047*	*41,897*	*16,960*	*58,857*
24. Currency and deposits	13,775	5,982	4,110	0	0	23,332	14,264	37,596
i. Customer deposits	13,200	5,049	3,800	0	0	22,049	14,194	36,243
ii. Interbank deposits	480	888	265	0	0	1,098	70	1,168
ii.i. Resident	140	225	200	0	0	30	70	100
Of which: among entities in DT2 group	***135***	***215***	***185***	***0***	***0***	***Eliminated***	–	–
ii.ii. Nonresident	340	663	65	0	0	1,068	0	1,068
iii. Other currency and deposits	95	45	45	0	0	185	0	185

Table 6A.2 Consolidation of Balance Sheets *(concluded)*

(Millions of US dollars, unless otherwise stated)	DT2	DT3	DT4	Non-DT1	Non-DT2	Step 1: DT2 Group Consolidated Data	DT1	Step 2: Sectoral Data
						F		H
	A	B	C	D	E	(= A + B + C + D + E ± Group Consolidated Adjustment)	G	(= F + G)
25. Loans	2,449	453	570	762	120	4,019	770	4,789
Of which: among entities in DT2 group	***25***	***40***	***50***	***130***	***90***	***Eliminated***	–	–
26. Debt securities	2,930	1,475	1,300	2,148	3,849	11,497	1,040	12,537
Of which: among entities in DT2 group	***60***	***85***	***0***	***60***	***0***	***Eliminated***	–	–
27. Other liabilities	1,321	289	200	350	78	2,238	838	3,076
Of which: among entities in DT2 group	0	0	0	0	0	***Eliminated***	–	–
28. Debt (= 24 + 25 + 26 + 27)	*20,475*	*8,199*	*6,180*	*3,260*	*4,047*	*41,086*	*16,912*	*57,998*
29. Financial derivatives and employee stock options	700	98	48	0	0	811	48	859
Of which: among entities in DT2 group	***35***	***0***	***0***	***0***	***0***	***Eliminated***	–	–
30. General and other provisions	0	0	0	0	0			
31. Capital and reserves	3,850	1,520	510	920	1,450	6,126	2,397	8,523
Of which: among entities in DT2 group		586	232	354	823	***Eliminated***	–	–
*32. **Balance sheet total** (= 23 + 31 = 14)*	*25,025*	*9,817*	*6,738*	*4,180*	*5,497*	*48,023*	*19,357*	*67,380*

Source: IMF staff estimates.

Note: DT = deposit taker.

Table 6A.3 Consolidation of Memorandum Series

	DT2	DT3	DT4	Non-DT1	Non-DT2	Step 1: DT2 Group Consolidated Data	DT1	Step 2: Sectoral Data
						F		H
Millions of US dollars, unless otherwise stated)	A	B	C	D	E	(= A + B + C + D + E ± Group Consolidated Adjustment)	G	(= F + G)
33. Tier 1 capital less corresponding supervisory deductions	3,003	1,040	395	680	980	4,103	1,925	6,028
34. Common Equity Tier 1 capital less corresponding supervisory deductions	2,102	728	276	476	686	2,714	1,348	3,621
35. Additional Tier 1 capital less corresponding supervisory deductions	901	312	118	204	294	1,829	578	2,407
Of which: among entities in DT2 group	***1,995***	***0***	***0***	***0***	***0***	***Eliminated***	–	–
36. Tier 2 capital less corresponding supervisory deductions	750	513	150	50	92	1,555	420	1,975
37. Tier 3 capital	0	0	0	0	0	0	0	0
38. Other supervisory deduction	0	0	0	0	0	0	0	0
39. Total regulatory capital (= 33 + 36+ 37- 38) (after intragroup adjustment)	3,753	1,553	545	730	1,072	5,658	2,345	8,003
40. Risk-weighted assets (after intragroup adjustment)	17,546	7,654	5,341	2,973	3,396	36,909	15,862	52,771
. . .								
46. Value of large exposures (after intragroup adjustment)	741	310	123	100	120	1,394	620	2,014
Series that provide a further analysis of the balance sheet								
47. Liquid assets	11,913	3,088	1,975	1,878	2,364	21,217	9,479	30,696
48. Short-term liabilities	10,530	4,208	3,038	1,239	1,619	20,633	10,698	31,331
49. Nonperforming loans (after intragroup adjustment)	367	255	94	55	103	875	241	1,115
50. Residential real estate loans	1,000	1,020	1,200	650	450	4,320	2,220	6,540
51. Commercial real estate loans (after intragroup adjustment)	2,000	890	750	0	0	3,640	1,200	4,840
52. Geographical distribution of loans (intragroup adjustment)	See addendum	See addendum	See addendum	See addendum	See addendum	See addendum	See addendum	See addendum

Table 6A.3 Consolidation of Memorandum Series *(concluded)*

	DT2	DT3	DT4	Non-DT1	Non-DT2	Step 1: DT2 Group Consolidated Data	DT1	Step 2: Sectoral Data
						F		H
Millions of US dollars, unless otherwise stated)	A	B	C	D	E	(= A + B + C + D + E ± Group Consolidated Adjustment)	G	(= F + G)
53. Foreign currency loans (after intragroup adjustment)	3,000	1,224	890	850	550	6,514	1,350	7,864
54. Foreign currency liabilities (after intragroup adjustment)	7,100	2,360	1,200	990	650	12,300	5,200	17,500
55. Net open position in foreign currency for on-balance-sheet items (after intragroup adjustment)	–2,540	–589	–200	78	85	–3,166	–1,500	–4,666
56. Total net open position in foreign currency (after intragroup adjustment)	–2,220	–120	–156	78	85	–2,333	–1,400	–3,733
. . .								
Addendum								
Geographical distribution of loans								
Total loans to nonresidents	2,650	1,246	980	0	1,300	6,176	1,080	7,256
Advanced economies	1,450	664	460	0	0	2,574	570	3,144
Emerging market and developing economies	1,200	582	520	0	1,300	3,602	510	4,112
Emerging and developing Asia	450	281	70	0	900	1,701	170	1,871
Emerging and developing Europe	250	301	0	0	0	551	55	606
Latin America and the Caribbean	0	0	0	0	0	0	0	0
Middle East and Central Asia	500	0	450	0	400	1,350	285	1,635
Sub-Saharan Africa	0	0	0	0	0	0	0	0

Source: IMF staff estimates.

Note: DT = deposit taker.

6.60 Once the adjustments are made, the data can be aggregated. The result appears as *Step 1* (column 6). As previously said, the last column will aggregate the data from column 6 (DT2 group) and column 7 (DT1) to compile the *sectoral* data (*Step 2*).

6.61 Adjustments in the balance sheets (Table 6.2)

6.62 The adjustments required to the balance sheets to eliminate intra-group financial assets and liabilities are:

- Deposits (among entities in DT2 group);
- Interbank loans (among entities in DT2 group);
- Non-interbank loans (among entities in DT2 group);
- Debt securities (among entities in DT2 group);
- Equity and investment fund shares (among entities in DT2 group);
- Financial derivatives and employee stock options (among entities in DT2 group);
- Other financial assets (among entities in DT2 group);
- Liability capital and reserves (among entities in DT2 group);

6.63 As in the prevision Section, once the adjustments are made, the data can be aggregated. The result appears as *Step 1* (column 6). The last column will aggregate the data from column 6 (DT2 group) and column 7 (DT1) to compile the *sectoral* data (*Step 2*).

6.64 Adjustments in the memorandum series (Table 6.3)

6.65 Regarding the memorandum series, the following adjustments are made in the DT2 group, offsetting claims on and liabilities to entities of the group:

- Regulatory capital, comprising Common Equity Tier 1 (CET1), Additional Tier 1 (AT1), Tier 2 capital, and Tier 3 capital; for the participation of the parent DT in the different tiers of the regulatory capital of its subsidiaries. (In the example, it is assumed that no claims/liabilities exit at the level of Tier 2 Capital)
- Risk-weighted assets comprising intra-group claims deducted from total risk- weighted assets of the group; memorandum series assets and liabilities (loans, debt securities, equity and investment fund shares, financial derivatives and employee stock options) deducted from the group totals.

6.66 As in the prevision Section, once the adjustments are made, the data can be aggregated. The result appears as *Step 1* (column 6). The last column will aggregate the data from column 6 (DT2 group) and column 7 (DT1) to compile the *sectoral* data (*Step 2*).

7 Specification of Core Financial Soundness Indicators for Deposit Takers

I. Introduction

7.1 This chapter brings together the concepts and definitions set out so far, to explain how core financial soundness indicators (FSIs) for deposit takers (DTs) are to be calculated.[1] The accounting principles and calculation methods for core FSIs presented in this chapter also apply to the additional FSIs for DTs. The availability of data reported to supervisory agencies will determine the scope of the data that can be compiled and disseminated.

7.2 For most of the FSIs, the *Guide* recommends that the data series be drawn from sectoral financial statements. For each reporting DT group, data need to be compiled on a consolidated basis as described in Chapter 6.[2]

Accounting Principles

7.3 The accounting principles are discussed in Chapter 4. Except where otherwise noted, the following principles should be applied when compiling the underlying series used to calculate FSIs:

- Transactions and positions should be recorded on an **accrual** basis, and only existing actual assets and liabilities should be recognized (paragraphs 4.10–4.13).
- Valuation methods should provide the most realistic assessment at any moment in time of the value of an instrument or item. **Market value** is the preferred basis of valuation of transactions, as well as for positions in traded securities. For positions in instruments not designated for trading or available for sale,[3] the *Guide* defers to International Financial Reporting Standards (IFRSs).
- **Provisions for loan losses** comprise specific provisions created to cover identified non-performing loans.[4]
- Transactions and positions in **foreign currency** should be converted into a single unit of account using the market exchange rate (see paragraphs 4.53–4.55).
- Short-term **maturity** is defined as three months or less (or payable on demand), (see paragraph 5.93).

Underlying Series

7.4 The underlying series to be used in calculating individual FSIs are defined in Chapter 5. In describing the FSIs, some brief illustrations of the underlying series are introduced, together with cross-references to the more detailed definitions provided in earlier chapters. In this, and subsequent chapters, reference is regularly made to the financial statements presented in Chapter 5.

7.5 As presented in the *Guide*, FSIs are compiled at an aggregated sector level and constructed as ratios where numerator and denominator are the sum of each DT group's underlying series. As such, they represent weighted averages for the whole financial system.[5]

---

[1] Some countries may also benefit from *EBA Guidance Note on Compiling the IMF Financial Soundness Indicators for 'Deposit-Takers' using the ITS on Supervisory Reporting*, https://eba.europa.eu/documents/10180/1460270/EBA+Guidance+Note+on+compiling+IMF+FSIs+%28July+2018+update%29.pdf/d2e22fc2-6602-4dd0-ad45-a914955f6883.

[2] The consolidation adjustments performed within the reporting groups will depend on the consolidation basis used to compile FSIs (see Chapter 6).

[3] In the terminology of the IFRS 9, these are instruments held to collect their contractual cash flows.

[4] Specific provisions are a memorandum series derived from the IFRS 9 calculation of expected credit loss (ECL), with the loan loss allowance allocated to specific provisions and general provisions in line with national supervisory guidance as described in Chapter 4. See BCBC *Regulatory treatment of accounting provisions—interim approach and transitional arrangements* (March 2017).

[5] The same FSIs recommended in the *Guide* for the whole sector can be compiled at the individual group level to support banking supervision.

Calculation of FSIs

7.6 Most FSIs consist of ratios of two underlying series. The calculation should use data with the same periodicity for both the numerator and the denominator, which, depending on the ratio being calculated, should be either flows recognized during the period, end-period, or average period positions.

7.7 The definitions underlying data series may differ across countries. Countries may also follow different conventions than those set out in the *Guide*. For transparency and cross-country comparability, the dissemination of FSI data should be accompanied of extensive metadata.

II. Core FSIs for DTs

7.8 The *Guide* recommends the compilation of 17 core FSIs for DTs (Table 1.1 of Chapter 1), which is a minimum set covering the most critical measures of financial soundness. However, for a more comprehen sive assessment of the health of the financial sector, they should be complemented with additional FSIs, including for other sectors of the economy.[6] Unless otherwise stated, all the "line" comments in this chapter refer to the financial statements and memorandum items of Table 5.1 in Chapter 5. Annex 7.1 summarizes the concepts, calculation methods, source data, and compilation issues of the core FSIs for DTs.[7]

Regulatory Capital to Risk-Weighted Assets

7.9 The FSI Regulatory capital to risk-weighted assets gauges DTs' capital strength to withstand shocks and absorb unexpected losses. This FSI is based, as described in Chapter 3, on the definitions of total regulatory capital (line 39) and risk-weighted assets (RWA) (line 40).

7.10 Compilers will rely on national supervisory definitions of the components of capital and specification of risk weights. The metadata should identify: (i) which version of the Basel Capital Accord has been implemented in the jurisdiction; (ii) use, if any, of the various elements of national discretion in the Basel standards; and (iii) any variations from the applicable Basel standard (other than specified elements of national discretion).

7.11 This FSI is a ratio where the numerator is total regulatory capital and the denominator is on- and off-balance-sheet assets weighted by risk. Total regulatory capital and RWA are defined in paragraphs 5.75–5.81 and paragraph 5.82, respectively, and use regulatory standards and concepts that do not correspond directly to balance sheet capital and assets.

7.12 Regulatory capital refers to a supervisory definition of capital developed by the Basel Committee on Banking Supervision (BCBS) and differs from accounting capital and reserve items. Current year results generally are excluded, while undisclosed reserves and valuation adjustments can be included in supplementary regulatory capital subject to specified restrictions. Goodwill, which is implicitly included in balance sheet capital, is deducted from regulatory capital. In addition, the definition adds several specified types of subordinated debt instruments that meet specified restrictions, as well as general provisions up to prescribed limits. Supervisory deductions are applied to the different components of regulatory capital, netting from its total. For a detailed treatment of the elements that constitute regulatory capital, see Chapter 3.

7.13 RWA refers to the DT's risk-weighted assets (for credit, market and operational risks) and off-balance-sheet exposures. The adopted regulatory framework (Basel I, II, or III) determines the specific way of calculating RWA. Basel I adopted a straightforward and simple way of weighting the assets with five pre defined factors for credit risk. Basel II introduced additional factors and some revised risk weighting in the Standardized Approach as well as advanced approaches that measure risk based on internal models. Basel III introduced a more granular approach to risk weights and alternatives to the use of external ratings in the Standardized Approach.

7.14 The BCBS has prescribed minimum regulatory capital of 8 percent of RWA for all internationally active banks. Basel III effectively raises this minimum to 10.5 percent through the introduction of the 2.5 percent capital conservation buffer. National supervisors may require a higher ratio and have leeway in establishing the specific standards for their economies.

[6] These additional FSIs are presented in Chapters 8, 9, and 10.
[7] Annex 7.4 describes the business model of Islamic Deposit Takers and provides guidance on how to map the financial information from the Islamic Deposit Takers' income statement and balance sheet to those of DTs to assist in the compilation of system FSIs for countries with dual DT systems.

7.15 As with other FSIs, when analyzing this indicator, it is important to consider how numerator and denominator affect its value. A higher capital adequacy ratio can be achieved either by increasing the amount of capital, or by reducing RWA, which can be done by restructuring the portfolio toward less risky assets, for example, by reducing lending and increasing holdings of low risk-weight securities (see Box 7.1).

Tier 1 Capital to Risk-Weighted Assets

7.16 The FSI **Tier 1 capital to RWA** focuses on the core capital concept of the BCBS. Tier 1 capital is the most solid and readily available layer of regulatory capital, as it is considered permanent and absorbs losses by ranking last in the hierarchy of claims in the event of insolvency. Compared to the regulatory capital to RWA ratio, this FSI measures the most freely and immediately available resources to absorb losses.

7.17 This FSI is a ratio where the numerator is Tier 1 capital and the denominator is RWA. The concepts of Tier 1 capital (line 33) and RWA (line 40) are defined in paragraphs 5.76, 5.77, and paragraph 5.82, respectively, and are derived from regulatory standards and concepts that do not correspond directly to capital and assets shown in the balance sheet. Under Basel I and II, the minimum Tier 1 requirement is 4 percent of RWA, while Basel III increased it to 6 percent.

7.18 Source data are consolidated Tier 1 capital and consolidated RWA of each DT group in the reporting population. Data are based on supervisory concepts. The metadata provided should describe the

Box 7.1 Interpreting Regulatory Capital Trends

These graphical examples highlight how numerator and denominator affect the capital adequacy ratio, and the need to look into the underlying series when interpreting this and other FSIs.

The banking systems of both Country A and Country B improved substantially their capital adequacy from very low levels. However, while in Country A, the increase in the *Regulatory capital to RWA* ratio was achieved increasing the stock of capital while at the same time increasing exposure; in Country B, the increase in the ratio was done basically by reducing banks' exposure through contracting lending and switching to less risky assets, such as government bonds. This can be seen observing the graphs on Total Regulatory Capital and RWA, with a base = 100 in the fourth quarter of Year 0.

Figure 7.1 Interpreting Regulatory Capital Trends

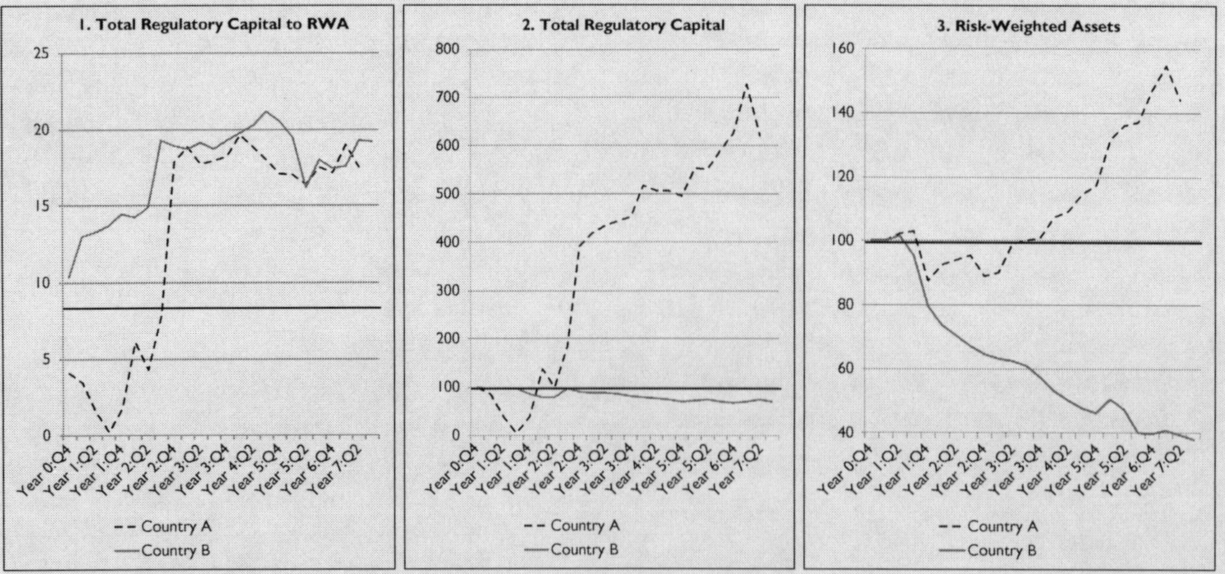

Source: IMF staff calculations.

Note: RWA = risk-weighted asset.

national treatment in Tier 1 capital of equity investments in other banks, other financial institutions, and insurance corporations; since under the BCBS, such investments may be excluded from Tier 1 capital at the discretion of the national authorities. Metadata should also indicate other elements of national discretion and any variations, other than elements of national discretion, from the version of the capital accord applied in the jurisdiction.

Common Equity Tier 1 Capital to Risk-Weighted Assets

7.19 The FSI **Common equity Tier 1 (CET1) capital to RWA** measures the capital adequacy of DTs based on the highest-quality capital defined by Basel III, Common Equity Tier 1 (CET1).[8] Countries that have not adopted Basel III are not required to compile this indicator. CET1 (which, together with additional tier 1 capital [AT1] is referred as "going-concern capital") is the most loss-absorbing form of capital. It is a measure of the amount of capital available to a bank to absorb losses while continuing operations.

7.20 This FSI is a ratio where the numerator is CET1 capital and the denominator is RWA. The concepts of CET1 capital (line 34) and RWA (line 40) are explained in paragraphs 3.27 and 3.32–3.35, and defined in paragraphs 5.77 and 5.82. They follow regulatory standards and concepts and do not correspond directly to capital and assets shown in the balance sheet.

7.21 As specified in Chapter 3, Basel III splits Tier 1 capital into two components: (1) CET1 and (2) AT1. CET1 capital consists predominantly of common shares issued by the bank, stock surplus, retained earnings, and accumulated other comprehensive income and other disclosed reserves. AT1 capital consists of instruments that are subordinated, have fully discretionary non-cumulative dividends or coupons, and have neither a maturity date nor an incentive to redeem. Basel III established a minimum of 4.5 percent for the CET1 to RWA ratio.

7.22 Source data, based on supervisory concepts, are the consolidated CET 1 capital and the consolidated RWA of each DT group in the reporting population.

[8]See Chapter 3, paragraphs 3.25–3.31.

Tier 1 Capital to Assets and the Basel III Leverage Ratio

7.23 The FSI **Tier 1 capital to assets** provides an indication of financial leverage that is, the extent to which assets are funded by other than own funds. It is another measure of capital adequacy of the DT sector. This ratio serves as a supplementary measure to the risk-based capital requirements. An adverse trend in the ratio may signal increased exposure to risk and possible capital adequacy problems.

7.24 This FSI is calculated by using Tier 1 capital as numerator, and total (nonfinancial and financial) balance sheet assets—without risk weighting—as denominator. Unweighted assets are used in this ratio to provide insights into leverage. The concepts of Tier 1 capital (line 33) and total assets (line 14) are defined in paragraphs 5.76 and 5.77 and paragraphs 5.33–5.35, respectively.[9]

7.25 For jurisdictions that have implemented Basel III, this indicator would be calculated using the new Basel III leverage ratio, defined in paragraph 3.46. In this ratio, the capital measure for the numerator is Tier 1 capital. The denominator comprises a new Basel III aggregate called "exposure" consists of all balance sheet assets (with an add on for potential future exposures of derivatives and securities financing transactions) and off-balance-sheet exposures (Supervisory-based memorandum series).[10] Off-balance-sheet exposures include commitments, unconditionally cancellable commitments, direct credit substitutes, acceptances, stand by letter of credit, trade letters of credit, failed transactions, and unsettled securities. Items that are deducted from capital are also deducted from the measure of exposure.

7.26 Regarding Tier 1 capital, source data and issues for compilers are discussed in the regulatory Tier 1 capital to RWA section. Data on total (financial and nonfinancial) assets are available from DTs' balance sheets. The capital measure required by the Basel III leverage ratio can be obtained from supervisory sources.

[9]The *2006 Guide* recommended to use balance sheet capital as numerator. This option is eliminated.
[10]See paragraph 3.46.

Nonperforming Loans Net of Provisions to Capital

7.27 The FSI **Nonperforming loans (NPLs) net of provisions to capital** is intended to gauge the potential impact on capital of the portion of NPLs not covered by specific provisions. If there is appropriate recognition of NPLs, this ratio can provide an indication of the capacity of bank capital to withstand losses on loans identified as non-performing but not fully provisioned. While NPLs net of specific provisions is considered to be the best estimate of the realizable value of the NPLs, there is uncertainty until individual NPLs have been either fully collected, or all collection options have been exhausted and any unrecovered portion written off. Since the actual losses that will be incurred, and thus the realizable value of the NPLs are not known, the estimates of required provisions may vary from actual experience.

7.28 This FSI is calculated by taking the value of NPLs (line 49) *less* the value of specific loan loss provisions against NPLs (line 18.ii) as the numerator,[11] and total regulatory capital as the denominator.

7.29 Loans are nonperforming when payments of principal and interest are past due by 90 days or more, or interest payments corresponding to 90 days or more have been capitalized, refinanced or rolled over. In addition, NPLs should also include those loans with payments less than 90 days past due, but for which evidence exists to classify them as nonperforming, such as if the debtor files for bankruptcy. After a loan is classified as nonperforming, it (or any replacement loan[s]) should remain so classified, until written-off or payments of interest or principal are received on this or subsequent loans that replace the original loan. Data on loans should exclude accrued interest on NPLs and lending among DTs in the reporting population that are part of the same group.[12]

7.30 Provisions are defined as specific loan loss provisions against NPLs. As described in Chapter 4, specific provisions refer to the portion of expected loss calculated for loans that are classified as impaired loans under IFRS9 or using an approach consistent with national supervisory guidance. The *Guide* relies on national practices in identifying specific provisions, which should be documented in the metadata. Provisions for the accrual of interest on NPLs should not be included under loan loss provisions, as they are identified within (and excluded from) net interest income.

7.31 Capital is measured as total regulatory capital (line 39 and defined in paragraph 5.75–5.80).[13] In measuring sector-wide regulatory capital, intra-sector equity investments are deducted from the overall capital in the sector, so that capital and reserves held within the sector are not double counted. In line with supervisory guidance, capital excludes the value of goodwill.

7.32 Information on NPLs and specific provisions for the reporting population are typically available from supervisory sources, although national definitions of NPLs can vary.[14] Similarly, regulatory capital data are available from supervisory sources.

7.33 The indicator requires the use of specific provisions when netting from NPLs. Some jurisdictions may not distinguish between specific and general provisions, which is consistent with the IFRS 9 ECL approach. This can result in negative values for the indicator if total (specific and general) provisions are higher than outstanding NPLs. In jurisdictions that do not allocate ECL to general and specific provisions, the subset ECL for non-performing loans, rather than total ECL, should be used if available to calculate the FSI, providing a more accurate indication of extent to which NPLs are covered by provisions. This emphasizes the importance of documenting national practices in the metadata if the dissemination of this FSI is not to be misleading.

Nonperforming Loans to Total Gross Loans

7.34 The FSI **nonperforming loans to total gross loans** is intended to identify problems with asset quality

[11] NPLs and specific provisions are defined in paragraph 5.94 and paragraph 5.48, respectively. The dissemination of data for this indicator should be supplemented with detailed metadata on national supervisory rules for classifying loans as nonperforming and for collateral.

[12] See Chapter 5, paragraph 5.94 to paragraph 5.96.

[13] Where a Domestic Location (DL) consolidation is used, countries have the flexibility to use total capital and reserves (line 31, defined in paragraphs 5.70–5.72) as denominator, because foreign-owned branches might not be required to hold regulatory capital.

[14] When national definitions deviate from the one presented in the *Guide*, they should be documented in the metadata.

in the loan portfolio, with an increasing ratio signaling a deterioration in the quality of banks' credit portfolio. For a proper interpretation, it should be used in combination with the FSIs *NPLs net of provisions to capital* ratio described earlier and *Provisions to NPLs* described further.

7.35 NPLs are identified only when problems emerge, so this FSI is a lagging indicator. Nevertheless, it shows a trend in the quality of DTs' portfolio over time. Appropriate recognition of NPLs is essential for this ratio to be meaningful and cross-country comparable. The indicator can be viewed together with those for the nonfinancial corporate sector, as a deteriorating financial position for nonfinancial corporations might foreshadow future deterioration of this ratio. Moreover, this indicator can also provide insights into the buildup of systemic credit risk, allowing for benchmarking of financial systems in normal times with no stress, to monitor changes over time, and to compare across jurisdictions.

7.36 This FSI is calculated by taking the value of NPLs as the numerator and the total value of the loan portfolio (including NPLs, and before the deduction of specific loan loss provisions) as the denominator. Also, and as noted in paragraph 7.29, the denominator should exclude lending among DTs in the reporting population that are part of the same group. NPLs (line 49) and loans (line 18.i) are defined in paragraphs 5.94–5.96 and paragraphs 5.41 and 5.43, respectively.

7.37 The guidance on the definition of NPLs is the same as that provided for the previous FSI in paragraph 7.29. Total loans correspond to the balance sheet concept (after consolidation within the banking group) and include all loans to resident and nonresident institutional units. Data on performing and NPLs should exclude accrued interest on NPLs. Since the goal of this FSI is to gauge banks' exposures arising from their loan portfolio, deposits with the central bank and other financial institutions should not be part of the denominator, even if national regulations allow to classify them as such.[15]

7.38 Information on loans should be available from the consolidated balance sheet of the reporting group and supervisory sources. Information on NPLs for the reporting population is typically available from supervisory sources, although national definitions on NPLs can vary. Equally, different legal frameworks may influence the length of time that NPLs must be kept on-balance sheet, distorting cross-country comparisons.[16] For instance, if banks are not allowed to write-off loans—even when they are fully provisioned and the losses already absorbed—until a legally established time has lapsed; their balance sheets will indicate a more vulnerable situation than if those loans had been taken off-balance sheet, without any effect on the solvency of the institutions.

Provisions to Nonperforming Loans

7.39 The FSI **provisions to NPLs** gauges the extent to which NPLs are already covered by specific provisions. This ratio complements the information provided by the two previous FSIs on NPLs, providing a measure of the amount of future losses that would be incurred if all NPLs were written-off.

7.40 This FSI is calculated by taking the value of specific provisions against NPLs (line 18.ii) as the numerator, and NPLs as the denominator. NPLs and specific provisions are defined in paragraphs 5.94–5.96 and paragraph 5.48, respectively.

7.41 As noted earlier the loan loss allowance that are derived from the IFRS9 calculation are allocated to specific provisions and general provisions in line with national supervisory guidance. In jurisdictions that treat all ECL as specific provisions, the subset ECL for non-performing loans, should be used for calculating the FSI. This should be documented in the metadata.

7.42 Regarding NPLs and specific provisions, source data and compilation issues are discussed for the FSI *nonperforming loans net of provisions to capital*. Due to different national standards for the classification of loans as nonperforming and the constitution of loan loss provisions, data disseminated for this indicator

[15] For instance, the EU Commission Implementing Regulation 2015/1278 includes as banks' exposures cash balances at central banks and other demand deposits. This treatment artificially inflates the denominator. Therefore, countries should follow the *Guide* definition and exclude such deposits when compiling this FSI.

[16] For this, and other cases where national frameworks differ, the availability of metadata is crucial for the interpretation of the indicators.

should be supplemented with detailed metadata on national supervisory rules for treatment of collateral in determining required provisions. The discussion in the previous section on general provisions included indistinctly from specific provisions also applies here.

Loan Concentration by Economic Activity

7.43 The FSI **Loan concentration by economic activity** is aimed at gauging the credit risk associated with excessive concentration of credit in a specific domestic sector or activity. A large concentration of aggregate credit exposure to a specific resident economic sector or activity may signal an important vulnerability of the DT sector to the level of activity, prices, and profitability in that sector or activity. If conditions in sectors where banks have an excessive credit concentration deteriorate, the quality of their loan portfolio will suffer, with negative consequences for their financial health.

7.44 This FSI is the ratio of DTs' lending to the largest three economic activities, as a proportion of their total gross loans to nonfinancial corporations. Lending by economic activity is based on the UN International Standard Industrial Classification of All Economic Activities, Rev 4 (ISIC Rev.4) at its higher level, which provides a widely accepted structure for the classification of economic activities. Box 7.2 presents a numerical example on how to calculate this indicator.

7.45 Data on loans are on a gross basis (i.e., before deducting specific loan loss provisions) and include NPLs. The availability of data on loans by economic activity might vary depending on supervisory practices, but it is expected that ISIC information will be readily available in most countries, facilitating cross-country comparability. If ISIC information is not available, an equivalent national classification by economic activity should be used and indicated in the metadata. Additional information on the three economic activities with the largest exposure will help interpret the results.

Return on Assets

7.46 The FSI **return on assets** (ROA) provides information on the DTs' profitability relative to total assets and can be an indicator of how efficiently the DTs manage their assets to generate earnings. The ratio may be interpreted in combination with the FSI on return on equity (ROE) described further.

7.47 This FSI is the quotient of net income and total (financial and nonfinancial) assets. The preferred definition of net income is the one before taxes (line 8), as it is not affected by cross-country tax differences and, thus facilitates cross-country comparability. Net income and its components are defined in paragraphs 5.13–5.30. Total assets (line 14) are not risk weighted and correspond to the balance sheet concept as defined in paragraphs 5.33 and 5.35.

7.48 Being a ratio of a flow (income) to a stock (assets), this FSI is subject to different methods of calculation. Compilers should report the income annualization choice in the metadata. The denominator should be the average of the stock of total assets during the reporting period. At a minimum, the denominator can be calculated by using the average of the beginning and end-period positions, but compilers are encouraged to use the most frequent observations available for averaging.

Box 7.2 Calculation of Loan Concentration by Economic Activity

The numerical example details the calculation of the FSI loan concentration by economic activity.

Country A Loans	Agriculture 170	Mining 155	Manufacturing 90	Total 1,000
Country B Loans	Mining 250	Construction 200	Accommodation 70	Total 1,000

For country A, the FSI would be $FSI_A = \frac{170+155+90}{1,000} = \frac{415}{1,000} = 41.5\%$

For country B, the FSI would be $FSI_B = \frac{250+200+70}{1,000} = \frac{520}{1,000} = 52\%$

Source: IMF staff estimates.

7.49 The data for net income available from supervisory sources may depend on the national commercial accounting practice, as might the extent to which they meet the definitions in the *Guide*. Net income is calculated based on commercial accounting and supervisory approaches.

7.50 Net income, as defined in the *Guide*, includes gains and losses on financial instruments valued at fair value through profit and loss, and gains and losses from the sales of fixed assets, which are measured as the difference between the sale value and the balance sheet value at the end of the previous period. Notably, compilers should be aware that the *Guide* recommends that interest income not include the accrual of interest on nonperforming assets (paragraph 5.14). It also encourages the inclusion of realized and unrealized gains and losses arising during each period on all financial instruments (financial assets and liabilities, in domestic and foreign currencies) valued at FVTPL.

Return on Equity

7.51 The FSI **return on equity** (ROE) is intended to measure DTs' efficiency in using capital. It also offers information on the ability of DTs to internally generate capital through retained earnings, and the attractiveness of the sector to new equity investment.

7.52 This FSI is the quotient of net income (flow) and total capital and reserves (stock) and therefore subject to different methods of calculations, which would produce different results. Compilers should report the income annualization choice in the metadata.

7.53 The *Guide* recommends net income after taxes (line 10), as this provides an indication of net operating income available for capitalization and profit distribution.

7.54 Net income and its components are defined in paragraphs 5.13–5.31. Capital is measured as total capital and reserves (line 31 and defined in paragraphs 5.70–5.72).

7.55 Differences in capital structure and business mix across countries affect bank performance and highlight the need to look at several operating ratios simultaneously. Banks with higher leverage (lower equity relative to assets) will generally report a higher ROE. Hence, an analysis of profitability based exclusively on ROE would tend to disregard the greater risks normally associated with high leverage. Regarding net income, data sources and compilation issues are discussed in the *ROA* indicator.

Interest Margin to Gross Income

7.56 The FSI **interest margin to gross income** measures the relative share of net interest income (interest earned *less* interest expenses) within gross income. This ratio is a gauge of the relative importance of the income generated by the intermediation business of DTs (mobilizing savings for investment).

7.57 This FSI is calculated by using net interest income (line 3) as the numerator and gross income (line 5) as the denominator. Net interest income and its components are defined in paragraphs 5.13–5.15, while gross income is defined in paragraph 5.16. Being a ratio of two flows, the *Guide* recommends accumulating the flows from the beginning of the year until the end of the reporting period.

7.58 Data for net interest income and gross income should be available from income statements and supervisory sources, but the extent to which they meet the definitions in the *Guide* could depend on national commercial accounting practice.

7.59 In the *Guide*, interest income should not include the accrual of interest on nonperforming assets (see paragraph 5.14). Gross income includes both net interest income and other gross income. As mentioned earlier, Other gross income items include realized and unrealized gains and losses arising during each period on all financial instruments (in domestic and foreign currencies) valued at FVPTL. Gains and losses on the sale of an associate or subsidiary (and disinvestment, of a reverse investment) are excluded from gross income (paragraph 5.19).

Noninterest Expenses to Gross Income

7.60 The FSI **noninterest expenses to gross income** measures the relation between non-intermediation expenses, often called overhead or operating expenses, and gross income (interest margin plus noninterest income). This FSI, often called the efficiency ratio, provides insights into the portion of gross revenues required to cover operating expenses, including personnel costs and occupancy expenses.

7.61 This FSI is calculated by using noninterest expenses (line 6 in Table 5.1) as the numerator and gross income (line 5) as the denominator. Noninterest expenses are defined in paragraph 5.25 and gross income in paragraph 5.16. The recommendation is for numerator and denominator to accumulate the flows from the beginning of the year until the end of the reporting period.

7.62 Noninterest expenses cover all expenses other than interest expenses. Provisions are not included in noninterest expenses but separately identified in the sectoral income and expense statement (line 7). Regarding gross income, issues for compilers are discussed in the interest margin to gross income summary.

7.63 The data for noninterest expenses and gross income available to supervisory sources may depend on national commercial accounting practice. Sources of gross income data are discussed in the section on *Interest margin to gross income.*

Liquid Assets to Total Assets

7.64 The FSI **liquid assets to total assets** provides an indication of the liquidity available to DTs to meet expected and unexpected cash outflows. The level of liquidity influences the ability of a banking system to withstand idiosyncratic funding shocks as well as more global market disruption.

7.65 This FSI is calculated by using the measure of liquid assets (line 47) as the numerator and total assets (line 14) as the denominator. Liquid assets are defined in paragraphs 5.90-5.92, and nonfinancial and financial assets are defined in paragraphs 5.33 and 5.35.

7.66 Data on liquidity should be available from supervisory sources. The extent to which national approaches to measuring liquidity meet the concepts in the *Guide* would require consideration. The available information may need to be aggregated to calculate both the numerator and denominator of this FSI.

Liquid Assets to Short-Term Liabilities and Liquidity Coverage Ratio

7.67 The FSI **liquid assets to short-term liabilities** is intended to capture the liquidity mismatch of assets and liabilities and provides an indication of the extent to which DTs could meet the short-term withdrawal of funds without facing liquidity problems.

7.68 This FSI is calculated by using the measure of liquid assets (line 47) as the numerator and the short-term liabilities (line 48) as the denominator. Liquid assets are defined in paragraphs 5.90–5.92, and short-term liabilities are defined in paragraph 5.93. Short-term liabilities are the short-term element (within three months or less) of DTs' debt liabilities (line 28) *plus* the net market value of the financial derivatives position[17] (liabilities line 29 *less* assets line 21); including liabilities to other DTs in the reporting population.

7.69 Sources of data on liquid assets are discussed in paragraph 7.66. Data on short-term liabilities for all debt instruments are often available on an original maturity, but not always on a remaining maturity basis.[18] Data on short-term liabilities on a remaining maturity basis might be available from supervisory sources. Data on financial derivatives should be available from accounting records and supervisory sources. The extent to which the data meet the concepts in the *Guide*, particularly about remaining maturity and financial derivatives, would require consideration. Any data should exclude positions within the same reporting group. The issues for compilers for liquid assets are the same as the ones described in the *liquid assets to total assets* section.

7.70 Jurisdictions that have implemented the liquidity standards of Basel III should compile both liquid assets to short term liabilities and the **liquidity coverage ratio** (LCR). If the LCR is applicable only to a subset of the DT sector, for example, large internationally active banks, the LCR should be compiled only for that subset. Liquid assets to short-term liabilities should continue to be compiled for the DT sector.

7.71 The LCR is an indicator of the ability of banks to survive a 30-day liquidity stress scenario. The

[17]The net market value position (liabilities *less* assets) of financial derivative liabilities should be included rather than the gross liability position. This is because of the market practice of creating offsetting contracts and the possibility of forward-type instruments switching between asset and liability positions from one period to the next.

[18]The IMF *External Debt Statistics—Guide for Compilers and Users* (2013) outlines the presentation of remaining maturity data for banks, on an external debt basis only.

numerator is High Quality Liquid Assets (HQLA), defined as assets that would be liquid in times of stress and ideally, eligible collateral for central bank liquidity facilities (line 42, defined in paragraph 5.85). The denominator is net cash outflows arising from the application of supervisor-prescribed run-off rates to different categories of funding, and supervisor-specified assumptions regarding the availability of banks' funding sources in the stress scenario (line 43, defined in paragraph 5.86).[19] Annex 7.2 provides a numerical example on how to calculate the LCR for one illustrative bank.

7.72 Source data for LCR's numerator and denominator are supervisory series reported in jurisdictions that have implemented Basel III. For the compilation of the indicator, data on HQLA and total net cash outflows calculated for each reporting group should be aggregated, to derive the ratio for the whole system. Application of the LCR will be challenging in many jurisdictions because of the dearth of highly rated assets traded in liquid markets that would meet the Basel definition of HQLA. This may result in national variations in definitions of HQLA. Also, there is no certainty that the Basel prescribed run-off rates and funding assumptions are appropriate for all jurisdictions, so these elements of the LCR may also be subject to national variations. The metadata should note any differences from the Basel LCR requirement in national implementation.

Net Stable Funding Ratio

7.73 The FSI **net stable funding ratio** (NSFR) replicates the indicator introduced under Basel III. It is an indicator of banks' ability to withstand market disruption over a one-year- time horizon. The NSFR is calculated by using the amount of available stable funding (ASF) (line 44, defined in paragraph 5.87) as the numerator, and the amount of required stable funding (RSF) (line 45, defined in paragraph 5.87) as the denominator.[20] The BCBS minimum requirement is that this ratio should be equal to at least 100 percent on an ongoing basis.

7.74 ASF is the portion of capital and liabilities expected to be available to the bank to fund its operations over a one-year period. It is calculated by applying supervisor-prescribed factors, presumed to reflect the stability of liabilities, to banks' liabilities and capital. There are five buckets with stability factors ranging from 100 percent (capital and borrowings with residual maturities of more than one year) to 0 percent (for highly volatile funding such as derivative liabilities).

7.75 RSF is measured based on the broad characteristics of the liquidity risk profile of an institution's assets and off-balance-sheet exposures. It is calculated by applying supervisor-prescribed factors intended to approximate the amount of each type of asset and off-balance-sheet exposure that would have to be funded over a one-year period. The factors range from 0 percent for assets that are self-funded such as central bank reserves to 100 percent of assets encumbered for one year or more (and thus unavailable as liquid assets).

7.76 Source data for numerator and denominator are supervisory series reported in jurisdictions that have implemented Basel III. If the NSFR has only been applied to a subset of the sector, for example, large internationally active banks, the NSFR should be compiled only for that subset. For the compilation of the aggregated indicator, data on ASF and RSF calculated for each reporting group should be added, obtaining a ratio for the whole system. As with the LCR, elements of NSFR may be subject to national variations. Metadata should indicate if any elements vary from the Basel standard. Annex 7.3 contains a numerical example on how to calculate the NSFR for one institution.

Net Open Position in Foreign Exchange to Capital

7.77 The FSI **net open position in foreign exchange to capital** is intended to identify DTs' exposure to exchange rate risk relative to capital. It measures the mismatch (open position) of foreign currency asset and liability positions to assess the potential vulnerability of the DT sector to exchange rate movements.

7.78 The most common measure of foreign exchange exposure is the net open position. Even if the sector as a whole does not have an open foreign exchange position, this might not be true for individual DTs or groups of DTs.

7.79 While a matched currency position will protect a DT against loss from movements in exchange rates, it will not necessarily protect its capital adequacy

[19] See BCBC *Basel III: The Liquidity Coverage Ratio and Liquidity Risk Monitoring Tools* (2013).
[20] See BCBS *Basel III: The Net Stable Funding Ratio* (2014).

Table 7.1 Example of Measuring the Net Open Position in Foreign Exchange

Yen	Euro	Pound Sterling	U.S. Dollar	Gold	Net Open Position
+100	+200	+300	−360	−70	+670

Source: IMF Staff estimates.

ratio. Even if a DT has a portfolio of foreign currency assets and liabilities that is completely matched, its capital/asset ratio will fall if the domestic currency depreciates.

7.80 To calculate this FSI, the numerator is either the net open position in foreign exchange for on-balance-sheet items (line 55) or the preferred approach using total (including off-balance-sheet items) net open position in foreign currency (line 56). Supervisory standards generally require inclusion of off-balance sheet items in the determination of net open position, so the total (line 56) will generally be available to compilers from supervisory sources. In disseminating data, it should be made clear which measure of the net open position is being employed. The denominator is total regulatory capital (line 39). Data for the net open position in foreign exchange and total regulatory capital from each reporting group should be aggregated to estimate the indicator for the whole system.

7.81 Deposit takers' net open position should be calculated in accordance with BCBS guidance: it includes the sum of the net position of on-balance-sheet foreign currency debt instruments; net positions in financial derivatives; on-balance-sheet holdings of foreign currency equity assets; net future foreign currency income and expenses not yet accrued but already fully hedged; foreign currency guarantees and similar instruments that are certain to be called and are likely to be irrecoverable; and, depending on the national commercial accounting practice, any other item representing a profit/loss in foreign currencies of the foreign currency positions set out in a single unit of account. The *Guide* describes the sum of the first three items listed earlier as the "net open position in foreign exchange for on-balance-sheet items." The extent to which the national approach to measuring the net open position varies from BCBS guidance should be disclosed in the metadata.

7.82 As described in paragraph 5.101, foreign currency items are those payable (receivable) in a currency other than the domestic currency (foreign currency denominated) and those payable in domestic currency but with the amounts to be paid linked to a foreign currency (foreign currency linked). Although by definition, gold held by DTs is a nonfinancial asset, due to its volatility and because DTs manage it similarly to foreign currency assets, the BCBS regards gold as foreign exchange when calculating this indicator.

7.83 To calculate the overall net open position, the nominal amount of the net position for each foreign currency and gold is first converted into the reporting currency using the spot rate.[21] The overall net open position is measured then by adding the sum of the net short positions or the sum of the net long positions, whichever is greater, plus the absolute value of the net position in gold.[22] In the example of Table 7.1, the net long position in foreign exchange results from adding the higher net open position (600 = 100 in yen + 200 in euro + 300 in pound sterling) and the absolute value of the net short position in gold (70), for an overall net open position of 670.[23]

[21] Where a DT is assessing foreign exchange risk on a cross-border consolidated basis, it may be technically impractical in the case of some marginal operations to include the currency positions of a foreign branch or subsidiary of the DT. In line with BCBS guidance, in such cases, the internal limit in each currency may be used as a proxy for the positions.

[22] See BCBS, 2005, *Amendment to the Capital Accord to Incorporate Market Risk*, Basel, p. 25. This method is called the "shorthand" method by the BCBS. At supervisory discretion, DTs could use internal models.

[23] This calculation method supersedes the recommendation of the *2006 Guide*, which calculated the numerator netting positive and negative open positions in foreign currencies and gold.

ANNEX

7.1 Summary of Core Financial Soundness Indicators for Deposit Takers

Definition	Source Data	Compilation Issues
Regulatory Capital to Risk-weighted Assets		
Ratio of total regulatory capital to risk-weighted assets (RWA).	– Supervisory data on aggregated total regulatory capital and RWA.	– Regulatory capital refers to a specific definition of capital developed by the Basel Committee on Banking Supervision (BCBS), as adopted by national authorities, with or without adjustments and exercise of national discretion. – RWA measured differently depending on the version of the Basel Accord adopted by national authorities, with or without adjustments.
Tier 1 Capital to Risk-weighted Assets		
Ratio of Tier 1 capital to RWA.	– Supervisory data on aggregated Tier 1 capital and RWA.	– National treatment in Tier 1 capital of equity investments in other banks, and other elements subject to national discretion, should be described in the metadata.
Nonperforming Loan Net of Provisions to Capital		
Ratio of total nonperforming loans (NPLs) *less* provision to total regulatory capital.	– Supervisory data on NPLs and total regulatory capital. Supervisory data on specific provisions.	– National treatment may vary. BCBS transitional guidance for International Financial Reporting Standards 9 recommends that national supervisory authorities specify the allocation of expected credit loss to specific and general provisions. – In some countries, general provisions are not separately identified from specific provisions.
Common Equity Tier 1 Capital to Risk-weighted Assets		
Ratio of CET1 capital to RWA.	– Supervisory data on aggregated CET1 capital and RWA.	– New to Basel III, timing of implementation will vary across jurisdictions.
Tier 1 Capital to Total Assets		
Ratio of Tier 1 capital to total assets. For economies that have implemented Basel III: Ratio of Tier 1 capital to total exposure.	– Supervisory data on Tier 1 capital, and balance sheet data on total assets. – Average of monthly leverage ratio over the quarter.	– Same as *Tier 1 capital to RWA*. – For Basel III leverage ratio, exposure includes both on- and off-balance-sheet items.
Nonperforming Loans to Total Gross Loans		
Ratio of total NPLs to total gross loans.	– Supervisory data on NPLs and balance sheet data on total gross loans.	– Loans exclude accrued interest on NPLs.

Provisions to Nonperforming Loans		
Ratio of provisions on NPLs to total NPLs.	– Supervisory data on NPLs and balance sheet data on specific provisions.	– On specific provisions, same as in NPLs net of specific provisions to capital.
Loan Concentration by Economic Activity		
Lending to the largest three economic activities, as a proportion of their total gross loans.	– Lending by economic activity is based on the UN International Standard Industrial Classification of All Economic Activities, Rev. 4 (ISIC Rev. 4).	– Limited availability of data on loans by economic activity.
Return on Assets		
Ratio of net income to total (financial and nonfinancial) assets.	– Balance sheet data on total assets, and income and expense data on net income.	– Annualization method for income should be reported in the metadata. – Total assets are the average of stocks from the beginning of the year until the end of the reporting period. – Gains and losses on the sale of an associate or subsidiary are excluded from income.
Return on Equity		
Ratio of net income to total capital and reserves.	– Balance sheet data on equity (capital and reserves), and income and expense data on net income.	– See compilation issues for return on assets.
Interest Margin to Gross Income		
Ratio of net interest income to gross income.	– Income and expense data for both interest margin and gross income.	– Data to be accumulated from the beginning of the year until the end of the reporting period. – Interest income should not include the accrual of interest on nonperforming assets. – Gross income includes both net interest income and other gross income.
Noninterest Expenses to Gross Income		
Ratio of non-interest expenses to gross income.	– Same as above.	– Numerator and denominator data accumulated from the beginning of the year until the end of the reporting period.
Liquid Assets to Total Assets		
Ratio of liquid assets to total financial and nonfinancial assets.	– Supervisory data on liquid assets, and balance sheet data on total assets.	– National definitions of liquid assets may differ.
Liquid Assets to Short-term Liabilities and Liquidity Coverage Ratio		
Ratio of liquid assets to short-term liabilities.	– Supervisory data on short-term liabilities and liquid assets.	– Short-term liabilities are the short-term element of deposit takers' debt liabilities plus the net market value of the net financial derivatives position.
For economies that have implemented Basel III: Liquidity Coverage Ratio.	– Stock of high-quality liquid assets as numerator, and total net cash outflows as the denominator.	– National definitions of high-quality liquid assets may vary.

Net Stable Funding Ratio		
Ratio of amount of available stable funding to required stable funding.	– Supervisory data on both available stable funding and required stable funding.	– The amount of available stable funding determined by applying supervisory-specified factors to liabilities and capital. The amount of required stable funding calculated by applying supervisor-specified factors to assets.
Net Open Position in Foreign Exchange to Capital		
Ratio of net open position in foreign currency to total regulatory capital.	– Supervisory data on both net open position in foreign exchange, and total regulatory capital.	– Numerator can be only the open position for on-balance-sheet items, or also include off-balance-sheet items. – Guidance for measuring the net open position based on that recommended by the BCBS.

*Residential Real Estate Prices are addressed in Chapter 10.

ANNEX

7.2 Numerical Example of Liquidity Coverage Ratio

Liquidity Coverage Ratio	Total Unweighted Value	Total Weighted Value	Weights (percent)
HQLA	**2,150**	**1,167**	
Level 1 HQLA	700	700	100
Level 2A HQLA	1,450	467	85
Level 2B HQLA			65
Cash outflows			
Retail deposits and deposits from small business customers	**5,700**	**323**	
Stable deposits	3,550	178	5
Term retail deposits over 30 days	700	0	0
Less stable deposits	1,450	145	10
Unsecured wholesale (corporate) deposits	3,200	1,280	40
Other unsecured wholesale funding	1,370	1,370	100
Secured wholesale funding	2,050	513	25
Additional requirements, of which:			
Outflows related to derivatives and collateral			100
Committed credit and liquidity facilities			100
Other contractual funding obligations			100
Other contingent funding obligations			100
Total expected cash outflows	12,320	3,485	
Cash inflows			
Secured lending (for example, reverse repos and securities borrowing)	1,420	1,065	75
Inflows from fully performing exposures			
From retail and small business counterparties	1,370	685	50
From wholesale counterparties	1,200	900	75
Total expected cash inflows	3,990	2,614	
Total HQLA	2,150	1,167	
Total net cash outflows	8,410	871	
Liquidity coverage ratio (%)		**134%**	

Note: The sum of total expected cash inflows is 2,650, but for calculating the liquidity coverage ratio they cannot be higher than 75 percent of cash outflows. HQLA = high-quality liquid assets.

Level 2B HQLA is capped to 40 percent of HQLA.

ANNEX

7.3 Numerical Example of Net Stable Funding Ratio

	Total Unweighted Value	Total Weighted Value	Weights (percent)
Available Stable Funding			
Capital Instruments			
Tier 1 and Tier 2 capital, before the application of capital deductions and excluding the proportion of Tier 2 instruments with residual maturity of less than one year	1,890	1,890	100
Capital instruments not included above with an effective residual maturity of one year or more			100
Deposits			
"Stable" (as defined in the LCR) demand and/or term deposits from retail and small business customers	3,500	3,325	95
"Less stable" (as defined in the LCR) demand and/or term deposits from retail and small business customers	2,200	1,980	90
Unsecured funding from nonfinancial corporates	5,000	2,500	50
Unsecured funding from central banks			50
Unsecured funding from sovereigns/PSEs/MDBs/NDBs			50
Unsecured funding from other legal entities (including financial corporates and financial institutions)	510	255	50
Secured borrowings and liabilities (including secured term deposits)	250	125	50
Derivatives			
NSFR derivative liabilities (derivative liabilities less total collateral posted as variation margin on derivative liabilities)			0
Other liability and equity categories			
Deferred tax liabilities			0
Minority interest			0
Trade date payables			0
Total Available Stable Funding	**13,350**	**10,075**	
Required Stable Funding			
Coins and banknotes			0
Central bank reserves			0
Loans to financial entities secured with level 1 assets			
Securities held where the institution has an offsetting reverse repurchase transaction when the security on each transaction has the same unique identifier and such securities are reported on the balance sheet of the reporting institutions			10
Operational deposits			
Deposits held at other banks			50
Unsecured loans to financial institutions	400	400	100
Securities			
Securities eligible as Level 1 HQLA for the LCR	2,000	100	5
Securities eligible for Level 2A HQLA for the LCR	1,000	150	15

	Total Unweighted Value	Total Weighted Value	Weights (percent)
Securities eligible for Level 2B HQLA for the LCR			50
Loans			
Residential mortgages of any maturity that would qualify for the 35% or lower risk weight under the Basel II standardised approach for credit risk	2,650	1,723	65
Other loans, excluding loans to financial insitutions, with a residual maturity of one year or greater that would qualify for the 35% or lower risk weight under the Basel II standardised approach for credit risk			65
Loans to retail and small business customers (excluding residential mortgages reported above) with a residual maturity of less than one year	3,800	1,900	50
Performing loans (except loans to financial institutions and loans reported in above categories) with risk weights greater than 35 percent under the Basel II standardised approach for credit risk	7,150	6,078	85
Loans to financial entities with a residual maturity of one year or more	400	400	100
Derivatives			
Twenty percent of derivative liabilities (where derivative liabilities exceed derivative assets)			100
Fixed assets, goodwill	**550**	**550**	**100**
Total Required Stable Funding	**17,950**	**11,300**	
Net Stable Funding Ratio		**89%**	

Note: HQLA = high-quality liquid assets; LCR = liquidity coverage ratio; MDB = multilateral development banks; NDB = new development bank; PSE = public sector entity.

ANNEX

7.4 Islamic Deposit Takers and Financial Soundness Indicators

A. Introduction

7.84 This annex describes the business model of Islamic Deposit Takers (IDTs) and how IDTs' financial instruments differ from conventional ones. The annex provides guidance to map IDTs' source data to the necessary balance sheet and income statement templates used to compile FSIs for systems with Islamic banking.

B. Islamic Financial System

7.85 Islamic finance refers to the provision of financial services in accordance with Shariah principles.[24] Shariah bans interest charges (Riba),[25] products with excessive uncertainty (Gharar), gambling (Maysir), short sales, as well as financing of prohibited activities considered harmful to society. It also requires parties to honor principles of fair treatment and the sanctity of contracts. Transactions must be underpinned by real economic activities, and there must also be sharing of risks in economic transactions.

7.86 Shariah principles have existed throughout Islamic history but only began to be applied in modern Islamic financial systems in the early 1960s, with the establishment of Egypt's Mitt Ghamar Savings Bank in 1963. Since then Islamic finance expanded rapidly in several countries in terms of value, market share, geographical reach, and number of institutions. As of end December 2017, Islamic banking had become systemically important in 13 jurisdictions, including Sudan and the Islamic Republic of Iran whose entire banking systems are Islamic banking.[26]

Islamic Deposit Takers' Structures

7.87 Islamic financial systems structures can be grouped into two broad categories:[27]

(a) A dual system, where both conventional deposit-takers (DTs) and IDTs coexist. The IDTs can be stand-alone entities, subsidiaries of conventional banks, or "Islamic windows."[28] Not all dual systems allow "Islamic windows" (e.g. Bahrain and Jordan).

(b) A full-fledged Islamic financial system with virtual absence of conventional DTs, where only full-fledged IDTs are licensed to operate – for example, in the Islamic Republic of Iran and Sudan.

7.88 The principles underpinning Islamic finance generate distinct operations and risk profiles and balance sheet structures that differ in important respects from conventional banks.[29] The differences may affect the compilation and meaning of the FSIs. Although the international prudential and accounting standards that apply to conventional banks are relevant, in significant measure, for IDTs, there is a need for some adjustments to address the specific features of DTs.

7.89 Standards for the Islamic banking industry have been developed in recent years to complement international conventional banking standards. Specifically, the Islamic Financial Services Board (IFSB)[30] has established standards and principles on

[24] The industry is termed "participation finance" or "noninterest-bearing finance" in some jurisdictions.

[25] Riba is an Arabic word, which is generally translated into English as "usury" or "interest."

[26] The Islamic Financial Services Board (IFSB) defines systemically important to be 15 percent or more of total banking system assets.

[27] See the *Revised Compilation Guide on Prudential and Structural Islamic Financial Indicators*, March 2011.

[28] An Islamic Window is a department, branch, or other dedicated unit of a conventional bank that offers Islamic financial services.

[29] For an elaboration of the unique risks posed by Islamic Finance, see IMF Staff Discussion Note. Islamic Finance: Opportunities, Challenges and Policy Options SDN/15/05.

[30] The IFSB, which is based in Kuala Lumpur, Malaysia, is a global standard setting body for Islamic finance, which prepares prudential standards and guidelines for the regulation of banking, capital markets and Islamic insurance *(Takaful)*. It was officially inaugurated on November 3, 2002 and started operations on March 10, 2003.

the regulation and supervision of Islamic financial intuitions and activities, including on capital adequacy, governance, risk management and the supervisory standards to supplement the Basel Committee on Banking Supervision (BCBS). In addition, the Accounting and Auditing Organization for Islamic Financial Institutions (AAOIFI)[31] has issued standards on accounting, auditing, governance, ethics, and Shariah standards on Islamic financial institutions. In order to harmonize the compilation of FSIs, this annex builds on the standard-setting framework for conventional banks.

C. Islamic Finance Business Model

7.90 Since IDTs are prohibited to pay interest, they are funded by financial instruments without a promised ex-ante return (e.g, Qard, Wadiah, or Amanah), as well as profit sharing investment accounts (PSIA) where investors receive returns that are determined *ex post* by the profitability of the IDT or the pool of assets financed by these accounts. Correspondingly, on the asset side, IDTs do not engage in interest-based lending, but in "financing" in the form of sales, lease, profit and loss-sharing financing, and fee-based services. On the treasury side, Islamic banks are restricted or prohibited, in many jurisdictions, from undertaking certain types of derivatives; as a result derivatives and hedging instruments tend to have limited and slowly developing markets.[32]

7.91 In addition to non-remunerative contracts such as Qard, Wadiah, and Amanah, IDTs earn income by charging fees for services (Wakala), by sharing profit (Mudaraba) or by leasing (Ijarah). Under a Wakala (agency) structure, an investor receives a profit return agreed between the parties at the outset; any profit in excess of the agreed return will be kept by the agent as a performance or incentive fee. In contrast, under a Mudaraba structure, profit/loss is divided between the investor and the bank according to pre-agreed ratios.

[31]The AAOIFI is a standard setting body for Islamic finance, which prepares accounting, auditing, and *Shariah* standards. It was established in 1991 and is based in Manama, Bahrain.

[32]The permissibility of Islamic banks to conduct derivatives transaction is subject to the Shariah rulings in a particular jurisdiction. In some jurisdictions it is permitted for banks to use derivatives transactions for hedging purposes. The derivatives are generally structured using Tawarruq and other parallel contracts.

7.92 Under profit and loss sharing (PLS) arrangements, the resources of the IDTs and investors are often pooled to undertake commercial ventures, and the total returns are shared among the IDTs and the investors based on a predetermined profit sharing arrangement. Profits earned could be disbursed during the life of the venture or upon its conclusion. These arrangements can also be generated by issuing securities, called PLS certificates (often classified as "other Shariah-compliant securities" – that is 'other' than Sukuk), that do not provide for either capital certainty or pre-fixed positive returns.

7.93 Profit and loss sharing activities are a distinguishing feature of the use of funds by IDTs, as the basis of Islamic finance is risk-sharing between the parties in an underlying asset-based transaction. IDTs use various Shariah compliant contracts (mode of finance or instrument) or, sometimes combination of contracts, when offering a spectrum of financial structures. The three broad modes of finance are:

(a) **Sale-based contracts**: IDTs provide immediate delivery of the goods or services sought by the customers in exchange for the customers promising to make a series of deferred payments to the IDTs equal to the cost of the goods or services plus a markup;

(b) **Lease-based contracts:** IDTs purchase assets and lease them to the customers in return for instalments that reflect the cost of holding and maintaining the assets; and

(c) **Equity-based or PLS contracts (Mudaraba and Musharaka)**: IDTs provide funds to an enterprise in return for a share of the profits generated by these PLS arrangements. Mudaraba contracts will be operated by the enterprise with remuneration of the IDT based on pre-agreed distributions of profits or losses, whereas Musharaka contracts a more fully partnership arrangements in which the IDT can participate in the enterprise's decision making.

7.94 The boxes 7.3. and 7.4. present a comprehensive list of Islamic financial instruments[33] and discuss their classification in the balance sheets and income

[33]The annex only discusses the main Islamic financial instruments and for FSI compilation.

statements of IDTs relative to those of conventional deposit takers.

D. The Capital Adequacy Requirements for Islamic Deposit Takers[34]

7.95 The computation of capital adequacy ratios (CAR) is similar to the BCBS formulae, but there are important variations in the recognition of eligible capital, risk-weighted assets, and the treatment of PSIA. In line with the global standard, the IFSB has provided more comprehensive guidance.

Eligible Capital

7.96 The definition of regulatory eligible capital to be used as the numerator in calculating the CAR is defined in Chapter 5. The PSIA are analogous to deposits and they should not be included in capital because they do not meet the requirement to constitute additional Capital (Tier 2).[35] The investment equalization reserves (IRR) and a portion of the profit equalization reserves (PER) that belong to the equity of investment account holders (IAH) are not part of the capital of the IDTs.[36] As the purpose of a PER is to smooth the profit payouts and not to cover losses, any portion of a PER that is part of the IDTs reserves should also not be treated as part of the regulatory capital of the IDTs.

7.97 Some types of Sukuk might qualify for inclusion in regulatory capital. Subject to Shariah approval, Musharaka Sukuk may be included as Additional Tier 1 if they meet loss-absorbency requirements. Also, Mudaraba or Wakala Sukuk may qualify as Tier 2 capital, if the underlying assets are convertible into common equity at the point of non-viability or insolvency.

[34]This section draws on Chapter 6 of the *Revised Compilation Guide on Prudential and Structural Islamic Financial Indicators*, March 2011, and on *IFSB-15: Revised CAS for institutions offering Islamic financial services (excluding Islamic insurance (Takaful) institutions and Islamic collective investment scheme, December 2013.*

[35]The requirements are loss absorbency, issuance process and procedure, maturity and callable option, distribution of profits, and unsecured in nature.

[36]Profit equalization reserves (PER) are allocated from operating income for smoothing returns to funders, prior to deducting the Mudarib's (IDT's) share. Investment risk reserves (IRR) are set aside from the income share of investment account holders as a cushion for future losses that they may incur.

Risk-weighted Assets

7.98 Islamic financial instruments are asset-based (Murabaha, Salam, and Istisna'a), equity-based (Musharaka and Mudaraba), leasing-based (Ijara), or Sukuk. The asset-based instruments bear market risk on the underlying assets and credit risk in respect to the counterparties. The risk exposure of an IDT transforms from market risk to credit risk when an asset is sold to its customer (Murabaha) as the price risk of holding that asset ceases and is replaced by credit risk. Risk-weighting requirements for equity-based instruments are based on credit risk requirements if they are loan-like instruments and market risk requirements if they are equity-like instruments. Sukuk may also be subject to differing approaches to risk-weighting. Sukuk held in the trading book are subject to credit and market-risk weighting requirements aligned with those for conventional instruments. For the Sukuk held in the banking book, the supervisory authorities have discretion to allow the IDTs that operate within their jurisdictions to specify the internal-rating based measurement approach to be used.

Profit Sharing Investment Accounts Treatment

7.99 A major difference between IDTs and conventional DTs relates to PSIA loss absorbency. Unless the IDT is guilty of misconduct or negligence, IAH are expected to bear the loss of earnings or investments that were made with their funds, but the IDT bears the costs of operations and thus might experience a net profit or loss. For the calculation of CAR, the IFSB standard provides two formulas: standard and discretionary. In the standard formula, the risk-weighted assets (RWA) exclude the assets financed by PSIA. The second formula, referred to as the supervisory discretionary formula, is designed to account for displaced commercial risk (DCR) as determined at the supervisor's discretion. The DCR is a risk specific to the Islamic banking that rises when an IDT is under pressure to pay its IAHs a rate of return higher than would be payable under the "actual' terms of the investment contact in order to remain competitive relative to other banks and thus retain customers. The IDTs have discretion to set aside some portion of the profits under special types of reserve, namely, PER

Box 7.3 Source of Funds

Type of Islamic financial instrument	Description	Equivalent classification in the balance sheet	Classification of the associated expense in the income statement[1]
Qard, Wadiah or Amanah[2]	Deposits can be withdrawn on demand, at par, without penalty or restriction, and are generally usable for making payments by check, draft, giro order, or other direct payment facilities. These types of deposits are not linked to any profit-making ventures and are not part of the profit and loss sharing schemes, hence IDTs have the flexibility to use the funds but are required to guarantee the nominal value of the deposits. With the foregoing characteristics, these deposits usually offer no (or very small) returns to the depositors on the basis of gift (*hibah*) and on the IDT's discretion.[3]	*Transferable deposits/ Other deposits.*	L.6
Mudaraba (also known as profit sharing investment account).	Is a contract between an investor and an IDT that, as a pass-through partner, invests the deposits in commercial ventures. Profit sharing of the venture is pre-determined based on the risk and return, and the IDT and investors share any profit generated from the venture. A Mudaraba can be entered into for a single investment or on a continuing basis with the IDT acting as a fiduciary. There are two types of Mudaraba investment accounts per AAOIFI FAS No. 27 (Investments Accounts), namely Unrestricted Mudaraba and Restricted Mudaraba.		
	Restricted Mudaraba is where an investor restricts the manner as to where, how, and for what purpose the funds are invested. No mixing of funds is allowed from other sources to ensure proper management and accountability of the funds. The IDT manages the Restricted Mudaraba either as Mudarib[4] or as an agent for a fixed fee and not participate in the investment results. A separate disclosure (off balance sheet) in the form of Statement of Restricted Mudaraba is required to be kept by the IDTs.	Off-balance sheet (In some jurisdictions, restricted Mudaraba are effectively controlled by the IDTs and thus are recorded on-balance sheet).	L.6
	Unrestricted Mudaraba is where the investor fully authorizes an IDT to invest the funds without restrictions as to where, how, and for what purpose the funds should be invested as long as it is deemed appropriate. Mixing of funds from other sources (including shareholders' funds) is permitted and separate disclosure in the financial statement is therefore required. Unrestricted Mudaraba can be divided into the following types:		
	• Mudaraba accepted without time frame (not fixed), hence the investors are free to withdraw their money at any time. This type of Unrestricted Mudaraba is similar to those of savings deposits at conventional financial institutions and is classified as *Other deposits;*	Unrestricted Mudaraba – *Other deposits*	L.2
	• Mudaraba accepted for a fixed period that provides an opportunity for IDTs to invest in more profitable long-term projects. This type of Unrestricted Mudaraba is similar to time deposits at conventional financial institutions and usually generates higher profits in comparison to the former type. For compiling FSIs, this type of Unrestricted Mudaraba is classified as *Other deposits*; and	Unrestricted Mudaraba – *Other deposits*	L.2
	• Mudaraba accepted for fixed terms and arranged through negotiable instruments (called investment deposit certificates or Mudaraba certificates). This type of Unrestricted Mudaraba has characteristics similar to those of debt securities and is classified as a *Debt security* or as *Equity* if part of capital base.	*Debt security or Equity*	L.2 if *Debt security* or L.12 if *Equity*

Box 7.3 Source of Funds *(concluded)*

Participation term certificates	Long-term investment instruments that entitle the holder to a share of a corporation's profit. These certificates should be classified as *Other deposits* if the certificates are treated as debt liability of an IDT, and as *Equity* if part of the capital base.	*Other deposits or Equity*	L.2 *if Other deposits* or L.12 if *Equity*
Profit and loss sharing certificates and investment deposit certificates, such as Mudaraba certificates	Investors' deposits that somewhat resemble shares in a company but do not provide a claim on the residual value of the IDT or participation in its governance. These instruments should be classified as *Other deposits*. If Mudaraba certificates are negotiable, they should be classified as a *Debt security*.	*Other deposits or Debt security*	L.2
Sukuk	Investment certificates issued by IDTs to obtain funding, Sukuk (plural of sakk, know as Islamic bonds) are certificates, with each sakk representing a proportional undivided ownership right in tangible and intangible assets, monetary assets, usufruct, services, debts or a pool of predominantly tangible assets, or a business venture (such as Mudaraba or Musharaka). These assets, which must be clearly identifiable, may be in a specific project or investment activity in accordance with Shariah rules and principles. Issuance of Sukuk, including the utilisation of funds raised through such issuance, should not involve any elements of interest (Riba), excessive uncertainty (Gharar), or activities prohibited by Shariah. The following three types of Sukuk contracts are the most prominent: (i) Sukuk Ijarah; (ii) Sukuk Musharaka; and (iii) Sukuk Murabaha, which are all negotiable instruments, except that Sukuk Murabaha becomes negotiable only when certain conditions are met. In recent years, Sukuk have become very popular as an alternative mean of raising funds for government through sovereign issues. A distinguishing feature of Sukuk is that the source of payments comes from either the revenues generated by the underlying assets (asset-backed Sukuk) or the originator/obligors' cash flows (asset-based Sukuk). Hence Sukuk holders claim an undivided beneficial ownership in the underlying assets. Governments, central banks, financial or nonfinancial corporations, and supranational organizations can issue Sukuk. For the purpose of compiling FSIs, Sukuk should be classified as debt securities, unless the owner of the security has a claim on the residual value of the issuing entity and thus it should be classified as *Equity*. For further details on the classification of Sukuk by type of underlying contract, see Annex 3 in the *Handbook on Securities Statistics*.	*Debt security or Equity*	L.2 if *Debt security* or L.12 if *Equity*
Wakalah	The IDT acts as an agent for investment of depositor's funds, usually against an agreed fee (as an absolute or percentage of a certain amount). Wakala should be recorded as off-balance sheet items if the agent does not bear the risk and funds raised are not comingled with other funds.	Off-balance sheet	L.6

Source: IMF staff estimates.

Note: AAOIFI FAS = Accounting and Auditing Organization for Islamic Financial Institution Financial Accounting Standard; IDT = international development targets; IFI = international financial institutions.

1 The line items correspond to the Table 5.1 in Chapter 5.

2 In some jurisdictions, this type of deposits is part of IDTs general pool.

3 The proposed classification is consistent with the current position of Task Force of the Islamic Financial Services Board (IFSB) on the Prudential and Structural Islamic Financial Indicators (PSIFIs). However, the classification of the Hibah under L.2 or L.6 depends on the underlying attributes of the Hibah whether it is paid on a regular and/or a nonvoluntary basis (L.2) or not (L.6).

4 A Mudarib is the party in the Mudaraba contract who provides the expertise to manage the capital with the purpose of earning profit that will be shared with the fund provider per a mutually agreed proportion

Box 7.4 Uses of Funds

Type of Islamic financial instrument	Description	Equivalent classification in the balance sheet	Classification of the associated income in the income statement[1]
Qard	A non-remunerative financing that is offered to needy individuals or for some social purpose. Qard financing is usually extended on a goodwill basis, and the debtor is required to repay only the principal amount of the financing. As a separate transaction, the debtor may, however, at his or her discretion, pay Hibah - an extra amount beyond the principal of the financing (without an obligation to pay it) as a token of appreciation to the creditor.	*Loan*	L.1
Murabaha	Per AAOIFI FAS No. 2 (Murabaha and Murabaha to the Purchase Orderer), is defined as a sale of goods at cost plus an agreed profit margin. A Murabaha sale in the above context means the selling of a product owned by the seller at the time of entering into a contract. In a Murabaha contract, an IDT purchases goods upon the request of a client, who makes deferred payments that cover costs and an agreed-upon profit margin for the IDT. The IDT handles payments to the supplier including direct expenses incurred (delivery, insurance, storage, fees for letter of credit, etc.). Operating expenses of the IDT are not included. Under Murabaha contracts, disclosure of cost of the underlying goods is necessary. Murabaha contracts resemble collateralized loans of conventional financial institutions, in which the underlying goods, such as properties or automobiles, are registered under the customer's name and are used as collateral. In compiling FSIs, Murabaha should be classified as loans.	*Loans*	L.1
Bai Muajjal	A type of financing provided by an IDT to its client by supplying desired commodities or services with deferred payments. In compiling FSIs, a Bai Muajjal is classified as a *Loan* as the supplied commodities or services are from third parties.	*Loan*	L.1
Bai Salam	A financing, per AAOIFI FAS No. 7 (Salam and Parallel Salam), is a short-term agreement in which an IDT makes full prepayments (spot payment) for future (deferred) delivery of a specified quantity of goods on a specified date. In practice, farmers usually need money to purchase seeds and fertilizers. An IDT and farmers in this case may engage in a Bai Salam contract, in which farmers agree to sell their crops to the IDT prior to harvesting. Generally, the agreed spot price is less than the future price of the commodities, in order for the IDT to make profits. A Bai Salam should be classified as a *Loan* given that the produced crops are not for the IDT's own use.	*Loan*	L.1
Istisna'a	Per AAOIFI FAS No. 10 (Istisna'a and Parallel Istisna'a), is a partnership between an IDT and an enterprise, usually manufacturer or construction company, in which the IDT places an order and provides financing to the enterprise to manufacture/construct and or supply certain goods or buildings. Upon or before the delivery of the order, IDTs usually enter into a contract with another party (the ultimate purchaser) at a price higher than the original contract of the Istisna'a, thus generating profits for the IDT. As a matter of practice, an Istisna'a is classified as a *Loan*, given that the produced goods or constructed buildings are not for the IDT's own use, but for the ultimate purchaser. If the goods or buildings are for the IDT's own use, an Istisna'a is classified as a trade credit and advance within *Other accounts receivables*.	*Loan/Other accounts receivables*	L.1

Box 7.4. Uses of Funds *(concluded)*

Ijarah	A lease-purchase contract in which an IDT purchases capital equipment or property and leases it to an enterprise. The IDT may either rent the equipment or receive a share of the profits earned through its use. According to AAOIFI FAS No. 8 (Ijarah and Ijarah Muntahia Bittamleek), there are two types of Ijarah, namely Operating Ijarah and Financing Ijarah (Ijarah Muntahia Bittamleek or Ijarah Wa Iktina). Under Operating Ijarah the title for the underlying asset is not transferred to the client (lessee), and ownership risks of the assets are borne by the IDT; expenses related to the use of the assets are the responsibility of the client. A Financing Ijarah involves two contracts (i.e., a lease over the lease period and transfer of ownership at the end of the contract). For compiling FSIs, an Operating Ijarah should be treated in the same way as a conventional operating lease. Financing Ijarah, which resembles conventional financial lease, should be classified as a *Loan*.	Operating lease Financing lease—*Loan*	L.4 L.1
Musharaka	Per AAOIFI FAS No. 4 (Musharaka financing), Musharaka is a partnership between an IDT and an enterprise in which both parties contribute to the capital (rab al maal) of partnership. In a Musharaka partnership, the IDT and client agree to share any profits generated from the venture according to the pre-agreed ratio; a loss is shared according to the ratio of contribution. Musharaka financing can be structured in two possible ways according to Islamic scholars: (i) *Musharaka* financing offered as a loan where the Islamic Financial Institution provides financing in the form of working capital to an entity but does not have a claim on the residual value of the debtor entity; and (ii) *Musharaka* financing offered as equity participation. In the context of compiling FSIs, a Musharaka financing is classified as a *Loan*, provided the IDT does not acquire a claim on the residual value of the enterprise.	*Loan/Equity*	L.1
Mudaraba	Per AAOIFI FAS No. 3 (Mudaraba Financing), Mudaraba is a partnership between an IDT and a client in which the IDT provides capital (rab al maal) and the client provides skillful labor. Mudaraba financing is a type of partnership whereby skill and money are brought together to conduct business. Profits generated from the business are shared according to the agreement, while losses are borne fully by the IDT as the capital provider, except when losses were due to misconduct, negligence or violation of the agreed conditions by the client. In the context of compiling FSIs, a Mudaraba financing is classified as a *Loan*. Although Mudaraba financing has features of *Equity*, it has a fixed-term nature and therefore represents a fixed-term claim on the client rather than a claim on any residual value.	*Loan*	L.1
Tawarruq (commodity Murabaha)[2]	A financial instrument in which a buyer purchases a commodity from an IDT on a deferred payment basis, and the buyer sells the same commodity to a third party on a spot payment basis. The use of Tawarruq by IDTs involves an extension of Murabaha whereby the IDT arranges for the sale of the good. The buyer basically borrows the cash needed to make the initial purchase. Later, when he secures the cash from the second transaction, the buyer pays the original seller the installment or lump sum payment he owes (which is cost plus markup, or Murabaha). Tawarruq is classified as a *Loan*.	*Loan*	L.1

Source: IMF staff.

Note: AAOIFI FAS = Accounting and Auditing Organization for Islamic Financial Institution Financial Accounting Standards; IDT = international development targets; IFI = international financial institutions.

[1] The line items correspond to the Table 5.1 in Chapter V.

[2] Tawarruq is used on both sides of the IDT balance sheet, for financing and deposits addressing various liquidity needs of the transacting parties. On the deposit side Islamic banks use Commodity Murabaha as a deposit mobilizing fund, where the client has excess liquidity and is looking for fixed return on it. In this case the client firstly buys a commodity and sells it to the IDTs on deferred basis. Effectively the client made a placement that resembles a fixed income deposit since he will be now receiving a fixed return. This structure in also known as a Reverse Tawarruq.

to mitigate the DCR. Hence, instead of excluding all the funds that belong to the PSIA from RWA, only a portion adjusted for the DCR is excluded because it can be borne by the IDT.[37] In some jurisdictions, the adjustment is made simply on the expectation that the IDT should carry greater amounts of capital as a protection for depositors. This portion of RWA is arbitrarily denoted by the Greek letter α "alpha". The quantification and use of this alpha parameter in the CAR calculation is subject to supervisory discretion and differs considerably across jurisdictions.

7.100 Due to the national discretion in the various implementation of Basel standards, the compilers will rely on national standards for the FSIs computation and should document in the metadata any departures. At time of publication, Islamic banks in various jurisdictions operate under Basel I, Basel II, or Basel III – the standard used should always be described in metadata.

E. Financial Soundness Indicators for Islamic Deposit Takers

7.101 The limited availability of statistical information on the Islamic financial services industry worldwide has hindered accurate and comprehensive analysis and assessment of developments in the industry. More specifically, the lack of cross-country historical data with sufficiently long time-series has been identified as one of the major challenges faced by the IFSB in developing its international prudential standards.

7.102 For this reason, the IFSB has developed FSI equivalents for IDTs—Prudential and Structural Islamic Financial Indicators (PSIFIs).[38] The *PSIFI Compilation Guide* was issued in 2008 and revised in March 2011. Furthermore, in November 2014 a supplement for the *PSIFI Compilation Guide* was issued to update the list of indicators to be compiled by IDTs under the IFSB's project on the implementation of PSIFIs.

7.103 The changes in the list of PSIFIs reflect lessons learned during the global financial crisis that began in 2007, revisions to global regulatory framework in Basel III and corresponding IFSB standards, modifications to the list of IMF's FSIs, proposals by the Statistical, Economic, and Social Research and Training Centre for Islamic Countries (SESRIC), and experiences of the IFSB and IMF in working with countries to compile and disseminate soundness indicators.

7.104 The prudential indicators are divided into core indicators and additional indicators. The core indicators, which closely correspond to the Core FSIs specified in the *Guide*, are commonly used banking indicators, and are analyzed in the IFSB's annual *Islamic Financial Services Industry Stability Report*.[39] The set of core indicators includes series related to Basel III items or which have demonstrated importance during the crisis. The structural indicators are indications of the size and structure of the Islamic banking sector. The IFSB recommended that all countries with Islamic banking should compile separate sets of prudential and structural indicators for stand-alone IDTs and Islamic windows of conventional DTs because of differences in their capital structure and liquidity arrangements. All the indicators remain the same for IDTs and Islamic windows except for some difference in the structural indicators.

F. Mapping Islamic Deposit Takers' Financial Statements[40]

7.105 This section provides guidance on how to map the financial information from the IDTs income statement, balance sheet, and other related information to the FSI's financial statements for deposit takers (income statement, balance sheet, and memorandum series) as recommended in this *Guide*.

7.106 Due to differences in business models across IDTs and DTs, some core FSIs for DTs, such as the margin between interest receipts and payments income and expense, do not apply to IDTs. However, for countries with dual DT systems, in order to compile the system's FSIs, there is a need to map the Islamic

[37] IFSB Guidance Note 15 provides more details.

[38] See the *Revised Compilation Guide on Prudential and Structural Islamic Financial Indicators*, March 2011.

[39] The IFSB also developed a series of structural indicators for IDTs to capture information on features of Islamic banking sectors not otherwise available; number of institutions, number of windows, total assets, total revenues, earnings, financing by type of Islamic financial instrument, assets of systemically important IDTs, etc.

[40] This section draws on Chapter 4 of the *Revised Compilation Guide on Prudential and Structural Islamic Financial Indicators*, March 2011.

financial instruments to the conventional ones. For example, the profits generated from loan and deposit-like instruments and Shariah-compliant securities, will be analogous to interest income/expense.

7.107 The reporting of the financial statements and the FSIs should be based on the table 5.1 of Chapter 5 which is intended to provide guidance to countries in preparing and producing the aggregated financial statements and the memorandum series for the whole deposit takers sector that encompass both IDTs and DTs. To ensure cross-country comparability Table 7.1 shows a suggested mapping of Islamic instruments to the required line items of the Table 5.1. These suggested items in *italic format* as mentioned in Table 7.1 are not to be reported but are shown as a guidance for compilers.

7.108 The mapping set out in the Table 7.1. specifies the data sources to draw from for the compilation of the full range of FSIs in this *Guide*. One key challenge is the classification of the PER and IRR. Unlike conventional banks, the IDTs undertake some risk-sharing activities with their fund providers and/or depositors. For harmonizing the FSIs compilation, it is necessary to consider the specificities of the Islamic finance and to classify the PER and IRR to best equivalent financial instruments. For the FSIs compilation, these instruments should be associated with their PSIA, under deposits.

7.109 One key issue in the compilation of FSIs for IDT is how to classify the returns on deposits/financing, financial lease, and Islamic bonds (Sukuk) as interest. In this section, as Islamic rules and principles (Sharia), prohibits usurious payment (riba), including predetermined returns on borrowed funds. Therefore, for FSI purposes, the term adopted to distinguish the Islamic return from conventional interest is *"financing and investment income."*[41]

7.110 Some of the series required to calculate the FSIs are not directly available from the financial statements. They are included as memorandum items to the financial statements. The supervisory-based items for the IDTs series are different from those of conventional banks, regarding the CAR. Although the Basel Capital Accord was not intended for IDTs, the IFSB developed a parallel Capital Adequacy Standard (CAS) for IDTs. Table 7.1 highlights selected memorandum series that require additional guidance information for compiling these series for the IDTs.

[41] Under the auspices of the Inter Secretariat Working Group on National Accounts (ISWGNA) work is ongoing to reconcile the classification of the property income associated with Islamic financial instruments as interest within the System of National Accounts (SNA) and the prohibition of interest in the Shariah law.

Table 7A.1 Islamic Deposit Taker

Income and Expense Statement[1,2]

1. Financing and investment income
   i. Gross financing and investment income
      o/w: *sale-based (Murabaha, Bai Muajjal, Bai salam, Istina'a)*
      o/w: *lease-based (Ijarah Muntahia bettamleek)*
      o/w: *equity-based (Musharaka)*
      Investments on sharia-compliant securities[3]
      o/w Sukuk
   ii. *Less* Provisions for accrued profit on nonperforming assets
2. Expenses accrued on funding and investment
   o/w: share of income attributable to on-balance sheet PSIA.
   o/w: share of income taken as PER.
   o/w: expense on Shariah-compliant securities issues[3]
3. *Net financing and investment income* (= 1 minus 2)
4. Other income
   i. Fees and commissions receivables
      o/w: bank's income for Wakala contract.
   ii. Gains or losses on financial Shariah compliant instruments
   iii. Prorated earnings
   iv. Other income
      o/w: rents from Ijarah
      o/w: bank's income as Mudarib from off-balance sheet RPSIAs
5. Gross income (= 3 + 4)
6. Expenses not related to funding and investment
   i. Personnel cost
   ii. Other expenses
      o/w: depreciation
      o/w: hibah
7. Provisions (net)
   i. Provision on financing, and receivable
   ii. Other financial asset provisions
   iii. Provision on non-performing investment
8. Net income (before taxes) (= 5 – (6 + 7))
9. Income tax
10. Net income after tax (= 8 – 9)[4]
11. Other comprehensive income (loss) net of tax
12. Dividends payable on Shariah compliant instruments
13. Retained earnings (= 10 – 12)

Balance Sheet[1,2]

14. ***Total assets (= 15+16 = 23+31)***
15. *Nonfinancial Assets*
    o/w: fixed assets held against Ijarah contracts
16. Financial assets (= 17 through 22)
17. Currency and deposits
    o/w: Wadiah or Amanah
    o/w: PSIA
18. Financing (after specific provisions)
    i. Gross financing (18.i – 18.ii)
       i.i. Interbank financing
          i.i.i. Resident
          i.i.ii. Nonresident
       i.ii. Noninterbank financing
          i.ii.i. Central bank
          i.ii.ii. General government
          i.ii.iii. Other financial corporations
    o/w: sale-based (Murabaha, Bai Muajjal, Bai salam, Istina'a)
    o/w: lease-based (Ijarah Muntahia bettamleek)
    o/w: equity-based or PLS contracts (Musharaka, Mudaraba)
          i.ii.iv. Nonfinancial corporations
             (same items as reported for other financial corporations)
          i.ii.v. Other domestic sectors
             (same items as reported for other financial corporations)
          i.ii.vi. Nonresidents
    ii. Specific provisions
       (same items as reported for other financial corporations)
19. Debt securities
    i. *o/w:* Sukuk holding
    ii. *o/w:* Participation term certificates
20. Equity and investment fund shares
21. Financial derivatives
22. Other financial assets
23. Liabilities (= 28+ 29 + 30)
24. Currency and deposits
    i. Customer deposits
       o/w: Qard, Wadiah and Amanah,
       o/w: PSIA
    ii. Interbank deposits
       ii.i. Resident
          (same items as reported for customer deposits)
       ii.ii. Nonresident
          (same items as reported for customer deposits)
    iii. Other currency and deposits
       (same items as reported for customer deposits)
25. Financing
    o/w: Tawarruq/commodity murabaha
    o/w: Other funding
26. Debt securities
    o/w: Sukuk issuances
    o/w: Participation term certificates
27. Other liabilities
28. Debt (=24+25+26+27)
29. Financial derivatives and employee stock options
30. General and other provisions
31. Capital and reserves
    o/w PER attributable to owner's equity
32. Balance sheet total (=23+31 =14)

Table 7A.1 Islamic Deposit Taker *(concluded)*

Memorandum Series for Balance Sheet IDTs[1,5]
Other series required to calculate FSIs
Supervisory-based series
33. Tier 1 capital less corresponding supervisory deductions
Tier 1 capital is defined as mentioned in Chapter 5.
34. Common Equity Tier 1 (CET1) capital less corresponding supervisory deductions
PSIA and PER allocated to shareholders are excluded.
35. Additional Tier 1 (AT1) capital less corresponding supervisory deductions
Musharaka Sukuk may be included.
36. Tier 2 capital less corresponding supervisory deductions
Mudaraba or Wakala Sukuk may be included in Tier 2.
40. Risk-weighted assets
The risk-weights should be adjusted for the assets funded by PSIA.

Source: IMF staff.

Note: IRR = investment risk reserve; PER = profit equalization reserve; PSIA = profit sharing investment accounts.

1 The purpose of this Table is to provide guidance for national compilers in preparing for the IDTs the Table 5.1 of Chapter 5.

2 The line-item series in this table are equivalent to those reported in the Table 5.1 of Chapter 5 which are required to be reported by the national compilers.

3 The details of the calculation are in Annex 5.2 of the *Monetary and Financial Statistics Manual and Compilation Guide*.

4 In some jurisdictions, net income should also exclude Zakah payment, which is obligatory payment made under Shariah on certain kinds of property and used for charitable and religious purposes. Its treatment in the financial statements should be analogous to tax.

5 Only selected memorandum series are shown from Table 5.1 Chapter 5 that require additional guidance for IDTs.

8 Specification of Additional Financial Soundness Indicators for Deposit Takers

I. Introduction

8.1 This chapter brings together the concepts and definitions previously set out—including accounting principles, underlying series, and calculation methods—to explain how additional FSIs for deposit takers (DTs) are to be calculated. Unless otherwise stated, all the "lines" mentioned in this chapter refer to Table 5.1.

8.2 Beyond the core FSIs for DTs discussed in Chapter 7, an additional set of indicators is recommended to provide additional information on deposit takers' financial health. Specifically, 12 additional FSIs for DTs are recommended by the *Guide*, which are listed in Table 1.1 and discussed in the rest of this chapter. Annex 8.1 summarizes the concepts, calculation methods, source data, and compilation issues for these additional FSIs for DTs.

II. Additional FSIs for DTs

Large Exposures to Capital

8.3 The FSI **Large exposures to capital** is intended to identify vulnerabilities arising from the concentration of credit risk. The assessment of large exposures aims at capturing the potential negative impact on financial institutions' capital if a few counterparties experience difficulties in servicing their obligations. As recognized by the Basel Committee on Banking Supervision (BCBS), "Banks did not always consistently measure, aggregate and control exposures to single counterparties or to groups of connected counterparties across their books and operations."[1]

8.4 This FSI is calculated by taking the value of large exposures (line 46) as the numerator, and Tier 1 capital (line 33) as the denominator. *Large exposures* refer to one or more credit exposures[2] to the same counterparty or group of connected counterparties that exceed a specified percentage of the DT's capital. The *Guide* recommendations are based on BCBS guidance, but national implementation may vary. Supervisory data will be the source for this FSI, and any national variations from the BCBS framework outlined further should be disclosed in the metadata.

8.5 The BCBS defines a large exposure as being equal to or larger than 10 percent of its Tier 1 capital as defined in Basel III.[3] The BCBS imposes an exposure limit of 25 percent of Tier 1 capital to a single counterparty or group of connected counterparties.

8.6 When calculating the aggregated FSI for the whole DT sector, the numerator is the sum of the large exposures after application of the eligible credit risk mitigation techniques of each DT group within the reporting population, while the denominator is the aggregated Tier 1 capital of all reporting DT groups. Data on large exposures should be available from supervisory sources. The BCBS stresses the need for banks to have methodologies in place for the measurement and control of large exposures, including the need for appropriate levels of large exposure limits, with special attention paid to connected lending.[4] Any national variance from the BCBS guidance with respect to definition of large exposures should be noted in the metadata.

Geographical Distribution of Loans to Total Gross Loans

8.7 The FSI **Geographical distribution of loans to total gross loans** provides information on the

[1] BCBS, *Supervisory Framework for Measuring and Controlling Large Exposures*, Basel, 2014, page 1.

[2] Net of specific provisions.

[3] See BCBS, *Supervisory Framework for Measuring and Controlling Large Exposures*, Basel, 2014, page 4. The BCBS establishes precise rules on how to measure different types of exposures, including its reduction via credit risk mitigation techniques. Banks have to report their largest 20 exposures.

[4] See BCBS, *Basel III: A Global Regulatory Framework for More Resilient Banks and Banking Systems*, Basel, 2011, paragraph 119.

geographical distribution of gross loans, by regional grouping of countries. It allows the monitoring of credit risk arising from exposures to a group of countries. Moreover, this FSI can help in assessing the impact of adverse events in these countries on the domestic financial system. If lending to any individual country or sub-region is particularly significant, further disaggregation—and identification of the country or sub-region—is welcome.[5]

8.8 The numerator of this FSI are loans to the different geographical regions, while the denominator is total gross loans. The loans in the numerator are gross loans to regional grouping of countries.

8.9 Information on total loans is available from the DTs' balance sheet, as described in paragraph 7.38. Gross loans (line 18.i of Table 5.1) are defined in paragraphs 5.41 to 5.43. Supervisory sources might have available information on the geographic distribution of loans (e.g., BIS's consolidated international banking statistics). Otherwise, additional data might be requested. In recording the geographic distribution of loans, claims are attributed to economies on the basis of the residency of the entity on which DTs have claims. Residency is based on the concept of economic territory, which is not always based strictly on physical or political borders (see paragraph 2.11). The suggested regional grouping of countries of Box 8.1 is based on the classification provided in the IMF's *World Economic Outlook*. Details of the countries included in each group of the *World Economic Outlook* are presented in Annex 8.2.

8.10 For *cross-border* consolidated data, lending is attributed based on the residence of the domestic reporting entity. Therefore, lending by any foreign branches or DT subsidiaries of the reporting group to residents of the local economy where they are located (including any local-currency-denominated lending) is classified as lending to nonresidents and allocated to the appropriate region of the world. Lending to residents of the economy for which the FSI data are being compiled is classified as lending to the domestic economy. For data compiled on a *domestic location* consolidation basis, any lending among DTs in the reporting population that are part of the same group should be excluded, but loans to DT branches and subsidiaries abroad are included in the data as lending to nonresidents.

Gross Asset Positions in Financial Derivatives to Capital

8.11 The FSI **Gross asset positions in financial derivatives to capital** is intended to gauge the exposure of DTs' asset positions in financial derivatives relative to capital. While net positions may be more readily available, and there are legitimate reasons to focus attention on them as a risk management tool, gross positions provide a more comparable metric across countries, markets, and products. Moreover, counterparty risk is particularly relevant in the financial derivative markets, and thus it is important to monitor the magnitude of the gross positions.

8.12 The gross asset position is calculated by using the market value of financial derivative assets (line 21 in Table 5.1) as the numerator and capital as the denominator. Capital is measured as total regulatory capital (line 39). Financial derivatives are defined in paragraphs 5.55–5.65.

8.13 Data on the market value position of financial derivative assets should be available from accounting records as well as supervisory sources. The coverage of financial derivatives includes forwards, futures, options and swaps of currency or interest rates, and instruments such as swaptions, among others, combining multiple derivative elements. Regarding capital, sources of data are discussed in 7.9–7.12.

Gross Liability Positions in Financial Derivatives to Capital

8.14 The FSI **Gross liability positions in financial derivatives to capital** is intended to gauge the exposure of DT's liability positions in financial derivatives relative to capital. It is the mirror indicator of the previous FSI, in this case measuring the liability exposure. In this regard, all the considerations on data sources and issues for compilers presented in the previous section also apply for this indicator.

[5] The Bank for International Settlements (BIS) collects and publishes international banking statistics on both a locational (residency) and consolidated basis for a group of economies with significant international banking activities. The definitions in the *Guide* are broadly consistent with those of the BIS. For countries compiling the BIS series "summary of foreign claims (immediate counterparty basis) by nationality of reporting bank," such data serve the purpose of this FSI. Annex 8.2 maps countries, which are the basis of the BIS series, to the regional groupings used for this FSI (see Box 8.1).

Box 8.1 Regional Grouping of Countries

Following the IMF's *World Economic Outlook*, the *Guide* recommends the following grouping of countries for the indicator on geographical distribution of loans.

- Advanced economies
  - Euro area
  - Major advanced economies (G7)
- Emerging market and developing economies
  - Emerging and developing Asia
  - Emerging and developing Europe
  - Latin America and the Caribbean
  - Middle East and Central Asia
  - Sub-Saharan Africa

Compilers are also encouraged to track lending to significant regional groupings that are relevant in their financial dealings; for example, East African Community (EAC) or Gulf Cooperation Council, (GCC), among others.

Source: *World Economic Outlook* (https://www.imf.org/external/pubs/ft/weo/2019/02/weodata/weoselgr.aspx).

8.15 Similarly to the previous indicator, this FSI is calculated by using the market value of financial derivative liabilities (line 21) as the numerator and total regulatory capital (line 39) as the denominator.

Trading Income to Gross Income

8.16 The FSI **Trading income to gross income** is intended to capture the share of DTs' income generated from financial market activities, including currency trading, and thus helps in assessing risks from the business model. The evolution of this FSI over time provides an indication of the DTs' reliance on activities other than intermediation to generate profits.

8.17 Data on gains and losses on financial instruments should be available from accounting records and be accessible to supervisors, but the extent to which they meet the definitions of the *Guide* could depend on national commercial accounting practices. Regarding gross income, sources of data are discussed in paragraphs 7.58–7.59. Since this a flow-based FSI, both for numerator and denominator, income should be accumulated from the beginning of the year until the end of the reporting period (month, quarter), as explained in paragraph 7.57.

8.18 This FSI is calculated by using gains or losses on financial instruments (line 4.ii of Table 5.1) as the numerator and gross income (line 5) as the denominator. Gains and losses on financial instruments are defined in paragraphs 5.19–5.21, and gross income is defined in paragraph 5.16.

8.19 *Gains and losses on financial instruments* are those arising during the period under review. Compilers should be aware that the *Guide* recommends the inclusion of gains and losses during each reporting period on all financial instruments (in domestic and foreign currency) valued at market or fair value through profit and loss; excluding equity in associates, subsidiaries, and any reverse equity investment that are designated at FVOIC where no recycle is allowed in accordance with IFRS 9 (see paragraph 5.19). The numerator calls for a net value, where gains and losses from trading income are netted out.

Personnel Expenses to Noninterest Expenses

8.20 The FSI **Personnel expenses to noninterest expenses** measures the incidence of personnel costs in total noninterest expenses (operating or overhead expenses). This FSI is used to gauge the management efficiency of a DT and its evolution over time. Different banking business models (wholesale corporate banking, investment banking, retail banking, micro-credit, personal banking, or others) require different staffing levels, so the ratio will heavily depend on the mix of models included in the reporting population. For instance, retail banking or personal banking require more staff per account, which will imply higher personnel costs and a larger value of the indicator compared to wholesale corporate banking or investment banking models. This fact should be highlighted when making cross-country and peer group comparisons.

8.21 This FSI is calculated by using personnel costs (line 6.i in Table 5.1) as the numerator and noninterest expenses (line 6 of Table 5.1) as the denominator. Noninterest expenses and personnel costs are defined in paragraphs 5.25–5.26.

8.22 Data for personnel costs are available from accounting records and should be accessible to supervisors. National practices will also determine the extent to which the data meet the definitions in the *Guide*. Regarding noninterest expenses, sources of data and issues for compilers are discussed in paragraph 7.62–7.63. Regarding employee stock options (see paragraph 5.63), the *Guide* recommends treating them as an increase in equity with a corresponding expense comprising the fair value of the stock options at the dates such options are granted.

Spread between Reference Lending and Deposit Rates

8.23 The FSI **Spread between reference lending and deposit rates (SLDR)** provides an indicator of the intermediation income earned by the DT sector. Spreads between lending and deposit rates can serve as indicators of trends in DTs' net interest income, and can also provide information on DTs' pricing behavior. However, further information would be required to understand the causes of that behavior. High spreads might signal less competitive pressures on banks; but they can also be attributable to bank inefficiency, higher counterpart risk, insufficient collateral, or weak protection by the judicial system.

8.24 This FSI is the difference (expressed in basis points) between the weighted average loan rate and the weighted average deposit rate, excluding interest charged on loans and deposits between DTs. To measure the SLDR, the Guide recommends one of two options. The first option entails calculating the weighted average of all lending and deposit interest rates (excluding loans and deposits among DTs) with the highest available frequency during the reference period (month or quarter) and reporting the spread between them as the indicator for that period. The second option consists on approximating weighted averages using interest income (line 1 of Table 5.1) divided by non-interbank gross loans (line 18.i.ii of Table 5.1) and interest expense (line 2 of Table 5.1) divided by customer deposits (line 24.i of Table 5.1), respectively (see Annex 8.3 for more details). While the first approach is more accurate, countries which are starting to report this indicator may choose the second approach because it is less computational intensive. Reporters should note their chosen approach in the metadata.

Spread between Highest and Lowest Interbank Rates

8.25 The FSI **Spread between highest and lowest interbank rates** measured in basis points is an indicator of the perceived risk of lending among DTs. Borrowing in the interbank market is the most immediate source of bank liquidity and interbank rates a key element of the monetary policy transmission mechanism. Interbank rates measure the cost of funds to DTs in the domestic interbank market, namely the cost of borrowing the excess reserves of other DTs. Interest-rate spreads, such as those between borrowers with different credit risk profiles, can serve to indicate the level of perceived risk within the financial system. Therefore, the spread between the highest and lowest interbank rates would help to capture banks' own perception of idiosyncratic problems and risks facing banks with access to the interbank market. Increasing spreads indicate increasing risk premium charged to DTs under stress (liquidity or solvency problems).[6]

8.26 This FSI is calculated as the spread between highest and lowest interbank rates, measured in basis

[6]Several studies conducted after the financial crisis of 2008–2009 indicate that counterparty risk played a prominent role in the pricing of the interbank market, with a significant increase in the spread charged to poorly performing banks. See, among others, Afonso, G., A. Kovner and A. Schoar; (2011) *Stressed, Not Frozen: The Federal Funds Market in the Financial Crisis*, Federal Reserve Bank of New York Staff Report, Number 437; or Angelini, P., A. Nobili and M.C. Picillo; (2009), *The Interbank Market after August 2007: What Has Changed and Why?*, Banca d'Italia Working Papers, Number 731.

points. Interbank rates are usually short-term in nature. Since this FSI provides information on DTs' own perceptions of risks facing other banks, and perceptions can change very quickly, the *Guide* encourages daily or weekly compilation of interbank rates for loans of the same maturity (overnight or weekly), and averaging them for the reporting period (month or quarter).

8.27 The source of these data is usually interbank dealers or brokers. The data might be available to supervisory authorities or the statistical departments of central banks.

Customer Deposits to Total (Non-interbank) Loans

8.28 The FSI **Customer deposits to total (non-interbank) loans** measures the share of DT's gross loans (excluding interbank activity) funded through customer deposits, which are generally presumed to be more stable than wholesale funding through the interbank market. When stable deposits are low relative to loans, there is greater funding risk: greater dependence on more "volatile" funding for DTs' portfolios.

8.29 This FSI is calculated by using customer deposits (line 24.i in Table 5.1) as the numerator and non-interbank loans (line 18.i.ii) as the denominator. Customer deposits are defined in paragraph 5.40, and loans are defined in paragraphs 5.41–5.43.

8.30 Supervisory sources will usually provide data that allow for the compilation of a measure of customer deposits consistent with the approach of the *Guide*. Regarding total loans, sources of data are the same as for the *NPLs to total gross loans* indicator, while loans to other DTs in the reporting population should be available from supervisors.

8.31 This FSI, which is the inverse of the loan to deposit ratio widely used by supervisors and analysts, provides a shorthand view of banks' reliance on volatile funding. A low value indicates greater reliance on non-deposit funding. More nuanced analysis requires more detail on the customer deposit base to assess the relative stability of the various types of deposits within the broader category of customer deposits.

8.32 The *Guide* recommends that the type of depositor be the primary factor in defining customer deposits, both because of its relevance and general applicability. Thus, customer deposits include all deposits (from residents and nonresidents) except those placed by other DTs and OFCs (resident or nonresident). Customer deposits considered to be a more stable financing source comprise current accounts (used for regular business transactions), time deposits with remaining maturity over one year, and deposits covered by deposit insurance schemes.

Foreign-Currency-Denominated Loans to Total Loans

8.33 The FSI **Foreign-currency-denominated loans to total loans** measures one aspect of DTs' exposure to exchange rate risk. This FSI is particularly relevant for countries where lending in foreign currency constitutes a significant share of total lending. Exchange rate changes will create holding gains or losses on the national-currency equivalent value of these loan positions. It is also important to monitor the ratio of foreign-currency-denominated loans to gross loans for residents, due to the increased credit risk associated with the ability of local borrowers to service their foreign-currency-denominated liabilities, particularly in the context of large devaluations or a lack of foreign currency earnings. This risk is ameliorated when borrowers' earnings are in foreign currency, such as the case of exporters, because a devaluation will have parallel effects on debt and earnings.

8.34 This FSI is calculated using the foreign-currency and foreign-currency-linked part of gross loans (line 53 in Table 5.1) to residents and nonresidents as the numerator, and gross loans (line 18.i) as the denominator.

8.35 Domestic currency is that which is legal tender in the economy and issued by the monetary authority for that economy or a common currency area. Any currencies that do not meet this definition are foreign currencies to that economy (see paragraph 4.53). Foreign currency instruments are those payable in a currency other than the domestic currency. In the special case where an economy uses as its only legal tender a foreign currency, this FSI could be compiled excluding borrowing in, and linked to, that foreign currency. A special case is presented by instruments payable in domestic currency but with their principal and interest linked to a foreign currency. These foreign-currency-linked instruments should be considered as if denominated in that foreign currency.[7]

[7] See *Balance of Payments and International Investment Position Manual*, sixth edition, paragraph 3.101 and *Monetary and Financial Statistics Manual and Compilation Guide*, paragraph 4.205. This treatment reflects a statistical rather than an accounting approach.

8.36 Data on foreign-currency-denominated loans should be available from supervisory sources because of the supervisory interest in banks' exposure to foreign currency. A difficultly can arise with data on foreign-currency-linked loans, since most probably they are reported as being denominated in the domestic currency, although in some countries they might be separately identified. Regarding total loans, the sources of data are the same as described in paragraph 7.38.

8.37 For cross-border consolidated data, the question of whether a currency is a foreign currency is determined by the residence of the parent entity of that specific consolidated group. The currency composition of assets (and liabilities) is primarily determined by the currency denomination of future payment(s).

8.38 Foreign-currency-linked loans are included in the numerator, as movements in the domestic exchange rate will affect their value in domestic currency terms (see paragraph 4.53). The most appropriate exchange rate to be used for conversion of a position into the unit of account is the market (spot) exchange rate prevailing on the reference date to which the position relates. The midpoint between buying and selling rates is preferred (see paragraph 4.55).

Foreign-Currency-Denominated Liabilities to Total Liabilities

8.39 The FSI **foreign-currency-denominated liabilities to total liabilities** measures the relative importance of funding in foreign currency within total liabilities. The magnitude of this ratio should be considered together with the value of the FSI *foreign-currency-denominated loans to total loans*. Exchange rate changes will create holding gains or losses on the national-currency equivalent value of these positions. Although it is desirable that domestically incorporated DTs have access to international markets, a high reliance on foreign-currency borrowing may signal that DTs are taking greater risks, by increasing their exposure to exchange rate movements and foreign currency funding reversals. It can also be a sign of residents' mistrust in the domestic currency and their preference for saving in a foreign currency. Extensive foreign currency lending funded by foreign currency borrowing in the same currency can help reduce the DTs' foreign exchange exposure. However, DTs could remain exposed if loans are being granted to domestic borrowers without foreign currency income as the debtors face difficulties servicing the loans in case of a large devaluation.

8.40 This FSI is calculated using liabilities denominated in foreign currency (line 54 in Table 5.1) as the numerator and total debt (line 28) *plus* financial derivative liabilities (line 29) *minus* financial derivative assets (line 21) as the denominator.

8.41 Data on foreign-currency-denominated liabilities should be available from supervisory sources. Total liabilities (line 23) may be sourced from accounting or supervisory data. If foreign-currency-linked loans comprise a significant volume of credit in a jurisdiction, the data should be available from supervisory sources.

8.42 The definitions of foreign currency, foreign-currency-denominated, and foreign-currency-linked instruments, as well as exchange rate conversion, are presented in paragraphs 4.52–4.56. They are the same as those set out in the issues for compilers in the previous section on *Foreign-currency-denominated loans to total loans*. Foreign currency liabilities are defined in paragraph 5.101, while financial derivatives are defined in paragraphs 5.55–5.62 and liabilities in paragraph 5.35. Metadata should disclose any national variation from these definitions.

8.43 For total liabilities, it is recommended that the net market value position (liabilities *less* assets) of financial derivatives be included, rather than the gross liability position, because of the market practice of creating offsetting contracts and the possibility of forward-type instruments switching between asset and liability positions from one period to the next. In the special case where an economy uses as its only legal tender a foreign currency, this ratio should be compiled excluding positions in, and linked to, this currency.

Credit Growth to Private Sector

8.44 The FSI **credit growth to private sector** is intended to capture emerging systemic risks and can serve as a forward-looking indicator of potential asset quality problems and vulnerabilities in the DT sector. Rapid credit expansion may, at times, exceed banks' capacity to assess credit risks, thereby leading to reduced asset quality and increased probability of default. Rapid credit growth can also be an indicator of deteriorating underwriting standards, leading to elevated risk in the portfolio.

Box 8.2 Co-circulation of Foreign Currency

Co-circulation—also commonly known as dollarization—results when a foreign currency (often the United States dollar, euro, or a regional currency) is used as a means of payment and store of value in parallel with the domestic currency. Several factors may affect the degree of co-circulation of an economy, among them its legal framework. While some countries do not allow deposits and loans in foreign currency, others accept them *de jure* or *de facto*. In extreme cases, some countries have adopted a foreign currency as the only legal tender.

Residents of countries with high and variable inflation may prefer to save and do business in a foreign currency whose value is more stable. The interest rate differential between instruments denominated in domestic and foreign currency also influences the preferences of the public, together with expectations of future exchange rate movements.

Both FSIs on foreign-currency-denominated loans and liabilities to total loans and total liabilities may serve as gauges of the level of co-circulation in an economy. High ratios for these FSIs can also result from high proportions of tourism or foreign trade in the economy. The graphs given next, constructed from data reported by countries for publication on the IMF's FSI website, show a sample of countries with different levels of co-circulation and its evolution through time

Figure 8.1.1.

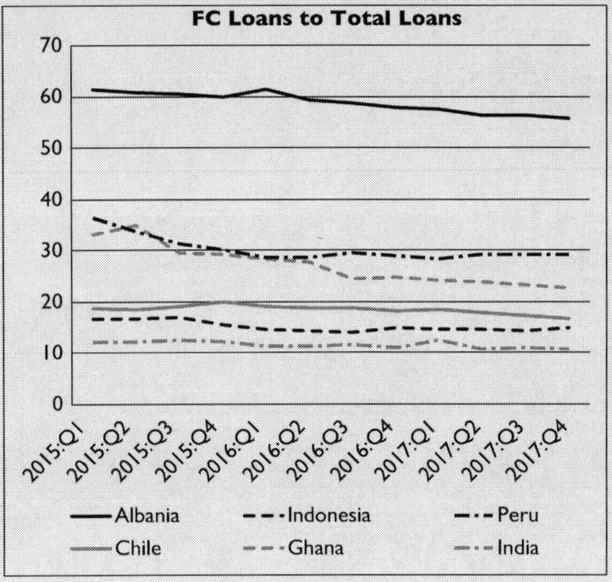

Source: IMF, Financial Soundness Indicators website.

Figure 8.1.2.

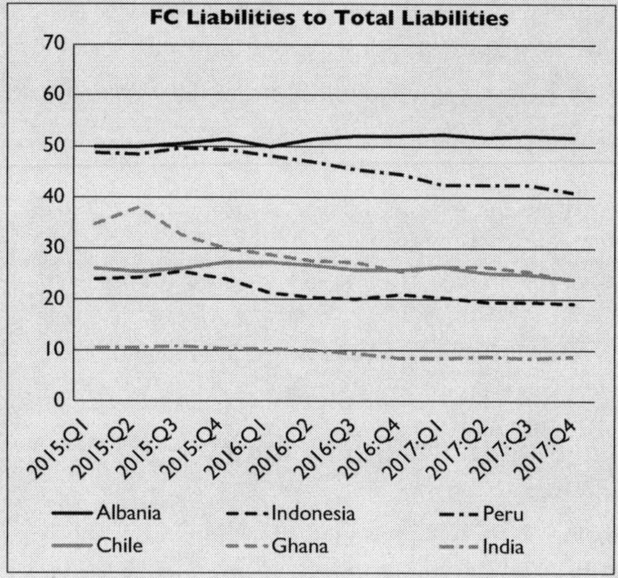

Source: IMF, Financial Soundness Indicators website.

8.45 Excessive credit growth, especially if concentrated in a few sectors, is an indicator of potential vulnerabilities in the financial sector. In fact, cross-country empirical studies of systemic bank distress suggest that banking crisis tend to be preceded by credit booms.[8] That is why, as discussed in Chapter 13, this indicator can be used as one input for macroprudential policies.

8.46 This FSI is calculated using the year-over-year growth rate of total credit to the nonfinancial private sector. The rate is computed as the difference between stocks of total credit to the non-financial private sector at the end of the reporting period and 12 prior months, divided by the stock of credit to the private sector a year earlier. The indicator is reported on a percentage basis.

8.47 *Credit to the private sector* (line 57) is defined in paragraph 5.103 and includes gross loans extended by DTs to the nonfinancial private sector, *plus* debt securities issued by private NFCs and held by DTs. Total credit is calculated on a gross basis, that is, excluding provisions for doubtful loans or debt securities.

8.48 Information on credit to the private sector is typically available from accounting records and supervisory sources.

[8]See: Demirgüç-Kunt, A. and Detragiache E., 2005, *Cross-Country Empirical Studies of Systemic Bank Distress: A Survey*, IMF Working Paper, Number 05/96; or Reinhart, C.M. and Rogoff K.S., 2011, "From Financial Crash to Debt Crisis," *American Economic Review*, Volume. 101, Number 5.

ANNEX

8.1 Summary of Additional Financial Soundness Indicators for Deposit Takers

Definition	Source Data	Compilation Issues
Large Exposures to Capital		
Ratio of large exposures to Tier 1 capital.	– Supervisory data on both value of large exposures and Tier 1 capital.	– The threshold used for calculating large exposures is intended to be applicable at the level of individual deposit takers (DTs).
Geographical Distribution of Loans to Total Gross Loans		
Lending to different economic regions as a percentage to total loans.	– Supervisory data on geographical distributions of loans, and balance sheet data on total gross loans.	– Lending is classified: (1) geographically based on the residence of the domestic reporting entity; (2) as lending to nonresidents if lending is by any foreign branches and/or deposit-taking subsidiaries of the reporting entity to residents of the local economy in which they are located.
Gross Asset Position in Financial Derivatives to Capital		
Market value of financial derivative assets to total regulatory capital.	– Balance sheet data on financial derivative assets. Supervisory data on regulatory capital.	– The coverage of financial derivatives includes forwards (including swaps) and options.
Gross Liability Position in Financial Derivatives to Capital		
Market value of financial derivative liabilities to total regulatory capital.	– Same as above.	– Same as above.
Trading Income to Gross Income		
Ratio of gains or losses on financial instruments to gross income.	– Income and expense data for both trading income and gross income.	– Trading income includes realized and unrealized gains and losses. – Gross income includes both net interest income and other gross income. – Gains and losses on the sale of an associate or subsidiary are excluded from gross income.
Personnel Expenses to Noninterest Expenses		
Ratio of personnel cost to noninterest expenses.	– Income and expense data on both personnel expenses and noninterest expenses.	– Noninterest expenses include all expenses other than interest expenses and provision expenses.
Spread between Reference Lending and Deposit Rates		
Difference (expressed in basis points) between the weighted average loan rate and the weighted average deposit rate.	– Data should be readily available from the accounting systems of DTs.	– Loans and deposits among DTs are excluded.

Definition	Source Data	Compilation Issues
Spread between Highest and Lowest Interbank Rates		
Difference between highest and lowest interbank rates, measured in basis points.	– Data might be available to supervisory authorities or the statistical departments of central banks.	– One outlier can change the value of the indicator substantially. The framework through which central banks provide liquidity to money markets influences the overall liquidity of these markets.
Customer Deposits to Total (Noninterbank) Loans		
Ratio of customer deposits to noninterbank loans.	– Balance sheet data for both customer deposits and total (noninterbank) loans.	– Interbank loans are excluded.
Foreign-currency-denominated Loans to Total Loans		
Ratio of foreign-currency and foreign-currency-linked part of gross loans to total gross loans.	– Balance sheet data for both foreign-currency-denominated loans and total loans.	– Foreign-currency-linked loans are included in the numerator. – If a foreign currency is used as legal tender, the financial soundness indicator is compiled excluding borrowing in, and linked to, that foreign currency.
Foreign-currency-denominated Liabilities to Total Liabilities		
Ratio of foreign-currency-denominated liabilities to total debt *plus* financial derivative liabilities *minus* financial derivative assets.	– Balance sheet data or supervisory data for both foreign-currency-denominated liabilities and total liabilities.	– Foreign-currency-linked liabilities are included. – For total liabilities, the net market value position of financial derivatives is included.
Credit Growth to Private Sector		
Year-over-year growth rate of total credit to the nonfinancial private sector.	– Balance sheet data on credit (loans) to private sector.	– The definition of credit refers to loans plus debt securities.

ANNEX

8.2 Geographical Distribution of Countries

The (October 2019) IMF's *World Economic Outlook* clusters countries in different groups, as described next.

Advanced Economies

Composed of 39 countries: Australia, Austria, Belgium, Canada, Cyprus, Czech Republic, Denmark, Estonia, Finland, France, Germany, Greece, Hong Kong Special Administrative Region, Iceland, Ireland, Israel, Italy, Japan, Korea, Latvia, Lithuania, Luxembourg, Macao Special Administrative Region, Malta, Netherlands, New Zealand, Norway, Portugal, Puerto Rico, San Marino, Singapore, Slovak Republic, Slovenia, Spain, Sweden, Switzerland, Taiwan Province of China, United Kingdom, and United States.

Euro Area

Composed of 19 countries: Austria, Belgium, Cyprus, Estonia, Finland, France, Germany, Greece, Ireland, Italy, Latvia, Lithuania, Luxembourg, Malta, Netherlands, Portugal, Slovak Republic, Slovenia, and Spain.

Major Advanced Economies (G7)

Composed of seven countries: Canada, France, Germany, Italy, Japan, United Kingdom, and United States.

Emerging Market and Developing Economies

Composed of 155 countries: Afghanistan, Albania, Algeria, Angola, Antigua and Barbuda, Argentina, Armenia, Aruba, Azerbaijan, The Bahamas, Bahrain, Bangladesh, Barbados, Belarus, Belize, Benin, Bhutan, Bolivia, Bosnia and Herzegovina, Botswana, Brazil, Brunei Darussalam, Bulgaria, Burkina Faso, Burundi, Cabo Verde, Cambodia, Cameroon, Central African Republic, Chad, Chile, China, Colombia, Comoros, Democratic Republic of the Congo, Republic of Congo, Costa Rica, Côte d'Ivoire, Croatia, Djibouti, Dominica, Dominican Republic, Ecuador, Egypt, El Salvador, Equatorial Guinea, Eritrea, Eswatini, Ethiopia, Fiji, Gabon, The Gambia, Georgia, Ghana, Grenada, Guatemala, Guinea, Guinea-Bissau, Guyana, Haiti, Honduras, Hungary, India, Indonesia, Islamic Republic of Iran, Iraq, Jamaica, Jordan, Kazakhstan, Kenya, Kiribati, Kosovo, Kuwait, Kyrgyz Republic, Lao P.D.R., Lebanon, Lesotho, Liberia, Libya, Madagascar, Malawi, Malaysia, Maldives, Mali, Marshall Islands, Mauritania, Mauritius, Mexico, Micronesia, Moldova, Mongolia, Montenegro, Morocco, Mozambique, Myanmar, Namibia, Nauru, Nepal, Nicaragua, Niger, Nigeria, North Macedonia, Oman, Pakistan, Palau, Panama, Papua New Guinea, Paraguay, Peru, Philippines, Poland, Qatar, Romania, Russia, Rwanda, Samoa, São Tomé and Príncipe, Saudi Arabia, Senegal, Serbia, Seychelles, Sierra Leone, Solomon Islands, Somalia, South Africa, South Sudan, Sri Lanka, St. Kitts and Nevis, St. Lucia, St. Vincent and the Grenadines, Sudan, Suriname, Syria, Tajikistan, Tanzania, Thailand, Timor-Leste, Togo, Tonga, Trinidad and Tobago, Tunisia, Turkey, Turkmenistan, Tuvalu, Uganda, Ukraine, United Arab Emirates, Uruguay, Uzbekistan, Vanuatu, Venezuela, Vietnam, Yemen, Zambia, and Zimbabwe.

Emerging and Developing Asia

Composed of 30 countries: Bangladesh, Bhutan, Brunei Darussalam, Cambodia, China, Fiji, India, Indonesia, Kiribati, Lao P.D.R., Malaysia, Maldives, Marshall Islands, Micronesia, Mongolia, Myanmar, Nauru, Nepal, Palau, Papua New Guinea, Philippines, Samoa, Solomon Islands, Sri Lanka, Thailand, Timor-Leste, Tonga, Tuvalu, Vanuatu, and Vietnam.

Emerging and Developing Europe

Composed of 16 countries: Albania, Belarus, Bosnia and Herzegovina, Bulgaria, Croatia, Hungary, Kosovo, Moldova, Montenegro, North Macedonia, Poland, Romania, Russia, Serbia, Turkey, and Ukraine.

Latin America and the Caribbean

Composed of 33 countries: Antigua and Barbuda, Argentina, Aruba, The Bahamas, Barbados, Belize, Bolivia, Brazil, Chile, Colombia, Costa Rica, Dominica, Dominican Republic, Ecuador, El Salvador, Grenada, Guatemala, Guyana, Haiti, Honduras, Jamaica, Mexico, Nicaragua, Panama, Paraguay, Peru, St. Kitts and Nevis, St. Lucia, St. Vincent and the Grenadines, Suriname, Trinidad and Tobago, Uruguay, and Venezuela.

Middle East and Central Asia

Composed of 31 countries: Afghanistan, Algeria, Armenia, Azerbaijan, Bahrain, Djibouti, Egypt, Georgia, Islamic Republic of Iran, Iraq, Jordan, Kuwait, Lebanon, Libya, Mauritania, Morocco, Oman, Pakistan, Qatar, Saudi Arabia, Somalia, Sudan, Syria, Tajikistan, Tunisia, Turkmenistan, United Arab Emirates, Uzbekistan, and Yemen.

Sub-Saharan Africa

Composed of 45 countries: Angola, Benin, Botswana, Burkina Faso, Burundi, Cabo Verde, Cameroon, Central African Republic, Chad, Comoros, Democratic Republic of the Congo, Republic of Congo, Côte d'Ivoire, Equatorial Guinea, Eritrea, Eswatini, Ethiopia, Gabon, The Gambia, Ghana, Guinea, Guinea-Bissau, Kenya, Lesotho, Liberia, Madagascar, Malawi, Mali, Mauritius, Mozambique, Namibia, Niger, Nigeria, Rwanda, São Tomé and Príncipe, Senegal, Seychelles, Sierra Leone, South Africa, South Sudan, Tanzania, Togo, Uganda, Zambia, and Zimbabwe.

ANNEX

8.3 Weighted Average Interest Rate for a Loan Portfolio

8.49 A method of calculating the weighted average lending rate described for the spread between reference lending and deposit rates consists of dividing the accrued amount of interest income on loans reported by DTs for a given period (numerator) by the average position of loans (denominator) for the same period. The weighted average deposit rate can be computed by dividing interest expense on deposits (numerator) by the average position of deposits (denominator) for the same period. Positions should be averaged using the most frequent observations available. Contracted interest rates (i.e., price data) can also be used to calculate weighted average interest rates for a given reference period, using the loan amounts as weights.[9]

8.50 In principle, using this method, the weighted average interest rate for a portfolio of n loans (types of deposits) can be constructed as follows:

$$\text{Weighted average interest rate} = \sum_{i=1}^{n} R_i L_i \Big/ \left(\sum_{t=0}^{T} S_t / T\right),$$ [10]

where R_i = Interest rate for Loan i that is outstanding during the period,[11]
L_i = Loan i,
S_t = Stock of loans observed at time t, and
T = Total number of observations during the period.

8.51 Under accrual accounting, interest costs accrue continuously on debt instruments, thus matching the cost of funds with the provision of funds. The rate at which these costs accrue is known as the interest rate, and for deposits and loans, it is typically established by contractual arrangement. For compiling the SLDR, annualized interest rates should be calculated.

8.52 Average-period interest rates are more closely related to profitability and pricing behavior than end-period rates and are not subject to the possibility of exceptional daily fluctuations. However, an SLDR based on end-period rates, directly measured, with appropriate metadata, provides reliable information. Such a spread between lending and deposit rates would be calculated as the difference between the weighted averages of end-period interest rates for the different types of loans and the different types of deposits (i.e., three-month and six-month). The weights for each type of loan and deposit would be calculated using end-period position data.

8.53 The *Guide* recommends at a minimum the compilation of an SLDR for outstanding business, as this is directly related to profitability. For the purposes of this FSI, *outstanding business* is the stock of deposits placed with DTs and the stock of loans extended by DTs, excluding deposits from, and loans to, other resident DTs.

[9] This method of calculation could minimize the reporting burden on DTs if data on accrued amounts of interest on loans and deposits are readily available from the accounting systems of DTs, as typically data on DTs' positions in loans and deposits are regularly reported to central banks in balance sheet reports required for the compilation of monetary statistics. Compilers need to ensure that the numerator and the denominator cover the same set of DTs. The ideal is to have frequent observations of positions, thus matching the data in the numerator. If less frequent observations of positions are available, then the numerator may capture flows unrelated to the amounts in the denominator. If loans or deposits in the denominator are valued at fair value, the implicit interest rate will move in line with changes in market rates.

[10] For example, if during the period of the first quarter, there are end-month observations for December (200), January (100), February (200), and March (300), then S_t is the sum of the four observations (800) and T is the number of observations (4), so the denominator in the equation would be 800/4 = 200.

[11] The amount of accrued interest in the numerator depends on the time over which the associated loans are outstanding. For instance, for a loan that is issued midway through the quarter, the numerator should capture accrued interest over one and one-half months only.

8.54 To reflect more closely, current market developments and DTs' pricing behavior, rather than outstanding business, countries could also compile an SLDR for new business, particularly if the necessary data are readily available. *New business* is defined as deposits placed with DTs and loans extended by DTs during the reference period. New business includes "rolled over" or renewed loans and deposits.

8.55 In Chapter 5, the *Guide* recommends that interest should no longer accrue on nonperforming loans, resulting in an implicit interest rate of zero. While there might be some analytical benefit in excluding NPLs from the SLDR calculation, the *Guide*'s preferred approach is to include such loans in the calculation. In other words, when compiling the interest rate on loans, positions in NPLs (less specific provisions against NPLs)[12] should be included in the denominator and zero interest included in the numerator. This approach has the benefit of reflecting the adverse impact on DT's yield on assets of high volumes of NPLs.

[12]Specific provisions have already reduced profits, as well as capital and reserves, and thus are deducted from the denominator (that is, from loans).

8.56 In some economies, a certain amount of lending by DTs can be directed to priority sectors at prescribed interest rates for economic development. As in the discussion on NPLs, the *Guide* prefers that such loans and the interest that accrues be included in the calculation of an SLDR, because excluding such business could give a misleading indication of profitability.[13]

8.57 As noted earlier, while the *Guide* recommends at a minimum the compilation of the SLDR on all outstanding business (excluding among DTs), this SLDR could be supplemented with information on various subcategories. In this context, the SLDR for all outstanding business could be supplemented with SLDRs for:

- both the nonfinancial corporations sector and the household sector;
- both short-term and long-term (original maturity) interest rates;
- peer groups, to ascertain the pricing behavior of different subgroups within the total resident DTs; or
- both domestic and foreign currency business.

[13]Nonetheless, if significant, another SLDR could be calculated that excludes such prescribed lending and the average interest rate received. In such circumstances, there may be analytical interest in information on the total amount of such lending.

9 Specification of Financial Soundness Indicators for Other Financial Corporations

I. Introduction

9.1 This chapter defines financial soundness indicators (FSIs) for the OFCs sector and three of its subsectors, explains how they are to be calculated, and deals with data sources and specific compilation issues.

9.2 The three subsectors include: money market funds (MMFs), insurance corporations (ICs), and pension funds (PFs). All other institutional units performing financial intermediation or auxiliary functions that do not include accepting deposits are combined in the OFCs sector. As explained in Chapter 2, the OFCs not enumerated earlier comprise a diverse group of units, including finance companies, financial leasing companies, non-MMF investment funds, securitization vehicles, and financial auxiliaries. For these units, only indicators of their share within the total financial system and their size relative to the gross domestic product (GDP) need to be compiled.

9.3 Countries are encouraged to compile for their own purposes data and indicators for additional financial sub-sectors when these are relevant to financial stability analysis. Non-MMF investment funds may be significant investors in financial and nonfinancial corporations.

II. Consolidation Basis

9.4 The two FSIs that measure the relative size of the OFC sector are calculated on a residency and institutional unit basis. Consequently, the data should be presented on an aggregated resident-based approach, except for countries with OFCs that have significant cross-border activities, for which cross-border consolidation may be relevant, as described in Chapter 6.

9.5 The *Guide* recommends compiling additional FSIs for ICs consolidating flows and positions of parent ICs with the flows and positions of their domestic and foreign branches and subsidiaries in the IC industry, following a cross-border, domestically incorporated (CBDI) consolidation basis approach.

9.6 For ICs whose parent is a resident DT, Chapter 6 discussed how data of ICs are not consolidated with flows and positions of their parent's DT when FSIs are compiled for deposit takers (DTs). Therefore, data from ICs are not captured in the core and additional FSIs for DTs. As a result, there are no issues of overlapping or risk of double counting between ICs and DTs.

9.7 The *Guide* recommends compiling additional FSIs for MMFs and PFs following an aggregated resident-based approach.

III. Calculation of Financial Soundness Indicators for OFCs

9.8 As for the deposit-taking (DT) sector, most FSIs for the other sectors are calculated by comparing two underlying series to produce a ratio. For some FSIs, when one or both of the underlying series can be defined in alternative ways, these alternatives are explained. Annex 9.1 summarizes the recommended FSIs for the OFC sector.

Other Financial Corporations

9.9 The list of additional FSIs for OFCs includes two indicators for the whole sector of OFCs, measuring their relative size within the financial sector and within the domestic economy. To assess the relevance of the three subsectors specifically identified in the *Guide*, the same indicators should be compiled for each of these subsectors.

9.10 The two indicators measuring the relative size of the OFC sector are:

- OFCs' assets to total financial system assets; and,
- OFCs' assets to GDP.

9.11 These two indicators are described further. The data to be used to calculate these FSIs are obtained either from aggregating individual balance sheets of each institutional unit of the OFC sector, or through estimates provided by the responsible supervisory authorities. If neither source is available, an alternative is flow of funds accounts, in which estimates of OFC assets may be built up from counterpart data.

Other financial corporations' assets to total financial system assets

9.12 The FSI **OFCs' assets to total financial system assets** provides a metric to gauge the relative magnitude of the OFCs sector within the domestic financial system.

9.13 This FSI is a ratio where the numerator is OFCs' total assets and the denominator is total financial system assets, excluding the central bank. As such, the denominator includes only the total assets owned by DTs and OFCs (including the sum of DT total assets, line 14 in Table 5.1; MMF total assets, line 10 in Table 5.2; IC total assets, line 14 in Table 5.3; and PF total assets, line 11 in Table 5.4 plus other OFCs not listed here).

9.14 The *Guide* recommends similar FSIs for the three subsectors of the OFCs sector. For MMFs, the numerator is total assets of this subsector; for ICs, it is the total assets of this subsector; and for PFs, their total assets. In all three cases, the denominator is total financial system assets, excluding the central bank, which is the same as the denominator for the whole OFC sector.

9.15 The FSI for OFCs' assets to total financial system assets and the FSIs for the three OFC subsectors are calculated using aggregated data of the resident financial institutions, or alternatively from flow of funds data in which estimates of OFC assets may be built up from counterpart data. Data for total assets of OFCs and DTs can be obtained from the aggregated balance sheets of each subsector and sector.

9.16 It should be noted that aggregated data of total DT assets will be different from total assets used for some core and additional FSIs for DTs, if the latter are calculated using a consolidation basis other than the aggregated resident-based approach, such as cross-border, cross-sector, domestically incorporated (CBCSDI) or cross-border, cross-sector, domestically-controlled (CBCSDC).

9.17 Data sources for the three targeted subsectors of the OFC sector are the aggregated balance sheets of those subsectors.

9.18 Data for one or more of the OFCs subsectors may not be available to compilers if these subsectors are not regulated or do not have an obligation to submit financial information to any authority. In cases where these subsectors are regulated by agencies other than the lead FSI agency, compilers should coordinate with those agencies the regular transmission of the needed information, ideally through a formal agreement.

Box 9.1 The Relative Size of the OFC Sector

The magnitude of the OFC sector, and hence its relative size within the financial sector, varies greatly across economies. The graph, based on a sample of data reported to the IMF's Statistics Department, shows participations going from as low as 6.7 percent (Albania) to 42.1 percent (Mexico) of the total financial system assets.

This FSI for OFCs provides compilers with a metric to assess the importance of devoting additional resources for the collection of data from the sector and its subsectors. Clearly, the larger the size of the OFC sector within the financial system, the higher the value added from additional information.

Figure 9.1.1. Total Financial System Assets of Selected Countries

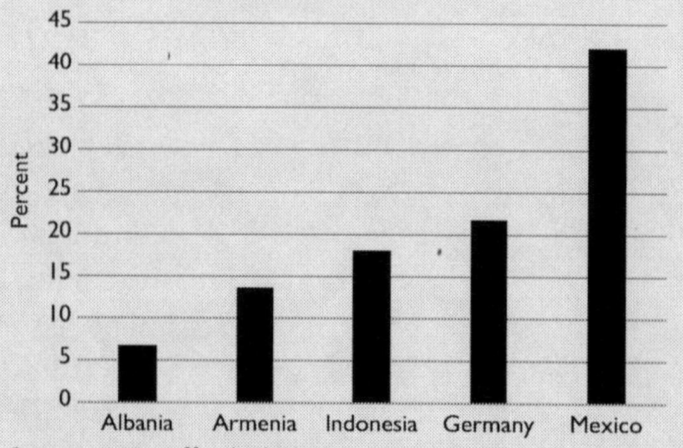

Source: IMF staff calculations.

Other financial corporations' assets to nominal gross domestic product

9.19 The FSI **OFCs' assets to nominal gross domestic product** provides a metric to gauge the volume of the OFCs sector within the overall economy.

9.20 This FSI is a ratio where the numerator is total assets of the OFCs sector and the denominator is nominal gross domestic product (GDP). Nominal GDP is an aggregate measure of production in the economy, equal to the sum of the gross value added of all resident institutional units engaged in production.

9.21 As for the previous FSI, indicators for the three subsectors can also be calculated as a ratio to nominal GDP.

9.22 Source data for the numerator are the same as elaborated in paragraph 9.13, with nominal GDP data for the denominator available from national accounts.

9.23 Compilation issues are the same as the ones elaborated in paragraphs 9.16 and 9.18 for total assets.

Money Market Funds

9.24 The systemic relevance of money market funds (MMFs) varies across countries and can have a substantial impact on financial stability. Like other mutual funds, investors in MMFs are considered as shareholders and they are entitled to receive the value of each share with its accumulated income, but the yield is not predetermined. MMFs compete with banks for funds although an important distinction is that investments in MMFs are generally not covered by deposit insurance schemes.

9.25 MMFs invest in high-quality, short-term, income instruments, such as treasury bills, commercial paper, certificates of deposits, and repurchase agreements. Despite the relatively high quality of the invested instruments, their maturity and their issuing sectors can have an impact on asset quality.

9.26 In some countries, MMFs and DTs are closely linked because the MMFs provide short-term funding to DTs by investing in instruments issued by DTs. In this case, a run on MMFs could have an impact on DTs' short-term liquidity. The maturity transformation through MMFs is also relevant for financial stability analysis, as some of MMFs' assets have maturities of more than 90 days while balances in their share accounts may be withdrawn on demand.

9.27 The *Guide* recommends compiling two FSIs to gauge the credit and liquidity risk of the investment portfolios of MMFs: (1) sectoral distribution of investments and (2) maturity distribution of investments.

Sectoral distribution of MMFs' investments

9.28 The FSI **sectoral distribution of MMFs' investments** provides some measure of the risk exposure faced by MMFs' investments. Although in principle, MMFs invest only in high-quality financial assets, their investments are nevertheless subject to counterparty risk. In particular, since MMFs' shares/units are not protected by deposit insurance, a perception that MMFs' investments are placed with subprime counterparts might intensify the risk of a run against MMFs in times of financial instability. Also, MMFs could be prone to runs if a significant shortfall emerges between the value of their underlying assets and their liabilities. This FSI gives information on the quality of assets held by MMFs based on the sectoral distribution of the issuers of those assets.

9.29 This FSI presents MMFs investments broken down into domestic economic sectors and nonresidents. Following the definitions of the System of National Accounts (SNA), the domestic economic sectors are grouped into: central bank, DTs (correspond to the SNA's sector *deposit-taking corporations except the central bank*), OFCs (all, including MMFs),[1] general government, and nonfinancial corporations. The investment by sector is presented as a ratio to the total MMFs' investments.

9.30 Source data for this indicator are the sectoral balance sheets of MMFs, which should identify their financial investments by counterpart economic sector. Total investment should be calculated from the asset side of the sectoral balance sheet (see Table 5.2). If the counterpart sectors of MMFs' investments are not identified in their balance sheets, memorandum series need to be compiled on the sectoral distribution of their investments.

9.31 Sectoral analysis is a concept used in national accounts that classifies institutional units according to the nature of their economic activity. For this reason, this indicator is a general measure of credit risk, but it

[1] Intra-MMF subsector positions are aggregated, not consolidated.

does not provide a measure of risk within an economic sector according to, for instance, the industry within the nonfinancial sector (e.g., extractive, commerce, tourism).

9.32 Availability of data for MMFs may vary by jurisdiction. Compilers may be able to obtain the data from the relevant regulatory authority, or directly from MMFs. In this case, similar considerations as the ones described for the two previous FSIs for OFCs apply here (see paragraphs 9.17 and 9.22).

Maturity distribution of MMFs' investments

9.33 The FSI **maturity distribution of MMFs' investments** provides a measure of the liquidity of MMFs' investments by breaking down the maturity structure of assets of the MMF sector. The maturity transformation through MMFs is relevant for financial stability analysis as MMFs' assets typically have longer maturities than their liabilities, which may be withdrawn on demand. The liquidity problems might be exacerbated if DTs also have investments in MMFs, as DTs may withdraw funds from their share accounts with MMFs to avoid potential losses.

9.34 Beyond the short-term analysis, the usefulness of this indicator is to show how the maturity of MMFs' assets is evolving through time, serving as an early warning of possible problems in cases where the term structure is deteriorating.

9.35 This FSI is defined as the distribution of MMFs' assets in three brackets: 1 to 30 days, 31 to 90 days, and more than 90 days (see Table 5.2, line 25 i–iii). This FSI is presented as a ratio, where the numerator is the volume of assets invested in each maturity bracket and the denominator is total investments of MMFs.

9.36 Source data for this indicator requires additional information not contained in the sectoral balance sheet of MMFs, as presented in Table 5.2. Memorandum series need to be reported by MMFs, breaking down their investments by maturity in the three brackets required for this indicator.

9.37 Compilers will need to rely on supervisory data or data collected directly from MMFs. In such cases, they will need to coordinate the reporting and data sharing of these supplementary series with the relevant supervisory authority, if any.

9.38 For this FSI, the preferred maturity is the remaining maturity of the MMFs' asset holdings. However, if remaining maturity is not available, original maturity can be reported, but it should be explained in the corresponding metadata.

9.39 Much of the earlier provided discussion also pertains on Non-MMF Mutual Funds. Countries are encouraged for their own purposes to compile similar FSIs for Non-MMF Mutual Funds when they are significant in their country. The Non-MMF Mutual Funds may present a wider range of financial stability issues because of the diversity of their investments, wide maturity range, currency mix, possible use of derivatives, and possible withdrawal restrictions.

Insurance Corporations

9.40 Insurance corporations provide financial benefits to policyholders through risk-sharing and risk-transfer contracts. Main types of insurance include:

- life or long-term insurance and
- nonlife insurance (including reinsurance).

9.41 The *Guide* recommends the compilation of specific FSIs separately for both the life and nonlife ICs, as the two industries are very different in terms of products they offer and resulting balance sheet structure as well as risks they face.

9.42 Insurance is based on probability theory, where the price (insurance premium) is set before knowing an exact cost of the product (insurance contract or policy). ICs broadly face two main types of risks: (i) technical risks and (ii) investment risks.

9.43 **Technical risks** stem from the very nature of insurance business. Policyholders buy protection against occurrence of defined events whose occurrence is uncertain, and insurers set reserves against the projected total cost of claims. Insurance liabilities are projected using actuarial techniques. If these projections are incorrect, premiums may be insufficient and liabilities may be understated, which may result in both solvency and liquidity problems.

9.44 **Investment risks** affect the value, performance, return, liquidity, and structure of ICs' investment portfolio. While liquidity risks are not dominant for ICs, they are exposed to market risks arising from changes in interest rates, exchange rates, and asset prices (equity, securities, and real estate); and counterparty credit risks.

9.45 ICs may also contract reinsurance, which is insurance provided by one insurer (usually specializing in reinsurance) to another, whereby the reinsurer agrees, in exchange for a premium, to indemnify the latter for losses on one or more contracts that it has issued. Much reinsurance business is cross-border and must be appropriately accounted for in the compiled data.

9.46 Against this backdrop, six FSIs for ICs are to be compiled, covering two broad categories of financial soundness separately for life and non-life IC: (i) capital adequacy and (ii) earnings and profitability. These six FSIs are presented in the following sub-sections.

Shareholder equity to invested assets (life and nonlife insurance)

9.47 The FSIs **shareholder equity to invested assets** are both a measure of capital adequacy and leverage. Unlike banking, there is no accepted international standard for capital adequacy for insurance companies. Regional or national standards for capital adequacy in advanced economies have common features of a ratio in which the numerator is an amount of capital determined for prudential purposes and not taken directly from financial statements, and a denominator which is a risk-based determination of the required amount of capital.[2] A ratio of 100 percent or above is usually required and expected in normal operating conditions. In contrast to the complex calculations within these types of capital adequacy frameworks, the Guide uses a balance sheet measure of capital and reserves (line 30 in Table 5.3), defined as the difference between total assets (line 14 in Table 5.3) and Liabilities (line 24 in Table 5.3), as an indicator of capital adequacy.

9.48 Capital adequacy is one of the key indicators of ICs' financial soundness, measuring the corporations' capital strength to absorb losses. This FSI focuses on the amount of capital that is available to meet potential losses from insurance corporations' investments. Additionally, this total provides an indication of the financial leverage of ICs; that is, the extent to which their assets are funded by sources other than their own capital.

9.49 This FSI uses IC capital and reserves (line 30 in Table 5.3) as the numerator. The denominator is the sum of ICs' holdings of currency and deposits, loans, debt securities, equity and investment fund shares, other financial assets, and financial derivatives (line 16 in Table 5.3), *plus* their nonfinancial assets held for investment purposes (line 15.ii in Table 5.3).

9.50 Source data are the sectoral balance sheets of life and nonlife ICs. Since the indicator is calculated using a CBDI consolidation basis, positions of domestically incorporated ICs vis-à-vis their resident and nonresident IC subsidiaries should be eliminated. Data of each domestically incorporated IC in the reporting population—consolidating its positions with its IC subsidiaries—should be available to supervisors.

9.51 Shareholder equity is measured as the accounting concept of capital and reserves (line 30 in Table 5.3). For CBDI consolidated data, investment in resident and nonresident subsidiaries is deducted from the overall capital in the sector, so that capital and reserves held within the sector are not double counted.

9.52 Unlike in the case of DTs, where total assets are included in the denominator, only invested assets are used to calculate the denominator here, excluding nonfinancial assets not held for investment purposes and reinsurance claims.

9.53 Compilers will likely require supervisory data. In cases where the lead agency for compiling FSIs is not also the insurance supervisor, compilers should coordinate with the relevant agency to ensure the regular transmission of the needed information, ideally through a formal agreement.

---

[2] Regional and national examples of measures of insurance capital adequacy requirements are: (i) the EU-wide Solvency II which has two measures of capital adequacy, the Solvency Capital Ratio (SCR) and Minimum Capital Ratio (MCR); (ii) the United States state-based insurance regulatory framework risk-based capital ratio which is calculated under different methodologies for the life insurance, property and casualty and health insurance industries; and (iii) the Canadian Life Insurance Capital Adequacy Test for life insurance companies, the Minimum Capital Test for property and casualty companies, and the Mortgage Insurance Capital Adequacy Test for mortgage insurance companies.

Combined ratio (nonlife insurance)

9.54 The FSI **combined ratio** should be calculated only for nonlife ICs.[3] This ratio measures the profitability of a given year's insurance underwriting, calculated as the sum of net incurred losses and underwriting expenses divided by net earned premiums, expressed as a percent. For nonlife insurers operating in a healthy market, this ratio should be less than 100 percent, indicating profitable underwriting. If the nonlife industry has combined ratios consistently over 100 percent, that is a sign of risk mispricing and an incentive to invest in riskier assets to try to make insurers profitable overall.

9.55 The FSI combined ratio for nonlife ICs is calculated using the sectoral income and expense statement of domestically incorporated nonlife ICs. The recommended CBDI consolidation basis requires eliminating intra-group flows between resident ICs and their resident and nonresident IC subsidiaries.

9.56 Net claims and underwriting expenses are part of the income and expense statement. Net claims are total claims (line 2.i in Table 5.3) *minus* claims paid by reinsurance (line 2.ii in Table 5.3), while underwriting expenses are a component of *other operating expenses* (line 7.ii in Table 5.3). Net premium earned is equal to gross premium earned (line 1.i in Table 5.3) *minus* premium ceded to reinsurers (line 1.ii in Table 5.3). If claims on reinsurance or premium ceded are not presented in the ICs' income and expense statement, supplementary information should be requested as a memorandum series.

9.57 This FSI is calculated as a ratio of two flows. To avoid sudden fluctuations from period to period and to foster cross-country comparability, the numerator and denominator should accumulate the flows from the beginning of the year until the reporting period, rather than be calculated only for the reporting period (month or quarter).

Return on assets (life insurance)

9.58 The FSI **return on assets (ROA)** is intended to measure the efficiency of life ICs in using their stock of assets. It is a common operating ratio used to assess a corporation's profitability. As for the case of similar indicators for DTs, this indicator may be interpreted in combination with the FSI on return on equity (ROE).

9.59 This FSI is a ratio where the numerator is defined as net income and the denominator is total assets. The preferred definition of net income is net income before taxes (line 10 in Table 5.3), which would produce a more comparable measure of efficiency across economies. The denominator is the balance sheet measure of total assets (line 14 in Table 5.3).

9.60 Source data for net income are the life ICs' consolidated sectoral income and expense statement, while source data for total assets are their consolidated sectoral balance sheet. To avoid double counting, life ICs' intragroup positions should be eliminated for data compiled on a CBDI consolidation basis.

9.61 Net income is calculated on an accounting and supervisory basis (see paragraphs 5.110–5.118), with premiums earned (line 1) and investment income (line 8) usually being the main source of income. Premiums earned are presented net of reinsurance ceded. Net income includes (1) gains and losses on revaluation of financial assets and liabilities (line 9); (2) gains and losses from the sales of fixed assets (line 5.iii, measured as the difference between the sale value and the balance sheet value at the previous end period); and (3) net change in technical reserves (line 3). The amount of technical reserves that need to be constituted in any specific period might not only be based on actuarial calculations, but also reflect supervisory guidelines.

9.62 The *Guide* recommends that investment income not include accrual of interest on nonperforming assets. It also recommends including realized and unrealized gains and losses arising during each period on all financial instruments valued at market or fair value through profit and loss, excluding equity in associates, subsidiaries, and any reverse equity investment.

9.63 Being a ratio of a flow (income) to a stock (assets), this FSI should be calculated in a way that facilitates time series and cross-country comparisons. For the numerator, net income should be annualized. The denominator should be a measure of the average stock of total assets either over the annualization period or, alternatively, from the beginning

[3] Much of the income of a life insurance company comes from invested assets, so the combined ratio is not a meaningful indicator of profitability in the life sector.

of the calendar year until the end of the reporting period, using the more frequent possible number of observations.[4]

Return on equity (life and nonlife insurance)

9.64 The FSI **return on equity (ROE)** should be separately calculated for life and non-life insurance due to the very different capital structures of life and non-life insurance companies. It is intended to measure the efficiency of ICs in using capital. It also indicates the ability of ICs to internally generate capital through retained earnings, and potentially attract new equity investment. The ratio needs to be interpreted in combination with FSIs on capital adequacy (*equity to invested assets*), because a high ROE could indicate high profitability but also low capitalization, while a low ratio could be caused by a high level of capitalization.

9.65 This FSI is a ratio where the numerator is defined as net income and the denominator is total capital. For life insurance, net income is the same concept as the numerator of *ROA*. Equity corresponds to capital and reserves of the sectoral balance sheet of ICs (line 30 in Table 5.3).

9.66 As for the case of *ROA* (see paragraph 9.60), the source data for this indicator are the consolidated sectoral income and expense statements and the sectoral balance sheets of ICs. ICs' intragroup positions should be eliminated for data compiled on a CBDI consolidation basis.

9.67 Since the main goal of this indicator is to measure the sustainability of a corporation, the *Guide* recommends using as numerator *net income after taxes* (line 12 in Table 5.3). Using two different measures of income for two different indicators enables compilers and analysts to better grasp the effect of income taxes on the final profitability of the enterprise. Also, net income after taxes provides a more cross-country comparable measure of profitability for the investor, which is the driving force for capital flows among economies: low (after tax) profitability may signal fundamental problems for ICs and may be considered as a leading indicator for solvency problems.

9.68 As with the FSI on *ROA*, net income flows should be annualized. Equity should be calculated averaging stocks over the annualization period or, alternatively, from the beginning of the year until the reporting period, using the most frequent observations available.

Pension Funds

9.69 Pension Funds (PFs) play an important role in the financial system in many countries and have a potential impact on the stability of financial markets in several ways, most significantly through their investment behavior. PFs hold a large amount of financial assets and, therefore, any sizable reallocation of their assets (e.g., between fixed income and equities) could have macrofinancial implications. The *Guide* recommends compiling two indicators to measure potential risks for PFs.

Liquidity ratio

9.70 The FSI **liquidity ratio** is intended to assess the adequacy of liquid assets held by PFs. In particular, this FSI gauges PFs' capacity to meet their financial obligations arising from pension payments over a one-year time horizon.

9.71 This FSI is a ratio where the numerator is defined as PFs' liquid assets (line 31 in Table 5.4) and the denominator is the estimated pension payments for the next 12 months (line 32 in Table 5.4). Pension payments are based on actuarial calculations.

9.72 Liquid assets are those assets readily available to an entity to meet a demand for cash. For a financial asset to be classified as liquid, the holder must have a reasonable certainty that it can be converted into cash at short notice, in large volumes, without substantially affecting their price.

9.73 For this indicator, liquid assets are defined in paragraph 5.132.

9.74 Whether an instrument is considered liquid or not depends on judgment and is influenced by market conditions. In particular, for securities, liquidity depends on the breadth of secondary

[4] Using the same example for data reported at end-May, the numerator should be the average of stock of total assets at the end of December of year 0, and January, February, March, April, and May of year 1.

markets. Compilation issues of liquid assets for PFs are the same as the ones already discussed for liquidity measures for DTs in Chapter 7 (see paragraph 7.66).

Return on assets

9.75 The FSI **return on assets (ROA)** is an indication of the yield on investments net of the costs of managing the fund. Since the costs of managing the fund generally are small relative to investment returns, unlike ROA for DTs and ICs, ROA for PFs provides little insight into efficiency. While a higher ROA could signal more efficient management, it could also result from higher yields on higher risk investments. For defined benefit schemes, a sound ROA—one reflecting appropriately balanced risk and return—indicates that the PFs will be able to fulfill future pension obligations. For defined contribution schemes, the obtained ROA will affect the level of future benefits to be paid by the PFs.

9.76 This FSI is a ratio where the numerator is the net income and the denominator is total assets of PFs. To foster cross-country comparability, the *Guide* recommends using net income before taxes (line 7 in Table 5.4). The denominator is the balance sheet measure of total assets (line 11 in Table 5.4).

9.77 Source data for net income are the resident-based sectoral income and expense statement of PFs, which are not being consolidated. Net income before taxes is calculated as net investment income (investment income from own financial and nonfinancial assets *less* investment expenses) *plus* other income *less* total administrative expenses and *plus* the net actuarial gains or losses of the period.

9.78 Total assets are sourced from the sectoral balance sheet of PFs, which is compiled using a resident-based approach. Total assets comprise financial and nonfinancial assets.

9.79 Net income is calculated on an accounting and supervisory approach. This is particularly important for long-term assumptions on actuarial gains or losses, which are subject to supervisory approval, including changes in benefits.

9.80 Similar considerations as the ones elaborated for the case of ICs regarding how to annualize net income and average total assets (see paragraph 9.63) apply for the case of PFs: (1) net income should be accumulated from the beginning of the year until the end of the reporting period and then annualized; (2) average total assets should make use of the most frequent available observations.

ANNEX

9.1 Summary of Financial Soundness Indicators for Other Financial Corporations

Definition	Source Data	Compilation Issues
Other Financial Corporations' Assets to Total Financial System Assets		
Ratio of other financial corporations' (OFCs') total assets to total financial system assets. OFC subsectors include money market funds (MMFs), other investment funds insurance companies, pension funds, other financial intermediaries, and financial auxiliaries.	– Aggregated sectoral balance sheets.	– Total financial and nonfinancial assets provide for more comprehensive coverage. – Data availability if some subsectors are unregulated or do not report financial information. – Coordination and data sharing with other supervisory agencies.
Other Financial Corporations' Assets to GDP		
Ratio of OFCs' total assets to gross domestic product.	– Aggregated sectoral balance sheets. – National accounts, for nominal GDP.	– Data availability if some subsectors are unregulated or do not report financial information. – Coordination and data sharing with other supervisory agencies. – Indicator is a ratio of a stock divided by a flow.
Sectoral Distribution of Money Market Funds' Investments		
Percentage distribution of MMFs' assets between the following economic sectors: central bank, deposit takers, OFCs (including MMFs), general government, nonfinancial corporations, and nonresidents.	– Sectoral balance sheets of MMFs. – Memorandum items might be needed if the sectoral balance sheet does not identify the counterpart sector of the investments.	– Indicator does not provide a measure of risk within an economic sector. – Coordination with supervisory agencies, or with the industry. – Data availability if MMFs are unregulated or do not report financial information.
Maturity Distribution of Money Market Funds' Investments		
Percentage distribution of MMFs' assets into three maturity brackets: 1–30 days; 31–90 days; and more than 90 days.	– Supplementary information directly provided by MMFs.	– Remaining maturity is recommended. – If remaining maturity is not available, original maturity can be used.
Insurance Corporations' Shareholder Equity to Total Invested Assets (life and nonlife insurance)		
Ratio of insurance corporations' shareholder equity to total invested assets.	– Consolidated sectoral balance sheet of insurance corporations.	– For CBDI data, investment in resident and nonresident subsidiaries has to be deducted from capital. – Total invested assets include nonfinancial assets held for investment purposes. – Cooperation with supervisory agencies may be required.

Definition	Source Data	Compilation Issues
Insurance Corporations' Combined Ratio (nonlife insurance only)		
Sum of net incurred losses and underwriting expenses, divided by net earned premiums.	– Sectoral income and expense statement of insurance corporations. – Memorandum series.	– Numerator and denominator should be the sum of flows from the beginning of the year until the end of the reporting period. – Consolidated data should eliminate intragroup flows.
Insurance Corporations' Return on Assets (life insurance only)		
Ratio of net income to total assets.	– Consolidated sectoral income statements and balance sheets of insurance corporations.	– Net income before taxes. – Numerator should be annualized net income. – Denominator should be the average stock of total assets.
Insurance Corporations' Return on Equity (life and nonlife insurance)		
Ratio of net income to total capital and reserves.	– Consolidated sectoral income statements and balance sheets of insurance corporations.	– Net income after taxes. – Same considerations for calculating flows and stocks as for return on assets.
Pension Funds' Liquidity Ratio		
Ratio of liquid assets to pension payments due in the next 12 months.	– Sectoral balance sheet, compiled using a resident-based approach. – Supplementary memorandum series, with data on core and broad liquid assets, and estimated pension payments.	– Data on liquid assets may not be readily available. – Data availability if pension fundshare unregulated or do not report financial information. – Coordination with supervisory agencies, or with the industry.
Pension Funds' Return on Assets		
Ratio of net income to total assets.	– Sectoral income and expense statement for net income. – Sectoral balance sheets for total assets. – Data compiled on a resident-based approach; that is, aggregation of individual financial statements without intragroup consolidation.	– Net income before taxes. – Same considerations for the calculation of flows and stocks as for insurance corporations' return on assets.

10 Specification of Financial Soundness Indicators for Nonfinancial Sectors

I. Introduction

10.1 Drawing on the definitions and concepts set out previously, this chapter explains how financial soundness indicators (FSIs) for the nonfinancial sectors are to be calculated and interpreted.

10.2 Nonfinancial sectors comprise nonfinancial corporations (NFCs), households, and real estate markets. This chapter covers these FSIs: consolidation basis, data sources, definition, analytical interpretation, and the calculation of their underlying series, as well as potential issues that compilers should be aware of.

10.3 In general, the accounting principles underlying source data calculation are similar to those recommended for deposit takers (DTs) and OFCs. NFCs and households are defined in Chapter 2. This chapter elaborates on real estate markets and prices. The accounting framework and accounting principles for FSIs are discussed in Chapter 4. The sectoral financial statements and memorandum items for NFCs and households, from which underlying series are derived, are covered in Chapter 5. Annex 10.1 summarizes the source data for compilers of recommended FSIs for the nonfinancial sectors.

II. Consolidation Basis

10.4 As described in Chapter 6, data for NFCs and households should be compiled on a resident-based approach, that is, data cover only resident institutional units without intra-group consolidation adjustments. This is because underlying data are mainly obtained from national accounts or other macroeconomic data sets, which are compiled based on the concept of institutional unit and do not consolidate intra-group positions and flows.[1]

[1] National compilation practices vary. In some jurisdictions, data on financial positions of nonfinancial sectors may be drawn from counterpart data, such as information on bank deposits and loans.

III. Calculation of Financial Soundness Indicators for NFCs

10.5 As with the deposit-taking sector, most FSIs for NFCs are calculated by comparing two underlying series to produce a ratio. For some FSIs, when one or both of the underlying series can be defined in alternative ways, these alternatives are explained.

10.6 Unlike in the case of DTs and OFCs, FSI compilers normally do not have access to accounting records of individual nonfinancial corporations. Therefore, it is often not possible to construct sectoral balance sheets and income statements aggregating the financial statements of all institutional units of the sector, as is the case for DTs. The series needed to calculate these FSIs can be drawn from national accounts-based data; or from specific surveys covering a representative sample of the sector (see Box 10.1). This restriction can pose additional challenges in terms of frequency and timeliness.

10.7 The *Guide* recommends compiling seven FSIs for the NFCs sector (see Table 1.1). These FSIs focus on NFCs' solvency, leverage (or gearing), profitability, and debt-servicing capacity. These indicators are useful in predicting corporate distress or failure. NFCs' poor financial performance will impair their capacity to service their obligations. To the extent that these NFC draw funding from DT's, NFCs' distress or failure may negatively impact DTs' asset quality.

10.8 Unless otherwise stated, all the line references in this section refer to Table 5.5 Nonfinancial Corporations. As already stated, the data to be used to calculate FSIs for this sector are not adjusted to eliminate intra-group positions and flows among NFCs in the reporting populations, but in some countries where these series are compiled from counterpart may be on a consolidated basis, which should be noted in metadata.

Box 10.1 European Central Balance Sheet Data Offices

The European Central Balance Sheet Data Offices provides an example of NFCs' data compilation based on individual accounting records, which eventually could be used to construct FSIs for NFCs.

The national data offices collect, store, and disseminate descriptive and accounting data of NFCs. Data collection is based on a sample of the corporations, which is afterwards expanded for the estimates of the whole population. Two-thirds of the data are collected on a mandatory basis, while the remaining one-third is obtained on a voluntary basis. Periodicity and timeliness vary across countries. The most frequent periodicity (over 60 percent of data sources) is annual, and the rest is collected on a quarterly basis. Almost three-quarters of the products and services are made available within one year of the reference period.

The Bank for Accounts of Companies Harmonized (BACH) database : https://www.bach.banque-france.fr/?lang=en collected by the European Committee of Central Balance Sheet Data Offices contains aggregated and relatively harmonized accounting data of NFCs for 12 European countries. These include 41 balance sheet items, 22 income statements items, and several economic and financial ratios collected at a national level. They complement national accounts data with a detail of subsets of institutional sectors.

Total Debt to Equity

10.9 The FSI for NFCs **total debt to equity** measures corporate leverage, that is, the extent to which activities are financed through liabilities other than own funds. Given the need to make interest and principal payments on debt, high corporate leverage increases the vulnerability of corporate entities in the event of economic, interest rate, or other financial market shocks and may impair their repayment capacity. More generally, the extent of corporate leverage—together with the volatility of the environment in which corporations operate—could be important indicators of the probability of corporate financial distress, as illustrated in Box 10.2.

10.10 This FSI is calculated by using debt (line 26 in Table 5.5) as the numerator, and capital and reserves (line 29 in Table 5.5) as the denominator. Debt is defined similarly as for DTs as the outstanding amount of those actual current and non-contingent liabilities (paragraph 5.69). Capital and reserves is the accounting concept defined in paragraph 5.144. It is assumed that capital is denominated in domestic currency.

10.11 As discussed, data should be compiled on a resident-based approach. NFCs' debt and capital and reserves can be drawn from national accounts-based data, more specifically from flow of funds accounts or similar frameworks Alternatively, they can be obtained from data collected from a representative sample of NFCs' financial statements.

10.12 Equity investments in associates and subsidiaries (and reverse investments) are to be recorded in the investor's balance sheet on the basis of the investor's proportionate share in the capital and reserves of the associate and subsidiary, and not using the market value of the traded equity.

External Debt to Equity

10.13 The NFCs **external debt to equity FSI** is a measure of NFCs' exposure to nonresident creditors. This indicator is useful for macroprudential analysis and systemic risk monitoring, as there are potential risks associated with a high exposure to nonresidents—usually denominated in foreign currency. As is well-documented, this funding has shown significant volatility, especially for emerging economies.[2]

10.14 This FSI is the ratio of total debt to nonresidents (line 32 in Table 5.5) to capital and reserves (line 29 in Table 5.5). Data on NFCs' external debt are readily available from external debt statistics if they are compiled with full-sector breakdown in accordance with the *External Debt Statistics: Guide for Compilers and Users* (2013). NFCs' external debt can also be sourced from the International Investment Position (IIP). If sourced from IIP, NFCs' external debt can be estimated by taking liabilities in the form of (a) direct investment intercompany lending, (b) debt securities under "portfolio investment," plus all items, except other equity,

[2] See, for instance, Bluedorn, John, Duttagupta, R., Guajardo, J. and Topalova, P., 2013, *Capital Flows Are Fickle: Anytime, Anywhere*, IMF Working Paper 13/183, August.

Box 10.2 Nonfinancial Corporations Debt to Equity in the United States

The graph, sourced from the United States Federal Reserve Bank of St. Louis, shows how a sharp increase in the ratio of NFCs' debt to equity (measured as NFCs' credit debt as a percentage of the market value of corporate equity) preceded recession periods in the United States.

Figure 10.2.1. Nonfinancial Corporate Business; Credit Market Debt as a Percentage of the Market Value of Corporate Equities

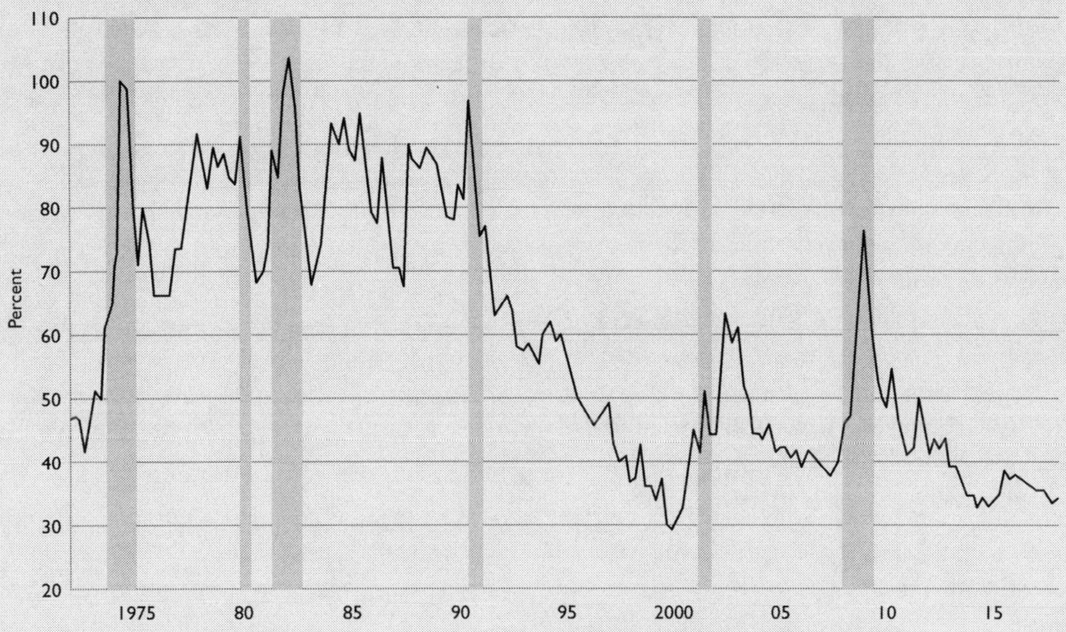

Source: Board of Governors of the US Federal Reserve System; Federal Reserve Bank of St. Louis.

Note: Shaded areas indicate US recessions.

under "other investment" for "other sectors." Due to its classification in the IIP, to identify liabilities of NFCs, the items of portfolio investment and other investment should deduct data for OFCs. Where available, NFC's external debt can be obtained from the sectoral accounts and balance sheet statistics. The extent to which the resulting data would be consistent with the concepts in the Guide would require further consideration.

10.15 If the FSI and external statistics compilation fall under the purview of different agencies, FSI compilers are encouraged to obtain the data from compilers of external sector statistics through a well-established data sharing arrangement.

10.16 Issues for compilers regarding NFCs' capital and reserves are discussed in the paragraphs 10.09–10.12. As data are compiled on a resident-based approach, resident parent NFCs' debt liabilities to any nonresident subsidiaries should be included. Issues for compilers regarding equity investments in associates and subsidiaries (and reverse investments) and goodwill, are also discussed in paragraphs 10.09–10.12.[3]

Foreign Currency Debt to Equity

10.17 The FSI for NFCs **foreign currency debt to equity** provides an indication of NFCs' total debt in foreign currency to both residents and nonresidents, compared with their capital. It is intended to gauge NFCs' exposure to potential foreign currency risk. High levels of foreign currency debt increase NFCs' foreign currency risk and, if the corporations' foreign currency debt is not offset by foreign currency receipts from exports or other sources, they may face difficulties in case of a sharp depreciation of the domestic currency. This could be partially or totally ameliorated if the foreign exchange risk is hedged.

[3] If data on NFCs' external debt are not available, but NFCs' total debt and domestic debt (debt to residents) are available, NFCs' external debt can be calculated as the difference between total debt and domestic debt.

10.18 This FSI is calculated by using total debt in foreign currency (line 33 in Table 5.5) as the numerator, and capital and reserves (line 29 in Table 5.5) as the denominator. Debt is defined in paragraph 5.69, capital and reserves is the accounting concept defined in paragraph 5.144, and foreign currency is defined in paragraph 5.37.

10.19 In cases where most debt to nonresidents is in foreign currency, external debt statistics and IIP may provide useful source data. Data on foreign currency debt vis-à-vis the resident central bank, DTs, and OFCs are available from the IMF's standardized report forms (SRFs) for monetary and financial statistics. SRFs provide data broken down by type of financial instrument, currency of denomination (domestic and foreign), and counterpart sector. If SRFs for the central bank, other depository corporations, and OFCs are available, NFCs' foreign currency debt to these financial corporations can be approximated as the sum of these financial corporations' claims on NFCs in the form of loans, debt securities, and other accounts receivable denominated in foreign currency.[4]

10.20 Issues for compilers regarding NFCs' capital and reserves are discussed in paragraphs 10.09–10.12.

10.21 Foreign currency debt among NFCs in the reporting population that are part of the same group are included, as FSIs for NFCs are compiled on a resident-based approach. Regarding equity investments in associates and subsidiaries (and reverse investments) as well as goodwill, issues for compilers are discussed in paragraphs 10.09–10.12.

Total Debt to GDP

10.22 The FSI for NFCs **total debt to GDP** is intended to measure the overall level of NFCs' indebtedness (both in domestic and foreign currency, to both residents and nonresidents) compared to the size of the economy. It should be analyzed together with other FSIs on NFCs' debt (see the previous three FSIs for NFCs). A high level of corporate debt in relation to gross domestic product (GDP) is a signal of increased vulnerability of corporations to shocks, which may impair their repayment capacity. This FSI is one of several measures of the NFCs' level of debt, which is also used to determine NFCs' debt sustainability (see Box 10.3 for an application of this ratio).[5]

10.23 This FSI is calculated by using debt (line 26 in Table 5.5) as the numerator, and annual GDP as the denominator. Debt data should be end-period stock and are defined in paragraph 5.69.

10.24 Issues on source data for total debt are discussed in paragraphs 10.09–10.12. If data on total debt are obtained from a sample of financial statements, the results must be extrapolated to estimate the value for the whole sector. GDP data are

[4] If complete SRFs for some countries are not accessible from the IMF's monetary statistics database, FSI compilers might obtain the data from monetary statistics compilers in their respective countries through a well-established data sharing arrangement. Another source of NFCs' foreign currency debt is the already described balance sheet databases.

[5] *2008 SNA*, paragraph 2.138 for a definition of GDP.

Box 10.3 Nonfinancial Corporations Debt to GDP by Instrument

This figure is presented in the IMF's *Regional Economic Outlook: Western Hemisphere (April 2016)*. It illustrates NFCs' indebtedness using the total debt to GDP ratio split by type of financial instrument, which makes it even more useful for analyzing corporate solvency risks.

As loans account for more than two-thirds of total debt in most of these countries, the focus is on ensuring the adequacy of buffers in the banking system, in terms of both provisions and capital.

Figure 10.3.1. Nonfinancial Corporate Debt by Instrument
(Percent of GDP, 2014)

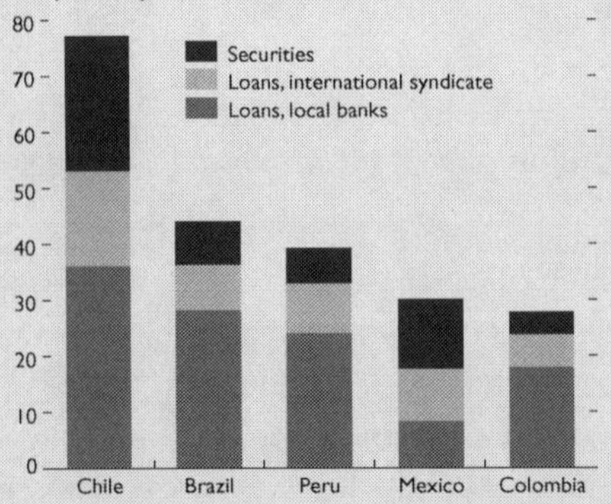

Sources: Bank for International Settlements; Dealogic; IMF, International Financial Statistics database; and IMF staff calculations.

available from national accounts sources. It should be noted that both underlying data series for this indicator already exist for compiling other FSIs on debt—e.g., "total debt" is the numerator for compiling *total debt to equity* for NFCs, while GDP is the denominator for compiling several FSIs for OFCs.

10.25 GDP data should be obtained from national accounts source. Regardless of which frequency is used to compile this FSI, the annualized GDP should be used as the denominator.

Return on Equity (ROE)

10.26 The FSI for NFCs **return on equity** is commonly used to capture NFCs' efficiency in using capital. It also indicates NFC's ability to internally generate capital through retained earnings and to potentially attract new equity investment. Profitability is a critical determinant of corporate strength, affecting capital growth, the ability to withstand adverse events and, ultimately, repayment capacity. Sharp declines in corporate sector profitability, for example, as a result of economic deceleration, may serve as a leading indicator of NFCs' financial difficulties and a potential credit risk exposure that will affect the financial corporations' asset quality. However, account should be taken of cyclical movements in corporate sector profitability and of market structure—that is, industry characteristics, competitive environment, and pricing flexibility. The diversified types of businesses within the NFC sector mean that the actual performance of subsectors is likely to vary widely from the overall NFCs' ROE. It is useful to examine the components of ROE to determine whether the change in NFC's positions is driven by leverage or net income.

10.27 The FSI is calculated by using net income after taxes (line 9 in Table 5.5) as the numerator and the average value of capital and reserves (line 29 in Table 5.5) over the same period as the denominator. As with DTs, net income after taxes is used in the calculation of this FSI because, in addition to be an indicator of profitability, ROE is a measure of return on shareholders' investments in NFCs—that is, shareholders' interest is on income after taxes. Net income is described in paragraphs 5.136–5.138. Capital and reserves is the accounting concept defined in paragraph 5.144.

10.28 Data can be drawn from national accounts-based data or, if available, from central balance sheet offices. For the large entities, data might be drawn from published corporate financial statements and aggregated to get both the numerator and the denominator for this FSI. However, the extent to which the resulting data would be consistent with the concepts in the *Guide* would require further consideration.

10.29 Regarding capital, issues for compilers—including the definitions of capital—are discussed in paragraphs 10.09–10.12. As data are collected on a resident-based approach, transactions and positions among NFCs in the reporting population that are part of the same group are not eliminated.

10.30 Being a ratio of a flow to a stock, the same considerations as for the case of DTs and insurance corporations for a similar indicator apply here. That is, net income should be annualized and compilers should report the income annualization method in the metadata. At a minimum, the denominator can be calculated by taking the average of the beginning and end-period positions (e.g., average of the beginning and the end of the reference quarter if this FSI is compiled on a quarterly basis), but compilers are encouraged to use the most frequent observations available in averaging the capital stocks.

Earnings to Interest and Principal Expenses

10.31 The FSI for NFCs **earnings to interest and principal expenses** measures NFCs' capacity to cover their debt-service payments (interest and principal). It serves as an indicator of the risk that NFCs may not be able to make the required payments on their debts. The NFCs' default on debt obligations will negatively affect the creditors' asset quality and profitability. This FSI thus is potentially a leading indicator of deterioration in the DT sector as NPLs may increase in future if the NFC sector has a low ratio of earnings to interest and principle expenses.

10.32 This FSI is calculated by using earnings (net income) before interest and tax (EBIT) (line 31 in Table 5.5) as the numerator, and debt-service payments (line 34 in Table 5.5) over the same period as the denominator. EBIT is a commonly used measure of earnings for the calculation of debt-service coverage. EBIT and interest receivable from other NFCs are defined in paragraph 5.146, and debt-service payments are defined in paragraph 5.149.

10.33 Data on earnings and debt-service payments may not be available from national accounts and, therefore, they should be obtained from other sources. Potential data sources include external debt statistics, which requires collection of data on debt service payments on external debt. Data on domestic debt-service payments need to be additionally collected. For the larger entities, data might be drawn from published corporate financial statements and aggregated to calculate both the numerator and the denominator for this FSI. Another source might be data stored by central balance sheet data offices, which will usually have a flow-of-funds-type framework. Specific survey data may be required.

10.34 Debt-service coverage, and particularly interest coverage, is a concept used in the analysis of corporate accounts. However, the extent to which the resulting data would be consistent with the concepts in the *Guide* would require consideration. Debt-service payments among NFCs in the reporting population, regardless of whether they are part of the same group or not, are included in the denominator. The numerator includes interest receivable (including those among NFCs in the reporting population that are part of the same group) from other NFCs. Therefore, the numerator and denominator have the same coverage.

10.35 The underlying flow data used to calculate this FSI should be reported on a cumulative basis—that is, data should be accumulated from the beginning of the reference year until the end of the reporting period.

Earnings to Interest Expenses

10.36 The FSI for NFCs **earnings to interest expenses** measures NFCs' capacity to cover interest payments, providing insights into the risk that NFCs may not be able to make the required interest payments. Lack of capacity to pay interest may constitute an early warning that NFCs might fail to pay overall debt obligations. As mentioned earlier, NFCs' default on debt services will lead to a deterioration of the lending financial corporations' asset quality and profitability (see Box 10.4).

10.37 In some cases, it is difficult to collect data on principal payments, while data on interest payments are generally available from accounting records.[6] For this reason, the FSI *earnings to interest expenses* is an alternative to report a debt-service ratio in case data on principal payments are not available. If data for both principal and interest payments are available, both FSIs *earnings to interest expenses* and *earnings to interest and principal expenses* should be compiled and disseminated.

10.38 This FSI is calculated by using EBIT (line 31 in Table 5.5) as the numerator and interest expenses (line 5 in Table 5.5) over the same period as the denominator.

10.39 Sources of data for both numerator and denominator are discussed in paragraphs 10.33–10.34.

10.40 Issues on reporting flow data and data definitions are the same as *earnings to interest and principal expenses* discussed earlier.

[6] Interest payments are recorded as a separate item in the income statement as they accrue and, therefore, are usually available. Principal payments are recorded on the balance sheet as a reduction of outstanding liabilities not separately identified. Without a more detailed record keeping, this information may not be readily available to FSI compilers.

Box 10.4 Earning to Interest Expenses

This figure is presented in the *Regional Economic Outlook: Western Hemisphere (April 2014)*. It illustrates the capacity of Latin American NFCs to cover interest payments, using the median of the ratio of EBIT to interest expenses. As EBIT were three to four times higher than interest payments in most of these countries during the reference period, the rise in leverage did not appear to have compromised the debt-servicing capacity of the corporations in the sample. However, these ratios are prone to marked declines in the event of a pronounced economic downturn or rise in interest rates. Moreover, statistics for the median firm conceal vulnerabilities in the weaker tail of the sample.

Figure 10.4.1. LA5 (Brazil, Chile, Colombia, Mexico, and Peru): Median Ratio of Earnings before Interest and Taxes to Interest Expenditure, 2003–13

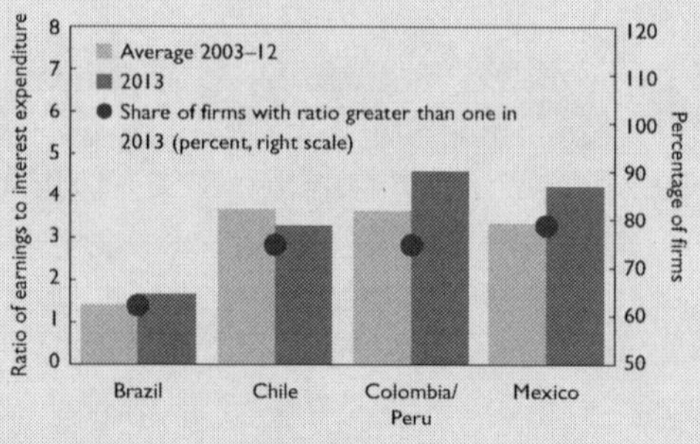

Source: IMF, *Regional Economic Outlook: Western Hemisphere*, April 2014.

Box 10.5 Household Debt to GDP

The graph shows the steep increase in the ratio of household debt to GDP in the United States in the years prior to the financial crisis; as well as its steady decline afterwards, as households reversed their consumption pattern from previous years.

Figure 10.5.1. Household Debt to GDP

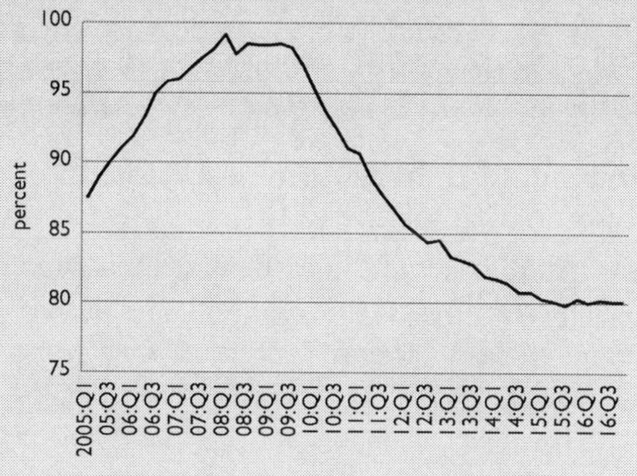

Source: IMF, Financial Soundness Indicators website.

10.41 The denominator includes interest payments to other NFCs (including payments among NFCs in the reporting population that are part of the same group). The numerator includes interest receivable from other NFCs (including those among NFCs in the reporting population that are part of the same group). Therefore, the numerator and denominator have the same coverage. Regarding the calculation of earnings and data consolidation, issues for compilers are discussed in paragraphs 10.33–10.35.

IV. Calculation of Financial Soundness Indicators for Households

10.42 The analysis of the household sector balance sheet is also key for financial stability considerations. Sharply rising household debt, for example, could lead to distress in DTs with considerable household exposure. Economic activity and interest rate shocks may impact the ability of households to service their debt, as well as the value of their collateral. As with FSIs for NFCs, FSIs for households serve as leading indicators of the expected evolution of DTs' asset quality.

10.43 The vulnerability of households may be assessed through the use of sectoral accounts, flow of funds, and other macroeconomic data. Indicators include the ratios of household debt to GDP, household debt to income, household debt service and principal payments to income, household debt to assets, and household debt to the value of collateral pledged. Household vulnerability on the asset side includes households' exposure to equity and real estate price movements.

10.44 Unless otherwise stated, all the line references in this section are to Table 5.6 Households. Data for households are compiled on a resident-based approach and no consolidation adjustments are required as they are not applicable to the household sector. The simplified presentation of Table 5.6 is based on information sourced from national accounts, which is derived from sample surveys subject to response and reporting errors. Obtaining data on the household sector is difficult and therefore coordination with the agency compiling national accounts statistics is essential.

Household Debt to GDP

10.45 The FSI for **household debt to GDP** measures the overall level of household indebtedness (usually related to consumer loans and mortgages) as a share of GDP. As with the NFC sector, a high rate of growth and level of borrowing increases the vulnerability of households to economic and financial market shocks and may impair their repayment capacity (see Box 10.5).

10.46 This FSI is calculated by using household debt (line 19 in Table 5.6) as the numerator, and GDP as the denominator. Debt data should be end-period stock. Household debt is defined in paragraph 5.156.

10.47 Both the numerator and the denominator should be compiled using national accounts data, which provide a broader coverage of household debt and GDP. If data on household debt are not available from national accounts sources, data from the financial sector sources can be used—although in this case, it would cover only household debt to resident financial corporations. Data sources should be documented in the metadata.

10.48 Data for household debt comprise debt incurred by resident households of an economy only. Regardless of which frequency is used to compile this FSI, the annualized GDP should be used as the denominator.

Household Debt-Service and Principal Payments to Income

10.49 The FSI for **household debt-service and principal payments to income** measures the capacity of households to cover their debt payments (interest and principal). It can also be used as a leading indicator of consumer spending growth: a high debt-service ratio over a period of time might be a sign of slow growth of personal consumption in the period ahead.

10.50 This FSI is calculated by using household debt-service and principal payments (line 22 in Table 5.6) as the numerator, and gross disposable income (line 6 in Table 5.6) over the same period as the denominator. Household debt-service payments are defined in paragraph 5.158, and gross disposable income is defined in paragraph 5.153.

10.51 Information on household disposable income should be available from national accounts sources. However, data on debt-service payments might not be available from national accounts sources and so additional data may need to be separately requested (see paragraph 5.150). Most likely, the household sector borrows from resident financial corporations, although some borrowing from abroad might exist, in which case there may be a need to capture cross-border borrowing activity. Additionally, households might obtain commercial or retail credit directly from NFCs, which in some economies could constitute an important part of household debt. The required data series on debt service could be included in household surveys. Alternatively, data from the resident financial sector can be used together with some assumptions about repayment schedules to estimate household debt service.[7]

10.52 Both the numerator and the denominator are flow data, which should be reported on a cumulative basis—that is, data should be accumulated from the beginning of the reference year until the end of the reporting period.

Household Debt to Income

10.53 The FSI for **household debt to income** is intended to assess the debt sustainability of the household sector, with a high or growing ratio signaling sector's vulnerabilities. A high level of household debt coupled with inadequate capacity to service could cause a shock to the country's financial sector. In this regard, this indicator should be analyzed together with the previous two FSIs for households.

10.54 This FSI is calculated using household debt (line 19 in Table 5.6) as the numerator and gross disposable income of households (line 6 in Table 5.6) over the same period as the denominator.

10.55 Information on household debt and disposable income should be available from national accounts sources (see paragraphs 5.153 and 5.156). If data on household debt are not available from national accounts sources, data from the financial sector source can be used—in this case covering only household debt to resident financial corporations.

10.56 Issues on both underlying series are the same as the previous two FSIs for households (paragraph 10.51).

10.57 Household debt should be measured as outstanding stock at the end of the reporting period, whereas the denominator is the households' annualized gross disposable income. Compilers should report the income annualization choice in the metadata.

V. Real Estate Markets

10.58 For macroprudential analysis, it is highly desirable to have indexes of real estate prices because deposit takers (DTs) may have large exposures (both direct and indirect) to real estate and may be affected by volatile price movements. Moreover, real estate assets are a major component of private sector wealth, a determinant of private consumption and, consequently, of economic activity.

10.59 Sharp drops in real estate prices affect DTs negatively due mainly to the impact they have on the value of collateral, the increase in the real estate loan to value ratio, the negative wealth effect on debtors, and therefore on the quality of DTs' loan portfolios. There is a well-documented relationship between real estate

[7] For instance, information can be obtained on possible repayment schedules based on remaining maturity data for loan debt and the pattern of credit card debt repayment, providing some rough estimates for debt service.

cycles and economic cycles, with rapid increases in real estate prices (bubbles) and excessive lending being early indicators of an impending financial crisis.[8] During an upswing in real estate prices, real estate may be used as collateral for extension of credit for further purchases. However, once conditions begin to reverse, such exposure could lead to a mutually reinforcing downward spiral.

10.60 DTs' exposure to real estate prices can arise through many channels: (1) ownership of real estate; (2) loans collateralized by real estate; (3) risk of prepayment; (4) holding of pass-through (or asset-backed) securities[9] backed by real estate (mortgage) loans; or (5) exposure to households and corporations that can be affected by changes in the servicing costs of real estate related borrowing or price movements in real estate markets.

10.61 The reasons why real estate prices are potentially volatile are varied. Real estate markets are illiquid, with final prices negotiated individually between the contracting parties and with high transactions costs. Supply is inelastic in the short-term owing to the time needed to plan projects and complete construction, making real estate markets cyclical.[10] Development is often subject to many legal or other restrictions, such as a shortage of urban land that can be developed. Under these conditions, the impact on prices of changes in demand is exacerbated. While international capital flows into or out of real estate can rapidly and unpredictably affect market sales and prices, price volatility is also endogenously induced through the provision and cost of domestic credit.

Measuring Real Estate Prices

10.62 International guidance in constructing representative real estate price indices is relatively limited. The first comprehensive overview of conceptual and practical issues related to the compilation of price indices for residential properties is available in the *Handbook on Residential Property Prices Indices (RPPIs)*, published in 2013.[11] And in 2019, the IMF will be issuing a *Practical Guide on the Compilation of the RPPI*. Methodological guidance on commercial property prices was at a developmental stage at the time the *Guide* was published.

10.63 Contrary to a general price index, where prices for identical goods and services can be observed over time, real estate markets are highly heterogeneous (both within and across countries), with properties having unique locations and structural characteristics. Furthermore, prices can only be observed sporadically—when properties are transacted. Consequently, the construction of a real estate price index is substantially more difficult than the construction of other price indexes based on a matched model methodology because:

- Because dwellings are not homogenous, there is normally no uniform market price for real estate.
- Diversity and lack of standardization result in the need to gather a wide range of data to compile indices to represent various market segments, with associated challenges to securing access to suitable data and high technical sophistication requirements.
- Representative real estate prices in residential and commercial markets can be hard to measure accurately given that there may be disparate prices for apparently similar properties, and prices may be volatile.
- Transactions of the same dwelling are infrequent.
- Experience has shown that there can be particular difficulties in acquiring representative source data for measuring commercial real estate prices across the economy.

10.64 When developing real estate price indices, compilers should be aware of a number of factors: (1) the wide range of differences among properties, leading to difficulties in identifying "a standard real estate unit"; (2) the mix of transactions by type,

[8] See, for instance, Gorton, Gary (2008), *The Panic of 2007*, paper prepared for the Federal Reserve Bank of Kansas City, Jackson Hole Conference, August.

[9] Pass-through securities are securities backed by a pool of loans (prominently, mortgage loans), where the interest and principal payments on the loans are directly passed through to the holders of the securities. Defaults on the interest or principal of the loans, or prepayments of the loans in the pool, are absorbed by the holders of the securities.

[10] See Mueller, Glenn (2002), "What Will the Next Real Estate Cycle Look Like?," in *Journal of Real Estate Portfolio Management*, January, pp. 115–125.

[11] The *Handbook* is a joint publication by Eurostat, the International Labour Organization (ILO), the IMF, the Organisation for Economic Co-operation and Development (OECD), the United Nations Economic Commission for Europe (UNECE), and the World Bank through the Inter-Secretariat Working Group on Price Statistics (IWGPS).

complicating the construction of weights to use in indices; and (3) different methods of compiling real estate price indices.

10.65 To capture changes in real estate price trends, the *Guide* advocates, at a minimum, quarterly compilation of data. Metadata describing in detail the content and coverage of—and the conceptual approach underlying—any price index disseminated is essential.

Residential property price indices

10.66 In the case of residential property, the objective for compilers is to construct a constant quality residential property price index (RPPI) that can control for differences in the characteristics of the properties sold over time. The goal is for changes in the RPPI to measure only price changes in the real estate market. Typically, the most important characteristics that need to be accounted for include (1) the location of the property; (2) the property type (e.g., detached house or apartment); (3) the size of the property (structure or plot); (4) the age of the structure; (5) the materials used in the construction; and (6) any other price determining characteristics.[12]

10.67 There are several methods to calculate RPPIs, all described in detail in Eurostat's *Handbook on Residential Property Prices Indices*, namely: (1) simple mean or median indices; (2) stratification or mix adjustment methods; (3) hedonic regression methods; (4) repeat sales methods; and (5) appraisal-based methods. Since this is an area beyond the scope of this *Guide*, it is sufficient to enumerate them and to make FSI compilers aware of the complexities involved in the calculation of RPPIs.

10.68 FSI compilers rely on other agencies or data providers for the source data used in producing the FSI measuring residential property prices. The quality, coverage, and detail of data will, to a very large extent, determine what RPPI might be used and, ultimately, the quality of the FSI. Ideally, the index should cover a large number of transactions nationally rather than just a subset (say for the capital city or only mortgage funded transactions); reflect actual transaction prices; and be timely, accurate, and continuously available over time.

[12]See Eurostat (2013), p. 25.

Commercial property price indices

10.69 The principles described for RPPIs also apply to commercial real estate, but with additional complexities. Commercial real estate comprises four very different types of properties: offices, retail, industrial, and residential (if developed for commercial purposes). Within these four categories, properties are heterogeneous and transactions irregular, hindering comparisons of average transaction prices for a fixed-quality bundle of properties over time. Even where repeat transactions can be used, the population of properties sold more than once in the period of the index can be very limited and unrepresentative of the total population of commercial properties.

10.70 For retail property, value depends heavily on the profits of the occupant's business, and therefore it will fluctuate with the economic cycle. Another complicating factor in compiling a CPPI is that statistical reporting systems often do not effectively pick up the relatively small number of commercial transactions—as they may involve privately negotiated sales—and the changing patterns of new construction. Rather, experience suggests that commercial real estate indices tend to be based on localities, such as big cities, where there are specific concentrations of properties available commercially. Consequently, the compiled CPPI may be unrepresentative of the whole economy.

10.71 Facilitating the process of compiling price indexes for commercial real estate is the fact that commercial real estate can be characterized as a commodity consisting of square meters of commercial space for which rental or use values can be estimated. Rental rates are often expressed in terms of the annual cost per unit of space, most commonly per square meter. Such measures can also be used for purposes of international comparisons of rental costs.

10.72 Two main types approaches have been developed for constructing CPPIs: (1) appraisal-based and (2) transaction-based indices.[13] Beyond methodological limitations, compilers of CPPIs face data availability problems. Data on commercial real estate are sparse and sometimes not available for some types of properties, especially for industrial property, and

[13]For a detailed treatment of these approaches, as well as the difficulties of compiling CPPIs, see Silver, Mick, 2013, "Understanding Commercial Property Price Indexes," *World Economics*, Volume 14, Number 3, July–September.

the mix of transactions can differ greatly over time. Currently, most price index series for commercial real estate are provided by private sector organizations. Indices disseminated by private sources may not disclose the methodology used for their calculation, hampering comparison between data sources. There is also possible bias if the private sector organization only covers certain segments of the market.

Financial Soundness Indicators for Real Estate Markets

10.73 The four FSIs for real estate markets are (1) residential real estate prices (a core FSI), (2) commercial real estate prices, (3) residential real estate loans to total gross loans, and (4) commercial real estate loans to total gross loans.

Residential real estate prices

10.74 The FSI **residential real estate prices** provides a metric to gauge the exposure of DTs in case of rapid increases in residential real estate prices, which can be followed by a sharp decline when credit conditions deteriorate (see Box 10.6).

10.75 This core FSI, which covers residential real estate price indices, is calculated as the percentage change in the index during the 12 months prior to the reporting period.

10.76 FSI compilers must rely on source data from third parties for this indicator. They usually do not determine the way RPPIs are estimated, as they use indices produced by other agencies and available to the public. Ideally, the index should have a broad coverage in terms of geography (country-wide, or the largest cities in the country), property type (detached homes, townhomes, apartments), and price-range coverage.

10.77 FSI compilers should be aware of the advantages and disadvantages of the four main methods for calculating RPPIs;[14] and ensure that comparable data are collected, stored, and compiled.

10.78 If more than one RPPI is disseminated, compilers of FSIs should acknowledge possible trade-offs between frequency, timeliness, accuracy, and coverage of the selected real estate price index. The coverage of the index should be as broad as possible, and its frequency should be at least quarterly. If a general aggregated price index with a comprehensive geographical coverage is not available, then FSI compilers should decide which of the narrower indices is the most representative of the residential real estate market and use it for the calculation of this core indicator. Metadata on this indicator must be also disseminated, clearly explaining the data sources and compilation methods used.

Commercial real estate prices

10.79 The FSI **commercial real estate prices** provides a metric to gauge the exposure of DTs in case of rapid increases in commercial real estate prices (often

[14]See Eurostat (2013).

Box 10.6 The Housing Bubble in the United States

The graph shows the evolution of the S&P Case-Shiller U.S. National Home Price Index, a generally accepted RPPI, in the run-up to the financial crisis of 2008.

Partly fuelled by a "loose" monetary policy, housing prices peaked in mid-2006 and reached levels 120 percent higher than 10 years prior. When the real estate bubble busted, prices dropped by almost 30 percent in the next six years.

The collapse of the housing market triggered a financial crisis in the United States that spread to the rest of the world. The U.S. government had to bail out the banking system through special loans and rescue packages.

Figure 10.6.1. S&P Case-Shiller U.S. National Home Price Index evolution

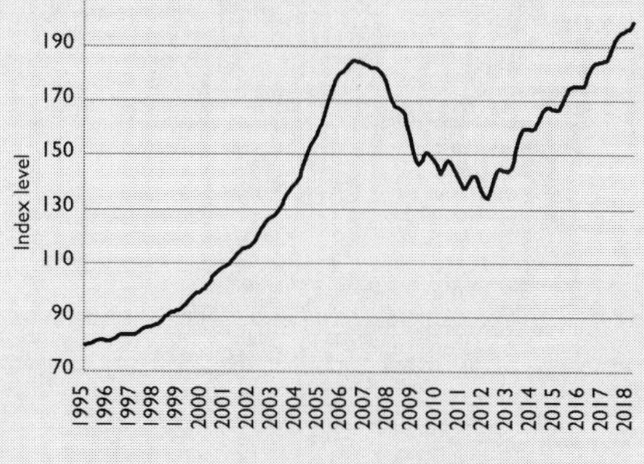

Source: S&P/Case-Shiller U.S. National Home Price Index.

fueled by expansionary monetary policy and capital inflows), which can be followed by a sharp decline in case of an economic downturn or when credit conditions deteriorate.

10.80 This FSI covers commercial real estate price indices. It is calculated as the percentage change in the commercial real estate price index during the 12 months prior to the reporting period.

10.81 For this indicator, FSI compilers must rely on indices produced by other public or private agencies. Shortcomings regarding geographical coverage and types of properties surveyed may negatively affect the quality of the index used. Contrary to the case of RPPIs, the main sources of data for CPPIs are often private sector organizations. This raises the issue about possible bias on the available data. Another source of information for CPPIs may be financial institutions active in lending to the commercial real estate market.

10.82 As explained earlier, the calculation of CPPIs involves the same difficulties as the estimation of RPPIs, and FSI compilers face similar issues as for the indicator on residential property prices. However, the differences are compounded by the fact that commercial real estate comprises four very different types of properties: offices, retail, industrial, and residential (if developed for commercial purposes), making it difficult to compare the prices.

10.83 The same considerations discussed for RPPIs regarding frequency, timeliness, and coverage of the indices apply also to CPPIs, and hence the need for extensive metadata on the CPPI used when calculating this indicator.

Residential real estate loans to total loans

10.84 The FSI **residential real estate loans to total loans** provides a metric to gauge the DTs' exposure to the residential real estate market. Experience has shown that, in many instances, a real estate boom characterized by a rapid rise in real estate prices has been preceded or accompanied by a boom in mortgage lending.[15] Following a subsequent tightening of these policies, and a collapse in market prices, there have been episodes of financial sector problems when debtors face difficulties meeting their payments. The drop in value of the residential real estate collateral worsens the situation.

10.85 This FSI is calculated by using residential real estate loans as the numerator (line 50 in Table 5.1), and gross loans (line 18.i in Table 5.1) as the denominator. Residential real estate loans are defined in paragraph 5.97 as all loans collateralized by real estate, while loans are defined in paragraphs 5.41–5.43. Household debt collateralized by real estate can be used alternatively as the numerator (line 23 in Table 5.6). While not all real estate lending to households is collateralized by residential real estate, such collateralized debt predominates.

10.86 The definition of this FSI requires not only data on residential real estate (mortgage) loans, but also data on all loans collateralized by residential real estate, regardless of the purpose of those loans. In many countries, loans collateralized by real estate may comprise a significant portion of credit to the household sector. National practices may differ on how these loans are classified. The required series are not available from the consolidated balance sheet of DTs but will need to be provided by DTs as supplementary memorandum series. Total loans can be sourced from the consolidated balance sheet of the DTs.

10.87 For *cross-border* consolidated data, data on residential real estate loans by subsidiaries abroad may need to be additionally requested, if not available from supervisory sources. The available information may need to be aggregated.

10.88 For data compiled on a *domestic location* consolidation basis, residential real estate loans may be available from monetary and financial statistics sources that provide an industrial classification of lending by type of economic activity. Otherwise, additional data may need to be separately requested.

10.89 The consistent application by DTs of a definition of residential real estate is central. This should include houses, apartments, and other dwellings (e.g., houseboats and mobile homes)—and any associated land—intended for occupancy by individual households. Furthermore, it is very important that all DTs follow the definition of residential real estate loans recommended by the *Guide*, namely not only residential real estate loans but also any other loan collateralized by residential real estate regardless of the purpose of those loans. Regarding total loans, issues

[15] See Gorton (2008).

for compilers are the same as for other core and additional FSIs for DTs where they are used as denominator, as discussed in Chapter 7.

Commercial real estate loans to total loans

10.90 The FSI **commercial real estate loans to total loans** provides a metric to gauge the DTs' exposure to the commercial real estate market. Many of the same considerations described earlier for residential real estate apply for commercial real estate.

10.91 This FSI is calculated by using loans collateralized by commercial real estate, loans to construction companies, and loans to companies active in the development of real estate (line 51 of Table 5.1) as the numerator; and gross loans (line 18.i) as the denominator. Commercial real estate loans are defined in paragraph 5.98 and loans are defined in paragraphs 5.41–5.43.

10.92 The definition of this FSI requires not only data on loans for commercial real estate but also data on all loans collateralized by commercial real estate, plus loans to construction companies and corporations active in the development of real estate. These series are not available from the consolidated balance sheet of DTs but will need to be provided by DTs as supplementary memorandum series.

10.93 For *cross-border* consolidated data, data on commercial real estate loans by subsidiaries abroad may need to be additionally requested, if not available from supervisory sources. The available information may need to be aggregated.

10.94 For data compiled on a *domestic location* consolidation basis, commercial real estate loans may be available from monetary and financial statistics sources that provide an industrial classification of lending by type of economic activity. If so, lending among resident DTs that are part of the same group should be deducted. Otherwise, additional data may need to be separately requested.

10.95 As with residential real estate loans, the consistent application by DTs of a definition of what constitutes commercial real estate lending is central. Commercial real estate lending among DTs in the reporting population that are part of the same group is deducted. Regarding total loans, issues for compilers are the same as for other core and additional FSIs for DTs where they are used as denominator, as discussed in paragraph 7.38.

ANNEX

10.1 Summary of Financial Soundness Indicators for Nonfinancial Sectors

Definition	Source Data	Issues for Compilers
Nonfinancial Corporations		
Total Debt to Equity		
Nonfinancial corporations' (NFCs') total debt as a percentage of capital and reserves.	- National accounts.	- Goodwill should not be deducted from capital and reserves.
External Debt to Equity		
NFCs' debt liabilities to nonresidents as a percentage of capital and reserves.	- External debt statistics. - International investment position. - National accounts.	- NFCs' debt liabilities to nonresident subsidiaries are included in external debt.
Foreign Currency Debt to Equity		
NFCs' debt in foreign currency as a percentage of capital and reserves.	- External debt statistics. - International investment position. - National accounts. - Standardized report forms (foreign-currency-denominated domestic debt).	- Issues on capital and reserves are discussed in *Total debt to equity.*
Total Debt to GDP		
NFCs' total debt as a percentage of GDP.	- National accounts. - For large corporations, data might be sourced from published financial statements.	- Denominator is annualized GDP.
Return on Equity		
NFCs' net income after taxes as a percentage of average capital and reserves.	- National accounts. - For large corporations, data might be sourced from published financial statements.	- Indicator is a ratio of a flow divided by a stock. Numerator is annualized net income after taxes. Denominator is average capital and reserves over the same period.
Earnings to Interest and Principal Expenses		
NFCs' earnings before interest and taxes as a percentage of debt service payments.	- Data might need to be obtained from sources other than national accounts. - For large corporations, data might be sourced from published financial statements.	- Interest payments among NFCs are included in both the numerator and denominator.
Earnings to Interest Expenses		
NFCs' earnings before interest and taxes as a percentage of interest service payments.	- Data might need to be obtained from sources other than national accounts. - For large corporations, data might be sourced from published financial statements.	- Interest payments among NFCs are included in both the numerator and denominator.

Definition	Source Data	Issues for Compilers
Households		
Debt to GDP		
Total household debt as a percentage of GDP.	- National accounts. - Monetary statistics (debt to resident financial corporations only)	- It covers only debt of resident households. - Annualized GDP should be used.
Debt-service and Principal Payments to Household Gross Disposable Income		
Household debt-service and principal payments as a percentage of household disposable income.	- National accounts. - Financial corporations or their regulatory agencies.	- Coordination with national statistical offices and financial corporation regulatory agencies is essential to obtain source data.
Debt to Household Gross Disposable Income		
Total household debt as a percentage of household gross disposable income.	- National accounts. - Financial corporations or their regulatory agencies.	- Annual gross disposable income covering the last 12 months ending in the reporting period. - Coordination with national statistical offices and financial corporations' regulatory agencies is essential to obtain source data.
Real Estate		
Residential Real Estate Prices		
Twelve-month percentage change in residential property price index.	- Official statistics. - Real estate agents. - Financial institutions active in lending to real estate market.	- Compilers usually rely on indices produced by other agencies. - Coverage of the index might not be sufficiently broad.
Commercial Real Estate Prices		
Twelve-month percentage change in commercial property price index.	- Private sector organizations. - Financial institutions active in lending to commercial real estate market	- Data availability. - Heterogeneity of types of commercial real estate properties hindering the comparability of prices.
Residential Real Estate Loans to Total Loans		
Deposit takers' (DTs') residential real estate loans as a percentage of their total loans.	- Supervisory data, when available. - DTs' internal records.	- Consistent application by DTs of a definition of residential real estate loans.
Commercial Real Estate Loans to Total Loans		
The sum of DTs' loans collateralized by commercial real estate plus loans to construction companies and to companies active in the development of real estate, as a percentage of DTs' total loans.	- Supervisory data, when available. - DTs' internal records.	- Consistent application by DTs of a definition of commercial real estate loans.

11 Compilation and Dissemination of Financial Soundness Indicators

I. Introduction

11.1 This chapter provides practical guidance on strategic and management considerations about the compilation of FSIs and dissemination practices, which can be adapted to meet specific country circumstances.

II. Strategic Issues

Legal and Institutional Requirements

Responsibility for data compilation and dissemination

11.2 Based on the experience of over a decade of FSI compilation and dissemination, as well as the experience of working with 140 FSI reporters, the *Guide* recommends that the primary responsibility for calculating and disseminating all FSIs should reside with the central bank, in collaboration with other relevant authorities. For DT data, the legal powers for imposing source data reporting normally reside in the central bank and the DT supervisor. For source data reporting of OFCs, separate agencies might be involved as in many countries, the central bank does not supervise all OFCs. Finally, for source data covering NFCs, the households and real estate prices, the responsibility is usually shared with the national statistical office. These agencies require appropriate legal powers to collect and disseminate the required data.

11.3 Whenever the compilation of FSIs involves multiple agencies, the *Guide* recommends that the relevant agencies sign a memorandum of understanding (MOU) providing a foundation for coordination and cooperation among them regarding source data collection and compilation.

Legal authority for data collection

11.4 The terms of the legal authority for data collection should cover the following:

- **Scope**. The type of entities compelled to report data should be clearly specified (e.g., DTs, OFCs, NFCs), and the rationale for targeting these entities should be explained (e.g., to monitor economic activity and financial transactions). Ideally, regulators could maintain a list of reporting institutions part of the reporting population.
- **Flexibility**. The legal authority should be clear as to the boundaries of the responsibilities of the compiling agencies, without being so restrictive that the agency lacks the freedom to adapt as new developments emerge.
- **Compliance**. To ensure the effectiveness of the reporting requirement, legislation could include the power to impose penalties on entities that fail to report.
- **Confidentiality**. Legislation should ensure the protection of confidential firm-level data.
- **Independence of statistical compilation**. Other government agencies should be prohibited from unduly influencing the content of statistical releases.

Adequacy of resources

11.5 National authorities are responsible for the allocation of resources for the compilation of FSIs. They are encouraged to provide adequate resources to compile the core and additional sets of FSIs. Resources will be needed for the collection and assessment of source data, as well as for the dissemination of FSIs. Moreover, authorities should strive to develop and retain over time a core contingent of qualified staff that is knowledgeable in statistical and financial soundness concepts and compilation methods.

11.6 In determining resource allocation, account should be taken of any needed improvements in data. Decisions may need to be made on updating existing report forms and questionnaires or developing new surveys (e.g., to strengthen real estate price information). After the initial development work is completed and data are being disseminated, a more detailed development work program can be produced in consultation with other agencies involved in the compilation work.

III. Managerial Issues

Data Quality

11.7 Data quality is a multidimensional construct encompassing the collection, processing, and dissemination of statistical information, in addition to the accuracy of the statistics themselves. High FSI data quality is supported by clear strategies processes including the following:

- *The principle of objectivity in the collection, processing, and dissemination of statistics be firmly adhered to.* Statistics should be collected and compiled on an impartial basis, with choices of sources and statistical techniques based solely on statistical considerations. The choice of methodologies should be justified, and information about the choices made should be readily available.
- *Validation checks within the data set and with other major data sets should be systematically undertaken.* Basic validation checks provide a first filter on the integrity of the source data and should be automated within the compiling agency. For the FSIs, emphasis should be put in ensuring consistency between the underlying series reported in the financial statements templates, the calculations of the indicators in the indicators' template, and the methodological choices documented in the FSI metadata.
- *Outlier detection can help identify breaks in the series due to reporting mistakes.* Plausibility tests should aim at identifying those data items that have reporting errors, even though they have passed the first validation checks.
- *Revision to FSI data, if needed, should follow a regular, well-established, and transparent schedule.* Since FSIs are intended to provide current actionable information to the public, supervisors, and policy officials, revisions covering all relevant periods should be introduced during the next dissemination round rather than wait for specific times (such as e.g., completion of annual audits).[1] Revisions should be analyzed by the compiling agency and fully explained to users.
- *Breaks in data series* should be clearly identified. Data supplying/producing agencies should also supply information on the shortcomings of the data.

Addressing Source Data Issues

11.8 A number of management challenges arise when compiling FSIs. First, procedures are needed to ensure that the concepts used and the data compiled are consistent with the methodology of the *Guide* in terms of instrument classification, sectorization, and valuation. The lead agency should establish key commonalities and differences in the source data and should be aware of any inconsistencies with the core concepts outlined in the *Guide*. The definitions of sectors and instruments should be assessed, as should the accounting and valuation rules.

11.9 Second, the coverage of the reporting population should be as comprehensive as possible, and ideally, it should be complete for all deposit takers. Some trade-offs might be necessary if some small institutions do not report their data in a timely manner, or do not report them at all. In such cases, a cost-benefit analysis should be undertaken to decide whether the missing data would materially affect the aggregated results. If not, it would not be necessary to devote additional resources to achieve complete coverage of the sector.

11.10 Third, the lead agency should be in close contact with the data providers, so that both sides understand the other's needs and problems. The timing, content, and formats of the data provided by the reporting units should be clearly established. Any changes in coverage, definition, or classification should be identified in advance of the provision of data so that there are no surprises during the data compilation process.

11.11 When addressing the issue of institutional coverage, particular attention should be given to

[1] Changes to data resulting from annual audits sometimes fall outside the on-going data reporting procedures. If this is the case, it is important that compilers devise additional methods to capture changes resulting from audits.

the provision of the applicable group-consolidated financial statements. Group-consolidation is recommended for DTs (CBCSDI) and for insurance corporations (CBDI). The lead agency should obtain from the relevant bank and insurance supervisory agencies information about the corporate groups that report on a consolidated basis and the consolidation approach used for each group. Information should also be obtained about groups that do not report on a consolidated basis. Knowledge about the consolidation approaches underlying the source data for the FSIs is critical when analyzing the FSIs and their implications for the soundness of the financial system.

11.12 FSIs are published on an aggregated basis. Some data are collected from individual institutions on a confidential basis. Most countries restrict the dissemination of individual entity source data. These confidentiality considerations should be incorporated when planning the strategy for compiling and disseminating FSIs, particularly when setting up data flows between relevant agencies. The lead agency should closely monitor the individual data supplied and should have the right to require that the data suppliers provide explanations regarding the data.

11.13 It is important that arrangements be put in place to facilitate formal and informal contacts among the staff of the different units responsible for FSI data collection and dissemination, to deal with any problems expeditiously and to avoid duplication of efforts. If there is only one agency involved (e.g., the central bank), compilers should have easy access to the underlying series managed by other departments that are needed for the calculation of FSIs. If more than one agency is involved (e.g., the central bank and a banking supervisory agency), cooperation and coordination between the data collecting agency and the agency in charge of compilation and dissemination of FSIs is of the utmost importance. Cooperation is also required with the national statistical office, or a similar agency, for FSIs for the nonfinancial sector.

Consultation with Reporters and Users

Consultation with reporters

11.14 Even though legal backing will support compilers' efforts to obtain the necessary information from the primary reporters of data (e.g., the individual deposit takers), it is essential that a "culture of reporting" be developed. This is not easily or quickly achieved but should be considered as an ongoing aspect of the work. Steps to encourage a culture of reporting include convening meetings with potential respondents and addressing their concerns, developing report forms that fit easily into existing management reporting systems and are not overly complex, and disseminating and promoting the FSIs in a transparent manner. Indeed, data reporters should see some benefit arising from the provision of data, such as obtaining information on financial sector conditions relevant for their own analysis. If data are collected and compiled in an efficient manner and the FSIs are viewed as important, experience suggests that data reporters are more likely to respond.

11.15 Thus, for example, when new data are to be collected, the compiler is advised to undertake report form testing—that is, obtain feedback from a sample of potential reporters on whether the instructions are clear and workable before they become operational. Moreover, seminars and workshops explaining the reporting requirements are valuable to both reporters and the compiling agency and are encouraged. The ongoing maintenance of an electronic register of contacts at the data reporting institutions provides information that can help ensure a well-run statistical operation. Through such a register, institutional memory at the statistical agency can be developed and maintained.

Consultation with users

11.16 There should be mechanisms to ensure that the FSIs continue to meet the needs of policymakers and other users. Feedback collected through this mechanism sometimes may warrant a revision of the FSIs and could be shared with the IMF to strengthen future editions of the *Guide*.

11.17 Meetings with policymakers and other data users should be periodically convened to review the comprehensiveness of the FSIs and to identify emerging data requirements. Similarly, consultation with regional and international organizations, including standard setters, would be helpful. New initiatives could be discussed with policy departments and statistical advisory groups; such discussions would provide justification for seeking additional resources. As with any new body of statistics, programs that reach out to users can be useful for promoting awareness and understanding of the data, as well as for identifying data quality issues and other user concerns.

IV. Compilation of FSIs: Practical Issues

Availability of Source Data

11.18 One of the first tasks in developing efficient systems for compiling the new FSIs is the identification of available source data. In the many jurisdictions that already have good coverage of the DT FSIs, data for the new and revised DT FSIs is likely to be available from the same supervisory sources. Obtaining data for FSIs outside the DT sector usually requires coordination among multiple agencies. When compared with the information needed to compile FSIs, this inventory of available information will inform decisions on resource needs and the development of work programs. Producing a comprehensive list of existing data will entail close coordination among potential compiling agencies, particularly those providing data on OFCs, NFCs, the household sector, and real estate prices. It is also essential that sources and methods be well documented for use when problems arise, for ensuring continuity of process when there is staff turnover or absence, and to support the development of metadata.

11.19 Experience with the FSIs indicates that coverage of DTs (as defined in Chapter 2) is generally quite good across more than 130 jurisdictions compiling FSIs. Coverage drops off significantly, however, for OFCs, NFCs, HHs, and real estate markets—data that is not normally obtained directly from DT supervisory sources by the lead agency. Addressing the gaps requires that the lead agency can either collect source data directly from different financial institutions/relevant entities or indirectly from relevant authorities/other agencies. Based on experience, the Guide recommends indirect collection as other agencies will generally have the required legal power and may already have much of the required data. The common indirect sources are relevant financial sector regulators for DTs and selected OFCs, national statistics offices (NSO), or other government agencies for other OFCs, NFCs, HHs, and real estate markets; relevant supervisors/regulators or private data sources for securities markets. In the event of the absence of source data, new surveys might be necessary.

11.20 Practical consideration may include the need to establish data sharing agreements with relevant agencies, including the NSO (which is most likely to collect data for NFCs/HHs and real estate markets). Data sharing and coordination between the compiler and other data-providing/producing agencies are necessary. Practical issues include smooth and timely flows of data and measures to protect data confidentiality agreements. The lead agency should also establish methods to ensure the accuracy and reliability of the data provided for compiling the FSIs, including to ensure consistency with the core concepts underlying the FSIs, such as definitions of sectors and instruments, accounting, and valuation rules.

V. Dissemination of FSIs and Related Data

Dissemination Practices

Dissemination channels

11.21 Decisions relating to the dissemination of data have important implications for a number of the compilation issues mentioned earlier. Publication deadlines help focus the work processes, which in turn affect resource allocation decisions. An important decision with regard to dissemination concerns periodicity. Also significant are decisions on the range of data to be disseminated, the timeliness of release, and the format of release. The preferred format for the electronic exchange of data is the Statistical Data and Metadata eXchange Standard (SDMX), which is fully supported by the IMF for the collection of FSI-related data.

11.22 Owing to the nature of FSIs and their importance for tracking vulnerabilities, countries might consider working toward disseminating core and additional FSIs as frequently as possible.

11.23 The *Guide* encourages dissemination on a single centralized website—the website of the lead agency—allowing simultaneous release to all users, general accessibility of the data, and transparency. To enhance the usefulness of FSIs, countries could consider supplement the dissemination of the FSIs with commentary on the main trends in the FSI data series and detailed metadata to support their understanding. In fact, some countries already imbed FSI commentary in their regular publications on financial stability issues. Additions could include discussions of relevant methodological issues. In parallel, countries are encouraged to regularly report core and additional FSIs for dissemination on the IMF's website. The IMF's web portal functions as a hub where users can easily access FSIs from a large number of countries compiled in accordance with international standards and containing detailed metadata, facilitating cross-country comparability.

Frequency and timeliness

11.24 It is recommended that FSIs be disseminated at least on a quarterly basis with a lag of one quarter, while monthly dissemination with one-month lag is strongly encouraged. The availability of information can vary among FSIs—for instance, information on interbank interest rates will be available more frequently than information on the geographic distribution of lending. Nonetheless, countries should work toward releasing most of the core FSIs and as many additional FSIs as possible on a quarterly basis, within one quarter of the reference date. The compilation and dissemination of additional FSIs depends on national circumstances. As with the core FSIs, the *Guide* recommends quarterly dissemination of the additional FSIs, with the national option for monthly dissemination.

Breaks in data series

11.25 It is particularly important to monitor and document breaks in data series because they can affect the analysis. One of the most frequent types of breaks arises from changes in the reporting population. For instance, new deposit takers can be licensed while others are closed. Moreover, mergers between deposit takers can have significant consequences.

11.26 In general, it is important for compilers to document mergers and any changes in underlying accounting rules that affect the continuity of the data series. Such information should be maintained over time.[2]

[2]Within a country, some DTs may be required to adopt Basel III, while some other DTs continue to follow Basel I or Basel II. Chapter 3 discusses a recommended aggregation of capital components under Basel III and Basel II (and/or Basel I) for deriving sectoral data.

Financial sector overview

11.27 The financial system structure will affect the range of data available for calculating FSIs and any assessment of FSIs that are disseminated. The dissemination of structural indicators for the deposit takers and OFCs discussed next might be relevant for any such assessment.

Deposit takers

11.28 To provide an overview of the size and ownership structure of the deposit-taking sector, thus supporting the interpretation of FSIs, the key structural indicators, such as number of deposit takers split by type and by ownership, their branches and subsidiaries could be disseminated.

11.29 The value of assets owned by the deposit-taking sector provides information on the size of the sector. Additionally, information on the net number of deposit takers entering or leaving the business and information from FSIs, such as the spread between deposit and lending rates, provides some indication of competitive pressures or whether the sector could be under stress. In addition, the number of branch outlets in the economy can be a source of information both on cost pressures and on the size of the deposit-taking industry within the economy.

11.30 In many economies, the deposit-taking sector may consist of specialized institutions, as described in Chapter 2. If so, the nature of the banking business undertaken by various types of specialized institutions may differ significantly. To further understand the structure of the financial system, compilers could distinguish structural information on commercial banks and on distinctive types of specialized banks such as savings banks, cooperative banks, and microfinance institutions.

11.31 FSIs for a sector as a whole may mask variations within the population of financial institutions. For example, the sector-wide capital asset ratio for deposit takers is an average ratio for the sector, but it does not reveal whether individual entities' capital ratios are clustered in a narrow range around the average value or are spread over a wide range. Hence, the publication of concentration and distribution measures (CDMs) is recommended (see Chapter 12 for guidance on the compilation of CDMs).

11.32 Finally, countries could disseminate information on their deposit insurance schemes, because the level of coverage of depositors' funds can affect economic behavior and thus have implications for financial stability.

Other financial corporations

11.33 Given the heterogeneity of institutions within the OFC sector, the *Guide* introduces disaggregated reporting for the OFC sector covering some of the key subsectors. This requires that compilers identify source data to compile the new FSIs for life and non life insurance corporations, pension funds, and money market funds, in addition to aggregate data on all OFCs.

Metadata

11.34 Metadata describes the content and coverage of the FSIs and the accounting conventions and other national guidelines reflected in the data. Given the diversity of standards and compilation practices between countries, compilers are urged to proactively assess whether disseminated metadata provide all relevant information needed by the public, researchers, and policy officials to properly understand the meaning and limitations of the disseminated FSIs.

11.35 Metadata should be publicly available along with FSI data. In particular, a brief description should be provided of the definitions for the numerator and denominator of each FSI, particularly if they are different from the definitions set out in the *Guide*. Other specific information that is useful to data users include the consolidation basis used to compile FSIs, regulatory framework (Basel I, Basel II, or Basel III), intra-group consolidation adjustments, and accounting rules such as asset/liability valuation and time of recognition, and exchange rates used for conversion of foreign-currency accounts into national currency value. In addition, compilers are encouraged to make public other information, such as source data and institutional coverage, and whether the numerator and denominator are available with the same periodicity, and if not, how this affects the use of the data. Metadata should also include explanation of any deviations of the national compilation practices from the *Guide's* recommendations.

11.36 When data are disseminated, provisional data should be clearly indicated and any major revisions explained by way of notes to the published tables or in the metadata. Breaks in series, for example, due to changes in the reporting population should be clearly identified and quantified where possible. Such explanations are particularly important given that the entrance or departure of a few institutions from the reporting sample could potentially have a significant impact on the FSIs. At the development stage, some FSIs may be calculated from data covering various subgroups that apply different accounting principles. Such situations should be highlighted in the metadata.

12 Concentration and Distribution Measures

I. Introduction

12.1 Financial soundness indicators for a sector may hide variations that could endanger the entire financial system. For example, the sector-wide capital-asset ratio for deposit takers is an average ratio for the system, but it does not reveal whether individual institutions' capital ratios are clustered around the average value or are spread over a wide range. Moreover, data for highly capitalized deposit takers could offset the data for undercapitalized deposit takers, such that the aggregate ratio may appear robust while masking significant vulnerabilities from weak deposit takers whose failure could lead to contagion throughout the system. For this reason, FSIs need to be supplemented by concentration and distributions measures (CDMs).

12.2 To address this concern, in 2009, the IMF/Financial Stability Board G-20 Data Gaps Initiative (DGI) called on the IMF "to investigate, develop, and encourage implementation of standard measures that can provide information on tail risks, concentrations, variations in distributions, and the volatility of indicators over time."[1] The concentration and distribution measures (CDMs) for selected FSIs aim at providing critical information about vulnerabilities in the financial system, not directly captured by simple averages.

12.3 This chapter provides a brief overview of the proposed CDMs for selected FSIs and guidance on their computation. The chapter also discusses ways to overcome confidentiality concerns about CDM reporting.

[1]See "The Financial Crisis and Information Gaps: Report to the G-20 Finance Ministers and Central Bank Governors," prepared by IMF Staff and the FSB Secretariat, October 29, 2009, recommendation number 3.

II. Background

The CDM Pilot Project

12.4 As part of the calls to develop and encourage the implementation of tail risk and concentration measures for FSIs, the IMF's Statistic Department conducted a pilot project to assess the feasibility of calculating and reporting (regularly) CDM data for *selected* deposit takers' FSIs. In addition, the pilot was undertaken to ascertain (1) the effectiveness of the pilot CDMs in monitoring financial sector vulnerabilities; (2) potential confidentiality concerns over their reporting; (3) the extent of the reporting burden; and (4) the procedures and resources the Fund would need to deploy in order to gather, compile, analyze, and disseminate the CDMs along with current FSI data and metadata.

12.5 Participation in the project was broadly based and there was a strong response to the request for volunteers—with 35 participants providing data. The comprehensiveness of reporting varied across countries, indicators, and time periods. Several participants engaged IMF staff to resolve methodological issues, including the computation of quartiles.

12.6 The pilot CDMs comprised (1) minimum, maximum, and mean; (2) weighted standard deviations and skewness; and (3) quartiles and the asset share of the bottom quartile. Also, a concentration (Herfindahl) index was calculated. The CDMs were requested for a subset of six FSIs for DTs (regulatory Tier 1 capital to risk-weighted assets, NPLs to total gross loans, return on assets [ROA], return on equity [ROE], liquid assets to short-term liabilities, and capital to total assets).

12.7 The results of the pilot provided useful insights to the analytical value of CDMs.[2] They suggested that

[2]See Crowley et al (2016).

Table 12.1 Concentration and Distributions Measures Indicators

Measure	Required Frequency
Sector concentration index (Herfindahl index)	Annual
Weighted quartiles	Monthly, quarterly, or annual
Weighted standard deviation	Monthly, quarterly, or annual
Weighted skewness	Monthly, quarterly, or annual
Weighted kurtosis	Monthly, quarterly, or annual

Source: IMF staff.

CDM data have analytical value that would justify efforts to compile and report them. CDMs provide important information that is not revealed by simple averages, can be used as a starting point in financial stability and performance assessments, and are useful tools for monitoring financial sector vulnerabilities. Participating countries did not report any significant resource burden associated with the compilation of CDMs.

The FSI Compilers' Perspective

12.8 When developing the work program for Phase 2 of the DGI, the IAG[3] agreed that the IMF should seek further input from FSI reporting countries and potential data users prior to taking a decision with moving ahead with the collection of FSI's CDMs.

12.9 In April 2017, the IMF conducted a workshop on FSIs, which brought together 75 participants from 36 countries and 7 international organizations, to secure an agreement on the collection of CDMs for a selected list of FSIs. Participants, which included a significant majority of FSI compilers, agreed with the benefits of the CDM project. Most participants observed that underlying bank-by-bank supervisory data are available, thus the data required for producing CDMs are, in many cases, readily available. They acknowledged that CDMs provide valuable insights for financial stability analysis, which supports efforts by member countries to compile and report them on a regular basis to the IMF. The list of CDMs and the underlying FSIs were discussed with the workshop participants and agreed upon.

III. Compilation of CDMs

12.10 This section provides a set of concrete recommendations and guidelines on the proposed CDM measures and their potential use. This would serve to harmonize and standardize different types of statistical methodologies (e.g., interpolation, estimation or approximation techniques, and software) available to users which in turn will facilitate cross-country comparability, reproducibility, and interpretability. The chapter also discusses how to address confidentiality concerns associated with their reporting.

12.11 The technique to compute CDMs may be a function of their ease of use, type of data available, and the type of information sharing agreements for the specific institutions. When it comes to public dissemination, some CDMs may prove particularly useful, as they can shed information on the system's vulnerabilities without revealing otherwise confidential information on individual institutions. To facilitate uniform and consistent reporting of the CDMs, the IMF is making available on its FSI website a template for the calculation of these CDMs.

12.12 To estimate concentration in the system, this Guide recommends the Herfindahl-Hirschman (thereafter Herfindahl) index. To gauge dispersion and related properties, the Guide recommends the following distribution measures: weighted standard deviation, weighted quartiles, weighted skewness, and weighted kurtosis (Table 12.1), for at least seven designated FSIs in the universe of a country's deposit-taking institutions (Table 12.2).

[3] The IAG was established in 2008 to coordinate international statistical work following the financial crisis.

Table 12.2 Subset of Financial Soundness Indicators Covered by Concentration and Distributions Measures

Solvency Indicator
Tier 1 capital to risk-weighted assets
Nonperforming loans net of specific provisions to capital
Asset Quality
Nonperforming loans to total gross loans
Provisions to nonperforming loans
Profitability
Return on assets
Return on equity
Leverage
Tier 1 capital to total assets

Source: IMF staff.

The Sample

12.13 CDMs should be computed for the same financial institutions for which the selected FSIs are reported according to the consolidation principles described in Chapter 6. The *Guide* also, prescribes a minimum number of DTs to ensure meaningful estimates and to preserve confidentiality, as described in section V of this chapter.

Concentration

12.14 Concentration in the banking sector has continued to increase in the recent times (e.g., BIS 2018). Some studies argued that concentration may promote financial stability (e.g., Beck et al., 2006; De Haan and Poghosyan, 2012; Evrensel, 2008), the rationale being that concentration may improve franchise value, leading to less risk taking, thus contributing to financial stability. At the same time, concentration is well-known to be linked to the moral hazard—*too big-to-fail problem*. The implicit assumption that large DTs in a concentrated sector will be bailed out by the government if they get into trouble provides an incentive to the DTs to acquire riskier assets and to operate with high levels of leverage, increasing the vulnerability of the financial system (e.g., Boyd and Runkle, 1993; Mishkin, 1999; O'Hara and Shaw, 1990).

12.15 Because of conflicting evidence on the concentration and stability nexus, it is important to start with a measure of the level of concentration in the financial system and then interpret the results considering additional country-specific factors for a more holistic view. There are several measures of concentration, ranging from heuristic measures (Herfindahl and Gini indices), to more sophisticated model and simulation-based approaches also known as granularity adjustments.[4] The *Guide* recommends the Herfindahl Index to estimate concentration in the financial system because of its ease of use. Furthermore, empirical evidence suggests that this measure does not yield significantly different estimates than more sophisticated and computation-intensive approaches.[5]

Herfindahl concentration index

12.16 The Herfindahl Index, *H*, is the percentage asset share of the system. It is calculated as the sum of squares of each financial institution's asset shares (measured in percent) in a sector: $H = \sum_{i=1}^{N} (a_i)^2$

where

$$a_i = \frac{\textit{Total assets of institution i}}{\textit{Total assets of the entire deposit taking sector}}.$$

12.17 Values of the index range from 1/N to 1.0, with higher values indicating greater concentration. In a situation where the sector has 100 institutions each

[4] There is vast literature on granularity adjustment, which was pioneered by Gordy (2003) in the context of credit risk concentration.

[5] See Deutsche Bundesbank (2006) and Grippa and Gornicka (2016). Equations 15 and 16 in Emmer and Tasche (2005) provide some theoretical background.

with an identical 1 percent share of the market, the index will be $H = 0.01$. In contrast, with perfect concentration, where one institution has a 100 percent market share, $H = 1.0$; that is, the contribution of the monopoly institution is $1.0 \times 1.0 = 1.0$. A rule of thumb sometimes used is that H below 0.1 indicates limited concentration, and H above 0.18 points to significant concentration. Table 12.3 illustrates how to compute H for a country consisting of 11 deposit takers. For this hypothetical example, the Herfindahl Index for the top-five DTs is equal to 0.1614.

Distribution: Dispersion Measures

12.18 FSIs include aggregated individual institution data as well as idiosyncratic elements in which the financial institutions operate. The extent to which these aggregates are good representatives of the entire sector is a function of factors such as the variability or dispersion among the underlying soundness of individual institutions. Given that large-scale disruptions to the financial stability might stem from difficulties in individual institutions, dispersion measures are needed to shed some light on such blind spots (e.g., Smaga, 2014; and Systemic Risk Centre RC, 2015).

12.19 There are various ways to measure dispersion, including variance, standard deviation, and quartiles. The *Guide* recommends (1) weighted standard deviation and (2) weighted quartiles as measures of dispersion, not just because of the ease of computation but also for their robustness.

Weighted standard deviation

12.20 The standard deviation (σ) estimates the variability (or spread) for an FSI among the different DTs. It indicates how close the indicators for the individual institutions are to the sectoral average. When the standard deviation is small, that is, close to zero, the values in a dataset are tightly bunched together, and consequently, the aggregate indicator is a good reflection of the overall system's soundness. On the other hand, when the individual values vary significantly, the standard deviation will be relatively large. And this difference can have a significant economic impact. For example, an aggregate Tier 1 capital to risk-weighted assets indicator with a large standard deviation indicates that some DTs could deviate significantly from the minimum capital requirement. However, standard deviation measures are not robust because they can be greatly influenced by outliers. In addition, they do not account for sample characteristics such as the relative asset or loan size of the different DTs.

12.21 To account for the relative asset or loan size of the different DTs, the *Guide* recommends weighing the standard deviation by the relative share of the variable in the denominator of the relevant FSI ratio. This weighting will account for the marginal contribution of DTs with larger assets, gross loans, and so on to the relevant FSI. For instance, the weighting variable of Tier 1 capital to risk-weighted assets is the relative share of risk-weighted assets of the individual

Table 12.3 Example of Computing the Herfindahl Index

Deposit Taker	Assets	Market Share (percent)	Market Share Squared
1	300	30	0.0900
2	200	20	0.0400
3	130	13	0.0169
4	90	9	0.0081
5	80	8	0.0064
6	50	5	0.0025
7	50	5	0.0025
8	40	4	0.0016
9	20	2	0.0004
10	20	2	0.0004
11	20	2	0.0004
Total	1,000	100	0.1692

Source: IMF staff estimates.

Table 12.4 Unweighted and Weighted Medians of Tier 1 Ratios for a Hypothetical Sample of 15 Deposit Takers

Deposit Taker	Tier 1 Ratio	Individual Deposit Taker's Assets
1	2.1	400,000
2	3.1	300,000
3	3.3	300,000
4	4.1	400,000
5	4.1	600,000
6	6.7	300,000
7	7.1	200,000
8	8.1	500,000
9	8.2	300,000
10	9.2	400,000
11	11.2	1,500,000
12	11.3	800,000
13	13.1	1,800,000
14	13.5	2,200,000
15	13.8	2,000,000
Unweighted median: 8.1		
Weighted median: 12.2		

Source: IMF staff estimates.

institutions. For the FSIs related to asset quality, the *Guide* recommends weighing the NPL indicator by the relative size of an institutions loans to total gross loans, and so on.

12.22 Specifically, the recommended weighted standard deviation is given by the positive square root of the weighted variance (σ^2). Finally, the weighted variance is calculated as follows:

$$\sigma^2 = \sum_{i=1}^{N}\left(FSI_i - \overline{FSI}\right)^2 \times \omega_i$$

where

$\overline{FSI}$ is the sector FSI[6] and ω is the weight used to calculate the average sector FSI.

Weighted quartiles

12.23 In addition, to understand the variability of financial soundness among the individual DTs, it is important to identify DTs' degree of exposure. The statistical method of quartiles which divides data into quarters (with the second quartile being the median) is useful in this regard.

12.24 Standard quantiles comprise the same number of institutions, irrespective of their contribution to the FSI in question. Therefore, with this approach, the important features of the distribution may be missed if the relative contribution of each data point is not properly accounted for in the compilation of the quantile.

12.25 In addition, adopting an unweighted approach where each quantile comprises the same number of institutions may affect cross-country comparability. For example, a country where 25 percent of the DTs are very small institutions with high NPLs will exhibit a fourth quartile with low asset quality, raising concerns about the stability of the system, even though the risk to the financial system as a whole may not be significant. This constitutes a major drawback of standard quantile analysis.

12.26 The *Guide* recommends the compilation of weighted quartiles. With weighted quartiles, the marginal contribution of the DTs to the FSI increases proportionally with their weights. Computing weighted quartiles require first mapping the DTs' specific asset, loan, or capital characteristics to the relevant FSI and

[6] The sector FSI is a weighted average.

Box 12.1 Step-by-step Instructions to Compute Weighted Quartiles

The practical computation of weighted quartiles can be thought of as following the three steps outlined here.

Let FSI_k be the value of the financial soundness indicator (FSI) for deposit taker (DT) k (k = 1, . . ., N), and let A_k refer to the total assets of DT_k, with N the number of institutions.

Step 1. Sorting

Sort the sequence $\{FSI_k\}$ in ascending order. As the sorting order will be the same for all the FSIs, the interpretation of the resulting quantiles will vary depending on the FSI. For the FSIs on Tier 1 capital, provisions to nonperforming loans (NPLs), returns on assets, and returns on equity, the value of the first quartile will point to institutions with relatively higher vulnerabilities, whereas for the FSIs on NPLs to gross loans and NPLs net of provisions to capital, the data for the first quartile will point to institutions with relatively lower vulnerabilities.

The sorting will result in a new sequence $\{FSI_j\}$ (j = 1, . . ., N) of the FSIs.[7]

Next to it, trace the corresponding sequence of assets $\{A_j\}$. Table 12.4 presents a sequence of FSIs sorted in an ascending order with their corresponding cumulative assets.

Step 2. Threshold Identification

Let T be the sum of the assets of DTs and W_i be the cumulative assets associated with each of the DTs in the distribution:

$$T = \sum_{j=1}^{N} A_j,\ W_i = \sum_{j=1}^{i} A_j \text{ (the assets cumulative frequency)}$$

Let "P" be the values of the asset that identify the theoretical thresholds that would define each of the quartiles.

Compute the following quantities for each quartile Q_p (p = 0.25, 0.50, *or* 0.75):

$P = T \times p$, and

Find the index W_i such that $W_i > P$ to identify the cutoff point for each of the quartile.

Step 3. Derivation of the Weighted Quartiles

Compute the weighted quartiles as follows:

$$Q_p = \begin{cases} \dfrac{FSI_{i-1} + FSI_i}{2} & \textit{if } W_{i-1} = P \\ FSI_i & \textit{Otherwise} \end{cases}$$

Thus, if the cumulative asset frequency (W_{i-1}) falls exactly on the cutoff point (P) for the quartile, the value for that quartile, say the first quartile, would be determined by the average of the FSI corresponding to the cumulative asset frequency W_i, and the next value. As a result, for the first quartile, 25 percent of the FSI values will be less than the value provided for the quartile, as intended. When $W_i > P$ (and $W_{i-1} < P$), then the value for the quartile is FSI_i. Table 12.5 shows the calculation steps to derive the weighted and unweighted median based on the data presented in Table 12.4.

then sorting out by quartile. This technique facilitates cross-country comparability of the measures, as each quartile will display the FSI for a comparable share of, say, total assets of the deposit-taking sector.

12.27 The difference between the unweighted and weighted quartiles may potentially be significant, as illustrated in Table 12.4 for the median of a fictitious sample of 15 deposit takers. While the unweighted median is 8.1, the weighted median is 12.2.[8]

[7] The new sequence is known as the sequence of order statistics.

[8] See step 3 on the derivation of the weighted quartiles.

12.28 Different approaches can be used to assign weights to each observation. The *Guide* recommends the weight by asset size approach, therefore providing a comparable weighing scheme across FSIs when defining the quartiles. In short, the point of this exercise is to construct cumulative weights according to the position of the DT's assets in the sector's distribution for the FSI and use these cumulative weights to identify the FSI quartiles. To provide concrete guidance on the compilation of weighted quartiles, Box 12.1 provides step-by step instructions for their computation.

12.29 The example in Table 12.5 illustrates the estimate differences under unweighted and weighted methodologies.

Distribution: Measures of Shape

12.30 Measures of variability and dispersion including standard deviations can help identify the presence of outlier individual institutions. However, several studies argue that these measures fail to capture fully the "true risk" of the distribution. Therefore, it is also important to identify the relative effect of the outliers.

12.31 The *Guide* recommends the use of (1) weighted skewness and (2) weighted kurtosis as additional distribution measures (DMs) for this purpose. Skewness and kurtosis are measures of shape of a distribution or dataset and widely applied in modern finance to study, for example, asset return risk.

Skewness

12.32 Skewness can indicate the extent to which FSIs of individual institutions are asymmetrically distributed relative to the sectoral mean. It serves a similar purpose as the standard deviation. In addition, skew, or skewness of a dataset, furthers our understanding of whether the outliers are tilted toward the low or high end of the spectrum, and whether the mass of the distribution is concentrated toward the left or right of the mean.

12.33 Specifically, the *Guide* recommends, the computation of weighted skewness is a function of the third moment of the distribution—with the weighting

Table 12.5 Calculation Steps of the Unweighted and Weighted Medians of Tier 1 Ratios for a Hypothetical Sample of 15 Deposit Takers

Deposit Taker	Tier 1 Ratio	Individual Deposit Taker's Assets	Cumulative Assets	Weights
1	2.1	400,000	400,000	
2	3.1	300,000	700,000	
3	3.3	300,000	1,000,000	
4	4.1	400,000	1,400,000	
5	4.1	600,000	2,000,000	
6	6.7	300,000	2,300,000	
7	7.1	200,000	2,500,000	
8	8.1	500,000	3,000,000	
9	8.2	300,000	3,300,000	W_9
10	9.2	400,000	3,700,000	
11	11.2	1,500,000	5,200,000	
12	11.3	800,000	6,000,000	
13	13.1	1,800,000	7,800,000	W_{13}
14	13.5	2,200,000	10,000,000	W_{14}
15	13.8	2,000,000	12,000,000	

P for the quantile 0.25: 3,000,000

P for the quantile 0.5: 6,000,000

P for the quantile 0.75: 9,000,000

$Q_{0.25} = \frac{8.1 + 8.2}{2}$; $Q_{0.50} = \frac{13.1 + 11.3}{2}$; $Q_{0.75} = 13.5$

Unweighted median: 8.1

Weighted median: 12.2

Source: IMF staff estimates.

Figure 12.1 Example of Right Skewed Distribution: Gamma Distribution with Parameters α = 2.5 and β = 0.5

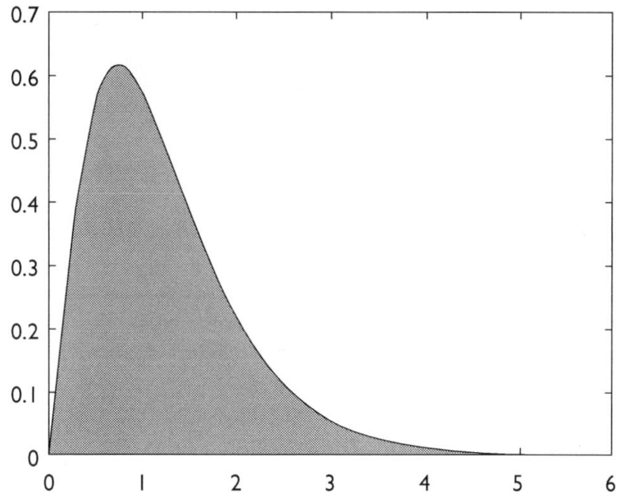

Source: IMF staff estimates.

variable being the denominator of the FSI ratio, similar to the approach recommended for the standard deviation:

$$\mu^3 = \frac{\sum_{i=1}^{N}\left(FSI_i - \overline{FSI}\right)^3 \times \omega_i}{\sigma^3}$$

12.34 Value of skewness can be positive, zero, or negative. Positive skewness indicates a longer right-hand-side tail of the distribution and the mass of the distribution concentrated toward the left of the mean as illustrated in Figure 12.1, while negative skewness indicates a longer left tail and mass of the distribution concentrated toward the right.

Kurtosis

12.35 Further, to get some insights on the proportional effect of the outliers, kurtosis may be calculated. Kurtosis estimates the degree of fatness of the tails of the FSI distribution compared to a normal distribution. Put simply, the kurtosis of distributions may be used to understand if the variability in the sectoral FSI is readily attributed to a few, extreme outliers (positive kurtosis) or several, modest deviations from the mean (negative kurtosis).

12.36 The *Guide* recommends weighted kurtosis for this purpose—with the weights constructed using the denominator of the FSI ratio. A common measure of kurtosis is the moment coefficient of kurtosis given by

$$\mu^4 = \frac{\sum_{i=1}^{N}\left(FSI_i - \overline{FSI}\right)^4 \times \omega_i}{\sigma^4}$$

12.37 As the normal distribution is often used as the standard for comparison, it is common to subtract its kurtosis from that of the distribution to estimate "excess kurtosis." The moment coefficient of kurtosis of a normal distribution equals 3.

- Positive excess kurtosis indicates that the distribution has fatter tails and sharper peak than the normal distribution. This is known as a "leptokurtic" distribution.
- Negative excess kurtosis indicates that the tails are "leaner" than the tails of the normal distribution. Such distributions are known as "platykurtic."
- The absence of excess kurtosis indicates that the distribution does not exhibit fat tails. This is referred to as "mesokurtic" distribution. For example, the student t-distribution (Figure 12.2) exhibits leptokurtosis.

Figure 12.2 Leptokurtic Distribution versus Normal Distribution

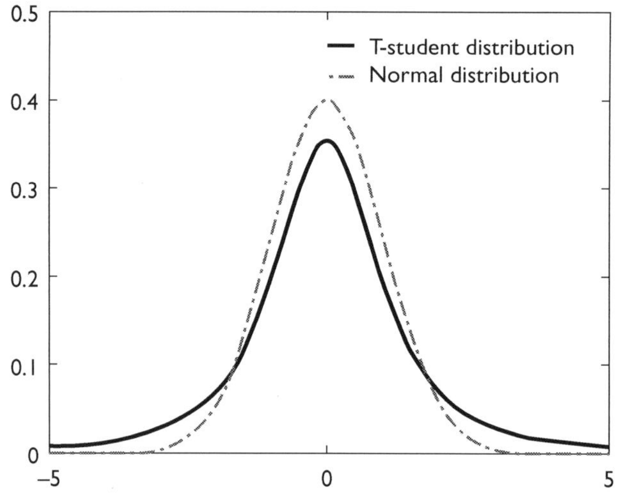

Source: IMF staff calculations.

IV. Use of CDMs

12.38 This section illustrates the use of CDMs as an early diagnostic for the assessment of financial stability with two examples.

12.39 Figure 12.3 shows the evolution of the interquartile range of the Tier 1 Capital to RWA ratio for a selected group of French banks. The gray band shows the inter-quartile range and quantifies the dispersion of this capitalization ratio for these banks. The lower and upper limits of the band represent, respectively, the lower and higher Tier 1 capitalization ratio among the banks (i.e., the 25th and 75th percentile, respectively). The wider the gray band, the higher the dispersion. The black dotted line shows the median (the 50th percentile) of this capitalization ratio for these banks.

12.40 Two things stand out from this distribution analysis. First, the black dotted line shows an increasing trend over time, indicating that major banks in France built up capital resources since the global financial crisis. The first quartile went from 7.7 percent in 2006 to 12.9 percent in 2016, exhibiting substantial improvement in Tier 1 capitalization over time. This very positive development could be, in part, the result of tighter regulation during this period. At the same time, from 2006 to 2016, we also observe a development that could merit closer analysis: the widening of the weighted interquartile capital range. As the widening of the gray band shows, this interquartile capital range went from 1.2 in 2006 to 2.2 in 2016, reflecting a wider spread across banks' capitalization.

12.41 Figure 12.4 shows the evolution of the return on assets (ROA), over time, for a sample of 20 randomly generated bank data. The weighted mean and median show a cyclical trend around 1.50 and 1.25, respectively, in dotted gray and solid black. The mean is larger than the median, indicating that the ROA distribution is skewed to the right.

12.42 In Figure 12.4, the gray line shows the weighted standard deviation, which quantifies how spread out are the ROAs of the individual banks around the mean for the sector. The standard deviation remains broadly stable indicating a low dispersion of the ROAs among the banks during the whole period.

12.43 The symmetry of the distribution around the mean is captured with the weighted skewness, which is represented with a dotted black line in the figure. Despite the overall low dispersion of the data, the skewness is rather volatile throughout the period of analysis. From 2015 onwards, the skewness becomes

Figure 12.3 Weighted Quartiles for Selected French Banks' Capital Adequacy Ratios (2006–2016)

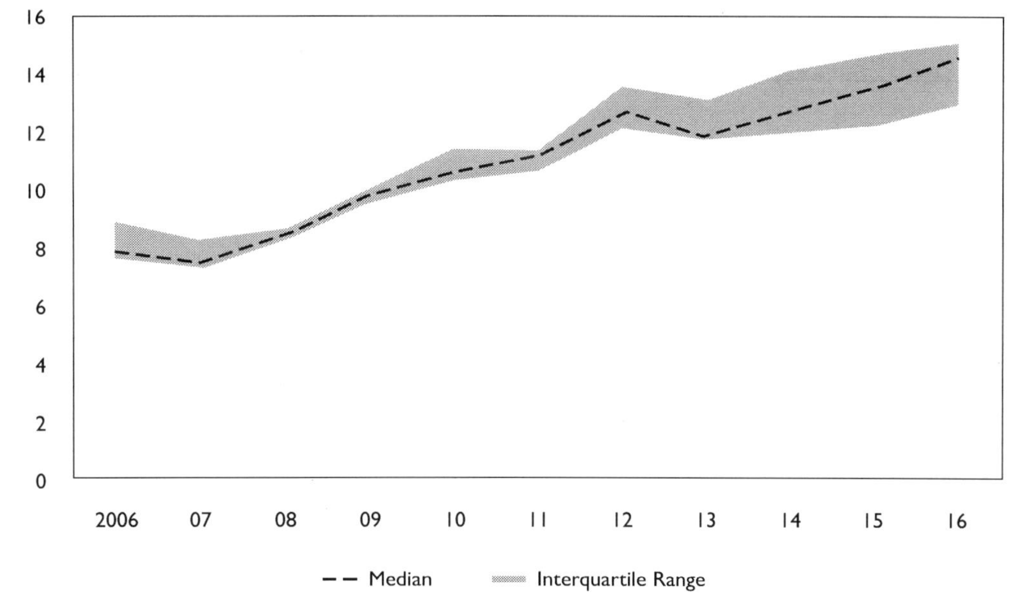

Source: Fitch Connect; and IMF staff calculations.

Figure 12.4 Distribution Measures Analysis for the Return on Assets

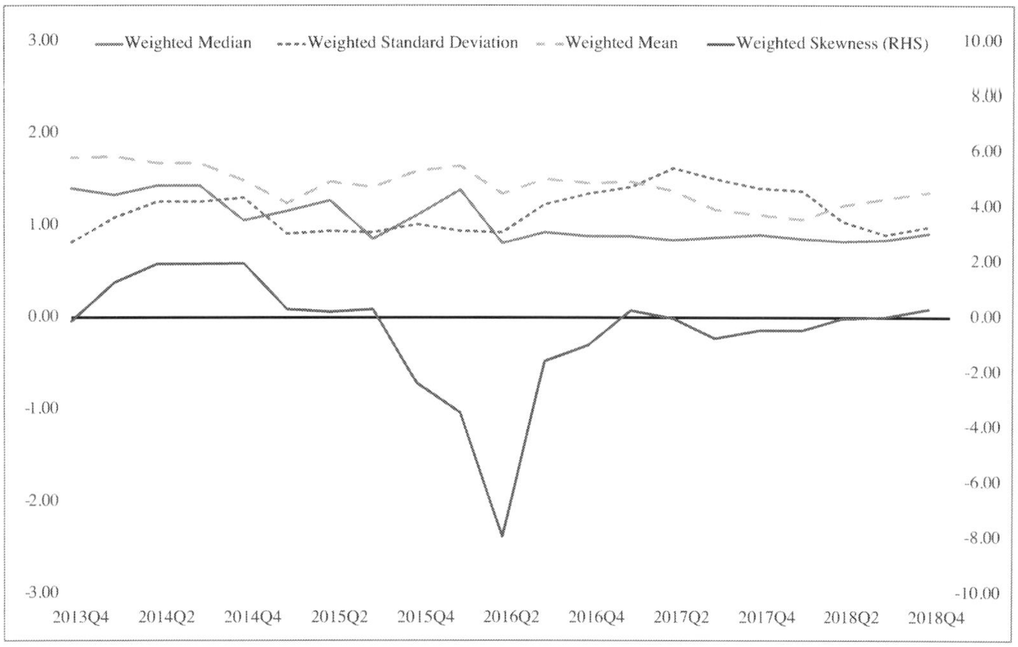

Source: IMF staff calculations.

negative, indicating ROA of one or more banks fall on the left-hand tail of the distribution. Put simply, this could possibly indicate an outlier—a bank with a large negative ROA. On a closer look at the underlying data, it appears that the ROA of one of banks fell from 0.25 in 2014Q4 to –30.90 in 2015Q4 while the assets declined by close to 300 percent, indicating financial difficulties. The strong impact of this bank's ROA on the weighted skewness of the sector warrants further investigation into the performance of the bank, the underlying causes of the stress and thus, identifies any potential risk of spillovers to the entire sector. If large interconnections exist among the banks, any adverse shock to this bank can rapidly transmit to the entire system.

V. Addressing Confidentiality Issues

12.44 As with any system that involves decomposition of aggregated data, dissemination of CDMs can be constrained by confidentiality issues. One way of addressing confidentiality issues is to establish, for each CDM, a minimum number of reporting institutions (reporting threshold) to a point where values of individual institutions cannot be derived. The *Guide* introduces stricter reporting thresholds for all CDMs to preserve data confidentiality (Table 12.6). In addition, the Guide recommends flexibility in reporting these measures for countries where financial systems are highly concentrated.

Table 12.6 Reporting Thresholds for Concentration and Distributions Measures

Measure	Required Minimum Number of Deposit Takers
Herfindahl concentration index	7
Weighted quartiles (weighted by shares of assets in total assets)	28
Weighted standard deviation	7
Weighted skewness	7
Weighted kurtosis	7

Source: IMF staff estimates.

ANNEX

12.1 CDM Template

Annex Figure 12.1.1 Concentration and Distribution Measures Template

CONCENTRATION AND DISTRIBUTION MEASURES

1. Sector Concentration (Herfindahl Index)	

	Tier 1 Capital to Risk-Weighted Assets	NPLs to Gross Loans	NPLs net of Provisions to Capital	Provisions to NPLs	Return on Assets	Return on Equity	Tier 1 Capital to Total Assets
2. Weighted Quartiles							
First Quartile (weighted)							
Second Quartile (weighted)							
Third Quartile (weighted)							
3. Weighted Standard Deviation							
4. Weighted Skewness							
5. Weighted Kurtosis							

Source: IMF staff.

13 Financial Soundness Indicators and Macroprudential Analysis

I. Introduction

13.1 This chapter provides an overview of the use of FSI data in macroprudential analysis. It begins with a brief review of approaches to financial stability analysis, macroprudential frameworks and macroprudential policies, and the role that FSIs can play in the supporting analysis. It continues with a more detailed discussion of the potential and current use of FSIs in macroprudential analysis, and a brief overview of related analytical approaches that commonly employ FSIs as inputs or outputs. The chapter concludes with a summary of key points.

13.2 One of the lessons from the Global Financial Crisis (GFC) was the need to put in place macroprudential frameworks which provide a system-wide perspective on risk (Borio 2014). In retrospect, it was clear that the build-up of imbalances in the financial system had not been adequately identified and measured in the period leading up to the crisis.

13.3 Macroprudential frameworks complement the traditional microprudential focus on individual institutions to contribute to financial stability. While many central banks, the Bank for International Settlements and the IMF, had included elements of a macroprudential perspective in assessing financial stability prior to the GFC,[1] this work took on a new prominence in the subsequent reform agenda. Increasingly, an explicit mandate for financial stability has come to be seen as an essential supplement to the traditional central bank mandate for price stability (Goodhart, 2014), although there is no single accepted definition of financial stability (Vlahović, 2014).

13.4 The macroprudential literature is still young, and as with financial stability, there is no common definition of macroprudential policy and its elements. One working definition in fairly widespread use is that macroprudential policy is the use of primarily prudential tools to limit systemic risk.[2] Efforts have focused on pragmatic approaches to a comprehensive framework for identifying and monitoring systemic risk despite the absence of theoretical consensus. The toolkit of macroprudential policy instruments is a work in progress, with no current consensus on optimal tools, calibration or triggers for use.

13.5 In this relatively new and developing field, despite variations in specific definitions and approaches, there has been convergence around four key elements of a macroprudential framework: (i) the objective of limiting systemic risk; (ii) a scope of analysis including the financial sector as a whole and its interaction with the real economy; (iii) a set of macroprudential tools and guidelines for their use including interactions with monetary policy; and (iv) the need for a macroprudential authority with a clear mandate, appropriate powers, and accountability. Macroprudential policies do not function in isolation from other elements of the financial stability framework and macroeconomic policies. Thus, the macroprudential framework supplements but does not replace a sound foundation for microprudential oversight and monetary and fiscal policies.

[1] References to macroprudential policy first emerged in the late 1970s and1980s in the work of the Bank for International Settlements, aimed at supporting the safety and soundness of the financial system as a whole, as well as the payments mechanism. Macroprudential policy assumed more importance in the early 2000s, and increased sharply with the onset of the Global Financial Crisis. For additional detail, see Borio (2003), and Galati and Moessner (2011).

[2] See IMF-FSB-BIS Elements of Effective Macroprudential Policies: Lessons from International Experience (2016) https://www.imf.org/external/np/g20/pdf/2016/083116.pdf. For a discussion of various working definitions, see Committee on the Global Financial System (2016), Claessens (2014), and Galati and Moessner (2011).

Figure 13.1 Analytic Framework for Financial Stability

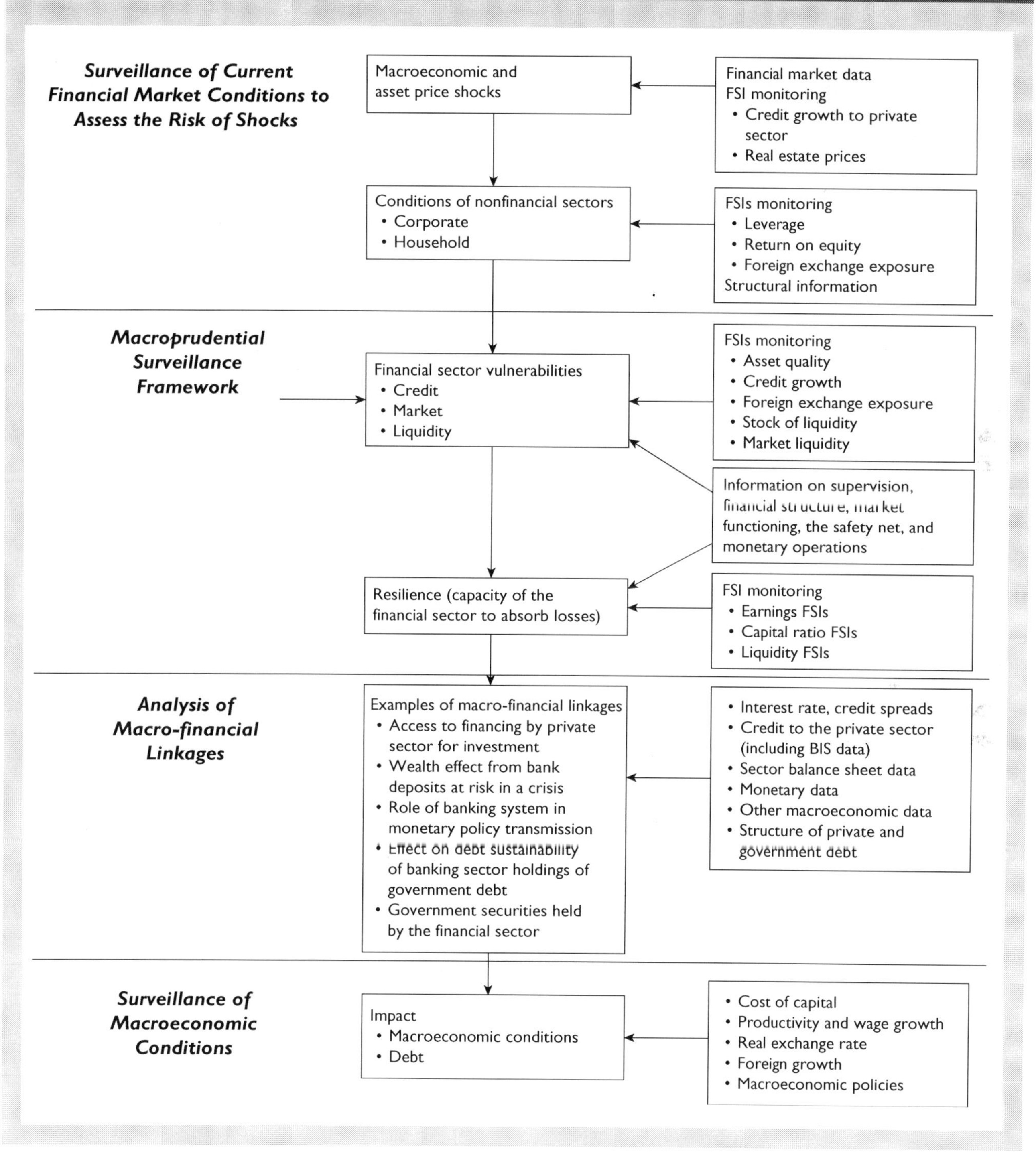

Source: Adapted from IMF 2003.

Note: BIS = Bank for International Settlements.

13.6 FSIs can play a central role an analytical framework that addresses the financial sector as a whole and its interaction with real economy (Figure 13.1). This begins with monitoring of markets and broader macro-economic conditions to identify potential shocks in the time dimension. In addition to financial market data, macro indicators such the difference between the credit-to-GDP ratio and its long-run trend (the credit-to-GDP gap), and other variables, some FSIs (growth of credit to the private sector, real estate prices) can provide insights into the potential emergence of asset price imbalances.

13.7 FSIs are also useful in monitoring the condition of the household and corporate sectors, potentially identifying vulnerabilities before they are reflected in financial sector performance. Excessive leverage, stressed debt-service levels, and exposure to foreign currency risk could be useful indicators of imbalances, which can help trigger the use of macroprudential tools.

13.8 The Core FSIs for deposit-takers provide a good overview of the resilience of the deposit-taking sector to potential shocks. Earnings-related FSIs provide an indication of the ability to internally generate capital, while the capital-related FSIs provide insights into the magnitude of losses that can be borne by system without falling into crisis. Liquidity FSIs similarly quantify the ability of the system to deal with market disruption over varying time horizons.

13.9 The FSIs have not played a major role in the other two elements of the analytical framework: analysis of macrofinancial linkages and surveillance of macroeconomic conditions. The first is targeted at understanding and assessing the various means by which shocks to the financial sector can result in a feedback loop to the real sectors, and contagion effects within the financial sector. The second is focused on monitoring the impact of these macrofinancial linkages on broader macroeconomic conditions, in the face of significant shock.

II. Macroprudential Policies

13.10 Macroprudential and microprudential approaches can be compared and understood using a number of criteria that reflect the inherent differences in focusing on risk in the financial system as a whole versus risk in individual institutions (Table 13.1). A systemic focus requires a broader analytical approach to identify the potential risks, assess resilience, and to calibrate and trigger the use of macroprudential tools. Macroprudential policies have to consider the build up of risks over time (the time dimension) as well as risks arising from the interlinkages among individual institutions—or financial markets—of potential systemic importance.

13.11 Taking steps to address excessive leverage or debt-service stress in the household or corporate sector and asset price imbalances can result in an orderly deceleration rather than a shock to the financial system. Similarly, taking a macro perspective on credit growth and liquidity may provide insights into needed interventions that may not be evident when only the condition of individual banks is considered.

13.12 Following the Global Financial Crisis, emphasis was placed on identification and supervision of systemically important financial institutions (SIFIs) whose size, behavior, and condition can affect the overall macroprudential environment—providing one type of bridge between micro- and macro- supervision and policy. The FSIs do not play a major role in identifying and assessing the important structural considerations arising from the presence of SIFIs within a financial sector.

13.13 There are three objectives to be met in operationalizing macroeconomic policies: (i) increasing resilience to aggregate shocks by building buffers; (ii) containing the buildup of systemic vulnerabilities;

Table 13.1 Comparison Between Macroprudential and Microprudential Policies

	Macroprudential	Microprudential
Proximate objective	Limit financial system-wide distress	Limit distress of individual institutions (solvency risk)
Ultimate objective	Minimize output costs	Consumer (investor/depositor) protection
Model of risk	Endogenous (in part)	Exogenous
Interconnectedness and substitutability	Important	Irrelevant
Calibration of prudential controls	In terms of system-wide distress; top-down	In terms of solvency risk; bottom-up

Source: Borio (2003).

and (iii) controlling structural vulnerabilities.[3] FSIs can play a useful role in the macroprudential analysis that supports achieving the first two of these objectives, both of which address the time dimension of macroprudential policies.[4]

III. Macroprudential Analysis

13.14 Macroprudential analysis incorporates a range of approaches and indicators to measure systemic risks in both the time and structural dimensions. Indicators include aggregate balance sheet and income statement-derived ratios; market-based indicators such as asset prices, spreads or market liquidity measures; broad macro indicators such as ratios of credit to GDP; and other quantitative and qualitative information available to country authorities. Stress testing and network analysis (measuring the relationships among potentially systemically important institutions) are examples of this additional quantitative information. Assessments of credit underwriting standards and the adequacy of banks' risk management processes are examples of qualitative information that may be incorporated into macroprudential analysis.

13.15 The need to capture systemic risks in the context of the financial cycle (time dimension) has led to greater use of macroeconomic variables, market data such as asset prices, measures of the linkages between the real and financial sector and monitoring of interactions between macroprudential policy with monetary policy (Table 13.2).[5] These macroprudential indicators, which include a number of the Additional FSIs and in some cases, can be derived using Core FSIs, potentially can be used to trigger and calibrate macroprudential tools to mitigate the build-up of imbalances in the financial sector. This emphasizes the importance of compiling the Additional FSIs in order to identify the build-up of risks outside the financial sector. Once buildup of systemic risks has been detected, the practical question then becomes what macroprudential tools are available, and when should they be deployed. Once deployed, when should the tools be further tightened or relaxed in response

[3] IMF *Staff Guidance Note on Macroprudential Policy* 2014.

[4] As aggregate statistics, FSIs provide limited insights into the third objective, which addresses the structural dimension of systemic risk. The concentration and distribution measures discussed in Chapter 12 can help to identify structural issues.

[5] Increased focus on macroprudential stability has raised the issue of how stability-oriented macroprudential policy interacts with monetary policy, both of which affect the condition of the banking sector. This has led to hybrid macroprudential/inflation targeting policy stances that recognize the mutual interactions between both types of policy.

Table 13.2 Macroprudential Indicators, Policy Tools and Financial Soundness Indicators

Core Macroprudential Indicators	Additional Macroprudential Indicators	Policy Tools	Relevant FSIs
Broad-based			
• Credit/GDP gap	• Growth in credit/GDP • Credit growth • Asset price deviations from long-term trends • Underpricing of risk in financial markets (low volatility/spreads) • Debt service to total income ratios • Leverage on individual loans or at the asset level • Increasing wholesale funding ratio (noncore funding) • Weakening exports and resulting current account deficits	• Countercyclical capital buffer • Leverage restrictions • General (dynamic) provisioning	• Residential real estate prices • Deposit takers customer deposits to total (non-interbank) loans • Nonfinancial corporations earnings to interest and principal expenses • Household debt service and principal payments to income • Commercial real estate prices • Growth in credit to the private sector

Table 13.2 Macroprudential Indicators, Policy Tools and Financial Soundness Indicators (*concluded*)

Core Macroprudential Indicators	Additional Macroprudential Indicators	Policy Tools	Relevant FSIs
Household			
• Household loan growth • Increasing house prices (nominal and real growth) • House price-to-rent and house price-to-disposable-income ratios • Increasing share of household loans to total credit	• Increasing house prices by regions and by types of property • Deteriorating lending standards • High loan-to-value ratios • High loan-to-income ratios • High debt-service-to-total-income ratios • Share of foreign-exchange-denominated loans and interest-only loans	Time varying limits on: • Debt service to income • Loan to income • Loan to value	Core FSIs • Loan concentration by economic activity Additional FSIs • Foreign-currency-denominated loans to total loans • Household debt service and principal payments to income
Corporate			
• Corporate loan growth • Increasing share of corporate loans to total credit • Increasing commercial property prices • Increasing commercial real estate credit • Increasing share of foreign-currency-denominated loans	• Increasing corporate leverage (debt-to-equity ratio) • Corporate credit gap • Increasing debt-service ratio • Deteriorating lending standards • Average debt service to total income on commercial real estate loans • Average loan-to-value ratios on commercial real estate loans • Average loan-to-value ratios on commercial real estate loans • Share of foreign-exchange-denominated loans and extent of natural hedges	Time varying limits on: • Debt service to income • Loan to income • Loan to value	Core FSIs • Loan concentration by economic activity Additional FSIs • Nonfinancial corporation's total debt to equity • Nonfinancial corporations earnings to interest and principal expenses • Commercial real estate prices • Foreign-currency-denominated loans to total loans
Liquidity			
• Increasing loan-to-deposit ratio • Increasing share of noncore funding to total liabilities	• Decreasing share of liquid assets • Worsening maturity mismatches • Increasing securities issuance • Increasing unsecured funding • Increasing foreign exchange positions • Increasing gross capital inflows	Time varying: • Liquidity buffer requirements • Stable funding requirements • Liquidity charges • Reserve requirements • Constraints on open foreign currency positions • Constraints on foreign currency funding	Core FSIs • Liquid assets to total assets • Liquid assets to short-term liabilities • Net stable funding ratio • Net open position in foreign exchange to capital Additional FSIs • Customer deposits to total (noninterbank) loans • Foreign-currency-denominated loans to total loans • Foreign-currency-denominated liabilities to total liabilities • Nonfinancial corporations net foreign exchange exposure to equity

Source: Adapted from IMF *Staff Guidance Note on Macroprudential Policy* (2014) and Table 1.1 in this Guide.

to changing circumstances? FSIs and other inputs can be used to trigger the deployment of macroprudential tools, as discussed next.

FSIs and the Calibration of Macroprudential Tools

13.16 A range of macroprudential tools have been identified (Table 13.2), with the availability and power to use such tools varying from country to country in accordance with national institutional structures and legal frameworks. Options can include restrictions on borrowers, instruments or activities, balance sheet restrictions, or capital or provisioning requirements. Macroprudential tools may have the objective of limiting the buildup of risks, or building additional buffers to enhance resilience. Many macroprudential tools, for example, restrictions on financial sector balance sheets or capital requirements, are in fact microprudential tools, but are deployed with a systemic perspective in mind (Gadanecz and Jayaram, 2015).

13.17 There are no broadly applicable standards or gauges to indicate when macroprudential tools should be deployed to address accumulating imbalances in the financial sector, but macroprudential policy cannot rely on rules and must be based on a continuous assessment of evolving risks.[6] In this regard, FSI data can contribute to identifying when particular macroprudential tools may be required, and to the ongoing measurement of their impact and hence decisions on tightening or relaxing. Trends and projections of FSIs can be used, in conjunction with other analysis, to inform the expert judgment exercised by the authorities with mandates for financial stability.

13.18 FSIs can provide insights into the resilience of the financial sector to potential vulnerabilities. Key indicators of resilience are capital as a measure of the capacity to absorb unexpected losses, and liquidity as a measure of capacity to deal with market disruption. The availability of FSIs provides a means for cross-country comparison and analysis.

13.19 The Core FSIs for deposit takers include total capital to risk-weighted assets, Tier 1 capital to risk-weighted assets and Common Equity Tier 1 capital to risk-weighted assets, all anchored in the international standard established by the Basel Capital Accord. These FSIs provide a view at a point in time, which can be used for trend analysis, of aggregate capital adequacy of the banking sector in a jurisdiction. This can be compared to the Basel standard, and to the ratios of other countries or regional peer groupings, providing a measure of resilience to unexpected losses. Non-performing loans net of provisions to capital provides an additional insight into resilience by identifying the ability of the banking system to absorb unexpected losses (provisions should cover expected losses) on already identified problem loans.

13.20 There originally were two liquidity measures in the Core FSIs for deposit takers—liquid assets to total assets, and liquid assets to short-term liabilities. Unlike capital measures, these FSIs are not anchored in an accepted international standard, but do provide indicators of the potential ability of the banking system to deal with market disruption. The Liquidity Coverage Ratio and Net Stable Funding Ratio, two new a Core FSIs, reflect the introduction in Basel III of an international standard for liquidity, effective January 2018. As with the capital FSIs, this will permit comparison to a clear nominal standard, as well as comparisons to other countries and peer groupings.

13.21 FSIs can also provide insights into the buildup of systemic vulnerabilities, allowing for benchmarking of financial systems in normal times with no stress, to monitor changes over time, and to compare across jurisdictions. The three asset quality Core FSIs address the buildup of credit risk (non-performing loans to total gross loans), risk concentrations (loan concentration by economic activity) within the banking sector and the adequacy of provisioning (provisions to non-performing loans). The liquidity FSIs, in addition to providing measures of resilience as discussed earlier, also provide insights into systemic vulnerabilities, as in the absence of healthy liquidity buffers, the banking sector is vulnerable to liquidity shocks. Net open position in foreign exchange to capital provides a measure of the vulnerability of the banking sector to foreign exchange shocks.

13.22 The Additional FSIs provide some further insights into potential vulnerabilities in the banking sector, and perhaps more importantly include measures of the leverage (debt to equity) and debt-service capacity (earnings to interest and principal expenses) of the nonfinancial corporations sector, and debt-service capacity (debt-service and principal payments to income) of the household sector. Together with the residential and commercial property price indices,

[6] IMF *Staff Guidance Note on Macroprudential Policy* (2014).

these offer the potential to detect vulnerabilities long before they become evident in the earnings, asset quality, and capital indicators of the deposit-taking sector.

13.23 In practice, FSIs are commonly used in the analysis supporting decisions to employ macroprudential tools. For example, The Hong Kong Monetary Authority (HKMA) relied in part on residential estate prices, then one of the Additional FSIs and now a Core FSI, in the analysis leading to the decision to deploy elements of the macroprudential toolkit in May 2017. In addition to prices exceeding previous peaks, the HKMA was motivated by the rate of turnover in the property market, which suggested that speculation may have been fueling the price increases, and concerns that intense competition by banks was leading to increased risk and lower resilience to shocks.[7] The HKMA introduced a 25 percent risk weight as a floor for residential mortgage risk weights, increased from the previous 10 percent, for banks using the internal ratings–based approach to determine their capital adequacy. This increase in the amount of capital required for mortgage loans was complemented by reducing the maximum allowable loan to value ratio and increasing the minimum permissible debt-service ratio.

13.24 The Iceland Financial Supervisory Authority similarly relied in part on residential real estate prices, then an Additional FSI and now a Core FSI, in its July 2017 decision to impose macroprudential restrictions. Other contributing factors were the inadequate supply of new housing, and concern that lenders were relaxing underwriting standards, evidenced by an increase in the average loan to value ratio and amortization period of new mortgage loans.[8] This led to the imposition of a loan to value limit of 85 percent in general, and 90 percent for first time homebuyers.

FSIs in Macroprudential Analysis

13.25 FSIs are most relevant for surveillance, providing near-contemporaneous indicators of risk and resilience. The Core FSIs provide a snapshot of the condition of the banking system. Trend analysis of some Core FSIs such as loan concentration by economic activity and liquidity ratios is potentially useful in identifying the build-up of systemic risks, providing insight into when to trigger macroprudential tools, and the tightening or relaxation of these tools once deployed. Some of the Additional FSIs are potentially more useful for their ability to provide insights into developments within a financial cycle, and thus as possible leading indicators of financial distress.

13.26 FSIs are used by the IMF in FSAPs, primarily in initial scoping and preliminary risk-assessment, and as inputs and outputs in stress testing. FSIs are also used in other surveillance, typically in the context of Article IV consultations. Most Article IV reports include the Core FSIs, and often include commentary on the soundness of deposit takers based on these indicators. When FSI data is not included, it is generally because of the lack of availability from the authorities. FSI data facilitates ongoing monitoring to determine whether more detailed review of financial stability is required. In most cases where there is detailed financial stability commentary provided as part of the Article IV, it is based on more in-depth analysis. Typically, this can include stress testing completed by the mission, recent FSAP or technical assistance findings, or asset quality reviews or financial stability reports produced by the authorities.

13.27 Other practical examples of the use of FSIs in financial stability analysis are readily found in country financial stability reports. Financial stability reports almost universally include discussion and analysis of macroprudential indicators, which in many cases overlap with the FSIs (Čihák; 2006, and Čihák et al., 2012). Use of FSIs ranges from being a central component and organizing framework for the analysis to reporting with little or no analysis of the data, to inclusion of some FSIs within broader reporting of macroprudential indicators.

13.28 The Islamic Financial Services Board (IFSB) has developed a parallel set of soundness indicators (called Prudential and Structural Indicators for Islamic Financial Institutions—PSIFIs) that apply to the Islamic banking sector in countries with Islamic banks. The indicators parallel the FSI core and additional indicators whenever feasible, with customization to reflect various differing practices in Islamic

[7] HKMA Press Release, May 19, 2017, http://www.hkma.gov.hk/eng/key-information/press-releases/2017/20170519-5.shtml accessed April 27, 2018.

[8] Iceland Financial Supervisory Authority Rules on Maximum Loan-to-Value Ratios for Mortgages, July 2017, https://en.fme.is/media/frettir/FME---LTV-Memorandum-July-2017.pdf accessed April 27, 2018.

Box 13.1 FSIs in the Macroprudential Literature

Financial and currency crises since the 1990s have spurred an extensive literature investigating the causes of crises, building from earlier work using financial ratios to predict distress in individual institutions. A small number of studies within the broader macroprudential analysis literature specifically address the use of FSIs. Recent work has tended not to specifically address FSIs, but rather a wider range of variables including macroeconomic and market-based data. Residential real estate prices, a Core FSI, and some of the Additional FSIs (commercial real estate prices, household and corporate leverage and debt service) are among the commonly used parameters in the quest for robust leading indicators.

Craig (2002) provides an early description of the use of FSIs in surveillance, highlighting the usefulness of the Additional FSIs for the nonfinancial corporate and household sectors to detect weakness at a relatively early stage. This can often be before weaknesses are reflected in FSIs of the financial sector that measure risk more directly, such as the non-performing loan ratio. FSI analysis as described was based on trend analysis, peer group comparisons and expert judgment. In a similar vein, Worrell (2004) noted that most FSI analysis uses expert judgment in conjunction with other analytical approaches, referring to the use of FSIs in individual country financial stability reports. He cited as an area for future work quantitative research to identify a statistically robust relationship between a variety of FSIs and financial system distress.

Jarle (2002) describes the use of FSIs by the Norges Bank (Norwegian Central Bank) in financial stability analysis. A key observation was the conclusion from practical experience that a set of FSIs for only the banking sector was too narrow. Even if problems showed up clearly in the banking sector FSIs, it was too late to take appropriate action to mitigate the buildup of systemic risk. This led Norges Bank in 1995 to introduce in its Financial Stability Report a number of additional FSIs for the nonfinancial sectors, facilitating an evaluation of the impact of macroeconomic conditions on the debt-service capacity of the household and non-financial corporate sector, and hence the likely impact on banking sector FSIs.

Čihák and Schaeck (2007) use selected FSIs compiled from FSAP and Article IV missions to explore the relationship between FSIs and banking problems. They conclude that there is evidence to suggest that FSIs provide signals of the buildup of imbalances in the banking sector and are of some benefit in determine the timing of crises. However, the authors stress a number of limitations in the data and the need for additional research.

Babahuga (2007) provides the first empirical work specifically using the FSI dataset. The paper establishes the link between selected FSIs and episodes of financial distress, finding that FSIs fluctuate strongly with the business cycle. Costa Navajas and Thegeya (2013) test the effectiveness of FSIs in predicting banking crises. Model results show correlation between some FSIs and banking crises. The findings are of limited use to policy-makers, however, as the most robust results are for contemporaneous or lagged variables, thus providing no lead time to deploy macroprudential tools to avert or mitigate the crisis. This finding highlights the need to compile the Core FSI residential real estate prices and Additional FSIs such as commerical real estate prices and household and corporate sector leverage and debt service, which have been more prominent in recent financial stability analysis due to their potential predictive ability.

More recent work tends to address FSIs less specifically, typically through incorporation of some FSIs into a broader set of macroprudential indicators. A useful overview of recent work is provided in IFC Bulletin No 46 (2017). While some of the papers do touch on the banking sector variables that underpin the Core FSIs, the bulk of current research: (i) stresses the importance of filling data gaps, particularly with respect to real estate and the household and corporate sector, and the shadow banking sector (this reinforces the importance of compiling the Additional FSIs); (ii) the use of market-based indicators including high frequency data; (iii) more granular analysis of potential vulnerabilities; and (vi) interconnectedness and potential contagion. This recent focus reflects that the Core FSIs on their own have limited predictive ability, but can be useful as monitoring tools and as inputs in a broader analytic approach.

banking. Thus, some countries will have two sets of indicators—one covering the entire banking system, and a second covering the Islamic banking subsector, which can permit analysis of relative stability conditions in the two subsectors.

13.29 Many country authorities have developed their own key indicators for financial stability analysis with varying degrees of overlap with the FSIs. While only two of the 27 Basel Committee member jurisdictions publishing financial stability reports routinely include the Core FSIs as a table or appendix (see Annex 13.1), almost all Basel Committee member jurisdictions make use of selected FSIs in three contexts. One is the incorporation of some FSIs—typically real estate prices, corporate and household sector leverage and debt-service—together with other parameters, into scenario-based or modeling approaches to identifying imbalances. The second is the use of some of the Core FSIs for deposit-takers—typically asset quality and sometimes liquidity—together with other indicators in the assessment of financial sector vulnerabilities. The third is to incorporate Core FSIs—usually some of the capital, earnings and liquidity-related ratios—into broader analysis of the resilience of the financial sector.

13.30 Most European Union countries report the Core and many of the Additional FSIs, and some are reflected in the European Systemic Risk Board dashboard.[9] The risk dashboard is a set of quantitative and qualitative indicators of systemic risk in the EU organized in seven categories: (i) interlinkages and composite measures of systemic risk; (ii) macro risk; (iii) credit risk; (iv) funding and liquidity; (v) market risk; (vi) profitability and solvency; and (vii) structural risk.

13.31 This risk dashboard, in common with approaches to macroprudential analysis in most highly developed financial systems, takes advantage of the availability of high-frequency market data, macro indicators, and details of individual exposures in addition to aggregate balance sheet and income statement data for banks and other financial institutions. The closest alignment of the risk dashboard with the FSIs is in the indicators of banking groups' profitability, solvency, liquidity, and balance sheet structure. These indicators are largely derived from supervisory data and thus bear close resemblance to the Core FSIs, with 6 of 12 included in the risk dashboard: (i) return on equity, (ii) return on assets, (iii) cost to income, (iv) net interest income to operating income, (v) NPLs to total gross loans, and (vi) liquid assets to short-term liabilities.

13.32 As explained in the last section, FSIs can play a more prominent role in macroprudential analysis. And a 2009 review of approaches to detecting systemic risk concluded that FSIs provided mixed results in predicting the global financial crisis, they were still useful in assessing systemic vulnerabilities when combined with other reliable data (GFSR April 2009, Chapter 3).

[9] See the European Systemic Risk Board, November 2017, *ESRB risk dashboard*.

IV. Related Analytic Approaches

13.33 Macroprudential analysis requires a number of complementary approaches, some of which employ FSIs as inputs or outputs. The most common of these is stress testing, in which outputs are frequently expressed as FSI capital ratios.

13.34 Stress testing can be done at the individual institution level as part of a bank's own internal risk management processes or as part of microprudential supervisory oversight (Basel Committee, 2017). Stress testing can also be done at the macro level, looking at the sector as a whole using either aggregate data (top-down) or by aggregating the results of stress testing individual institutions (bottom-up).[10] Top-down stress testing by the IMF is a common feature of FSAPs and may also be used in other surveillance (Jobst, Ong and Schmieder, 2013).

13.35 Many countries have incorporated stress testing into their macroprudential analysis. FSIs often figure prominently in balance-sheet approaches as inputs (increases in NPL ratios, declines in liquidity ratios) and outputs (capital adequacy ratios). More complex models also often incorporate FSIs among their inputs, and almost invariably have capital adequacy ratios among the outputs.

13.36 Network analysis is a subset or variation on stress testing approaches, which investigates the relationships between individual institutions, or in cross-border network analysis, relationships between financial systems.[11] It requires detailed information on bilateral exposures in order to construct a web or network, which can provide insights into the structural dimension of systemic risk. This is done using scenario analysis to assess the impact of default by one or more institutions, or in the case of cross-border analysis, financial distress in one or more jurisdictions, on the other institutions or jurisdictions in the network. While the analysis is based on detailed information on institutional exposures that is not captured in the FSIs, the outputs of network analysis are frequently expressed as FSI capital or liquidity ratios.

[10] For a useful and easy to use bottom-up stress testing model that has been adapted for use in a number of countries, see Čihák, 2014.

[11] For more detailed discussion, see "The Network Analysis Approach" in *A Guide to IMF Stress Testing: Models and Methods* 2014.

V. Challenges to Enhance FSIs for Macroprudential Analysis

13.37 The Core FSIs provide measures of both the buildup of risks (asset quality, credit concentration, liquidity stress, foreign currency exposure, residential real estate prices) and resilience (capital, leverage and liquidity buffers) within the banking system. Additional FSIs for deposit takers provide further insights into risks (risk concentrations, reliance on non-deposit funding, and foreign currency exposures). The Additional FSIs for the non-financial sectors are potentially highly useful in identifying vulnerabilities (high leverage, high debt- service ratios, and real estate prices) before these are evident in the Core FSIs, which more directly measure risk in the financial system. This provides an opportunity for policy-makers to use macroprudential tools to mitigate the risks prior to crystallization into a crisis.

13.38 FSIs have been most widely used as macroprudential indicators and organizing frameworks in jurisdictions, which introduced their formal approach to financial stability analysis after the introduction of the FSIs. In other jurisdictions there is often overlap between the set of macroprudential indicators used on an ongoing basis and the FSIs. Particularly in jurisdictions where data gaps persist, in the absence of high frequency market data and the detail required for network analysis, the FSIs can play a key role in macroprudential analysis.

13.39 There are several challenges to be overcome to enhance macroprudential analysis using FSIs. First, significant data gaps remain despite the steadily increasing number of countries disseminating FSIs. While many countries provide all or most of the Core FSIs, availability drops off rapidly for the Additional FSIs, particularly those not derived from supervisory data. This frequently reflects capacity constraints in national statistics agencies, and also challenges in domestic coordination between the supervisory authorities or central banks often responsible for the complication of FSIs, and statistics agencies, which may play the leading role in compilation of indicators for the non-financial sectors.

13.40 Integrity of data from supervisory sources is an ongoing concern. The Core FSIs, like all supervisory data, are vulnerable to inadvertent or willful misreporting. This is a particular concern due to evidence that often emerges through FSAPs of under-reporting of adverse loan classifications and provisions (Andrews, 2017). Under-provisioning has the effect of reducing expenses and increasing income, thus distorting the profitability and capital-related FSIs in addition to the impact on asset quality indicators.

13.41 Lack of "forward-lookingness" is a common issue in macroprudential analysis. Many financial stability reports tend to rely on the current levels of some key FSIs, such as capital and asset quality-related indicators, and trend analysis (Čihák, 2006). FSIs are historical data, at best providing a picture of the system as it existed three months earlier. This is a problem familiar to bank supervisors everywhere, which has resulted in ratio-based analysis being augmented by additional data and qualitative assessments to become more forward looking. As with microprudential supervision, in macroprudential analysis data extending beyond the Core FSIs, and judgment, are required to better identify vulnerabilities and lack of resilience while there is still time to take action.

13.42 Some key FSIs can provide a foundation to address the lack of "forward lookingness." As noted in early work by Norges Bank and the IMF, FSIs for the household and nonfinancial corporate sector potentially can identify vulnerabilities before they are evident in the Core FSIs, providing an opportunity to employ the macroprudential toolkit to mitigate accumulating risks. Asset price data, particularly for real estate, offers similar promise as a leading indicator. The Additional FSI growth of credit to the private sector can be used to calculate the credit to GDP gap, one of the few robust leading indicators of financial distress.[12]

13.43 As these and other Additional FSIs become more widely available, they will facilitate analysis of variations from long-term trends that potentially can detect buildup of systemic risk with sufficient lead time for policy-makers to act. There will still be challenges, however, which preclude a simple rules-based

[12] For further detail, see Gadanecz and Jayaram (2015), Drehmann and Juselius, (2013), and *Staff Guidance Note on Macroprudential Policy—Considerations for Low Income Countries*, 2014.

approach driven by empirical models. Even when relying on some of the best performing indicators, judgment is still required to determine when to act. For example, some research suggests that the credit to GDP gap tends to continue to rise for some quarters after the onset of the crisis, and price to rent and residential property price gaps tend to peak before the onset of the crisis (Gadanecz and Jayaram, 2015). While the available data may never support rules-based decisions, it can still be extremely useful in informing the expert judgment of the authorities with financial stability mandates.

13.44 In less developed financial systems, improvements in supervisory capacity and data availability will generally need to be given priority to lay the foundation for effective macroprudential policy.[13] A sound microprudential framework can help to address concerns over the integrity of the Core FSIs. Further, in the bank-dominated financial systems common in low-income countries, there will be few sources of systemic risk outside the banking system. Thus, sound microprudential supervision and the capacity and will to act when weaknesses are detected are essential components of a framework for financial stability.

[13] IMF *Staff Guidance Note on Macroprudential Policy—Considerations for Low Income Countries*, 2014.

13.45 It is important to include a range of methodologies in the macroprudential approach, so FSI analysis should be supplemented by stress testing, other quantitative indicators where available, and qualitative assessments using expert judgment. FSIs do not provide insights into the structural dimension of systemic risk, so it is especially important to use other approaches in assessing the potential systemic risks of individual institutions and financial markets infrastructures.

13.46 Use of FSIs for macroprudential analysis has been hampered by lack of availability, particularly for those not derived from supervisory returns. As the additional FSIs for the nonfinancial sectors are particularly useful as leading indicators that can help to trigger and calibrate the use of macroprudential tools, when seeking to fill the data gaps, authorities should give priority to nonfinancial corporations debt to equity, earnings to interest and principle expenses, household debt-service and principal payments to income, and residential and commercial real estate price changes. Following the GFC, the G20 urged countries to give priority to development of multisector balance sheet and accumulation accounts (often described briefly as "flow of funds accounts"), which can be constructed to incorporate relevant macroprudential information. This is, however, a large statistical undertaking that might be beyond the resources of some countries.

ANNEX

13.1 Financial Soundness Indicators in the Financial Stability Reports of Members of the Basel Committee

Argentina	Some FSIs included in published risk indicators for D-SIBs (capital, earnings). Additional FSI (corporate leverage) used in assessing risks.
Australia	Most core FSIs (capital, asset quality, earnings, liquidity) referenced in the assessment of the financial system. Additional FSIs (real estate prices, corporate and household debt service and leverage) used in assessing risks.
Belgium	Some FSIs included in key figures for banks and credit institutions. Most core FSIs used in the review of the banking system (capital, assets quality, earnings, liquidity); some additional FSIs (real estate prices, corporate and household debt service and leverage) used in assessing risks.
Brazil	FSIs included in statistical appendix. Many core FSIs (capital, earnings, asset quality, liquidity) referenced in the financial system overview. Some additional FSIs (corporate debt service and leverage) used in risk assessment.
Canada	Additional FSIs (corporate leverage and debt service) used in risk assessment.
China	Some core FSIs referenced in the soundness assessment of the banking sector (capital, asset quality, earnings, liquidity).
European Union	Some FSIs (capital, asset quality, earnings) referenced in description and analysis. Additional FSIs (real estate prices, corporate leverage) used in vulnerability assessment.
France	The Banque de France *Financial Stability Review* is entirely thematic, and the FSIs may have limited relevance to the selected theme of a specific review.
Germany	Some core FSIs (capital, earnings) referenced in the assessing risks in the banking sector. Core FSI (nonperforming loans) and additional FSIs (corporate and household leverage and debt service) used in identifying vulnerabilities.
Hong Kong SAR	Some core FSIs included in Key Performance Indicators of the banking sector. Most core FSIs (capital, asset quality, earnings, liquidity) used in assessing banking sector performance. Some additional FSIs (real estate prices, household and corporate debt and leverage) used to assess external environment.
India	Additional FSI (residential real estate prices) used in assessing macrorisks. Selected FSIs referenced in assessing financial institutions' soundness and resilience (capital, asset quality, earnings). FSIs provide main inputs to the banking stability map methodology.
Indonesia	Most core FSIs referenced in the overview of the banking sector and risks (capital, asset quality, earnings, net open position).
Italy	Some additional FSIs (real estate prices, household and corporate sector leverage, number of bankruptcy proceedings) used in assessing macroeconomic risks. Some core FSIs (capital, asset quality, earnings, liquidity) used to assess financial sector risks.
Japan	FSIs not specifically included or used extensively other than as inputs to or outputs from stress testing. One core FSI (sectoral distribution of loans) used in describing developments in intermediation. Two additional FSIs (corporate leverage and number of bankruptcies) used as inputs in assessing credit risk of the system.
Korea	Some additional FSIs (household debt service, corporate leverage and debt service) used in the assessment of risks. Most core FSIs (capital, asset quality, earnings, liquidity) referenced in discussion of financial institutions' risk conditions and resilience.
Mexico	FSIs not specifically included or used extensively other than as inputs to or outputs from stress testing.

Netherlands	Some core (leverage ratio, Common Equity Tier 1 ratio) and additional FSIs (household and corporate leverage, real estate prices) included in Macroprudential Indicator Appendix. Some core (capital, asset quality) and additional FSIs (real estate prices used in the assessment of financial stability).
Russia	FSIs not specifically included, and little referenced with the Central Bank of Russia relying on analysis generally employing more disaggregated ratios and alternative approaches.
Saudi Arabia	Several core FSIs (capital, asset quality, earnings, liquidity) used in assessing risks and resilience in the banking sector.
Singapore	FSIs published in the statistical appendix. Some core FSIs (capital, asset quality, liquidity) are used in the review of the Singapore financial sector. Some additional FSIs (number of bankruptcies, household debt service) are used in the assessment of risks in the corporate and household sectors.
South Africa	Many of the core FSIs are included in the Selected Indicators Annex. Some core FSIs are referenced in the analysis of financial institutions (earnings, liquidity), and some additional FSIs are used in the analysis of the corporate and household sectors (debt service, real estate prices).
Spain	Some core FSIs used in assessing banking sector risks (capital, asset quality, earnings, liquidity).
Sweden[1]	Riksbank: Some core FSIs (capital, asset quality, liquidity) are used in the analysis of banking sector risks. Some additional FSIs used in the assessment of broader risks and vulnerabilities (household leverage and debt service, real estate prices). Finansinspektionen: FSIs not specifically included. Some core FSIs (capital, liquidity) are used in financial stability assessment of the banking sector. Some additional FSIs (real estate prices) are used in the assessment of the household and corporate sectors.
Switzerland	Some Core FSIs (capital, liquidity) are used in the overall assessment of domestic banks, and in the assessments of risks and vulnerabilities. Additional FSIs (real estate prices) are used in assessing the macroeconomic environment.
Turkey	Many Core FSIs (capital, asset quality, earnings) are used in the analysis of specific risks to the financial sector.
United Kingdom	The Core Indicators Index Annex includes some core FSIs (Tier 1 capital, Common Equity Tier 1 capital, leverage, return on assets) and additional FSIs (household debt service, real estate prices). Some additional FSIs (corporate and household debt service, real estate prices) are cited in the overall assessment. Some core FSIs are used in the assessment of the resilience of the banking sector (capital, liquidity).
United States[2]	Office of Financial Research: FSIs not specifically included. Some core (capital, earnings, liquidity) and additional FSIs (household and corporate debt service) included among 56 key indicators considered. Financial Stability Oversight Council: FSIs not specifically included. A number of core FSIs (capital, asset quality, earnings) and some additional FSIs (household debt service, real estate prices) considered in the assessment of financial developments.

Sources: Published financial stability reports, 2017 unless otherwise noted. Please see bibliography for full citations.

Notes: Luxembourg does not publish a financial stability report. D-SIB = domestically systemically important banks. Residential real estate prices was an Additional FSI when 2017 financial stability reports were published. It is now a Core FSI.

[1] Both the Riksbank (Central Bank) and Finansinspektionen, the supervisory authority, publish financial stability reports.

[2] Both the Office of Financial Research and Financial Stability Oversight Council publish financial stability reports.

Bibliography

Afonso, Gara, Kovner Anna, and Schoar Antoinette. 2011. "Stressed, Not Frozen: The Federal Funds Market in the Financial Crisis." Federal Reserve Bank of New York Staff Report, Number 437.

Andrews, Michael A. 2017. "Experience with Financial Soundness Indicators; A Practitioner's Perspective." Paper prepared for the IMF Statistics Department Workshop on Financial Soundness Indicators, Washington, DC, April 25–26.

Angelini, Paolo, Nobili Andrea, and Picillo M. Cristina. 2009. "The Interbank Market After August 2007: What Has Changed and Why?" Banca d'Italia Working Papers, Number 731.

Babihuga, Rita. 2007. "Macroeconomic and Financial Soundness Indicators: An Empirical Investigation." IMF Working Paper 07/115, International Monetary Fund, Washington, DC.

Bank for International Settlements. 2018. *Annual Economic Report*. https://www.bis.org/publ/arpdf/ar2018e.pdf

Bank Indonesia. 2017. *Financial Stability Report*, Indonesia. https://www.bi.go.id/en/publikasi/perbankan-dan-stabilitas/kajian/Pages/KSK_0917.aspx

Bank of Canada. 2017. *Financial Stability Report*, Canada. https://www.bankofcanada.ca/wp-content/uploads/2017/11/fsr-november2017.pdf

Bank of England. 2016. *The Financial Policy Committee's Approach to Setting the Countercyclical Capital Buffer*. London.

Bank of England. October 17, 2018. *Financial Stability Report*. Accessed April 27, 2018. https://www.bankofengland.co.uk/financial-stability

Bank of France. 2018. *Financial Stability Report*, France. https://publications.banque-france.fr/sites/default/files/medias/documents/financial_stability_review_22.pdf

Bank of Italy. 2017. *Financial Stability Report*, Italy. https://www.bancaditalia.it/pubblicazioni/rapporto-stabilita/2017-2/en-FSR-2-2017.pdf?language_id=1

Bank of Japan. 2018. *Financial Stability Report*, Japan. https://www.boj.or.jp/en/research/brp/fsr/data/fsr180419a.pdf

Bank of Korea. 2017. *Financial Stability Report*, Korea. http://www.bok.or.kr/broadcast.action?menuNaviId=2578

Bank of Singapore. 2017. *Financial Stability Report*, Singapore. http://www.mas.gov.sg/~/media/resource/publications/fsr/FSR%202017.pdf

Bank of Spain. 2017. *Financial Stability Report*, Spain. https://www.bde.es/f/webbde/Secciones/Publicaciones/InformesBoletinesRevistas/InformesEstabilidadFinancera/17/IEF_Noviembre2017Ing.pdf

Bank of Uganda. 2016. *Financial Stability Report*. https://www.bou.or.ug/bou/bou-downloads/financial_stability/Rpts/All/Financial-Stability-Report--June-2016.pdf.

Basel Committee on Banking Supervision (BCBS). 1988. *International Convergence of Capital Measurement and Capital Standards*. Basel, Switzerland: Bank for International Settlements.

Basel Committee on Banking Supervision (BCBS). 1992. *Minimum Standards for the Supervision of International Banking Groups and their Cross-border Establishments*. Basel, Switzerland: Bank for International Settlements.

Basel Committee on Banking Supervision (BCBS). 1996. *Amendment to the Capital Accord to Incorporate Market Risks*. Basel, Switzerland: Bank for International Settlements.

Basel Committee on Banking Supervision (BCBS). 2003a. *New Basel Capital Accord: Third Consultative Paper*. Basel, Switzerland: Bank for International Settlements.

Basel Committee on Banking Supervision (BCBS). 2003b. *Overview of the New Basel Capital Accord*. Basel, Switzerland: Bank for International Settlements.

Basel Committee on Banking Supervision (BCBS). 2006. *International Convergence of Capital Measurement and Capital Standards*. Basel, Switzerland: Bank for International Settlements.

Basel Committee on Banking Supervision (BCBS). 2011. *A Global Regulatory Framework for More Resilient Banks and Banking Systems*. Basel, Switzerland: Bank for International Settlements.

Basel Committee on Banking Supervision (BCBS). 2012a. *Core Principles for Effective Banking Supervision*. Basel, Switzerland: Bank for International Settlements.

Basel Committee on Banking Supervision (BCBS). 2012b. Models and Tools for Macroprudential Analysis." Working Paper No. 21. Basel, Switzerland: Bank for International Settlements.

Basel Committee on Banking Supervision (BCBS). 2013. *Basel III: The Liquidity Coverage Ratio and Liquidity Risk Monitoring Tools*. Basel, Switzerland: Bank for International Settlements.

Basel Committee on Banking Supervision (BCBS). 2014a. *Basel III: The Net Stable Funding Ratio*. Basel, Switzerland: Bank for International Settlements.

Basel Committee on Banking Supervision (BCBS). 2014b. *Minimum Capital Requirements for Market Risk (2016)*. Basel, Switzerland: Bank for International Settlements.

Basel Committee on Banking Supervision (BCBS). 2014b. *Supervisory Framework for Measuring and Controlling Large Exposures*. Basel, Switzerland: Bank for International Settlements.

Basel Committee on Banking Supervision (BCBS). 2017a. *Finalization of Post Crisis Reforms*. Basel, Switzerland: Bank for International Settlements.

Basel Committee on Banking Supervision (BCBS). 2017b. *Supervisory and Bank Stress Testing: Range of Practices*. Basel, Switzerland: Bank for International Settlements.

Basel Committee on Banking Supervision (BCBS). 2017c. *Regulatory Treatment of Accounting Provisions–Interim Approach and Transitional Arrangement*. Basel, Switzerland: Bank for International Settlements.

Basel Committee on Banking Supervision (BCBS). 2019. *Minimum Capital Requirements for Market Risk*. Basel, Switzerland: Bank for International Settlements.

Beck Thorsten, Demirgüç-Kunt Asli, and Levine Ross. 2006. "Bank Concentration, Competition, and Crises: First Results." *Journal of Banking and Finance* 30(5): 1581–603.

Bergo, Jarle. 2002. "Using Financial Soundness Indicators to Assess Financial Stability." Paper presented at Challenges to Central Banking from Globalized Financial Systems, IMF Washington, DC, September 16–17.

Bessis, Joel. 2015. *Risk Management in Banking*, fourth edition. West Sussex: John Wiley & Sons.

Bluedorn, John, Rupa Duttagupta, Jaime Guajardo, and Petia Topalova. 2013. "Capital Flows Are Fickle: Anytime, Anywhere." IMF Working Paper 13/183, August, International Monetary Fund, Washington, DC.

Borio, Claudio. 2003. "Towards a Macroprudential Framework for Financial Supervision and Regulation?" BIS Working Papers No 128. Basel, Switzerland: Bank for International Settlements.

Borio, Claudio. 2014. "Macroprudential Frameworks: (Too) Great Expectations?" In *Macroprudentialism*, edited by Dirk Schoenmaker. London: Centre for Economic Policy Research, pp. 29–46.

Borio, Claudio, and Mathias Drehmann. 2009. "Towards an Operational Framework for Financial Stability: "Fuzzy" Measurement and Its Consequences." BIS Working Papers No. 248. Basel, Switzerland: Bank for International Settlements.

Borio, Claudio, Mathias Drehmann, and Kostas Tsatsaronis. 2012. "Stress Testing Macro-Stress Testing: Does It Live Up to Expectations?" BIS Working Papers No. 369. Basel, Switzerland: Bank for International Settlements.

Boyd, John H., and David E. Runkle. 1993. "Size and Performance of Banking Firms: Testing the Predictions of Theory." *Journal of Monetary Economics* 31(1): 47–67.

Bundesbank. 2017. *Financial Stability Report*, Germany. https://www.bundesbank.de/Redaktion/EN/Downloads/Publications/Financial_Stability_Review/2017_financial_stability_review.pdf?__blob=publicationFile

Bussière, Matthieu. 2013. "In Defense of Early Warning Signals." Working Paper No. 420. Paris: Banque du France.

Cabello, Miguel, Jose Lupu, and Minaya Elias. 2017. "Macroprudential Policies in Peru: The effects of Dynamics Provisioning and Conditional Reserve

Requirements." Working Paper No. 2017-002. Lima: Banco Central de Reserva Del Peru.

Carson, Carol. 2001. "Toward a Framework for Assessing Data Quality." IMF Working Paper 01/25. International Monetary Fund, Washington, DC.

Catalán, Mario, and Dimitri Demekas. 2015. "Challenges for Systemic Risk Assessment in Low-Income Countries." *Journal of Risk Management in Financial Institutions* 8(2): 118–29.

Central Bank of Argentina. 2017. *Financial Stability Report*, Argentina. http://www.bcra.gob.ar/Pdfs/PublicacionesEstadisticas/ief0217i.pdf

Central Bank of Brazil. 2017. *Financial Stability Report*, Brazil. http://www.bcb.gov.br/?fsr201710

Central Bank of Nigeria. 2016. *Financial Stability Report*. Accessed December 27, 2017. https://www.cbn.gov.ng/out/2017/fprd/fsr%20december%202016%20(2).pdf

Central Bank of the Republic of Turkey. 2017. *Financial Stability Report*, Turkey. http://www.tcmb.gov.tr/wps/wcm/connect/6c95b5fe-4815-4064-a9a4-80ff33b51906/fulltext25.pdf?MOD=AJPERES&CACHEID=ROOTWORKSPACE-6c95b5fe-4815-4064-a9a4-80ff33b51906-m52f977.

Central Bank of Russia. 2017. *Financial Stability Report*, Russia. http://www.cbr.ru/Eng/publ/Stability/OFS_17-02_e.pdf

Choudhry, Moorad. 2012. *The Principles of Banking*. Singapore: John Wiley & Sons.

Čihák, Martin. 2006. "How Do Central Banks Write on Financial Stability." IMF Working Paper 06/163. International Monetary Fund, Washington, DC.

Čihák, Martin. 2014. "Stress Tester: A Toolkit for Bank-By-Bank Analysis." In *A Guide to IMF Stress Testing: Models and Methods*, edited by Li Ong (Washington, DC: International Monetary Fund).

Čihák, Martin, Sonia Muñoz, Shakira Teh Sharifuddin, and Kalin Tintchev. 2012. "Financial Stability Reports: What Are They Good For?" IMF Working Paper 12/1. International Monetary Fund, Washington, DC.

Čihák, Martin, and Klaus Schaech. 2007. "How Well Do Aggregate Bank Ratios Identify Banking Problems." IMF Working Paper 07/275. International Monetary Fund, Washington, DC.

Claessens, Stijn. 2014. "An Overview of Macroprudential Policy Tools." IMF Working Paper 14/214. International Monetary Fund, Washington, DC.

Committee on the Global Financial System. 2010. "Macroprudential Instruments and Frameworks: A Stocktaking of Issues and Experience." CGFS Paper No. 28. Basel, Switzerland: Bank for International Settlements.

Committee on the Global Financial System. 2016. "Objective-Setting and Communication of Macroprudential Policies" CGFS Paper No. 57. Basel, Switzerland: Bank for International Settlements.

Costa Navajas, Matias, and Aaron Thegeya. 2013. "Financial Soundness Indicators and Banking Crises." IMF Working Paper 13/263. International Monetary Fund, Washington, DC.

Craig, Sean R. 2002. "Role of Financial Soundness Indicators in Surveillance: Data Sources, Users and Limitations." IFC Bulletin No. 12. Basel, Switzerland: Bank for International Settlements, pp. 199–209.

Crowley, Joseph, Plapa Koukpamou, Elena Loukoianova, and André Mialou. 2016. "Pilot Project on Concentration and Distribution Measures for a Selected Set of Financial Soundness Indicators." IMF Working Paper WP/16/26. International Monetary Fund, Washington, DC.

De Haan, Jakob, and Poghosyan Tigran. 2012. "Bank Size, Market Concentration, and Bank Earnings Volatility in the US." *Journal of International Financial Markets, Institutions and Money* 22(1): 35–54.

De Nederlandsche Bank. 2017. *Financial Stability Report*, Netherlands. https://www.dnb.nl/en/binaries/OFS_Autumn%202017_tcm47-363954.pdf

Demirgüç-Kunt, Asli, and Enrica Detragiache. 2005. "Cross-Country Empirical Studies of Systemic Bank Distress: A Survey." IMF Working Paper 05/96. International Monetary Fund, Washington, DC.

Deutsche Bundesbank. 2006a. *Concentration and Risk in Credit Portfolios*, Monthly Report, June.

Deutsche Bundesbank. 2006b. *Financial Stability Review*, November. https://www.bundesbank.de/resource/blob/621872/a0c2a5a4a9bae205a74b7149f7e709b2/mL/2006-finanzstabilitaetsbericht-data.pdf

Drehmann, Mathias, and Mikael Juselius. 2013. "Evaluating Early Warning Indicators of Banking Crises: Satisfying Policy Requirements." BIS Working Papers No. 42. Basel, Switzerland: Bank for International Settlements.

Emmer, Susanne, and Dirk Tasche. 2005. "Calculating Credit Risk Capital Charges with the One-factor Model." *The Journal of Risk* 7(2): Winter.

European Commission. 2015. "Commission Implementing Regulation (EU) 2015/1278." Brussels.

European Commission. 2018. "Commission Implementing Regulation (EU) 2018/292." Brussels.

European Parliament. 2009. "Solvency II, Directive 2009/138/EC." *Official Journal of the European Union*, Brussels, pp. L335/1–L335/155.

European Systemic Risk Board. 2017. *ESRB Dashboard* (November).

European Union. 2017. *2017 Financial Stability Report*, European Union. https://www.ecb.europa.eu/pub/pdf/other/ecb.financialstabilityreview201711.en.pdf?7a775eed7ede9aee35acd83d2052a198

Eurostat. 2013. *Handbook on Residential Property Prices Indices*. Luxembourg.

Evans, Owen, Alfredo Leone, Mahinder Gill, and Paul Hilbers 2000. *Macroprudential Indicators of Financial System Soundness*. Occasional Paper 192. Washington, DC: International Monetary Fund.

Evrensel, Ayşe. 2008. "Banking Crisis and Financial Structure: A Survival-Time Analysis." *International Review of Economics and Finance* 17(4): 589–602.

Fjármálaeftirlitið (Iceland Financial Supervisory Authority), Rules on Maximum Loan-to-Value Ratios for Mortgages. July 2017. https://en.fme.is/media/frettir/FME---LTV-Memorandum-July-2017.pdf.

Gadanecz, Blaise, and Jayaram Kaushik. 2015. "Macroprudential Policy Frameworks, Instruments and Indicators: A Review." IFC Bulletin No. 41. Basel, Switzerland: Bank for International Settlements.

Galati, Gabriele and Richhild Moessner. 2011. "Macroprudential Policy—A Literature Review." BIS Working Papers No. 337. Basel, Switzerland: Bank for International Settlements.

Goodhart, Charles. 2014. "The Use of Macroprudential Instruments." In *Macroprudentialism*, edited by Dirk Schoenmaker (London: Centre for Economic Policy Research), pp. 11–20.

Gordi, Michael B. 2003. "A Risk Factor Model Foundation of Ratings-based Bank Capital Rules." *Journal of Financial Intermediation* 12(3): 199–232.

Gorton, Gary. 2008. "The Panic of 2007." Working Paper No. 14358. The National Bureau of Economic Research.

Grippa, Pierpaolo, and Lucyna Gornica. 2016. "Measuring Concentration Risk—A Partial Portfolio Approach." IMF Working Paper WP/16/158. International Monetary Fund, Washington, DC.

Hong Kong Monetary Authority. May 19, 2017. "Press Release." http://www.hkma.gov.hk/eng/key-information/press-releases/2017/20170519-5.shtml.

Hong Kong Monetary Authority. 2018. *Financial Stability Report*, Hong Kong SAR. http://www.hkma.gov.hk/media/eng/publication-and-research/quarterly-bulletin/qb201803/E_Half-yearly_201803.pdf

Hull, John C. 2015. *Risk Management and Financial Institutions*, fourth edition. Hoboken, NJ: John Wiley & Sons.

Hyndman, Rob J., and Yanan Fan. 1996. "Sample Quantiles in Statistical Packages." *The American Statistician* 50(4): 361–65.

IFC Bulletin No. 41. 2016. *Combining Micro and Macro Statistical Data for Financial Stability*. Basel, Switzerland: Bank for International Settlements.

IFC Bulletin No. 46. 2017. *Data Needs and Statistics Compilation for Macroprudential Analysis*. Basel, Switzerland: Bank for International Settlements.

International Accounting Standards Board. 2004. "Provisions, Contingent Liabilities and Contingent Assets." *International Financial Reporting Standards 37*.

International Accounting Standards Board. May 2011. "Fair Value Measurement." *International Financial Reporting Standards 13*.

International Accounting Standards Board. July 2014. *International Financial Reporting Standards 9*.

International Accounting Standards Board. 2018. "*Conceptual Framework for Financial Reporting*." Paragraph 4.54.

International Monetary Fund, European Commission, Organization for Economic Cooperation and Development, United Nations, and the World Bank. 2009c. *2008 System of National Accounts*. New York.

International Monetary Fund, Financial Stability Board, and Bank for International Settlements. 2016a. *Elements of Effective Macroprudential Policies: Lessons from International Experience*. https://www.imf.org/external/np/g20/pdf/2016/083116.pdf.

International Monetary Fund. 2003a. *External Debt Statistics: Guide for Compilers and Users*. Washington, DC.

International Monetary Fund. 2003b. *Financial Soundness Indicators*. http://www.imf.org/external/np/sta/fsi/eng/2003/051403.htm

International Monetary Fund. 2006. *Financial Soundness Indicators Compilation Guide*. Washington, DC.

International Monetary Fund. 2009a. *Balance of Payments and International Investment Position Manual*. https://www.imf.org/external/pubs/ft/bop/2007/pdf/bpm6.pdf

International Monetary Fund. 2009b. *The Financial Crisis and Information Gaps: Report to the G-20 Finance Ministers and Central Bank Governors*. https://www.imf.org/external/np/g20/pdf/102909.pdf

International Monetary Fund. 2009c. *Global Financial Stability Report*. https://www.imf.org/~/media/Websites/IMF/imported.../GFSR/2009/01/.../_textpdf.ashx

International Monetary Fund. 2013a. *External Debt Statistics Guide for Compilers and Users*. Washington, DC.

International Monetary Fund. 2013b. *Modifications to the Current List of Financial Soundness Indicators*. http://www.imf.org/external/np/pp/eng/2013/111313.pdf

International Monetary Fund. 2013c. *Modifications to the Current List of Financial Soundness Indicators—Background Paper*. https://www.imf.org/external/np/pp/eng/2013/111313b.pdf

International Monetary Fund. 2014a. *Rising Challenges, Regional Economic Outlook*. Washington, DC.

International Monetary Fund. 2014b. *Government Finance Statistics Manual*. Washington, DC.

International Monetary Fund. 2014c. *Staff Guidance Note on Macroprudential Policy*. http://www.imf.org/external/np/pp/eng/2014/110614.pdf

International Monetary Fund. 2014d. *Staff Guidance Note on Macroprudential Policy—Considerations for Low Income Countries*. http://www.imf.org/external/np/pp/eng/2014/110614b.pdf

International Monetary Fund. 2014e. *Sustaining the Momentum: Vigilance and Reforms, Regional Economic Outlook*. Washington, DC.

International Monetary Fund. 2015. *The Handbook on Securities Statistics*. Washington, DC.

International Monetary Fund. 2016b. *Financial Stability Report*, Mexico. http://www.banxico.org.mx/publicaciones-y-discursos/publicaciones/informes-periodicos/reporte-sf/%7B838A2500-845F-2BC0-DF4A-167F4601542F%7D.pdf

International Monetary Fund. 2016c. *Financial Stability Report*, China. http://www.pbc.gov.cn/english/130736/3130899/index.html

International Monetary Fund. 2016d. *Managing Transitions and Risks, Regional Economic Outlook*. Washington, DC.

International Monetary Fund. 2016e. *Monetary and Financial Statistics Manual and Compilation Guide*. Washington, DC.

International Monetary Fund. 2017. "Experience with Financial Soundness Indicators; A Practitioner's Perspective." Paper prepared for the IMF Statistics Department Workshop on Financial Soundness Indicators, Washington, DC, April 25–26.

International Monetary Fund. 2018. *World Economic Outlook*. http://www.imf.org/external/pubs/ft/weo/2018/01/weodata/weoselagr.aspx.

Islamic Finance Services Board. 2013. *Revised Capital Adequacy for Institutions Offering Islamic Financial Services*. Kuala Lumpur, Malaysia.

Islamic Finance Services Board. 2017. *PSIFI Compilation Guide*. Kuala Lumpur, Malaysia.

Israël, Jean-Marc, Patrick Sandars, Aurel Schubert, and Björn Fischer. 2013. "Statistics and Indicators for Financial Stability Analysis and Policy." Occasional Paper Series No. 145. Frankfurt: European Central Bank.

Jobst, Andreas, Li Ong, and Christian Schmieder. 2013. "A Framework for Macroprudential Bank Solvency Stress Testing: Application to S-25 and Other G-20 Country FSAPs." IMF Working Paper 13/68. International Monetary Fund, Washington, DC.

Maino, Rodolfo, and Steven Barnett, eds. 2013. *Macroprudential Frameworks in Asia*. Washington, DC: International Monetary Fund.

Mishkin, Frederic S. 1999. "International Experiences with Different Monetary Policy Regimes." NBER Working Paper No. 6965.

Mueller, Glenn. 2002. "What Will the Next Real Estate Cycle Look Like?" *Journal of Real Estate Portfolio Management* 8(2): 115–25.

National Bank of Belgium. 2017. *Financial Stability Report*, Belgium. https://www.nbb.be/doc/ts/publications/fsr/fsr_2017.pdf

National Bank of Georgia. 2011. *Financial Stability Report*. https://www.nbg.gov.ge/uploads/publications/finstability/finans_stabil_web_2011new.pdf.

O'Hara, Maureen, and Wayne Shaw. 1990. "Deposit Insurance and Wealth Effects: The Value of Being 'Too Big to Fail.'" *Journal of Finance* 45(5): 1587–600.

Ong, Li. 2014. *A Guide to IMF Stress Testing: Methods and Models*. Washington, DC: International Monetary Fund.

Parzen, Emanuel. 1979. "Nonparametric Statistical Data Modeling." *Journal of the American Statistical Association* 74(365): 105–21.

Reinhart, Carmen M., and Kenneth N. Rogoff. 2011. "From Financial Crash to Debt Crisis." *American Economic Review* 101(5): 1676–706.

Reserve Bank of Australia. 2018. *Financial Stability Report*, Australia. http://www.rba.gov.au/publications/fsr/2018/apr/

Reserve Bank of India. 2017. *Financial Stability Report*, India. https://rbidocs.rbi.org.in/rdocs/PublicationReport/Pdfs/0FSR201730210986ADDA44E2A946A3F6C4408581.PDF

Reserve Bank of South Africa. 2018. *Financial Stability Report*, South Africa. https://www.resbank.co.za/Lists/News%20and%20Publications/Attachments/8420/FSR%20First%20Edition%202018.pdf

Saudi Arabia Monetary Authority. 2017. *Financial Stability Report*, Saudi Arabia. http://www.sama.gov.sa/en-US/EconomicReports/Financial%20Stability%20Report/Financial%20Stability%20Report%202017-EN.PDF

Schmieder, Christian, Claus Puhr, and Maher Hasan. 2011. "Next Generation Balance Sheet Stress Testing." IMF Working Paper 11/83. International Monetary Fund, Washington, DC.

Silver, Mick. 2013. "Understanding Commercial Property Price Indexes." *World Economics* 14(3): 27–41.

Smaga, Pawel. 2014. "The Concept of Systemic Risk." SRC Special Paper No. 5. London School of Economics.

Sundararajan, Vasudevan, Charles Enoch, Armida San Jose, Paul Louis Ceriel Hilbers, Russell Krueger, Marina Moretti, and Graham Slack. 2002. "Financial Soundness Indicators: Analytical Aspects and Country Practices." Occasional Paper No. 212. International Monetary Fund, Washington, DC.

Sveriges Riksbank. 2017. *Financial Stability Report*, Sweden. https://www.fi.se/contentassets/3613a7a9f24e425c8b6dfe6e861d6567/stab2-17_engny.pdf and https://www.riksbank.se/en-gb/financial-stability/financial-stability-report/2017/financial-stability-report-20172/

Swiss National Bank. 2017. *Financial Stability Report*, Switzerland. https://www.snb.ch/en/mmr/reference/stabrep_2017/source/stabrep_2017.en.pdf

United Nations. 2008. *International Standard Industrial Classification of All Economic Activities*, Statistical Papers, Series M, Number 4/Rev.4 (New York). https://unstats.un.org/unsd/publication/seriesm/seriesm_4rev4e.pdf

United States Treasury. 2017. *Financial Stability Report*, United States. https://www.financialresearch.gov/financial-stability-reports/files/OFR_2017_Financial-Stability-Report.pdf and https://www.treasury.gov/initiatives/fsoc/studies-reports/Documents/FSOC_2017_Annual_Report.pdf

Worrell, DeLisle. 2004. "Quantitative Assessment of the Financial Sector: An Integrated Approach." IMF Working Paper 04/153. International Monetary Fund, Washington, DC.

Glossary

Accrual Accounting: Accrual accounting records flows and changes in the corresponding stocks at the time economic value is created, transformed, exchanged, transferred, or extinguished. Under accrual accounting, flows and positions are recorded when a change in economic ownership takes place.

Additional Tier 1 Capital (AT1): Supervisory concept defined in Basel III, consisting of subordinated instruments with no maturity and neither secured nor covered by a guarantee of the issuer (Refer to *Basel III: A Global regulatory framework for more resilient banks and banking systems* for complete details).

Aggregate Resident-Based Approach: Under an aggregate resident-based approach, the headquarters office consolidates its transactions and positions with resident branch offices only, that is, not with any subsidiaries, associates, or nonresident branches. This is the approach adopted in the 2008 SNA, the sectoral balance sheets in monetary statistics, and related national accounts methodologies.

Aggregation: Refers to the summations of position or flow data. For sector-level data, aggregation is the sum of the positions and flows of all individual reporting groups/entities within the sector. The sectoral financial statements described in Chapter 5 are aggregates, where positions and flows are the sums of flows and positions of all the reporting units in the sector.

Amortized Cost: Amount advanced originally plus all accrued but not paid interest, less any repayment of principal, less any allowance for impairment or non-collectability (IFRS concept).

Arrears: When principal or interest payments are not made when due (e.g., on a loan) arrears are created. Arrears should continue to be recorded from their creation date, until they are extinguished, such as when they are repaid, rescheduled, or forgiven by the creditor. Arrears should continue to be recorded in the underlying instrument, with the exception of interest on nonperforming loans (see paragraph 5.14).

Asset: Store of value, over which ownership rights are enforced and from which their owners may derive economic benefits by holding them over a period of time.

Associates: Corporations over which the investor has a significant degree of influence, being the power to participate in the financial and operating policy decision of the investee; but not control or joint control as is the case of subsidiaries. Significant influence is usually assumed to arise when the investor controls between 10 and 50 percent of the shareholders' voting power.

Available Stable Funding: Supervisory concept defined in Basel III as the portion of a banks' capital and liabilities that are expected to remain with the bank in a stress scenario over a one-year horizon. Calibration of the presumed degree of stability considers both the funding tenor, and the funding type and counterparty. *Required stable funding* is institution specific, reflecting the liquidity characteristics and residual maturities of its assets and its off-balance-sheet exposures. Compilers will rely on supervisory data and will not generally need to be familiar with the highly detailed specification of available stable funding and required stable funding.

Balance Sheet: Corresponds to IAS 1 concept of *statement of financial position*, is the statement of assets, liabilities, and capital at the end of each accounting period.

Basel Committee on Banking Supervision: Established by the Central Bank Governors of the Group of Ten (G–10) countries at the end of 1974, the BCBS formulates broad supervisory standards and guidelines. It also recommends standards of best practice in the expectation that individual authorities will take steps to implement them through detailed arrangements—statutory or otherwise—that are best suited to their own national systems. It encourages convergence toward common approaches and common standards.

Basel II: The BCBS's *International Convergence of Capital Measurement and Capital Standards—A Revised Framework*, released in June 2004, is a comprehensive revision of the Basel capital adequacy standards. It includes three "pillars" for ensuring the strength of banking institutions. The first pillar covers the minimum capital requirements for banks, including changes in the risk weights for assets of banks in order that they better reflect the underlying risk incurred, and it includes alternative methodologies for assessing risk, based on banks' internal risk assessment procedures. The second pillar focuses on enhancing the supervisory review process. The third pillar focuses on enhancing market discipline over banking institutions through increased disclosures.

Basel III: The BCBS's *A Global Regulatory Framework for More Resilient Banks and Banking Systems* and the *International Framework for Liquidity Risk Measurement, Standards and Monitoring*, both released in 2010, together with *Basel III: Finalising Post-Crisis Reforms* (2017) is an internationally agreed set of measures developed by the Basel Committee on Banking Supervision in response to the financial crisis of 2007–2009. These measures aim to strengthen the regulation, supervision, and risk management of banks.

Book Value: Value of an asset as recorded in an entity's balance sheet.

Branches: Operating entities that do not have a separate legal status from their parent corporations and are thus integral part of them. A branch of a nonresident DT is identified for statistical purposes as a separate institutional unit in the economy where it operates.

CAMELS Framework: CAMELS is a commonly used supervisory framework that groups indicators of bank soundness into six categories. The categories are (1) capital adequacy, (2) asset quality, (3) management capability, (4) earnings, (5) liquidity, and (6) sensitivity to market risk

Capital Adequacy Ratio: The capital adequacy ratio is the central feature of the Basel Capital Accord. It is an analytical construct in which regulatory capital is the numerator and risk-weighted assets are the denominator. The minimum ratio of regulatory capital to risk-weighted assets is set at 8 percent (the core regulatory capital element should be at least 4 percent, increased to 6 percent in Basel III). These ratios are considered the minimum necessary to achieve the objective of securing over time soundly based and consistent capital ratios for all internationally active banks.

Capital and Reserves: Capital and reserves is the difference between total assets and total liabilities in the balance sheet. It represents the equity interest of the owners in an entity and is the amount available to absorb unidentified losses.

Capital Conservation Buffer: Extra capital that, under Basel III, a financial institution is required to hold to absorb losses during downturns.

Central Bank: National financial institution exercising control over key aspects of the financial sector. Its functions generally include: (1) issuing currency, (2) conducting monetary policy, including by regulating money supply and credit, (3) managing international reserves, (4) providing credit to deposit-taking corporations, and (5) acting as banker to government, by holding central government deposits and providing credit in the form of overdrafts, advances, and purchases of securities. Central banks frequently are the supervisory authority for the deposit-taking sector and payments systems, and less commonly, for other elements of the financial system. FSIs are not computed for the central bank.

Commercial Real Estate Loans: Loans collateralized by commercial real estate, loans to construction companies, and loans to companies active in the development of real estate (including those companies involved in the development of multi-household dwellings). Commercial real estate includes buildings, structures, and associated land used by enterprises for retail, wholesale, manufacturing, or other such purposes.

Common Equity Tier 1 capital (CET1): Supervisory concept defined in Basel III as the highest quality capital capable of absorbing losses on a going concern basis. It comprises (1) common shares, (2) retained earnings and accumulated other comprehensive income, and (3) other disclosed reserves. (Refer to *Basel III: A Global regulatory framework for more resilient banks and banking systems* for complete details).

Consolidation: The elimination of positions and flows that occur among institutional units that are grouped together for statistical purposes. For FSI purposes, reporting on a consolidated group basis preserves the integrity of capital by eliminating its double counting.

Consolidation Basis: The consolidation basis determines which ownership related units report data as if they formed a single encompassing entity, offsetting positions and flows between units of the same group. The consolidation basis determines the reporting population for FSI compilation. Which units are included under a specific consolidation basis depends, among other factors, on ownership and control, including whether a unit is a branch, subsidiary, or associate, and whether it is domestic or foreign controlled.

Contingencies: Many types of contractual financial arrangements between institutional units do not give rise to unconditional requirements, either to make payments or to provide other economic assets. In this context, "conditional" means that the claim becomes effective only if a stipulated condition (or conditions) arise. Contingencies are not recognized as financial assets (liabilities) on balance sheet because they are not actual claims (or obligations). However, these arrangements can potentially affect financial soundness.

Contingent Liability: Obligation that does not arise unless a particular, discrete event(s) occurs in the future.

Countercyclical Capital Buffer: Extra capital charge to be implemented based on national authorities' assessments of the build-up of system-wide risks and geographical credit exposure of internationally active banks.

Control of a Corporation: It exists when an entity is exposed, or has rights, to variable returns from its involvement with the corporation and has the ability to affect those returns through its power over the corporation. This IFRS definition encompasses but is somewhat broader than existing monetary and national statistics definitions of control: the ability to determine its general corporate policy and operations by choosing (or removing) appropriate directors.

Credit to the Private Sector: For DTs, gross loans extended by DTs to the private nonfinancial sector, plus debt securities issued by private NFCs and held by DTs. The data should be compiled on a domestic consolidated basis. The private sector comprises private NFCs, HHs, and NPISHs.

Credit Risk: The risk that one party to a financial contract will fail to discharge an obligation and thus cause the other party to incur a financial loss.

Cross-Border Consolidation: It involves a parent DT and its nonresident subsidiaries and branches, in addition to the resident ones. A branch or subsidiary may be resident in another economy than its parent. When such units are included in the group reporting, the data are referred to as *cross-border data*.

Cross-Sector Consolidation: It involves a parent DT and its financial subsidiaries (DT and non-DT). If such non-DT subsidiaries (e.g., a leasing company or a money market fund) are included in the group data of its parent DT, the data are referred to as *cross-sector data*.

Deferred Tax Assets: Difference between current tax charges/credits recognized by tax authorities and taxes recorded in financial statements.

Deposit-Taking Corporation (Excludes the Central Bank): Financial corporation that has financial intermediation as its principal activity and obtains funds through the acceptance of deposits or other financial instruments (e.g., short-term certificates of deposits) that are close substitutes for deposits.

Domestically Controlled Deposit Takers: If they are directly or indirectly controlled by resident shareholders. In the rare instances that the parent is located in both the domestic and a foreign economy, such subsidiaries are classified as domestically controlled.

Domestic Currency: Currency that is legal tender in the economy and is issued by the central bank or government of that economy or of the common currency area to which the economy belongs.

Economic Ownership: The economic owner of nonfinancial and financial assets and liabilities is the institutional unit entitled to claim the benefits associated with their use by virtue of accepting the associated risks.

Economic Territory: Area or jurisdiction under the effective economic control of a single government, for which statistics are required. It includes special zones.

Exposure at Default: The sum of debt outstanding and irrevocable commitments at the time a counterparty defaults.

External Debt: The outstanding amount of those actual current, noncontingent, and liabilities that require payments of principal or interest by the resident debtor to nonresident creditors at some point(s) in the future.

Face Value: Amount of principal to be repaid, also known as "par value" or simply "par."

Fair Value: Market-equivalent value defined as the amount for which an asset could be exchanged, or a liability settled, between knowledgeable, willing parties in an arm's length transaction.

Financial Assets: Subset of economic assets that are financial instruments and are unconditional creditor claims on economic resources of other institutional units, which give rise to corresponding liabilities of debtors. See Chapter 5 for definitions of different types of financial assets.

Financial Auxiliary: Financial corporation principally engaged in activities associated with transactions in financial assets and liabilities or with providing the regulatory context for these transactions but in circumstances that do not involve the auxiliary taking ownership of the financial assets and liabilities being transacted.

Financial Corporation (FC): Corporation principally engaged in providing financial services, including insurance and pension fund services, to other institutional units.

Foreign-Controlled Deposit Takers: DT subsidiaries or branches of a foreign parent DT, or a regulated or unregulated holding company controlled by nonresident shareholders, either directly or indirectly as described in paragraph 6.11.

Foreign Currency: Any currency other than the domestic currency.

Foreign Currency Debt: Debt that is payable in a currency other than the domestic currency and those that are payable in domestic currency but with the amounts to be paid linked to a foreign currency (foreign currency linked).

Foreign-Currency-Linked Instrument: Instruments payable in domestic currency but with the amounts payable linked to a foreign currency.

Financial Sector Assessment Program (FSAP): A joint IMF and World Bank program introduced in May 1999, the FSAP aims to increase the effectiveness of efforts to promote the soundness of financial systems in member countries. The objective of FSAP reviews is to gauge the stability and soundness of the financial sector and to assess its potential contribution to growth and development.

General Government Sector: It consists of resident institutional units that fulfill the functions of government as their primary activity. Government units are unique kinds of legal entities established by political processes that have legislative, judicial, or executive authority over other institutional units within a given area.

Goodwill: The excess of the fair (paid) value for a business entity over the book value of the acquired net assets. Accounting standard setters consider goodwill to be an asset. However, goodwill is an intangible asset, and as such not available to absorb losses.

Gross Recording: Refers to the presentation of assets and liabilities at their full value, that is, where claims on a particular institutional unit or group of units are not netted against the liabilities to that unit or group. (*Net recording* refers to the offsetting of these assets and liabilities, and is not recommended by the *Guide*; however, compilation on a net basis may be unavoidable due to lack of source data.)

Hedge Accounting: Accounting for gains and losses on financial assets and liabilities included in hedging relationships, recognizing the offsetting effects on profit or loss of changes in the fair values of the hedged instruments.

Hedging: Investment designed to offset the risk of adverse price movements in an asset.

Herfindahl Index: Measure of industry concentration calculated as the sum of the squares of the market shares of all firms in the industry.

High-Quality Liquid Assets: Supervisory concept defined in Basel III as unencumbered assets that can be converted easily and immediately into cash at little or no loss of value. The Basel III text sets out specific market-related characteristics and operational requirements that high-quality liquid assets should possess or satisfy.

Historic Cost: Cost at the time of acquisition, and sometimes it also may reflect occasional revaluations.

Holding Companies (for DTs): Units that hold the assets of subsidiary corporations but do not undertake any management activities. Their principal activity is to own and direct the group and they are not directly engaged in deposit taking.

Household: Group of persons who share the same living accommodation, pool some, or all, of their income and wealth and consume certain types of goods and services collectively, mainly housing and food.

Income and Expense Statement: Corresponds to the IAS 1 concept of statement of comprehensive income, presented as a single statement or as two statements: statement of profit or loss and a statement of other comprehensive income. The profit or loss section represents the traditional profit and loss concepts, while the other comprehensive income section presents items of income and expense that are not recognized in profit or loss, such as foreign currency translation gains or losses, as required or permitted by other IFRSs

Institutional Sector: Institutional units are allocated to different institutional sectors according to the nature of the economic activity they undertake. The resident institutional units of the economy are grouped into five mutually exclusive sectors: (1) FCs; (2) nonfinancial corporations; (3) general government; (4) households; and (5) NPISHs.

Institutional Unit: Economic entity capable, in its own right, of owning assets, incurring liabilities and engaging in economic activities and in transactions with other entities.

Insurance Corporation: Financial entity whose principal function is to provide life, accident, sickness, fire, or other forms of insurance coverage to individual institutional units or groups of units, or reinsurance services to other insurance corporations.

Internal Ratings–Based Approach: Methodology for determining the capital required for credit risk using credit ratings produced internally by a financial institution.

International Accounting Standard Board (IASB): Independent standard-setting body of the International Financial Reporting Standard Foundation. Its members are responsible for the development and publication of IFRSs and for approving interpretations of IFRSs.

International Banking Statistics (IBS): These data cover international banking business and are compiled and disseminated by the BIS on a quarterly basis. The IBS system has two main datasets: locational banking statistics, for which reporting banking institutions provide data on a residence basis; and consolidated banking statistics, which provide data on a worldwide consolidated basis.

International Financial Reporting Standards (IFRSs): Relevant international accounting and reporting principles for preparing general purpose financial statements, issued by the IASB.

Investments in Unconsolidated Subsidiaries: Holdings in affiliated financial institutions, which exceed 10 percent of equity of the parent bank.

Kurtosis: Measure of dispersion that estimates the degree of fatness of the tails of the distribution.

Large Exposures: The sum of all exposure values of a DT to a counterparty or to a group of connected counterparties, if it is equal to or above 10 percent of the DT's eligible capital base. Specific principles are outlined for the measurement of exposure values. Off-balance-sheet exposures should be converted into credit exposure equivalents through the use of credit conversion factors.

Legal or Social Entity: Institutional unit whose existence is recognized by law or society independently of the persons, or other entities, that may own or control it.

Legal Ownership: The legal owner of nonfinancial and financial assets and liabilities is the institutional unit entitled by law and sustainable under the law to claim the associated benefits.

Leptokurtic Distribution: Distribution with fatter tails and sharper peak than the normal distribution.

Leverage: Having access to the full benefits arising from holding a position in a financial asset without having to fully fund the position with own funds. It can be built up by borrowing (on-balance-sheet leverage, commonly measured by debt-to-equity ratios) or by using financial derivatives.

Leverage Ratio: Relation between Tier 1 capital to all balance sheet assets and off-balance-sheet commitments. The ratio is to be calculated as the average monthly leverage ratio over the quarter.

Liability: Established when one unit (the debtor) is obliged, under specific circumstances, to provide funds or other resources to another unit (the creditor).

Liquid Assets (of DTs): Assets that are readily available to an entity to meet a demand for cash. In the *Guide*, *liquid assets* comprise (1) currency; (2) deposits and other financial assets that are available either on demand or within three months or less; and (3) securities that are traded in liquid markets (including repo markets) that can be readily converted into cash, with insignificant risk of change in value under normal business conditions.

Liquidity: In terms of markets, liquidity generally refers to the ability to buy and sell assets quickly and in large volume without substantially affecting the asset's price. In terms of instruments, liquidity generally refers to those assets that can be converted into cash quickly without a significant loss in value.

Liquidity Coverage Ratio (LCR): A supervisory requirement defined in Basel III intended to promote resilience to potential liquidity disruptions over a 30-day horizon. The LCR estimates the short-term liabilities that would have to be covered by asset sales if access to funding were lost. Composition floors and haircuts ensure that high-quality liquid assets can be liquidated even in times of stress.

Liquidity Risk: The risk that assets may not be readily available to meet a demand for cash. Because deposit takers' assets are typically of longer maturity than their liabilities, monitoring deposit takers' liquidity risk through FSIs (e.g., liquidity assets to total assets and liquid assets to short-term liabilities) is important for financial soundness indicators.

Loss Given Default: Percentage of exposure lost when a counterparty defaults.

Macroprudential Analysis: It incorporates a range of approaches and indicators to measure systemic risks in both the time and structural dimensions. Indicators include aggregate balance sheet and income statement-derived ratios; market-based indicators such as asset prices, spreads or market liquidity measures; broad macro indicators such as ratios of credit to GDP; and other quantitative and qualitative information available to country authorities.

Market Risk: Risk of losses on financial instruments arising from changes in market prices. Market risk covers interest rate, foreign exchange, equity price, and commodity price risk.

Market Value: Value at which nonfinancial and financial assets are exchanged or else could be exchanged for cash (currency or transferable deposits).

Memorandum Series: Series required to calculate the FSIs that are not directly available from the financial statements. They are included as memorandum items to the financial statements. These series fall into two categories: (1) supervisory-based series and (2) series that provide a further analysis of the balance sheet

Mesokurtic Distribution: Distribution that does not exhibit fat tails.

Money Market Funds (MMFs): Collective investment schemes that raise funds by issuing shares or units to the public. The proceeds are invested primarily in money market instruments, MMF shares or units, transferable debt instruments with a residual maturity of not more than one year, bank deposits, and instruments that pursue a rate of return that approaches the interest rates of money market instruments.

Mortgage Servicing Rights: Capitalization of future income streams from the servicing of sold or purchased mortgage loans (as required by accounting standards).

Net Stable Funding Ratio (NSFR): A supervisory requirement defined in Basel III aimed at limiting over-reliance on short-term wholesale funding. The NSRF requires a minimum quantity of stable funding relative to relative to the liquidity profile of the bank.

Nominal Value: Outstanding amount that at any moment the debtor owes to the creditor. It reflects the funds originally advanced, plus any subsequent advances, plus interest that has accrued, less any repayment.

Nonfinancial Corporation (NFC): Corporation or a quasi-corporation whose principal activity is the production of market goods or nonfinancial services.

Non-MMF Investment Funds: Collective investment scheme that raises funds by issuing shares or units to the public. The proceeds are invested predominantly in long-term financial assets, such as equity shares, bonds, and mortgage loans, and nonfinancial assets, such as real estate.

Nonperforming Loans (NPLs): Loans for which (1) payments of interest or principal are past due by 90 days or more; or (2) interest payments equal to 90 days or more have been capitalized or delayed by agreement; or (3) evidence exists to reclassify a loan as nonperforming even in the absence of a 90-day past due payment, such as when the debtor files for bankruptcy.

Nonprofit Institution Serving Households (NPISHs): Legal entity principally engaged in the production of non-market services for households or the community at large, and whose main resources are voluntary contributions.

Nonprofit Institution: Legal or social entity created for the purpose of producing or distributing goods and services, but they cannot be a source of income, profit, or other financial gain for the institutional units that establish, control, or finance it.

Nonresident Unit: Institutional unit that has its center of predominant economic interest outside the economic territory under consideration.

Off-Balance-Sheet Exposures: Contractual financial arrangements often referred to as contingencies that are not financial assets or liabilities. These arrangements comprise commitments (including liquidity facilities), unconditionally cancellable commitments, direct credit substitutes, acceptances, standby letters of credit, trade letters of credit, failed transactions, and unsettled securities. Off-balance-sheet items are a source of potentially significant leverage.

Offshore Bank: Deposit-taking corporations established in jurisdictions that provide legal and fiscal advantages, such as low or no taxation and less stringent regulations in terms of reserve requirements or foreign exchange restrictions.

Operational Risk: Risk of loss resulting from inadequate internal processes or external events.

Original Maturity: Period from the date of issue until the final contractually scheduled payment.

Other Depository Corporation (ODC): For monetary statistics purposes, a financial corporation (other than the central bank) that incurs liabilities included in broad money.

Other Financial Corporation (OFC): Financial corporation that is not classified as central bank or deposit takers.

Pension Fund: Financial entity that provides retirement benefits for specific groups of individuals. To be classified as a pension fund, the entity must have its own separate sets of pension-fund assets and liabilities, with specific obligations to its contributors.

Platykurtic Distribution: Distribution with leaner tails than the normal distribution.

Positions: Level of assets or liabilities at a particular point in time. Also called stocks.

Quartile: Observation in a distribution below which lies 25 percent of the data.

Regulatory Capital: Equity and subordinated debt meeting specified conditions, defined in three tiers under Basel I and Basel II and two tiers under Basel III, that financial institutions are required to hold.

Remaining Maturity: Period from the reference date until the final contractually scheduled payment; also referred to as residual maturity.

Residence: The residence of an institutional unit is the economic territory with which it has the strongest connection, expressed as its center of predominant economic interest.

Residential Real Estate Loans: Loans collateralized by residential real estate. Residential real estate includes houses, apartments and other dwellings (e.g., houseboats and mobile homes), and any associated land intended for occupancy by individual HHs.

Required Stable Funding: See *Available Stable Funding.*

Risk-Weighted Assets: On- and off-balance-sheet exposures weighted according to their perceived risk. Basel I allocates different types of assets to four predefined risk-weights: 0, 20, 50, or 100 percent. Basel II introduced a more granular standardized approach using external credit ratings and an option for banks, subject to supervisory approval, to use internal models to determine risk weights.

Settlement Date: Time of delivery of a financial asset.

Skewness: Measure of dispersion that indicates the extent to which data are asymmetrically distributed around the mean.

Stable funding: Supervisory concept defined in Basel III as the portion of equity and liability financing expected to be reliable sources of funds over a one-year time horizon under conditions of extended stress.

Standardized Approach (for Credit Risk): Approach that determines risk weights using credit ratings produced by an external agency.

Subsidiaries: Entities controlled by another entity. A corporation is said to be a subsidiary of its parent when the parent is exposed, or has rights, to variable returns from its involvement with the corporation and has the ability to affect those returns through its power over the corporation.

Supervisory Deductions: Deductions from regulatory capital adjust for assets that are likely to be worthless in liquidation and to prevent the multiple use of the same capital resources. These deductions include: (1) goodwill; (2) deferred tax assets; (3) defined benefit plan deficits; (4) excess minority interest in subsidiaries; (5) profit revaluation of own debt; and (6) thresholds deductions. Deductions are applied to the different elements of capital (Tier 1, Tier 2, CET1) as prescribed by the relevant version of the Basel Capital Accord.

Systemic Risk Surcharge: Surcharge designed to provide additional safeguards around the banks classified as global systemically important banks (also known as "too big to fail") to deal with cross-border negative externalities posed by such institutions that are not fully addressed by current regulatory policies.

Tier 1 Capital: Supervisory concept introduced in Basel I. It consists of equity capital and disclosed reserves that are considered freely available to meet claims against the bank. It comprises paid-up shares and common stock, and disclosed reserves created or increased by appropriation of retained earnings or other surplus. Goodwill is deducted from Tier 1 capital.

Tier 2 Capital: Supervisory concept introduced in Basel I including financial instruments and reserves that are available to absorb losses, but which might not be permanent or have uncertain value. It consists of (1) unsecured subordinated debt with a minimum original maturity of at least five years; (2) stock surplus resulting from the issuance of some instruments; (3) instruments issued by subsidiaries that are consolidated with the bank; (4) general provisions up to 1.25 percent of risk-weighted assets; and (5) regulatory adjustments.

Total Net Cash Outflows: Supervisory concept defined in Basel III as the total expected cash outflows minus total expected cash inflows in the specified stress scenario for the subsequent 30 calendar days.

Value at Risk: Maximum likely loss in a given period of time in the event of extreme market moves.

Transaction: Interaction between institutional units by mutual agreement or through the operation of the law, involving an exchange of value or transfer.

Transaction Date: Time of change in ownership of a financial asset. Also called trade date.

Variance: A measure of dispersion around the mean calculated as the sum of squared deviations of each observation from the mean divided by the number of observations (for population variance) or the number of observations minus one (for sample variance).

Volatility: The tendency of quantities or prices to vary over time. Usually measured by the variance or annualized standard deviation of changes, volatility is said to be high if quantities or prices move significantly both up and down. The higher the volatility usually the higher the risk, as the ability to convert an asset into cash quickly without a significant loss in value is less certain.

Index

Numbered locators refer to paragraph numbers in chapters, appendices, and boxes, figures, or tables.

D

E

Made in United States
Orlando, FL
05 November 2026

90281941R00120